D1122874

The Raw and the Cooked

the text of this book is printed
on 100% recycled paper

Claude Lévi-Strauss

THE RAW
and the COOKED

Introduction to a Science of Mythology: I

TRANSLATED FROM THE FRENCH BY
JOHN AND DOREEN WEIGHTMAN

HARPER COLOPHON BOOKS
Harper & Row, Publishers
New York, Hagerstown, San Francisco, London

Figures numbered 1, 4, 5, 6, 7, 8, 10, 11, 16, 17, 18, 20 were executed at the Laboratoire de cartographie de l'Ecole Pratique des Hautes Etudes, under the direction of M. Jacques Bertin.

Bestiary pictures numbered 1–4, 6–9, 11, 12, 14, 16–18, 21, 23, 24, 26, 27, 29–32, 34–36, 39, 40 are taken from R. von Ihering, *Dicionário dos animais do Brasil*, São Paulo, 1940; 5, 10, 13, 15, 20, 22, 25, 28, 33, 37, 38 are from Carl Vogt, *Les Mammifères*, Paris, 1884; and 19 is from M. Bouyer, *La Guyane française*, Paris, 1867.

This work was first published in France under the title
Le Cru et le Cuit © 1964 by Librairie Plon.

First HARPER COLOPHON edition published 1975.

STANDARD BOOK NUMBER: 06-090441-0

LIBRARY OF CONGRESS CATALOG CARD NUMBER: 67-22501

77 78 79 80   12 11 10 9 8

TO MUSIC

Mè — re du sou-ve- nir — et nour ri — ce — du rê — ve, C'est toi
— qu'il nous plait au — jour — d'hui, d'in-vo-quer sous ce toit! —

(Mother of memory and feeder of dreams, Thee would we fain invoke today beneath this roof!)

"TO MUSIC"
Chorus for female voices with solo
(for a friend's housewarming)
Words by EDMOND ROSTAND
Music by EMMANUEL CHABRIER

Contents

Illustrations

PLATES

(Photographs by the author)

Table of Symbols

{ △	man
{ ○	woman

△ = ○   marriage (disjunction of marriage : #)

△   ○   brother and sister (their disjunction : |— —|)

△ , ○   father and son, mother and daughter, etc.

T   transformation

⟶   is transformed into

{ :	is to . . .
{ ::	as . . .

/   contrast

{ ≡	congruence, homology, correspondence
{ ≢	noncongruence, nonhomology, noncorrespondence

{ =	identity
{ ≠	difference

≈   isomorphism

{ U	union, reunion, conjunction
{ //	disunion, disjunction

{ ⟶	conjoins with . . .
{ #⟶	is in a state of disjunction with . . .

ƒ   function

$x^{(-1)}$ inverted x

+ , −   these signs are used with various connotations depending on the context: plus, minus; presence, absence; first or second term of a pair of opposites

The Raw and the Cooked

Overture

I

The aim of this book is to show how empirical categories—such as the categories of the raw and the cooked, the fresh and the decayed, the moistened and the burned, etc., which can only be accurately defined by ethnographic observation and, in each instance, by adopting the standpoint of a particular culture—can nonetheless be used as conceptual tools with which to elaborate abstract ideas and combine them in the form of propositions.

The initial hypothesis demands therefore that from the outset we place ourselves at the most concrete level—that is, in the heart of a community or of a group of communities sufficiently alike in regard to their habitat, history, and culture. However, while this is undoubtedly an essential methodological precaution, it cannot mask or restrict my intention. Using a small number of myths taken from native communities which will serve as a laboratory, I intend to carry out an experiment which, should it prove successful, will be of universal significance, since I expect it to prove that there is a kind of logic in tangible qualities, and to demonstrate the operation of that logic and reveal its laws.

I shall take as my starting point *one* myth, originating from *one* community, and shall analyze it, referring first of all to the ethnographic context and then to other myths belonging to the same community. Gradually broadening the field of inquiry, I shall then move on to myths from neighboring societies, after previously placing them, too, in their particular ethnographic context. Step by step, I shall proceed to more remote communities but only after authentic links of a historical or a geographic nature have been established with them or can reasonably be assumed to exist. The present work will describe only the initial stages of a long journey through the native mythologies of the New World, starting in the heart of tropical America and leading, as I can already foresee, to the furthermost regions of North America. The connecting thread throughout will be a myth of the Bororo Indians of central Brazil; this is not because this particular myth is more archaic than others that will be examined later, or because I consider it to be simpler or more complete. It attracted my attention in the first place for reasons that are largely contingent. And if I have tried to make the explanation of my synthesis correspond as far as possible to the analytical procedure by which I have arrived at it, this is because I felt that the close link I observe in such matters between their empirical and systematic aspects would be brought out all the more clearly if the method followed exemplified it in the first place.

In fact, the Bororo myth, which I shall refer to from now on as the key myth, is, as I shall try to show, simply a transformation, to a greater or a lesser extent, of other myths originating either in the same society or in neighboring or remote societies. I could, therefore, have legitimately taken as my starting point any one representative myth of the group. From this point of view, the key myth is interesting not because it is typical, but rather because of its irregular position within the group. It so happens that this particular myth raises problems of interpretation that are especially likely to stimulate reflection.

Even though I have thus stated my aims clearly, there is some danger that my project may meet with preliminary objections on the part of mythographers and specialists of tropical America. It cannot be contained within precise territorial limits or within the framework of any one system of classification. However it is approached, it spreads out like a nebula, without ever bringing together in any lasting or systematic way the sum total of the elements from which it blindly derives its substance, being confident that reality will be its guide and show it a surer road than any it might have invented. Starting with a myth chosen not so much arbitrarily as through an intuitive feeling that it was both rich and rewarding, and then, after analyzing it in accordance with rules laid down in previous works (L.-S. 5, 6, 7, and 9),* I establish the group of transformations for each sequence, either within the myth itself, or by elucidation of the isomorphic links between sequences derived from several myths originating in the same community. This itself takes us beyond the study of individual myths to the consideration of certain guiding patterns situated along a single axis. At each point on the axis where there is such a pattern or schema, we then draw, as it were, a vertical line representing another axis established by the same operation but carried out this time not by means of apparently different myths originating from a single community, but by myths that present certain analogies with the first, although they derive from neighboring communities. As a result, the guiding patterns are simplified, made more complex, or transformed. Each one becomes a source of new axes, which are perpendicular to the first on different levels, and to which will presently be connected, by a twofold prospective and retrospective movement, se-

* See Bibliography, pages 361–370, for full information on this and other references.

quences derived either from myths originating in more remote communities or from myths initially neglected because they seemed useless or impossible to interpret, even though they belonged to peoples already discussed. It follows that as the nebula gradually spreads, its nucleus condenses and becomes more organized. Loose threads join up with one another, gaps are closed, connections are established, and something resembling order is to be seen emerging from chaos. Sequences arranged in transformation groups, as if around a germinal molecule, join up with the initial group and reproduce its structure and determinative tendencies. Thus is brought into being a multidimensional body, whose central parts disclose a structure, while uncertainty and confusion continue to prevail along its periphery.

But I do not hope to reach a stage at which the subject matter of mythology, after being broken down by analysis, will crystallize again into a whole with the general appearance of a stable and well-defined structure. Apart from the fact that the science of myths is still in its infancy, so that its practitioners must consider themselves fortunate to obtain even a few tentative, preliminary results, we can already be certain that the ultimate state will never be attained, since were it theoretically possible, the fact still remains that there does not exist, nor ever will exist, any community or group of communities whose mythology and ethnography (and without the latter the study of myths is ineffectual) can be known in their entirety. The ambition to achieve such knowledge is meaningless, since we are dealing with a shifting reality, perpetually exposed to the attacks of a past that destroys it and of a future that changes it. For every instance recorded in written form, there are obviously many others unknown to us; and we are only too pleased with the samples and scraps at our disposal. It has already been pointed out that the starting point of the analysis must inevitably be chosen at random, since the organizational principles governing the subject matter of mythology are contained within it and only emerge as the analysis progresses. It is also inevitable that the point of arrival will appear of its own accord, and unexpectedly: this will occur when, a certain stage of the undertaking having been reached, it becomes clear that its ideal object has acquired sufficient consistency and shape for some of its latent properties, and especially its existence as an object, to be definitely placed beyond all doubt. As happens in the case of an optical microscope, which is incapable of revealing the ultimate structure of matter to the observer, we can only choose between various degrees of enlargement: each one reveals a level of organization which has no more than a relative truth and, while it lasts, excludes the perception of other levels.

The above remarks go some way toward explaining the nature of a book which might otherwise be considered paradoxical. While it is complete in itself and leads to conclusions that, I hope, the reader will accept as answers to the problems posed at the beginning, it makes reference to a second volume, beyond which can be glimpsed the outline of yet a third. But if these works ever see the light of day, they will not be so much a continuation as a different handling of the same material, a new attack on the same problems, in the hope that they will bring out hitherto blurred or unnoticed features, by means of different lighting or by a different coloring of histological cross sections. Therefore, if my inquiry proceeds in the way I hope, it will develop not along a linear axis but in a spiral; it will go back over previous findings and incorporate new objects only in so far as their examination can deepen knowledge that had previously existed only in rudimentary form.

Moreover, it must not be considered surprising if this work, which is avowedly devoted to mythology, draws unhesitatingly on material provided by folk tales, legends, and pseudo-historical traditions and frequently refers to ceremonies and rites. I cannot accept overhasty pronouncements about what is mythology and what is not; but rather I claim the right to make use of any manifestation of the mental or social activities of the communities under consideration which seems likely to allow me, as the analysis proceeds, to complete or explain the myth, even though it may not constitute an obbligato accompaniment of the myth in a musician's sense of the term (on this point cf. L.-S. 5, chap. 12). On another level—and in spite of the fact that my inquiry is centered on the myths of tropical America, which supply most of the examples—the analysis itself, as it progresses, demands that use be made of myths originating in more remote regions, just as primitive organisms, although enclosed within a membrane, still retain the ability to move their protoplasm within this covering and to achieve such extraordinary distention that they put forth pseudopodia; their behavior appears less strange, once we have ascertained that its object is the capture and assimilation of foreign bodies. Finally I have been careful to avoid grouping the myths into preconceived classifications, under such headings as cosmological, seasonal, divine, heroic, technological, etc. Here again the myth itself, on being put to the test of analysis, is left to reveal its nature and to show the type to which it belongs; such an aim is beyond the scope of the mythographer if he relies on external and arbitrarily isolated characteristics.

In short, the peculiarity of this book is that it has no subject: it is restricted in the first place to the study of one myth; yet to achieve even partial success, it must assimilate the subject matter of two hundred others. Anxious though I am to keep within a clearly defined geographic and cultural area, I cannot prevent the book from taking on, from time to time, the appearance of a general treatise on mythology. It has no beginning, since it would have developed along similar lines if it had had a different starting point; and it has no end, since many problems are dealt with in summary fashion, and others are simply mentioned in the hope that they may be treated more fully at some later date. In order to draw my map, I have been obliged to work outward from the center: first I establish the semantic field surrounding a given myth, with the help of ethnography and by means of other myths; and then I repeat the operation in the case of each of these myths. In this way the arbitrarily chosen central zone can be crisscrossed by various intersecting lines, although fewer overlappings occur as we move further out. In order to make the grid or mesh even, one would have to repeat the process several times, by drawing more circles around points situated along the periphery. But at the same time this would increase the size of the original area. And so we see that the analysis of myths is an endless task. Each step forward creates a new hope, realization of which is dependent on the solution of some new difficulty. The evidence is never complete.

I must, however, admit that the curious conception underlying this book, far from alarming me, seems rather to be a sign that I have perhaps succeeded in grasping certain fundamental properties of my subject, thanks to a plan and a method that were not so much chosen by me as forced upon me by the nature of the material.

Durkheim has said (p. 142) of the study of myths: "It is a difficult problem which should be dealt with in itself, for itself, and according to its own particular method." He also suggested an explanation of this state of affairs when later (p. 190) he referred to the totemic myths, "which no doubt explain nothing and merely shift the difficulty elsewhere, but at least, in so doing, appear to attenuate its crying illogicality." This is a profound definition, which in my opinion can be extended to the entire field of mythological thought, if we give it a fuller meaning than the author himself would have agreed to.

The study of myths raises a methodological problem, in that it cannot be carried out according to the Cartesian principle of breaking down the difficulty into as many parts as may be necessary for finding the solution. There is no real end to mythological analysis, no hidden unity to be grasped once the breaking-down process has been completed. Themes can be split up *ad infinitum*. Just when you think you have disentangled and separated them, you realize that they are knitting together again in response to the operation of unexpected affinities. Consequently the unity of the myth is never more than tendential and projective and cannot reflect a state or a particular moment of the myth. It is a phenomenon of the imagination, resulting from the attempt at interpretation; and its function is to endow the myth with synthetic form and to prevent its disintegration into a confusion of opposites. The science of myths might therefore be termed "anaclastic," if we take this old term in the broader etymological sense which includes the study of both reflected rays and broken rays. But unlike philosophical reflection, which claims to go back to its own source, the reflections we are dealing with here concern rays whose only source is hypothetical. Divergence of sequences and themes is a fundamental characteristic of mythological thought, which manifests itself as an irradiation; by measuring the directions and angles of the rays, we are led to postulate their common origin, as an ideal point on which those deflected by the structure of the myth would have converged had they not started, precisely, from some other point and remained parallel throughout their entire course. As I shall show in my conclusion, this multiplicity is an essential characteristic, since it is connected with the dual nature of mythological thought, which coincides with its object by forming a homologous image of it but never succeeds in blending with it, since thought and object operate on different levels. The constant recurrence of the same themes expresses this mixture of powerlessness and persistence. Since it has no interest in definite beginnings or endings, mythological thought never develops any theme to completion: there is always something left unfinished. Myths, like rites, are "in-terminable." And in seeking to imitate the spontaneous movement of mythological thought, this essay, which is also both too brief and too long, has had to conform to the requirements of that thought and to respect its rhythm. It follows that this book on·myths is itself a kind of myth. If it has any unity, that unity will appear only behind or beyond the text and, in the best hypothesis, will become a reality in the mind of the reader.

But I shall probably incur the severest criticism on the ethnographic level. Although the book is carefully documented, I have disregarded certain sources of information, and some others have proved inaccessible.[1] Those I have made use of do not always appear in the final draft. To avoid making the demonstration too unwieldy, I had to decide which myths to use, to opt for certain versions, and in some measure to simplify the variants. Some people will accuse me of having adapted the subject matter of my inquiry to suit my own purposes. If I had selected, from the vast quantity of available myths, only those that were most likely to support my thesis, my argument would have lost much of its force. It might therefore be said that I ought to have gone through all the known myths of tropical America before venturing to embark on a comparison between them.

The objection may seem particularly telling in the light of the circumstances that delayed the appearance of this book. It was almost completed when the publication of the first volume of the *Enciclopédia Boróro* was announced; and I waited until the work had reached France and I had studied it before putting the finishing touches to my text. But, following the same line of reasoning, I ought perhaps to have waited another two or three years for the second volume, which will deal with myths and will include a section on

[1] Certain works, such as *Die Tacana* by Hissink and Hahn (Stuttgart, 1961) have been only skimmed through, because of their relatively recent publication; while others, which did not reach France until after the completion of this book, have not been consulted at all: e.g., J. Wilbert, *Indios de la región Orinoco-Ventuari* (Caracas, 1963); and *Warao Oral Literature* (Caracas, 1964); and N. Fock, *Waiwai, Religion and Society of an Amazonian Tribe* (Copenhagen, 1963). However, in this last book I have already noted a myth about the opossum which confirms my analyses in the third and fourth parts. This new material will be utilized in a later volume.

proper names. Actually the study of the volume already to hand suggested a different conclusion, in spite of the wealth of detail it provides. The Salesians, who record their own changes of opinion with great serenity, when they do not simply fail to mention them, can be harshly critical if a piece of information published by some author does not coincide with their own most recent findings. In both cases they are committing the same methodological error. The fact that one item of information contradicts another poses a problem but does not solve it. I have more respect for the informants, whether they are our own or those who were employed in the old days by the missionaries, and whose evidence is consequently of particular value. The merits of the Salesians are so indisputable that, without failing in the debt of gratitude that is owed them, we can voice one slight criticism: they have an unfortunate tendency to believe that the most recent piece of information cancels out everything else.

I do not doubt for a moment that further information already available or as yet unpublished will affect my interpretations. Some that are no more than tentative will perhaps be confirmed; others will be abandoned or modified. No matter; in a subject such as this, scientific knowledge advances haltingly and is stimulated by contention and doubt. Unlike metaphysics, it does not insist on all or nothing. For this book to be worthwhile, it is not necessary in my view that it should be assumed to embody the truth for years to come and with regard to the tiniest details. I shall be satisfied if it is credited with the modest achievement of having left a difficult problem in a rather less unsatisfactory state than it was before. Nor must we forget that in science there are no final truths. The scientific mind does not so much provide the right answers as ask the right questions.

I can go further. If critics reproach me with not having carried out an exhaustive inventory of South American myths before analyzing them, they are making a grave mistake about the nature and function of these documents. The total body of myth belonging to a given community is comparable to its speech. Unless the population dies out physically or morally, this totality is never complete. You might as well criticize a linguist for compiling the grammar of a language without having complete records of the words pronounced since the language came into being, and without knowing what will be said in it during the future part of its existence. Experience proves that a linguist can work out the grammar of a given language from a remarkably small number of sentences, compared to all those he might in theory have collected (not to mention those he cannot be acquainted with because they were uttered before he started on his task, or outside his presence, or will be uttered at some later date). And even a partial grammar or an outline grammar is a precious acquisition when we are dealing with unknown languages. Syntax does not become evident only after a (theoretically limitless) series of events has been recorded and examined, because it is itself the body of rules governing their production. What I have tried to give is an outline of the syntax of South American mythology. Should fresh data come to hand, they will be used to check or modify the formulation of certain grammatical laws, so that some are abandoned and replaced by new ones. But in no instance would I feel constrained to accept the arbitrary demand for a total mythological pattern, since, as has just been shown, such a requirement has no meaning.

Another more serious objection is possible. Someone may question my right to choose myths from various sources, to explain a myth from the Gran Chaco by means of a variant from Guiana, or a Ge myth by a similar one from Colombia. But structural analysis—however respectful it may be of history and however anxious to take advantage of all its teachings—refuses to be confined within the frontiers already established by historical investigation. On the contrary, by demonstrating that myths from widely divergent sources can be seen objectively as a set, it presents history with a problem and invites it to set about finding a solution. I have defined such a set, and I hope I have supplied proof of its being a set. It is the business of ethnographers, historians, and archeologists to explain how and why it exists.

They can rest assured that, as regards the explanation of the group nature of the myths assembled here (and which have been brought together solely for the purposes of my investigation), I do not expect that historical criticism will ever be able to reduce a system of logical affinities to an enormous list of borrowings, either successive or simultaneous, made by contemporary or ancient communities from each other, over distances and intervals of time often so vast as to render any interpretation of this kind implausible, and in any case impossible to verify. From the start then, I ask the historian to look upon Indian America as a kind of Middle Ages which lacked a Rome: a confused mass that emerged from a long-established, doubtless very loosely textured syncretism, which for many centuries had contained at one and the same time centers of advanced civilization and savage peoples, centralizing tendencies and disruptive forces. Although the latter finally prevailed through the working of internal causes and as a result of the arrival of the European conquerors, it is nonetheless certain that a set, such as the one studied here, owes its character to the fact that in a sense it became crystallized in an already established semantic environment, whose elements had been used in all kinds of combinations—not so much, I suppose, in a spirit of imitation but rather to allow small but numerous communities to express their different originalities by manipulating the resources of a dialectical system of contrasts and correlations within the framework of a common conception of the world.

Such an interpretation, which I shall leave in this tentative form, is obviously based on historical conjecture: it supposes that tropical America was inhabited in very early times; that numerous tribes were frequently in movement in various directions; that demographic fluidity and the fusion of populations created the appropriate conditions for a very old-established syncretism, which preceded the differences observable between the groups; and that these differences reflect nothing or almost nothing of the archaic conditions but are in most cases secondary or derivative. Therefore, in spite of its formal approach, structural analysis establishes the validity of ethnographic and historical interpretations that I put forward more than twenty years ago; at the time they were thought to be somewhat rash (cf. L.-S. 5, p. 118 ff. and all of chap. 6), but they have continued to gain ground. If any ethnographic conclusion is to be deduced from the present work, it is that the Ge, far from being the "marginal" people they were supposed to be in 1942, when Volume I of *The Handbook of South American Indians* came out (I protested at the time against this assumption), represent a pivotal element in South America, whose function is comparable to the part played in North America by the old settlements along the Fraser and Columbia rivers, and their survivors. When I extend my inquiry to the northern areas of North America, the basis for the comparison will appear more clearly.

It was necessary to mention at least the concrete results achieved by structural analysis (certain others, relating only to the peoples of tropical America, will be explained in the course of this book) to put the reader on his guard against the charge of formalism, and even of idealism, that has sometimes been leveled against me. It may be said that the present book, even more than my previous works, takes ethnographic research in the direction of psychology, logic, and philosophy, where it has no right to venture. Am I not helping to deflect ethnography from its real task, which should be the study of native communities and the examination, from the social, political, and economic points of view, of problems posed by the relations among individuals and groups within a given community? Such misgivings, which have often been expressed, seem to me to arise from a total misunderstanding of what I am trying to do. And what is more serious, I think, is that they cast doubt on the logical continuity of the program I have been pursuing since I wrote *Les Structures élémentaires de la parenté,* a work about which the same objection cannot reasonably be made.

The fact is, however, that *La Pensée sauvage* represented a kind of pause in the development of my theories: I felt the need for a break between two bursts of effort. It is true that I took advantage of the situation to scan the scene before me, to estimate the ground covered, to map out my future itinerary, and to get a rough idea of the foreign territories I would have to cross, even though I was determined never to deviate for any length of time from my allotted path and—apart from some minor poaching—never to encroach on the only too closely guarded preserves of philosophy. . . . Nevertheless, the pause that some people misinterpreted as marking a conclusion was meant to be a merely temporary halt between the first stage that had been covered by *Les Structures* and the second, which the present work is intended to open.

Throughout, my intention remains unchanged. Starting from ethnographic experience, I have always aimed at drawing up an inventory of mental patterns, to reduce apparently arbitrary data to some kind of order, and to attain a level at which a kind of necessity becomes apparent, underlying the illusions of liberty. In *Les Structures,* behind what seemed to be the superficial contingency and incoherent diversity of the laws governing marriage, I discerned a small number of simple principles, thanks to which a very complex mass of customs and practices, at first sight absurd (and generally held to be so), could be reduced to a meaningful system. However, there was nothing to guarantee that the obligations came from within. Perhaps they were merely the reflection in men's minds of certain social demands that had been objectified in institutions. If so, their effect on the psychological level would be the result of mechanisms about which all that remains to be determined is their mode of operation.

The experiment I am now embarking on with mythology will consequently be more decisive. Mythology has no obvious practical function: unlike the phenomena previously studied, it is not directly linked with a different kind of reality, which is endowed with a higher degree of objectivity than its own and whose injunctions it might therefore transmit to minds that seem perfectly free to indulge their creative spontaneity. And so, if it were possible to prove in this instance, too, that the apparent arbitrariness of the mind, its supposedly spontaneous flow of inspiration, and its seemingly uncontrolled inventiveness imply the existence of laws operating at a deeper level, we would inevitably be forced to conclude that when the mind is left to commune with itself and no longer has to come to terms with objects, it is in a sense reduced to imitating itself as object; and that since the laws governing its operations are not fundamentally different from those it exhibits in its other functions, it shows itself to be of the nature of a thing among things. The argument need not be carried to this point, since it is enough to establish the conviction that if the human mind appears determined even in the realm of mythology, *a fortiori* it must also be determined in all its spheres of activity.[2]

In allowing myself to be guided by the search for the constraining structures of the mind, I am proceeding in the manner of Kantian philosophy, although along different lines leading to different conclusions. The ethnologist, unlike the philosopher, does not feel obliged to take the conditions in which his own thought operates, or the science peculiar to his society and his

[2] "If law is anywhere, it is everywhere." Such was the conclusion reached by Tylor in the passage that I used seventeen years ago as an epigraph for *Les Structures élémentaires de la parenté.*

period, as a fundamental subject of reflection in order to extend these local findings into a form of understanding, the universality of which can never be more than hypothetical and potential. Although concerned with the same problems, he adopts an opposite approach in two respects. Instead of assuming a universal form of human understanding, he prefers to study empirically collective forms of understanding, whose properties have been solidified, as it were, and are revealed to him in countless concrete representational systems. And since for him, belonging as he does to a given social milieu, culture, region, and period of history, these systems represent the whole range of possible variations within a particular type, he chooses those that seem to him to be the most markedly divergent, in the hope that the methodological rules he will have to evolve in order to translate these systems in terms of his own system and vice versa, will reveal a pattern of basic and universal laws: this is a supreme form of mental gymnastics, in which the exercise of thought, carried to its objective limits (since the latter have been previously explored and recorded by ethnographic research), emphasizes every muscle and every joint of the skeleton, thus revealing a general pattern of anatomical structure.

I am perfectly aware that it is this aspect of my work that Ricoeur is referring to when he rightly describes it as "Kantism without a transcendental subject."[3] But far from considering this reservation as indicating some deficiency, I see it as the inevitable consequence, on the philosophical level, of the ethnographic approach I have chosen; since, my ambition being to discover the conditions in which systems of truths become mutually convertible and therefore simultaneously acceptable to several different subjects, the pattern of those conditions takes on the character of an autonomous object, independent of any subject.

I believe that mythology, more than anything else, makes it possible to illustrate such objectified thought and to provide empirical proof of its reality. Although the possibility cannot be excluded that the speakers who create and transmit myths may become aware of their structure and mode of operation, this cannot occur as a normal thing, but only partially and intermittently. It is the same with myths as with language: the individual who conscientiously applied phonological and grammatical laws in his speech, supposing he possessed the necessary knowledge and virtuosity to do so, would nevertheless lose the thread of his ideas almost immediately. In the same way the

[3] P. Ricoeur, "Symbole et temporalité," *Archivio di Filosofia,* Nos. 1-2 (Roma, 1963), p. 24. Cf. also p. 9: "A Kantian rather than a Freudian unconscious, a combinative, categorizing, unconscious . . ."; and p. 10: "a categorizing system unconnected with a thinking subject . . . homologous with nature; it may perhaps be nature. . . ."

With his customary subtlety and insight Roger Bastide (pp. 65–79) anticipated the whole of the preceding argument. The coincidence of our views is a most eloquent indication of his clearsightedness, since I did not see his work (which he himself kindly sent me) until I was busy correcting the proofs of this book.

practice and the use of mythological thought demand that its properties remain hidden: otherwise the subject would find himself in the position of the mythologist, who cannot believe in myths because it is his task to take them to pieces. Mythological analysis has not, and cannot have, as its aim to show how men think. In the particular example we are dealing with here, it is doubtful, to say the least, whether the natives of central Brazil, over and above the fact that they are fascinated by mythological stories, have any understanding of the systems of interrelations to which we reduce them. And when by appealing to such myths we justify the existence of certain archaic or colorful expressions in our own popular speech, the same comment can be made, since our awareness is retrospective and is engineered from without and under the pressure of a foreign mythology. I therefore claim to show, not how men think in myths, but how myths operate in men's minds without their being aware of the fact.

And, as I have already suggested, it would perhaps be better to go still further and, disregarding the thinking subject completely, proceed as if the thinking process were taking place in the myths, in their reflection upon themselves and their interrelation.[4] For what I am concerned to clarify is not so much what there is *in* myths (without, incidentally, being in man's consciousness) as the system of axioms and postulates defining the best possible code, capable of conferring a common significance on unconscious formulations which are the work of minds, societies, and civilizations chosen from among those most remote from each other. As the myths themselves are based on secondary codes (the primary codes being those that provide the substance of language), the present work is put forward as a tentative draft of a tertiary code, which is intended to ensure the reciprocal translatability of several myths. This is why it would not be wrong to consider this book itself as a myth: it is, as it were, the myth of mythology.

However, this code, like the others, has neither been invented nor brought in from without. It is inherent in mythology itself, where we simply discover its presence. One ethnographer working in South America expresses surprise at the way in which the myths were conveyed to him: "The stories are told differently by almost every teller. The amount of variation in important details is enormous." Yet the natives do not seem to worry about this state of affairs: "A Caraja, who traveled with me from village to village, heard all sorts of variants of this kind and accepted them all in almost equal confidence. It was not that he did not see the discrepancies, but they did not matter to him . . ." (Lipkind 1, p. 251). A naïve observer from some other planet might more justifiably (since he would be dealing with history, not myths) be amazed that in the mass of works devoted to the French Revo-

---

[4] The Ojibwa Indians consider myths as "conscious beings, with powers of thought and action." (W. Jones, "Ojibwa Texts," *Publications of the American Ethnological Society,* Vol. III, Part II [New York, 1919], p. 574, n. 1.)

lution the same incidents are not always quoted or disregarded, and that the same incidents are presented in different lights by various authors. And yet these variants refer to the same country, the same period, and the same events, the reality of which is scattered throughout the various levels of a complex structure. The criterion of validity is, therefore, not to be found among the elements of history. Each one, if separately pursued, would prove elusive. But some of them at least acquire a certain solidity through being integrated into a series, whose terms can be accorded some degree of credibility because of their over-all coherence.

In spite of worthy, and indeed indispensable, attempts to become different, history, as its clearsighted practitioners are obliged to admit, can never completely divest itself of myth. What is true for history is, therefore, *a fortiori* truer still in regard to myth itself. Mythological patterns have to an extreme degree the character of absolute objects, which would neither lose their old elements nor acquire new ones if they were not affected by external influences. The result is that when the pattern undergoes some kind of transformation, all its aspects are affected at once. And so if one aspect of a particular myth seems unintelligible, it can be legitimately dealt with, in the preliminary stage and on the hypothetical level, as a transformation of the homologous aspect of another myth, which has been linked with the same group for the sake of the argument, and which lends itself more readily to interpretation. This I have done on more than one occasion: for instance, by explaining the episode of the jaguar's closed jaws in M_7 by the reverse episode of the wide-open jaws in M_{55}; or the episode of the genuine willingness to help shown by the vultures in M_1 by their false willingness in M_{65}. The method does not, as one might expect, create a vicious circle. It merely implies that each myth taken separately exists as the limited application of a pattern, which is gradually revealed by the relations of reciprocal intelligibility discerned between several myths.

I shall no doubt be accused of overinterpretation and oversimplification in my use of this method. Let me say again that all the solutions put forward are not presented as being of equal value, since I myself have made a point of emphasizing the uncertainty of some of them; however, it would be hypocritical not to carry my thought to its logical conclusion. I therefore say in advance to possible critics: what does this matter? For if the final aim of anthropology is to contribute to a better knowledge of objectified thought and its mechanisms, it is in the last resort immaterial whether in this book the thought processes of the South American Indians take shape through the medium of my thought, or whether mine take place through the medium of theirs. What matters is that the human mind, regardless of the identity of those who happen to be giving it expression, should display an increasingly intelligible structure as a result of the doubly reflexive forward movement of two thought processes acting one upon the other, either of which can in turn provide the spark or tinder whose conjunction will shed light on both.

And should this light happen to reveal a treasure, there will be no need of an arbitrator to parcel it out, since, as I declared at the outset (L.-S. 9), the heritage is untransferable and cannot be split up.

II

At the beginning of this introduction I explained that I had tried to transcend the contrast between the tangible and the intelligible by operating from the outset at the sign level. The function of signs is, precisely, to express the one by means of the other. Even when very restricted in number, they lend themselves to rigorously organized combinations which can translate even the finer shades of the whole range of sense experience. We can thus hope to reach a plane where logical properties, as attributes of things, will be manifested as directly as flavors or perfumes; perfumes are unmistakably identifiable, yet we know that they result from combinations of elements which, if subjected to a different selection and organization, would have created awareness of a different perfume. Our task, then, is to use the concept of the sign in such a way as to introduce these secondary qualities into the operations of truth.

It was natural that the search for a middle way between aesthetic perception and the exercise of logical thought should find inspiration in music, which has always practiced it. Nor did the parallel suggest itself only from a general point of view. At a very early stage, almost from the moment of beginning to write, I realized that it was impossible to organize the subject matter of this book according to a plan based on traditional principles. The division into chapters not only did violence to the movement of thought; it weakened and mutilated the thought itself and blunted the force of the demonstration. The latter, to be convincing, seemed, paradoxically enough, to require greater suppleness and freedom. I also came to see that the documentary data could not be presented in unilinear fashion, and that the different stages of the commentary were not interlinked merely in order of sequence. Certain devices of composition were indispensable to provide the reader from time to time with a feeling of simultaneity; the impression would no doubt remain illusory, since an expository order had to be respected, but a near equivalent to it might be achieved by an alternation in style between the discursive and the diffuse, by varying the rhythm between fast and slow, and by sometimes piling examples one on top of another and sometimes giving them separate presentation. I saw that the process of analysis would take place along different axes: there would be the sequential axis, of course, but also the axis of relatively greater densities which would involve recourse to forms comparable to solos and *tutti* in music; there would be the axis of expressive tensions and the axis of modulation codes, and during the process of composition these would bring about contrasts similar to the alternation between melody and recitative or between instrumental ensembles and arias.

It followed, from the liberty I was thus taking in developing my themes in several dimensions, that the division into isometric chapters must give way to a pattern involving parts of unequal length, fewer in number but also more voluminous and complex, and each one of which would constitute a whole by virtue of its internal organization according to a certain unity of inspiration. For the same reasons the various parts could not all be cast in the same mold; rather, in respect to tone, genre, and style, each would have to obey the rules dictated by the nature of the material being used and of the technical devices employed in each particular case. Consequently here, too, musical form offered the possibility of diversity already standardized by experience, since comparison with models such as the sonata, the symphony, the cantata, the prelude, the fugue, etc., allowed easy verification of the fact that constructional problems, analogous to those posed by the analysis of myths, had already arisen in music, where solutions had been found for them.

But at the same time I could not avoid another problem—that of the fundamental causes of the initially surprising affinity between music and myths (structural analysis of the latter does no more than emphasize their properties, while taking them over and transposing them onto another plane). And undoubtedly a great step forward had been made in the direction of finding a reply when I realized a constant of my own personal history which had remained unaffected through all vicissitudes, even withstanding during adolescence those two shattering revelations *Pelléas et Mélisande* and Stravinsky's *Les Noces* ("The Wedding"): I mean my reverence, from childhood on, for "that God, Richard Wagner." If Wagner is accepted as the undeniable originator of the structural analysis of myths (and even of folk tales, as in *Die Meistersinger*), it is a profoundly significant fact that the analysis was made, in the first instance, *in music.*[5] Therefore, when I suggested that the analysis of myths was comparable with that of a major musical score (L.-S. 5, p. 234), I was only drawing the logical conclusion from Wagner's discovery that the structure of myths can be revealed through a musical score.

However, this preliminary tribute confirms the existence of the problem more than it solves it. The true answer is to be found, I think, in the characteristic that myth and music share of both being languages which, in their different ways, transcend articulate expression, while at the same time—like articulate speech, but unlike painting—requiring a temporal dimension in which to unfold. But this relation to time is of a rather special nature: it is

[5] In recognizing this influence, I should be guilty of ingratitude if I did not at the same time admit other debts: in the first place, to the work of Marcel Granet, so rich in insights of genius and then, last but not least, to M. Georges Dumézil; and to M. Henri Grégoire's *Asklèpios, Appollon Smintheus et Ruda* (Mémoires de l'Académie Royal de Belgique, classe des Lettres . . . tome XLV, fasc. 1, 1949).

as if music and mythology needed time only in order to deny it. Both, indeed, are instruments for the obliteration of time. Below the level of sounds and rhythms, music acts upon a primitive terrain, which is the physiological time of the listener; this time is irreversible and therefore irredeemably diachronic, yet music transmutes the segment devoted to listening to it into a synchronic totality, enclosed within itself. Because of the internal organization of the musical work, the act of listening to it immobilizes passing time; it catches and enfolds it as one catches and enfolds a cloth flapping in the wind. It follows that by listening to music, and while we are listening to it, we enter into a kind of immortality.

It can now be seen how music resembles myth, since the latter too overcomes the contradiction between historical, enacted time and a permanent constant. But to justify the comparison fully, it must be carried much further than I took it in a previous study (L.-S. 5, pp. 230–33). Like a musical work, myth operates on the basis of a twofold continuum: one part of it is external and is composed in the one instance of historical, or supposedly historical, events forming a theoretically infinite series from which each society extracts a limited number of relevant incidents with which to create its myths; and in the other instance, the equally infinite series of physically producible sounds, from which each musical system selects its scale. The second aspect of the continuum is internal and is situated in the psychophysiological time of the listener, the elements of which are very complex: they involve the periodicity of cerebral waves and organic rhythms, the strength of the memory, and the power of the attention. Mythology makes demands primarily on the neuromental aspects because of the length of the narration, the recurrence of certain themes, and the other forms of back references and parallels which can only be correctly grasped if the listener's mind surveys, as it were, the whole range of the story as it is unfolded. All this applies, too, in the case of music. But the latter appeals not only to psychological time but also to physiological and even visceral time; this appeal is not absent in the case of mythology, since the telling of a story may be of "breathtaking" interest, but it is not as essential as in music: any piece of counterpoint includes a silent part for the rhythmic movements of heart and lungs.

To simplify the argument, let us restrict ourselves for the moment to visceral time. We can say that music operates according to two grids. One is physiological—that is, natural: its existence arises from the fact that music exploits organic rhythms and thus gives relevance to phenomena of discontinuity that would otherwise remain latent and submerged, as it were, in time. The other grid is cultural: it consists of a scale of musical sounds, of which the number and the intervals vary from one culture to another. The system of intervals provides music with an initial level of articulation, which is a function not of the relative heights of the notes (which result from the perceptible properties of each sound) but of the hierarchical relations among them on the scale; the division into fundamental, tonic, dominant, and leading notes expresses relations that the polytonal and atonal systems complicate but do not destroy.

The composer's mission is to modify the discontinuity without challenging its principle: his melodic inventiveness either creates temporary lacunae in the grid or temporarily stops up or reduces the intervals. Sometimes it increases the perforation; at other times it closes the gaps. And what is true of the melody is also true of the rhythm since, by means of the latter, the theoretically constant intervals of the physiological grid are missed out or extended, anticipated or caught up with after some delay.

The musical emotion springs precisely from the fact that at each moment the composer withholds or adds more or less than the listener anticipates on the basis of a pattern that he thinks he can guess, but that he is incapable of wholly divining because of his subjection to a dual periodicity: that of his respiratory system, which is determined by his individual nature, and that of the scale, which is determined by his training. If the composer withholds more than we anticipate, we experience a delicious falling sensation; we feel we have been torn from a stable point on the musical ladder and thrust into the void, but only because the support that is waiting for us was not in the expected place. When the composer withholds less, the opposite occurs: he forces us to perform gymnastic exercises more skillful than our own. Sometimes he moves us, sometimes he forces us to make the movement ourselves, but it always exceeds what we would have thought ourselves capable of achieving alone. Aesthetic enjoyment is made up of this multiplicity of excitements and moments of respite, of expectations disappointed or fulfilled beyond anticipation—a multiplicity resulting from the challenges made by the work and from the contradictory feeling it arouses that the tests it is subjecting us to are impossible, at the same time as it prepares to provide us with the marvelously unpredictable means of coping with them. The intention of the composer, ambiguous while still in the score, which offers:

> . . . irradiant un sacre
> Mal tu par l'encre même en sanglots sibyllins,[6]

becomes actual, like that of myth, through and by the listener. In both instances the same reversal of the relation between transmitter and receiver can be observed, since in the last resort the latter discovers its own meaning through the message from the former: music has its being in me, and I listen to myself through it. Thus the myth and the musical work are like conductors of an orchestra, whose audience becomes the silent performers.

If it is now asked where the real center of the work is to be found, the answer is that this is impossible to determine. Music and mythology bring

---

[6] TRANSLATORS' NOTE: The conclusion of Mallarmé's sonnet in honor of Wagner. Literally: "[The god Richard Wagner] radiating a coronation, inadequately kept silent by the ink itself in sibylline sobs." The meaning may be that the aesthetic triumph of Wagner's work belies the mysterious sadness of the music as it is actually written.

man face to face with potential objects of which only the shadows are actualized, with conscious approximations (a musical score and a myth cannot be more) of inevitably unconscious truths, which follow from them. In the case of myth we can guess the reason for this paradoxical situation: it is a consequence of the irrational relation between the circumstances of the creation of the myth, which are collective, and the particular manner in which it is experienced by the individual. Myths are anonymous: from the moment they are seen as myths, and whatever their real origins, they exist only as elements embodied in a tradition. When the myth is repeated, the individual listeners are receiving a message that, properly speaking, is coming from nowhere; this is why it is credited with a supernatural origin. It is therefore comprehensible that the unity of the myth should be projected onto a postulated center, beyond the conscious perception of the listener through whom for the time being it is merely passing, up to the point at which the energy it radiates is consumed in the effort of unconscious reorganization that it has itself previously prompted. Music raises a much more difficult problem, because we know nothing of the mental conditions in which musical creation takes place. In other words, we do not understand the difference between the very few minds that secrete music and the vast numbers in which the phenomenon does not take place, although they are usually sensitive to music. However, the difference is so obvious, and is noticeable at so early an age, that we cannot but suspect that it implies the existence of very special and deep-seated properties. But since music is a language with some meaning at least for the immense majority of mankind, although only a tiny minority of people are capable of formulating a meaning in it, and since it is the only language with the contradictory attributes of being at once intelligible and untranslatable, the musical creator is a being comparable to the gods, and music itself the supreme mystery of the science of man, a mystery that all the various disciplines come up against and which holds the key to their progress.

It cannot be argued that poetry raises a problem of the same order. Not everyone is a poet, but the vehicle of poetry is articulate speech, which is common property. Poetry merely decrees that its particular use of language will be subject to certain restrictions. Music, on the contrary, has its own peculiar vehicle which does not admit of any general, extramusical use. Theoretically, if not in fact, any adequately educated man could write poems, good or bad; whereas musical invention depends on special gifts, which can be developed only where they are innate.

Devotees of painting will no doubt protest against the privileged position I have accorded to music, or at least will claim the same position for the graphic and plastic arts. However, I believe that from the formal point of view the materials used—that is, sounds and colors—are not on the same level. To justify the difference, it is sometimes said that music is not normally imitative or, more accurately, that it never imitates anything but itself; whereas the first question that springs to the mind of someone looking at a picture is: what does it represent? But if the problem is formulated in this way at the present time, we are faced with the anomaly of nonfigurative painting. In defense of his efforts, would not the abstract painter be justified in appealing to the precedent of music and in claiming the right to organize forms and colors, if not with absolute freedom, at least in accordance with a code independent of sense experience, as is the case in music with its sounds and rhythms?

Anyone proposing this analogy has fallen victim to a serious illusion. Whereas colors are present "naturally" in nature, there are no musical sounds in nature, except in a purely accidental and unstable way; there are only noises.[7] Sounds and colors are not entities of the same standing, and the only legitimate comparison is between colors and noises—that is, between visual and acoustic modes of nature. And it happens that man adopts the same attitude to both, since he is unwilling to allow either to remain in a random state. There are confused noises just as there are medleys of color; but as soon as it is possible to perceive them as patterns, man at once tries to identify them by relating them to a cause. Patches of color are seen as flowers nestling in the grass, crackling noises must be caused by stealthy movement or by the wind in the trees, and so on.

There is no true equality, then, between painting and music. The former finds its materials in nature: colors are given before they are used, and language bears witness to their derivative character through the terms that describe the most subtle shades—midnight blue, peacock blue, petrol blue; sea green, jade green; straw color, lemon yellow; cherry red, etc. In other words, colors exist in painting only because of the prior existence of colored objects and beings; and only through a process of abstraction can they be separated from their natural substrata and treated as elements in an independent system.

It may be objected that what applies to colors is not true of forms. Geo-

[7] If, through lack of verisimilitude, we dismiss the whistling of the wind through the reeds of the Nile, which is referred to by Diodorus, we are left with little but bird songs—Lucretius' *liquidas avium voces*—that can serve as a natural model for music. Although ornithologists and acousticians agree about the musicality of the sounds uttered by birds, the gratuitous and unverifiable hypothesis of the existence of a genetic relation between bird song and music is hardly worth discussing. Doubtless man is not the only producer of musical sounds, if he shares this privilege with the birds, but the fact has no bearing on my argument since, unlike color which is a natural phenomenon, musical tone, in the case of both birds and men, is a social phenomenon. The so-called songs of birds are on the frontiers of language; their purpose is to express and communicate. Therefore it is still true that musical sounds are part of culture. However, the dividing line between culture and nature is not identical, as used to be thought, with any of the lines of demarcation between human and animal nature.

metrical forms and all others derived from them have already been created by culture when the artist becomes aware of them; they are no more the product of experience than musical sounds are. But an art limited to the exploitation of such forms would inevitably take on a decorative character. Without ever fully existing in its own right, it would become anemic, unless it attached itself to objects as adornment, while drawing its substance from them. It is, then, as if painting had no choice but to signify beings and things by incorporating them in its operations or to share in the significance of beings and things by becoming incorporated with them.

It seems to me that this congenital subjection of the plastic arts to objects results from the fact that the organization of forms and colors within sense experience (which, of course, is itself a function of the unconscious activity of the mind) acts, in the case of these arts, as an initial level of articulation of reality. Only thanks to it are they able to introduce a secondary articulation which consists of the choice and arrangement of the units, and in their interpretation according to the imperatives of a given technique, style, or manner—that is, by their transposition in terms of a code characteristic of a given artist or society. If painting deserves to be called a language, it is one in that, like any language, it consists of a special code whose terms have been produced by combinations of less numerous units and are themselves dependent on a more general code. Nevertheless, there is a difference between it and articulate speech, with the result that the message of painting is grasped in the first place through aesthetic perception and secondly through intellectual perception, whereas with speech the opposite is the case. As far as articulate speech is concerned, the coming into operation of the second code wipes out the originality of the first. Hence the admittedly "arbitrary character" of linguistic signs. Linguists emphasize these aspects when they say that "morphemes, which are significant elements, break down into phonemes, which are articulatory elements without significance" (Benveniste, p. 7). Consequently, in articulate speech the primary nonsignifying code is a means and condition of significance in the secondary code: in this way, significance itself is restricted to one level. The dualism is re-established in poetry, which incorporates in the second code the potential, signifying value of the first. Poetry exploits simultaneously the intellectual significance of words and syntactical constructions and aesthetic properties, which are the potential terms of another system which reinforces, modifies, or contradicts this significance. It is the same thing in painting, where contrasts of form and color are perceived as distinctive features simultaneously dependent on two systems: first, a system of intellectual significances, the heritage of common experience and the result of the subdivision and organization of sense experience into objects; second, a system of plastic values which only becomes significant through modulating the other and becoming incorporated with it. Two articulated mechanisms mesh to form a third, which combines the properties of both.

It can thus be understood why abstract painting and more generally all schools of painters claiming to be nonfigurative lose the power to signify: they abandon the primary level of articulation and assert their intention of surviving on the secondary one alone. The attempt to establish a parallel between certain contemporary experiments and Chinese calligraphic painting is particularly instructive. In these experiments, the forms used by the artist have no prior existence on a different level with their own systematic organization. It is therefore impossible to identify them as elementary forms: they can be more accurately described as creations of whim, fictitious units, which are put together in parodic combinations. Calligraphic art, on the contrary, rests wholly on the fact that the units it selects, puts into position, and translates by means of the conventions of a particular kind of writing or of a personal sensibility, rhythm, or style, have an independent existence as signs and fulfill other functions within a certain graphic system. Only in these circumstances can a pictorial work be part of a language, because it then results from the contrapuntal relation between two levels of articulation.

It can also be seen why the comparison between painting and music would be acceptable, at a pinch, only if limited to calligraphic painting. Like the latter—but because it is a sort of secondary form of painting—music refers back to a primary level of articulation created by culture: in the one instance, there is a system of ideograms; in the other, a system of musical sounds. But by the mere fact of its creation, the pattern makes explicit certain natural properties: for instance, graphic symbols, particularly those of Chinese writing, display aesthetic properties independent of the intellectual meanings they are intended to convey; and it is these properties that calligraphic art exploits.

This is an essential point, because contemporary musical thought, either formally or tacitly, rejects the hypothesis of the existence of some natural foundation that would objectively justify the stipulated system of relations among the notes of the scale. According to Schönberg's significant formula, these notes are to be defined solely by "the total system of relations of the sounds with one another." However, the lessons of structural linguistics should make it possible to overcome the false opposition between Rameau's objectivism and the conventionalism of modern theorists. As a result of the selection made in the sound continuum by each type of scale, hierarchical relations are established among the notes. These relations are not dictated by nature, since the physical properties of any musical scale considerably exceed in number and complexity those selected by each system for the establishment of its distinctive features. It is nevertheless true that, like any phonological system, all modal or tonal (or even polytonal or atonal) systems depend on physical and physiological properties, selecting some from among the infinite number no doubt available, and exploiting the contrasts and combinations of which they are capable in order to evolve a code that

serves to distinguish different meanings. Music, then, just as much as painting, supposes a natural organization of sense experience; but it does not necessarily accept this organization passively.

We must not forget, however, that painting and music stand in opposite
relations to nature, although nature speaks to them both. Nature spontaneously offers man models of all colors and sometimes even their substance in a
pure state. In order to paint he has only to make use of them. But, as I have
already emphasized, nature produces noises not musical sounds; the latter
are solely a consequence of culture, which has invented musical instruments
and singing. The difference is reflected in language: we do not describe
shades of color and sound in the same way. In the case of the former, we
almost always proceed by means of implicit metonymies, as if a given yellow
were inseparable from the visual perception of straw or lemon, or a given
black from the burnt ivory used in its making, or a given brown from
pounded earth. On the other hand, metaphors are widely used in the world
of sounds: for instance, *les sanglots longs des violons/de l'automne* "the
long sobbing of the violins of autumn," *la clarinette, c'est la femme aimée*
"the clarinet is like the beloved," etc. No doubt culture sometimes discovers
colors that are thought not to come from nature; it would be more accurate
to say that it rediscovers them, since nature in this respect is literally in-
exhaustible. But apart from the instance of bird song already referred to,
man would be unacquainted with musical sounds if he had not invented
them.

Therefore, it is only at a later stage, and retroactively as it were, that music
recognizes physical properties in sounds and selects certain of these properties
with which to build its hierarchical structures. Can it be said that, in so doing,
music proceeds like painting which also recognized, at a later stage, that
there is a physical science of color, on which it is now, more or less openly,
based? But, in doing this, painting, through the instrumentality of culture,
gives intellectual organization to a form of nature which it was already
aware of as a sense pattern. Music follows exactly the opposite course: culture
is already present in it, but in the form of sense experience, even before it
organizes it intellectually by means of nature. It is because the field of operation of music is cultural that music comes into being, free from those
representational links that keep painting in a state of subjection to the world
of sense experience and its organization in the form of objects.

It is precisely in the hierarchical structure of the scale that the first level
of articulation of music is to be found. It follows that there is a striking
parallel between the ambitions of that variety of music which has been
paradoxically dubbed concrete and those of what is more properly called
abstract painting. By rejecting musical sounds and restricting itself exclusively to noises, *musique concrète* puts itself into a situation that is comparable, from the formal point of view, to that of painting of whatever kind:
it is in immediate communion with the given phenomena of nature. And,

like abstract painting, its first concern is to disrupt the system of actual or potential meanings of which these phenomena are the elements. Before using the noises it has collected, *musique concrète* takes care to make them unrecognizable, so that the listener cannot yield to the natural tendency to relate them to sense images: the breaking of china, a train whistle, a fit of coughing, or the snapping off of a tree branch. It thus wipes out a first level of articulation, whose usefulness would in any case be very limited, since man is poor at perceiving and distinguishing noises, perhaps because of the overriding importance for him of a privileged category of noises: those of articulate speech.

The existence of *musique concrète* therefore involves a curious paradox. If such music used noises while retaining their representative value, it would have at its disposal a first articulation which would allow it to set up a system of signs through the bringing into operation of a second articulation. But this system would allow almost nothing to be said. To be convinced of this, one has only to imagine what kind of stories could be told by means of noises, with reasonable assurance that such stories would be both intelligible and moving. Hence the solution that has been adopted—the alteration of noises to turn them into pseudo-sounds; but it is then impossible to define simple relations among the latter, such as would form an already significant system on another level and would be capable of providing the basis for a second articulation. *Musique concrète* may be intoxicated with the illusion that it is saying something; in fact, it is floundering in non-significance.

Far be it from me to make the inexcusable mistake of confusing this phenomenon with the case of serial music. Serial music, which keeps firmly to sounds and has a subtle grammar and syntax at its disposal, remains of course within the bounds of music proper and may even be helping to prolong its life. But although the problems it faces are of another kind and arise on a different level, they nevertheless offer some resemblance to those discussed in the previous paragraph.

The serial approach, by taking to its logical conclusion that whittling down of the individual particularities of tones, which begins with the adoption of the tempered scale, seems to tolerate only a very slight degree of organization of the tones. It is as if one were trying to find the lowest level of organization compatible with the retention of a series of sounds handed down by tradition, or, more accurately, to destroy a simple organization, partly imposed from without (since it results from a choice among pre-existing possibilities), to leave the field open for a much more supple and complex, yet declared code:

> The composer's thought, operating in accordance with a particular methodology, creates the objects it needs and the form necessary for their organization, each time it has occasion to express itself. Classical tonal thought is based on a world defined by gravitation and attraction, serial thought on a world which is perpetually expanding." (Boulez.)

In serial music, according to the same writer, "there is no longer any pre-conceived scale or preconceived forms—that is, general structures into which a particular variety of musical thought can be inserted." It should be noted that the adjective "preconceived" is used ambiguously here. It does not follow from the fact that the structures and forms imagined by the theoreticians have been proved to be most often artificial and sometimes mistaken that no general structure exists; a more effective analysis of music, which would take into account all its geographic and temporal manifestations, might some day reveal such a structure. Where would linguistics now be if it had concluded, from its criticism of the grammars of any given language formulated by philologists at different periods, that the particular language had no inherent grammar? Or if the differences in grammatical structure among individual languages had discouraged it from pursuing the difficult, but essential task of evolving a general grammar? Above all, one must ask oneself in dealing with this conception, what has happened to the first level of articulation, which is as indispensable in musical language as in any other, and which consists precisely of general structures whose universality allows the encoding and decoding of individual messages. Whatever the gulf between *musique concrète* and serial music in respect of intelligence, the question arises whether both are not deceived by the utopian ideal of the day: one concentrates on matter; the other on form; but both are trying to con-struct a system of signs on a single level of articulation.

The exponents of the serial doctrine will no doubt reply that they have abandoned the first level to replace it by the second, but they make up for the loss by the invention of a third level, which they count on to perform the function previously fulfilled by the second. Thus, they maintain, they still have two levels. We have had in the past the ages of monody and poly-phony; serial music is to be understood as the beginning of a "polyphony of polyphonies"; through it the previous horizontal and vertical readings are integrated in an "oblique" reading. But in spite of its logical coherence, this argument misses the essential point: the fact is that, in the case of any language, the first articulation is immovable, except within very narrow limits. And it is certainly not interchangeable. The respective functions of the two forms of articulation cannot be defined in the abstract and in relation to each other. The elements raised to the level of a meaningful function of a new order by the second articulation must arrive at this point already endowed with the required properties: that is, they must be already stamped with, and for, meaning. This is only possible because the elements, in addi-tion to being drawn from nature, have already been systematized at the first level of articulation: the hypothesis is faulty, unless it is accepted that the system takes into account certain properties of a natural system which creates *a priori* conditions of communication among beings similar in nature. In other words, the first level consists of real but unconscious relations which, because of these two attributes, are able to function without being known or correctly interpreted.

In the case of serial music, however, such rootedness in nature is uncertain and perhaps nonexistent. Only ideologically can the system be compared to a language, since unlike articulate speech, which is inseparable from its physiological or even physical foundation, it is a system adrift, after cutting the cables by which it was attached. It is like a sailless ship, driven out to sea by its captain, who has grown tired of its being used only as a pontoon, and who is privately convinced that by subjecting life aboard to the rules of an elaborate protocol, he will prevent the crew from thinking nostalgically either of their home port or of their ultimate destination. . . .

I do not deny that the choice may have been dictated by the hardness of the times. It may even happen that the hazardous journey undertaken by painting and music will lead them to new lands, preferable to those where they have lived throughout the centuries, and where the harvests were thinning out. But if such is the outcome, it will be without the knowledge or agreement of the navigators because, as we have seen, the possibility is indignantly denied by the exponents of serial music at least. It is not a question of sailing to other lands, the whereabouts of which may be unknown and their very existence hypothetical. The proposed revolution is much more radical: the journey alone is real, not the landfall, and sea routes are replaced by the rules of navigation.

Be this as it may, what I want to emphasize is a different point. Even when they seem to be moving along side by side, painting and music are separated by an obvious disparity. Without realizing it, abstract painting is taking over, more and more, the functions that were formerly fulfilled in society by decorative painting. It is therefore being divorced from language conceived as a system of meaning; whereas serial music clings to speech, continuing and exaggerating the lieder tradition—that is, a genre in which music, forgetting that it is itself a sovereign, irreducible language, puts itself at the service of words. Does not this dependence on a different idiom betray a feeling of anxiety that, in the absence of a fairly apportioned code, complex messages may be inadequately received by those people to whom they have, after all, to be addressed? Once a language has been unhinged, it inevitably tends to fall apart, and the fragments that hitherto were a means of reciprocal articulation between nature and culture drift to one side or the other. The listener notices this in his own way, since the composer's use of an extraordinarily subtle syntax (which allows combinations all the more numerous, since the twelve halftones can arrange their patterns at will in a four-dimensional space defined by height, duration, intensity, and timbre) affects him either on the natural or the cultural level, but rarely on both at once. Sometimes all he derives from the instrumental parts is the flavor of the timbres, acting as a natural stimulant of sensual feeling; sometimes the use of wide intervals, which kills any budding desire for melody, gives the vocal part the doubtless false appearance of a mere expressive reinforcement of articulate speech.

In the light of the foregoing remarks, the reference to an expanding universe that I quoted from the writings of one of the most eminent thinkers of the serial school takes on a remarkable significance. It shows that this particular school has chosen to risk its fate, and the fate of music, on a gamble. Either it will succeed in bridging the traditional gap between listener and composer and—by depriving the former of the possibility of referring unconsciously to a general system—will at the same time oblige him, if he is to understand the music he hears, to reproduce the individual act of creation on his own account. Through the power of an ever new, internal logic, each work will rouse the listener from his state of passivity and make him share in its impulse, so that there will no longer be a difference of kind, but only of degree, between inventing music and listening to it. Or something quite different will happen, since we have no guarantee, alas, that bodies in an expanding universe are all moving at the same rate or in the same direction. The astronomical analogy to which I am appealing suggests rather the opposite. It may therefore turn out that serial music belongs to a universe in which the listener could not be carried along by its impetus but would be left behind. In vain would he try to catch up; with every passing day it would appear more distant and unattainable. Soon it would be too far away to affect his feelings; only the idea of it would remain accessible, before eventually fading away into the dark vault of silence, where men would recognize it only in the form of brief and fugitive scintillations.

The reader is in danger of being put off by this discussion of serial music, which is hardly appropriate, it would seem, at the beginning of a work devoted to the myths of the South American Indians. Its justification lies in my intention to treat the sequences of each myth, and the myths themselves in respect of their reciprocal interrelations, like the instrumental parts of a musical work and to study them as one studies a symphony. The legitimacy of this procedure depends on the demonstration of the existence of an isomorphism between the mythic system, which is of a linguistic order, and the system of music which, as we know, constitutes a language, since we understand it, but whose absolute originality and distinguishing feature with regard to articulate speech is its untranslatability. Baudelaire (p. 1213) made the profound remark that while each listener reacts to a given work in his own particular way, it is nevertheless noticeable that "music arouses similar ideas in different brains." In other words, music and mythology appeal to mental structures that the different listeners have in common. The point of view I have adopted involves, therefore, reference to general structures that serialist doctrine rejects and whose existence it even denies. On the other hand, these structures can only be termed general if one is prepared to grant them an objective foundation on the hither side of consciousness and thought, whereas serial music sets itself up as a conscious product of the mind and an assertion of its liberty. The argument is complicated by problems of a philosophical nature. Because of its vigorous theoretical ambitions, its very strict methodology, and its brilliant technical achievements, the serialist school provides a much better illustration than do the various forms of nonfigurative painting of a current in contemporary thought, which has to be distinguished from structuralism with special care, since they have so many features in common: a resolutely intellectual approach, a bias in favor of systematic arrangements, and a mistrust of mechanistic or empirical solutions. However, by virtue of its theoretical presuppositions, the serialist school is at the opposite pole from structuralism and stands in a relation to it comparable to that which used to exist between free thought and religion—with the difference, however, that structural thought now defends the cause of materialism.

Consequently, far from being a digression, my comparison with serialist thought takes up again and develops themes that were broached in the first part of this introduction. I have thus completed my demonstration of the fact that, whereas in the public mind there is frequently confusion between structuralism, idealism, and formalism, structuralism has only to be confronted with true manifestations of idealism and formalism for its own deterministic and realistic inspiration to become clearly manifest.

What I state about any language seems to me to be still truer when the language under consideration is music. If, of all human products, music strikes me as being the best suited to throw light on the essence of mythology, the reason is to be found in its perfection. Mythology occupies an intermediary position between two diametrically opposed types of sign systems—musical language on the one hand and articulate speech on the other; to be understood it has to be studied from both angles. However, when one decides, as I have done in this book, to look from myth to music rather than from myth to language—as I tried to do in previous works (L.-S. 5, 6, 8, 9)—the exceptional position occupied by music is brought out still more clearly. In making the comparison, I referred at the outset to an attribute that the myth and the musical work have in common: they operate through the adjustment of two grids, one internal, the other external. But, in the case of music these grids, which are never simple, become complex to the point of reduplication. The external, or cultural, grid formed by the scale of intervals or the hierarchical relations among the notes, refers back to an inherent discontinuity: the discontinuity of musical sounds that are already wholly cultural objects in themselves, since they stand in contrast to noises, which are the only elements given *sub specie naturae*. The inner, or natural, grid, which is a function of the brain, is reinforced symmetrically by a second and, one might say, still more wholly natural grid: that constituted by the visceral rhythms. Consequently, in music the mediation between nature and culture that occurs within every language becomes a hypermediation; the connections are strengthened on either side. Since music is established at the point where two different spheres overlap, its writ runs well beyond boundaries that the other arts are careful not to overstep. In the two opposite directions of nature and culture, it is able to go much farther than they can. This explains the principle (though not the genesis and functioning, both of which, as I have already said, remain the great mysteries of the science of man) of music's extraordinary power to act simultaneously on the mind and the senses, stimulating both ideas and emotions and blending them in a common flow, so that they cease to exist side by side, except insofar as they correspond to, and bear witness to, each other.

No doubt mythology offers only a weaker imitation of this force. Yet it is the language that has most in common with that of music, not only because their very high degree of internal organization creates a bond between them, but for deeper reasons also. Just as music makes the individual conscious of his physiological rootedness, mythology makes him aware of his roots in society. The former hits us in the guts; the latter, we might say, appeals to our group instinct.[8] And to do this, they make use of those extraordinarily subtle cultural mechanisms: musical instruments and mythic patterns. In music, the duplication of the mechanisms, which can be both instrumental and vocal, reproduces, through their union, the union of nature and culture, since it is a fact that singing differs from the spoken language in demanding the participation of the whole body, but according to the strict rules of a particular vocal style. As a result, here again music asserts its claims in a more coherent, systematic, and total fashion. However, myths are often sung or chanted; and even when they are recited, the process is usually marked by certain physical rules: the reciter or the listener is forbidden to fall asleep, to remain seated, etc.

In the course of this book (Part One, I, *d*) I shall establish the existence of an isomorphism between two oppositions; that of nature and culture and that of continuous and discrete quantities. My thesis can therefore be supported by the fact that innumerable societies, both past and present, have conceived of the relation between the spoken language and singing or chanting as analogous to that between the continuous and the intermittent. This is tantamount to saying that, within culture, singing or chanting differs from the spoken language as culture differs from nature; whether sung or not, the sacred discourse of myth stands in the same contrast to profane discourse. Again, singing and musical instruments are often compared to masks; they are the acoustic equivalents of what actual masks represent on the plastic level (and for this reason, in South America especially, they are associated, mentally and physically, with masks). Through this particularity, too, music and the mythology illustrated by masks are brought into symbolic proximity.

---

[8] TRANSLATORS' NOTE: The original reads: *L'une nous prend aux tripes, l'autre, si l'on ose dire, "au groupe."*

All these comparisons result from the closeness of music and mythology to each other on the same axis. But since along this axis music stands in opposition to articulate speech, it follows that music, which is a complete language, not reducible to speech, must be able to fulfill the same functions on its own account. Looked at in the round and in its relation to other sign systems, music is close to mythology. But, so far as the mythic function is itself an aspect of speech, it must be possible to discover in musical discourse some special function that has a particular affinity with myth—an affinity that, we might say, serves to illustrate the general affinity I have already noted between the two categories, myth and music, when they are considered in their entirety.

It is immediately obvious that there is a correspondence between music and language in respect of the variety of their functions. In both cases it is necessary to make a preliminary distinction according to whether the function relates principally to the sender or to the receiver. The term "phatic function," that Malinowski introduced, is not strictly applicable to music. Yet it is clear that almost all folk music, such as choral singing or singing as an accompaniment to dancing, as well as a considerable part of chamber music, gives pleasure in the first place to the performers—that is, the senders. It is, we may say, a subjectivized phatic function. Amateur musicians who get together to play quartets are not much concerned whether they have an audience; and it is probably the case that they prefer not to have one. The explanation must be that even in this instance the phatic function is accompanied by a conative one, the group performance creating a harmony of gesture and expression which is one of its aims. This conative function takes precedence over the other in the case of military marches and dance music, the main object of which is to regulate the behavior of other people. In music, even more than in linguistics, the phatic and conative functions are inseparable. They are on the same side, at the opposite pole from the cognitive function. The latter is predominant in theater or concert music, which aims primarily—though again not exclusively—at transmitting information-loaded messages to an audience which acts as a receiver.

The cognitive function, in its turn, can be broken down by analysis into several forms, each of which corresponds to a particular kind of message. These forms are approximately the same as those distinguished by the linguist under the headings of "metalinguistic," "referential," and "poetic" functions (Jakobson 2, chap. 11 and p. 220). Only by recognizing that there are several kinds of music can we explain the apparently self-contradictory fact that we like very different composers. Everything becomes clear, once we realize that there is no point in trying to put them in an order of preference (by seeking, for instance, to establish their relative degrees of "greatness"); in reality they fall into separate categories according to the nature of the information they convey. In this respect composers can be divided up, roughly speaking, into three groups, which are combined and interrelated in all manner of ways.

In this classification, Bach and Stravinsky appear as musicians concerned with a "code," Beethoven—but, Ravel too—as concerned with a "message," and Wagner and Debussy as concerned with "myth." The first use their messages to expound and to comment on the rules of a particular musical discourse; the second group tell a tale; the third group code their messages by means of elements that already partake of the nature of narrative. Of course, no piece of music by these composers can be entirely reduced to one or the other of these formulas, which are not intended as a complete definition of the musician's work but rather serve to emphasize the relative importance attributed to each function. It is also for the sake of simplicity that I have quoted only three pairs, each including an older and a more modern musician.[9] But even in the case of dodecaphonic music, the distinction remains enlightening, since it allows us to see the relative positions of Webern, Schönberg, and Berg: the first belongs to the category of the code, the second to that of the message, and the third to that of myth.

As for the emotive function, it too exists in music; and where it exists as a constituent element, musicians refer to it in their professional jargon by the German term *Schmalz*. However, for the reasons already indicated, it is clear that its role would be even more difficult to determine precisely than in the case of articulate speech, since we have seen that, theoretically if not always in practice, emotive function and musical language are coextensive.

I shall deal much more rapidly with another feature of my book: the occasional use of apparently logico-mathematical symbols, which should not be taken too seriously. There is only a superficial resemblance between my formulas and the equations of the mathematician, because the former are not applications of rigorously employed algorisms, allowing the demonstrations of the various points to be interlinked or condensed. Their purpose is quite different. Certain analyses of myths are so long and detailed that it would be impossible to carry them through to the end, if one did not have at one's disposal some abbreviated form of writing—a kind of shorthand which allows one to indicate rapidly the intellectual course to be pursued; it can be grasped intuitively in broad outline, but one cannot follow it with the certainty of not going astray, unless it has first been reconnoitered piecemeal. The formulas that I have written with the help of symbols borrowed

[9] Needless to say, I took the first six names that came to mind. But this was perhaps not entirely an effect of chance, since it turns out that when one lists these composers in chronological order, the special functions to which they relate form a closed cycle, as if to demonstrate that in the space of two centuries tonal music has exhausted its internal possibilities of renewal. The older composers give the sequence: code → message → myth; and the more modern ones, the opposite sequence: myth → message → code; always supposing, however, that one is prepared to see some significance in the relatively slight intervals between the dates when the latter were born (Debussy 1862, Ravel 1875, Stravinsky 1882).

from mathematics (chiefly because these symbols are already available in typography) are not intended to prove anything; they are meant rather to suggest in advance the pattern of some discursive account, or to sum up such an account, by bringing within a single purview complex groups of relations and transformations, the detailed description of which may have sorely tried the reader's patience. Far from replacing such a description, their function is merely to illustrate it in a simplified form, which I think is helpful but which some people will no doubt consider superfluous and perhaps even likely to obscure the main argument by adding one form of indefiniteness to another.

I am as conscious as anyone of the very loose senses in which I have employed terms such as "symmetry," "inversion," "equivalence," "homology," "isomorphism," etc. I have used them to refer to large bundles of relations which we vaguely perceive to have something in common. But if the structural analysis of myths has any future, the way in which it chooses and uses its concepts in the initial stages must be subjected to severe criticism. Each term must be defined afresh and limited to a particular use. Above all, the rough classifications that I have used because they were the instruments that came to hand must be refined by analysis into more subtle categories and applied methodically. Only then will it be possible to subject myth to a genuine logico-mathematical analysis; and in the light of this profession of humility, I may perhaps be excused for having thus naïvely attempted to sketch the outlines of such an analysis. After all, the scientific study of myth must involve some very formidable difficulties, since people have hesitated so long to undertake it. However ponderous a volume this may be, it does not claim to have done more than raise a corner of the veil.

My overture therefore comes to a close on a few melancholy chords, after the, by now, ritual thanks that I must offer to collaborators of long standing: M. Jacques Bertin, in whose laboratory the maps and diagrams were drawn; M. Jean Pouillon for his lecture notes, since part of the book formed the subject of a lecture course; Mlle. Nicole Belmart who helped me with documentation and the index; Mme. Edna H. Lemay who did the typing; and my wife and M. Isac Chiva, who read the proofs. But it is time to conclude as I said I would. When I look back over these confused and indigestible pages, I begin to doubt whether the public will have the sensation of listening to a musical work, as the plan and chapter headings try to suggest. What the reader is about to embark on is more likely to remind him of those commentaries on music that are written with an abundance of tedious paraphrase and misguided abstractions—as if music could be the object of linguistic discourse, when its peculiar quality is to express what can be said in no other way. In neither case, therefore, is music present. After making this disillusioned statement, I may at least be allowed the consolation of hoping that when the reader has crossed the bounds of irritation and boredom and is moving away from the book, he will find himself carried toward that music which is to be found in myth and which, in the complete versions, is preserved not only with its harmony and rhythm but also with that hidden significance that I have sought so laboriously to bring to light, at the risk of depriving it of the power and majesty that cause such a violent emotional response when it is experienced in its original state, hidden away in the depths of a forest of images and signs and still fresh with a bewitching enchantment, since in that form at least nobody can claim to understand it.

PART ONE

THEME AND VARIATIONS

1

Bororo Song

a. THE BIRD-NESTER'S ARIA

The following is one of many myths told by the Bororo Indians of central Brazil, whose territory used to extend from the upper reaches of the Paraguay River to beyond the valley of the Araguaya:

M₁ (key myth). Bororo: o xibae e iari. "The macaws and their nest"

In olden times the women used to go into the forest to gather the palms used in the making of *ba*. These were penis sheaths which were presented to adolescents at their initiation ceremony. One youth secretly followed his mother, caught her unawares, and raped her.

When the woman returned from the forest, her husband noticed feathers caught in her bark-cloth belt, which were similar to those worn by youths as an adornment. Suspecting that something untoward had occurred, he decreed that a dance should take place in order to find out which youth was wearing a similar adornment. But to his amazement he discovered that his son was the only one. The man ordered another dance, with the same result.

Convinced now of his misfortune and anxious to avenge himself, he sent his son to the "nest" of souls, with instructions to bring back the great dance rattle (*bapo*), which he coveted. The young man consulted his grandmother who revealed to him the mortal danger that such an undertaking involved; she advised him to obtain the help of the hummingbird.

When the hero, accompanied by the hummingbird, reached the aquatic region of souls, he waited on the shore, while the hummingbird deftly stole the rattle by cutting the short cord from which it was hanging. The instrument fell into the water, making a loud noise—*jo*. Alerted by this noise, the souls fired arrows from their bows. But the hummingbird flew so fast that he reached the shore safe and sound with the stolen rattle.

The father then ordered his son to fetch the small rattle belonging to the souls; and the same episode was repeated, with the same details, only this time the helpful animal was the quick flying juriti (*Leptoptila* species, a kind of dove). During a third expedition, the young man stole some buttore; these are jingling bells made from the hoofs of the caititu (*Dicotyles torquatus,* a type of wild pig), which are strung on a piece of rope and worn as anklets. He was helped by the large grasshopper (*Acridium cristatum,* EB, Vol. I, p.

780), which flew more slowly than the birds so that the arrows pierced it several times but did not kill it.

Furious at the foiling of his plans, the father invited his son to come with him to capture the macaws, which were nesting in the face of a cliff. The grandmother did not know how to ward off this fresh danger, but gave her grandson a magic wand to which he could cling if he happened to fall.

The two men arrived at the foot of the rock; the father erected a long pole and ordered his son to climb it. The latter had hardly reached the nests when the father knocked the pole down; the boy only just had time to thrust the wand into a crevice. He remained suspended in the void, crying for help, while the father went off.

Our hero noticed a creeper within reach of his hand; he grasped hold of it and with difficulty dragged himself to the top of the rock. After a rest he set out to look for food, made a bow and arrows out of branches, and hunted the lizards which abounded on the plateau. He killed a lot of them and hooked the surplus ones to his belt and to the strips of cotton wound round his legs and ankles. But the dead lizards went bad and gave off such a vile smell that the hero fainted. The vultures (*Cathartes urubu, Coragyps atratus foetens*) fell upon him, devoured first of all the lizards, and then attacked the body of the unfortunate youth, beginning with his buttocks. Pain restored him to consciousness, and the hero drove off his attackers which, however, had completely gnawed away his hindquarters. Having eaten their fill, the birds were prepared to save his life; taking hold of his belt and the strips of cotton round his arms and legs with their beaks, they lifted him into the air and deposited him gently at the foot of the mountain.

The hero regained consciousness "as if he were awaking from a dream." He was hungry and ate wild fruits but noticed that since he had no rectum, he was unable to retain the food, which passed through his body without even being digested. The youth was at first nonplussed and then remembered a tale told him by his grandmother, in which the hero solved the same problem by molding for himself an artificial behind out of dough made from pounded tubers.

After making his body whole again by this means and eating his fill, he returned to his village, only to find that it had been abandoned. He wandered around for a long time looking for his family. One day he spotted foot and stick marks, which he recognized as being those of his grandmother. He followed the tracks but, being anxious not to reveal his presence, he took on the appearance of a lizard, whose antics fascinated the old woman and her other grandson, the hero's younger brother. Finally, after a long interval, he decided to reveal himself to them. (In order to re-establish contact with his grandmother, the hero went through a series of transformations, turning himself into four birds and a butterfly, all unidentified; Colb. 2, pp. 235–6.)

On that particular night there was a violent wind accompanied by a thunder storm which put out all the fires in the village except the grandmother's. Next morning everybody came and asked her for hot embers, in particular the second wife of the father who had tried to kill his son. She recognized her stepson, who was supposed to be dead, and ran to warn her husband. As if there were nothing wrong, the latter picked up his ceremonial rattle and welcomed his son with the songs of greeting for returned travelers.

However, the hero was full of thoughts of revenge. One day while he was walking in the forest with his little brother, he broke off a branch of the api tree, which was shaped like a deer's antler. The child, acting on his elder brother's instructions, then managed to make the father promise to order a collective hunt; in the guise of a mea, a small rodent, he secretly kept watch to discover where their father was lying in wait for the game. The hero then donned the false antlers, changed into a deer, and rushed at his father with such ferocity that he impaled him on the horns. Without stopping, he galloped toward a lake, into which he dropped his victim, who was immediately devoured by the Buiogoe spirits who are carnivorous fish. All that remained after the gruesome feast were the bare bones which lay on the bottom of the lake, and the lungs which floated on the surface in the form of aquatic plants, whose leaves, it is said, resemble lungs.

When he returned to the village, the hero took his revenge on his father's wives (one of whom was his own mother).

This myth provides the theme of a song, called *xobogeu*, belonging to the Paiwe clan of which the hero was a member (Colb. 3, pp. 224–9, 343–7).

An older version ends as follows. The hero declared: "I no longer want to live with the Orarimugu who have ill-treated me, and in order to have my revenge on them and my father, I shall send them wind, cold, and rain." Then he took his grandmother into a beautiful and distant land, and returned to punish the Indians as he said he would (Colb. 2, p. 236).

b. Recitative

1. It is well known that the model Bororo village consists of eight collective huts, each one housing several families and all arranged round an open space, in the center of which stands the men's house. A line running from east to west divides the village into two moieties. To the north are the Cera comprising (from east to west) the four huts belonging respectively to the following clans: *badegaba cobugiwu* "upper chiefs"; *boḳodori* "large armadillo"; *ḳi* "tapir"; *badegeba cebgiwu* "lower chiefs." To the south are the Tugare, comprising (west to east) the four huts of the following clans: *iwaguddu* "the azure jay" [Portuguese: *gralha azul* (*Cyanocorax caecrulus*)]; *arore* "larva"; *apibore* "acuri palm tree" (*Attalea speciosa*); *paiwe* or *paiwoe* "howler monkey" (*Alouatta* species). In either direction the east-west axis is supposed to extend to the "villages of the souls" over which reign (in the west) the culture hero, Bakororo, whose emblem is the transverse wooden trumpet (*iḳa*), and (in the east) the culture hero, Itubore, whose emblem is the resonator (*panna*) made from hollowed gourds pierced with holes and stuck together with wax.

In all observed cases the clans were for the most part subdivided into subclans and lineages; others had disappeared, and the general pattern was more complex. In order to illustrate the social structure of the Bororo, we are therefore obliged to choose between three possibilities: either, as we have done here, make a theoretical and simplified model; or give the plan of one

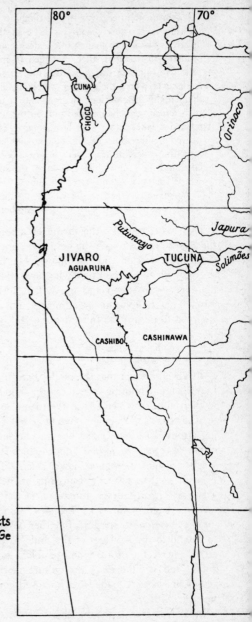

Area covered by Ge linguistic group

Area covered by Tupi dialects of tribes bordering on the Ge

URUBU Tupi-speaking tribes

Gran Chaco

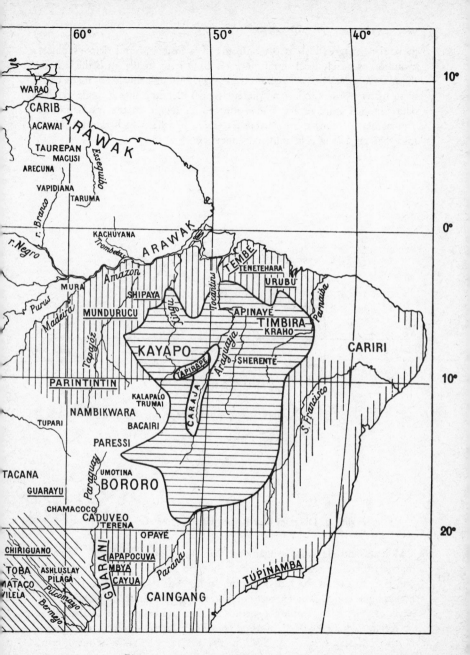

Figure 1. Geographical distribution of the chief tribes mentioned.

particular village which is the outcome of a historical and demographical evolution of purely local significance (L.-S. O.); or finally, as is the case in the *Enciclopédia Boróro* (Vol. I, pp. 434–44), although this is not made clear in so many words, produce a syncretic model blending into a single pattern data obtained from several native sources. In regard to the translation of clan names, I follow the *Enciclopédia* (*ibid.*, p. 438), which clarifies meanings that for a long time remained uncertain.

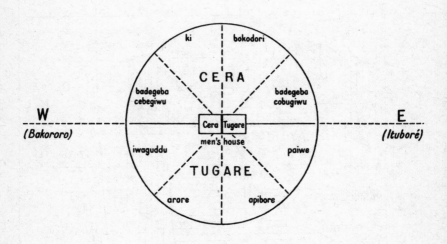

Figure 2. Diagram of a Bororo village (from C. Albisetti).

Moieties and clans are exogamous, matrilineal, and matrilocal. When he marries, therefore, each man crosses the line separating the two moieties and goes to live in the hut belonging to his wife's clan. But in the men's house, into which women are not allowed to penetrate, he continues to have his place in the sector assigned to his clan and his moiety. In the village of Kejara, where I stayed in 1935, the men's house was situated along a north-south axis (plan in L.-S. O, p. 273, and 3, p. 229). Without offering either explanation or comment, the *Enciclopédia Boróro* (pp. 436, 445) presents things in the same way; yet from 1919 to 1948 Colbacchini and Albisetti, either together or separately, continued to maintain that the men's

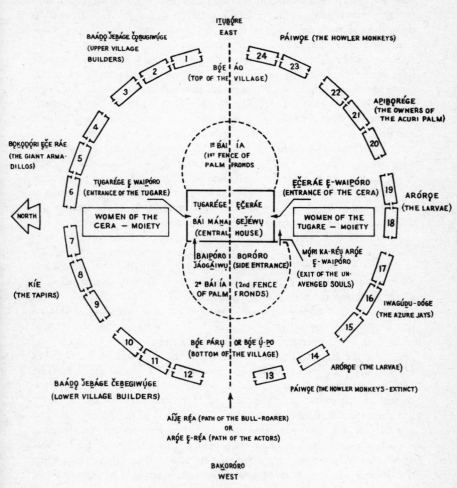

ITUBÓRE
EAST

BAÁDǪ ᴊEBÁGE ĮǪBUGIWÚGE
(UPPER VILLAGE
BUILDERS)

BǪE ᴊÁO
(TOP OF THE VILLAGE)

PÁIWǪE (THE HOWLER MONKEYS)

24 23

1

2

3

22

21

20

APIBǪRÉGE
(THE OWNERS OF
THE ACURI PALM)

4

BǪKǪDǪRI ᴇᴄᴇ RÁE
(THE GIANT ARMA-
DILLOS)

5

6

1ª BÁI ᴊÁ
(1ST FENCE OF
PALM FRONDS)

NORTH

TUGARÉGE Ę WAIPÓRO
(ENTRANCE OF THE TUGARE)

EᴄᴇRÁE Ę-WAIPÓRO
(ENTRANCE OF THE CERA)

19

ARÓRǪE
(THE LARVAE)

WOMEN OF THE
CERA — MOIETY

TUGARÉGE   EᴄᴇRÁE

BÁI MÁ IA   GEᴊÉWᵾ
(CENTRAL HOUSE)

WOMEN OF THE
TUGARE — MOIETY

18

7

BAIPÓRO   BORÓRO
ᴊÁOGÁIWᵾ   (SIDE ENTRANCE)

MǪRI KA-RÉᵾ ARǪE
Ę-WAIPÓRO
(EXIT OF THE UN-
AVENGED SOULS)

17

8

9

KÍE
(THE TAPIRS)

2ª BÁI ᴊÁ
OF PALM FRONDS)

(2nd FENCE
OF PALM FRONDS)

16

15

IWAGÚDU-DÓGE
(THE AZURE JAYS)

10

11

12

BǪE PÁRᵾ   OR BǪE Ú-PO
(BOTTOM OF THE VILLAGE)

14

13

ARÓRǪE (THE LARVAE)

BAÁDǪ ᴊEBÁGE ᴄEBEGIWÚGE
(LOWER VILLAGE BUILDERS)

PÁIWǪE (THE HOWLER MONKEYS-EXTINCT)

Aᴊᴇ RÉA (PATH OF THE BULL-ROARER)
OR
ARǪE Ę-RÉA (PATH OF THE ACTORS)

BAKORÓRO
WEST

Figure 3. Diagram of a Bororo village
(from the *Enciclopédia Boróro*, Vol. I, p. 436).

house was situated along an east-west axis. One may speculate endlessly about this belated change of opinion, which confirms my observations but contradicts all that the Salesians have been writing on the subject for more than forty years. Can it be that during all those years they based their arguments on data derived purely from the village of Rio Barreiro (photos taken in 1910, in Colb. 2, pp. 7, 9), which was built near the mission station at the instigation of the Fathers and presents several anomalies (a square, rather than a round, ground plan, since "the Indians hardly differentiate between the circle and the square" (*sic*); a men's house with four entrances corresponding to the cardinal points and with thirteen paths leading up to them)? But even if this were so, more recent evidence does not necessarily invalidate observations made long ago. In reading the *Enciclopédia Boróro,* one often gets the impression that the authors and their predecessors have been enthusiastically pursuing a single and absolute truth which, so far as the Bororo Indians are concerned, probably never existed. Although respectful of the evidence supplied by their informants on these matters, the Salesians were perhaps less willing to accept their differences. Politely but firmly they would invite the natives to form a council and to reach some agreement about what should be the accepted dogma. This explains why from Colbacchini 1 to Colbacchini 2 and again to Colbacchini 3 and finally to the *Enciclopédia Boróro* by way of Albisetti, there can be detected a dual process of enrichment and impoverishment: detailed information is piled up and will culminate finally in what promises to be the tremendous storehouse of the *Enciclopédia;* yet at the same time the outlines harden, and old indications and suggestions disappear, without it always being possible to know whether this is because mistakes have been duly rectified, or because truths have been abandoned through an inability to accept the view that the realities of Bororo life might be multiform. Nevertheless if, as the Salesians themselves discovered, between the upper courses of the Itiquira and the Correntes rivers the bones of the dead were laid in grottoes in the rock face instead of being immersed in water as was the general custom, and if the practice survived until relatively recent times, as is suggested by the state of preservation of the remains that have been found (EB, Vol. I, pp. 537–41), what a tremendous variety of customs it must be possible to envisage in other spheres, which the Indian undoubtedly considered no more vital than the question of funeral rites. In several places the *Enciclopédia Boróro* expresses the opinion that the Bororo are the descendants of a tribe that came originally from Bolivia and was therefore culturally more advanced than the existing tribe and, in particular, was acquainted with the use of precious metals. It would be absurd to imagine that during this migratory process the natives were able to retain all the characteristics of their former mode of life, and that it did not undergo many and various changes according to locality and the kind of terrain occupied (the Bororo are still divided into eastern and western groups, and the first group subdivides into those who live on the sandy plateau and those who live in the marshy valleys); finally, it must have come under the influence of the neighboring communities—to the east, the west, the north, and the south—which are themselves characterized by great differences in culture.

2. The clans are distinguished one from another by the place they occupy in the social hierarchy, by their emblems, by the privileges and taboos relating to the technique and style of manufactured objects, and, finally, by the ceremonies, songs, and proper names peculiar to each. In this respect the names of the chief characters in the key myth provide valuable indications,

which I propose to group together provisionally, pending publication of the second volume of the *Enciclopédia Boróro* which, as is known, will deal with proper names.

The hero is called Geriguiguiatugo. This name, which is mentioned by the *Enciclopédia Boróro* (Vol. I, p. 689), does not figure on the list of names of the Paiwe clan given in Colbacchini 3 (glossary of proper names, pp. 441–6). It can be split up into: *atugo* "painted," "decorated," an adjective that, used substantively, refers to the jaguar; and *geriguigui* "land tortoise" (*djerighighe* "kágado," B. de Magalhães, p. 33; *jerigigi* "name of a variety of *cagado*," EB, Vol. I, p. 689) or "the constellation Corvus" (Colb. 1, pp. 33–4; 2, p. 220; 3, pp. 219, 420). This last meaning, which was discarded by the *Enciclopédia Boróro* (Vol. I, pp. 612–13) in favor of a different constellation, will be discussed at length later (see Part Four, II). The hero also bears the name Toribugo, no doubt from *tori* "stone"; compare Colbacchini 3, glossary (p. 446): *tori bugu,* masculine and feminine, *como pedra* ("like stone"). It transpires from the *Enciclopédia Boróro* (Vol. I, p. 981) that in sacred language the *jerigigi* tortoise is called *tori tabowu* "the creature (whose shell is) like a stone"—a detail that creates a link between the two names. The tortoise is one of the eponyms of the Paiwe clan (Colb. 3, p. 32), to which we know the hero belonged. By virtue of the matrilineal law of consanguinity, it must also have been his mother's clan. His mother's name was Korogo. According to the *Encyclopédia Boróro* (Vol. I, p. 746), the word *koroge* refers in fact to an enemy tribe, conquered and subsequently assimilated as a Paiwe subclan.

The mother and son being Tugare, the father belonged to the other moiety, since the moieties were exogamous: he must have been a Cera. According to the glossary of proper names given in Colbacchini 3 (p. 441), his name Bokwadorireu, sometimes spelled Bokuaddorireu (from *bokwaddo* "jatoba tree"?), belonged to the *badegeba cebegiwu* clan, "lower chiefs," which is precisely in the Cera moiety.

The father's second wife was called Kiareware. The name is simply mentioned in passing in the *Enciclopédia Boróro* (Vol. I, p. 716).

3a. The myth begins with a reference to the initiation rites. According to Colbacchini 3, these lasted a whole year; according to the *Enciclopédia Boróro,* several months (Vol. I, pp. 624–42) and until someone in the village died, so that the final phase of the initiation could coincide with the funeral rites. In spite of this discrepancy, which perhaps does not present any insuperable problem, both sources agree about the grueling experiences the novices suffered during the journey several hundred miles long (*dezenas e dezenas de léguas,* EB, Vol. I, p. 641), which they made under the guidance of the older men. When they were finally brought back, hirsute, emaciated, and completely covered with leaves, their respective mothers had to identify them before taking them off to wash and shave them and do their hair. The novices performed ritual leaps over a fire, and the ceremony of the return ended with everyone bathing in the river (Colb. 3, pp. 239–40).

Mothers greeted their sons by "weeping bitterly and uttering cries and lamentations as if for the death of some loved one. They wept because, from now on, the boy, having been emancipated, would leave the women to go to live with the men. Also from now on until the end of his life, the young man would wear the *ba*, or penis sheath. . . ." (Colb. 3, pp. 171–2; EB, Vol. I, pp. 628, 642).

3b. The penis sheath occurred originally in myth. The natives attributed its invention to the hero Baitogogo, whose acquaintance we shall make presently (M2 on page 49). Formerly, "they did not pierce their lower lip and did not wear sheaths; they did not use any of the adornments they wear today and did not paint their bodies with urucu. . . ." (EB, Vol. I, p. 61). The word *ba* could apparently also mean "egg" or "testicle" (B. de Magalhães, p. 19); but the *Enciclopédia Boróro* (Vol. I, p. 189) maintains that this was in fact a different word.

3c. According to the oldest versions of the myth, "it was the women who, on the day preceding the initiation ceremony, went into the forest to gather branches of the babassu palm (*Orbignya* species) to make the *ba* intended for the young boy. The women made it, the men fixed it in position . . ." (Colb. 3, p. 172). This reading is vigorously denied by the *Enciclopédia Boróro* (Vol. I, p. 641), which maintains that the gathering of the palm branches was also carried out by "grandmothers and uncles, or to be more exact by the nearest relatives of the novice's mother."

The discrepancy poses a curious problem. As a matter of fact, the original wording of the myth and the juxtalinear Italian translation do not admit of any ambiguity:

> ba-gi maerege e   maragoddu-re.   Korogo
> *Il ba gli antenati essi lavorarono.   Korogo* (mother's name)
>
> ǧameddo aremme e-bo[1] u-ttu-re
> *anche donne   colle essa ando*

The following work (in Portuguese) by the Salesian Fathers, written in collaboration by Colbacchini and Albisetti (Colb. 3), upholds this version in its entirety. Nevertheless, if we refer to the Bororo text, which is quoted again in the second part, we discover that the beginning of the myth has been changed:

> Koddoro gire maregue e maragoddure.   Korogue utture
> *Esteira ela antepassados eles trabalhavam.   Korogue foi*
> aremebo jameddo.
> *mulheres com tambem.*   (Colb. 3, p. 343.)

---

[1] *Sott. 'a cercare foglie di palma per costruire i bá.* (Colb. 2, p. 92 and n. 4.) Later (pp. 107–8) the author comments: *Per fare questi bá in occasione d'un 'iniziazione, le donne vanno alla foresta a cercare foglie della palma uaguassù, come appare anche dalla leggenda di Gerigigiatugo.*

In other words, even though there has been no change either in the free Portuguese version or in the ethnographic commentary, the Bororo text and its juxtalinear translation are no longer quite the same: it is still the women who go into the forest, but the aim of the expedition, instead of being to gather palm leaves for the penis sheaths, is to collect straw with which to make rush mats, *esteira*. Are we to understand that this is another version of the myth, obtained subsequently from a different informant? Not at all. Apart from the point noted, the two versions—the 1925 one and the 1942 one—are identical. Furthermore, both are incomplete, and both break off at exactly the same point. The alteration in the 1942 wording must therefore be attributed to a native scribe (the Salesians were helped in turn by two or three educated informants). In retranscribing a myth, he probably noticed that a certain detail did not correspond to customs which he himself had observed or which had been described to him, and took it upon himself to alter the text in order to make it correspond to what he considered to be the ethnographic reality. His action, which passed unnoticed in 1942, must have been spotted later. This would explain the change of opinion in the *Enciclopédia Boróro* and confirms the interpretation I put forward above, about another change of the same kind. We can thus forecast that both the text and the commentary of the key myth, in the form in which they will appear in the second volume of the *Enciclopédia Boróro,* will definitely eliminate all reference to any kind of participation by the women in the making of the penis sheaths.

It is regrettable that such liberties should be taken with the wording of a myth. As I have shown elsewhere (L.-S. 6), a myth may well contradict the ethnographic reality to which it is supposed to refer, and the distortion nevertheless forms part of its structure. Or it may be the case that the myth perpetuates the memory of customs that have disappeared or still persist in another part of the tribal territory. In this particular instance the original reading is especially noteworthy, since the new material and new interpretations found in the *Enciclopédia Boróro* strengthen the link, which is testified to, actually or symbolically, in the myth, betweeen the fixing in place of the penis sheath and the organization of sexual relations characteristic of the Bororo community. Only after he had been fitted with the *ba* was the young man allowed to marry (p. 628). Not only must the "sponsor" entrusted with the making and fitting on of the sheath belong to the opposite moiety from that of the novice—"the subclans from which the young man can choose his bride are always taken into consideration, too; the sponsor must also be a member of one of these" (p. 639). Among the Bororo Indians, in fact, not only does exogamy prevail between the two moieties; there are also preferences about the subclans and lineage groups among which marriages should take place (p. 450). At the end of the ceremony "the novice offers food to his sponsor, observing the same ritual conventions as would a wife with her husband" (p. 629).

This last point is of fundamental importance, because Colb. 2 assumed the opposite kind of relation between novice and sponsor. Commenting on an account of the initiation rites in Bororo language:

emma-re-u   ak'oredduğe-re-u
esso proprio (ecco qui) la tua moglie costui,

the author concluded that "in the minds of the Indians, it would seem that the *jorubbadare* (sponsor) represented the future wife" (p. 105 and n. 4). Colb. 3 (p. 172) upholds the same interpretation.

Using as evidence a new description written by an educated informant, the *Enciclopédia Boróro* maintains that this is a misinterpretation and that the sexual symbolism of the *ba* is more complex. According to the new account, the novice's grandfathers and elder brothers first of all take a bud (or a young shoot, Portuguese *brôto*) from the babassu palm and offer it to the man whom they have chosen to play the part of sponsor, saying to him: "This (bud) will in truth be your bride." Helped by his elder and younger brothers (the novice's future "brothers-in-law"), the sponsor then loses no time in making the leaves into penis sheaths, which the novice wears around his head all night, strung together in the form of a crown. Next morning the sponsor is led back to the novice who is still wearing his crown, and the formula is repeated. Thereupon one sheath is picked out, and the novice at first holds it between his teeth; he has to keep his eyes raised when it is being fitted, so that he sees nothing of the operation, which takes place in two stages: there is a provisional fitting, then a permanent one.

If the theory that "the young babassu shoot and the penis sheath . . . represent the female organ, since they are called the sponsor's brides" (EB, Vol. I, p. 640) were confirmed, it would completely alter our ideas about the symbolism of the penis sheath, in both South America and elsewhere. Without venturing to develop this idea, I would nevertheless like to stress one of its implications: the rite seems to identify the penis sheath and the substance of which it is made, not with the feminine sex in general, but with the women of the moiety and even of the clan and subclan to which the novice belongs and with which the sponsor's subclan prefers to intermarry—in other words, with those women who might be the sponsor's "brides" and who, according to the contested version of the myth, play an active part in the gathering of the palms, a detail that suggests the same identification figuratively.

However, in the present state of our knowledge, the interpretation given by the *Enciclopédia Boróro* cannot be accepted as final. The ritual formula *emmareu ak-oreduje* "this one will be your wife" refers to a subject whose identity remains somewhat uncertain. At first Colbacchini thought that the sponsor was the subject of the sentence. But even if, as it seems, the sponsor is not the subject, "this one" could refer to the novice or the bud

1. A view of the rock formations of the *chapada* where the Bororo look for macaw's nests.

2. A macaw fledgling.

or the sheath; and the comment already quoted from page 629 would appear to favor the first solution.

Whatever the truth of the matter, the answer to this problem is not essential for the point I am trying to prove, which merely requires that the expedition into the forest at the beginning of the narrative be of a specifically feminine nature. Now this remains true in the modified, as well as in the original, version, since both maintain that the hero's mother went into the forest "along with the other women." The collecting of straw for the purpose of making rush mats, which is referred to in the modified version, would, if necessary, confirm this invariant feature, since among the Bororo Indians, the plaiting of straw was a feminine occupation, whereas weaving was done by the men (Colb. 1, pp. 31–2).

4. The Bororo Indians like to catch young macaws, which they then feed in the village and pluck periodically. The rock faces where the birds nest rise to a height of 200 or 300 meters above the low-lying marshy land. They form the southern and western edges of the central plateau, which slopes gradually to the north as far as the Amazon basin.

5. The macaws occupy an important place in native thought processes for two reasons. Their feathers, which are carefully preserved along with those of other birds (toucan, egret, harpy eagle, etc.) in wooden caskets, are used in the making of diadems and crowns and to decorate bows and other objects. At the same time the Bororos believe in a complicated system of trans-migration of souls: the latter are thought to become embodied for a time in the macaws.

6. The arousing of the father's suspicions by the mere sight of the feathers clinging to his wife's girdle after the rape can be explained by the contrast between masculine and feminine attire among the Bororo. Apart from their penis sheaths, the men are naked; but in the ordinary course of events (and always on festive occasions) they like to wear elaborate ornaments made of fur, multicolored feathers, or bark painted with various designs. The women's attire consists of a slip made from white bark (black when they are unwell: B. de Magalhães, pp. 29, 30; EB, Vol. I, p. 89) and a high girdle, almost a corset, also made of bark, but dark in color. Feminine ornaments consist for the most part of cotton straps colored with red urucu (*Bixa orellana*) dye, which quickly fades, and of pendants and necklaces made from jaguar's fangs or monkey's teeth, worn only on feast days. The creamy whiteness of the necklaces discreetly sets off the yellows, browns, and somber reds of the women's costume, the almost austere soberness of which is in striking con-trast to the brilliant display of color among the men.

7a. Several animal species occur in the key myth: the hummingbird, the dove, the grasshopper, the lizard, the vulture, and the deer. We will come back to them later. The mea, "cotia" (Colb. 3, p. 430), *Dasyprocta aguti*, is a rodent mentioned among the eponyms of the Paiwe clan (*ibid.*, p. 32).

7b. The data so far available does not make it possible to identify with any accuracy the *pogodóri* (*bobotóri,* Colb. 2, p. 135), "a kind of potato" with which the hero made himself a new set of buttocks. According to the *Enciclopédia Boróro* (Vol. I, p. 882), it is a kind of edible tuber like the *cara,* and its leaves can be smoked in place of tobacco: on page 787 it is referred to more specifically as a "woodland dioscorea." This episode will be discussed further in a future work, in which I shall deal with what American mythographers refer to as the "anus stopper." It is widely distributed throughout the New World, since it is found in North America from New Mexico to Canada, and it is mentioned with special frequency in the tribal mythology of Oregon and Washington (Coos, Kalapuya, Kathlamet, etc.).

7c. We are equally uncertain about the species of tree which the hero used for making the false antlers, and which is called *api* in Bororo. The glossary in Colb. 3 (p. 410) gives *app'i* "sucupira," a meaning confirmed by the *Enciclopédia Boróro* (Vol. I, p. 77): *appi* "sucupira" (Ormosia species); but see also page 862: *paro i* "sucupira" (a leguminous plant). In fact, the term, which is of Tupi origin, covers several species—in particular, *Bowdichia virgilioides,* whose hardness and branch formation correspond fairly well to the use described in the myth, and *Pterodon pubescens* (Hoehne, p. 284).

7d. On the other hand, there is no doubt about the identity of the cannibal spirits: *buiogue,* plural of *buiogo; piranha* (*Serrasalmus* genus, EB, Vol. I, p. 520), which haunt the lakes and rivers of central and southern Brazil and whose voracity is justly renowned.

8. The song mentioned at the end of the myth was published by Albisetti (pp. 16–18) in what is referred to as "archaic" language and therefore is untranslatable even by the Salesians. The song seems to be about a battle between white men and Indians; the murder of the red-headed urubu by his younger brother, the japuira bird (an oriole); the expedition made by the bird-nester to the rock face: his transformation into a deer, so that he could kill his father; and the plunging of the latter into the waters of the lake, "as if he had been an egret."

c. FIRST VARIATION

The initial theme of the key myth is the incest committed by the hero with the mother. Yet the idea that he is "guilty" seems to exist mainly in the mind of the father, who desires his son's death and schemes to bring it about. The myth itself, however, does not render a verdict, since the hero begs for and obtains help from his grandmother, thanks to whom he survives all the ordeals. In the long run, it is the father who appears guilty, through having tried to avenge himself, and it is he who is killed.

This curious indifference toward incest appears in other myths; for example, in the myth in which the wronged husband is also punished:

M₂. Bororo. "*The origin of water, adornments, and funeral rites*"

In olden times, when the two village chiefs belonged to the Tugare moiety (and not, as they do today, to the Cera moiety) and were respectively members of the Arore clan and the Apibore clan, there was a principal chief, called Birimoddo "pretty skin" (Cruz 1; Colb. 3, p. 206) and nicknamed Baitogogo (the meaning of the word will be discussed later).

One day when Baitogogo's wife—a member of the Bokodori clan in the Cera moiety—was setting off into the forest to look for wild fruit, her young son asked to go with her; and as she refused, he secretly followed her.

He thus saw his mother being raped by an Indian from the Ki clan, a member of the same moiety as her own (and consequently her "brother," according to native terminology). Informed by the child of what had happened, Baitogogo first took revenge on his rival, by shooting arrows at him which pierced in turn his shoulder, his arm, his hip, his buttock, his leg, and his face and finally finished him off with a wound in the side; after this, Baitogogo strangled his wife with a bowstring during the night. Helped by four different species of armadillo or *tatu*—*bokodori* (giant armadillo, *Priodontes giganteus*); *gerego* (*tatu-liso*, EB, Vol. I, p. 687, *tatu-bola, Dasypus tricintus*, B. de Magalhães, p. 33); *enokuri* (*tatu-bola-do-campo*, EB, Vol. I, p. 566); *okwaru* (a variety of *tatu-peba, ibid.*, p. 840)—he dug a trench just below his wife's bed and buried the body there, taking care to fill up the hole and to cover it over with a mat, so that no one should discover his crime.

The little boy nevertheless went on looking for his mother. Emaciated and tearful, he became exhausted through following the false tracks suggested by the murderer. Finally one day when Baitogogo was taking the air with his second wife, the child turned into a bird in order to search more effectively for his mother. He deliberately allowed his droppings to fall on Baitogogo's shoulder, where the excrement germinated and grew into a huge tree (the jatoba, *Hymenea courbaril*).

Hampered and humiliated by this burden, the hero left the village and lived a wandering existence in the bush. But every time he stopped to rest, he caused lakes and rivers to appear, for at that time there was no water on the earth. At each new appearance of water the tree shrank and finally disappeared.

Nevertheless, Baitogogo was enchanted by the verdant landscape he had created, and decided not to return to the village but to leave the chieftainship to his father. The second chief who governed in his absence did likewise and followed him: thus both halves of the chieftainship fell to the Cera moiety. Having now become the two culture heroes, Bakororo and Itubore (cf. pp. 37, 42), the former chiefs never returned to visit their fellow tribesmen, except to bring adornments, ornaments, and instruments which they invented and manufactured during their voluntary exile.[2]

When they reappeared in the village for the first time in their superb attire, their fathers, who had succeeded them, were frightened at first and

[2] From a historical point of view, it is interesting to compare this myth with the episode in the Apapocuva myth where the Fai brothers, wearing loincloths and rich costumes, distribute adornments and ornaments among men (Nim. 1, pp. 37–8).

then welcomed them with ritual songs. Akario Bokodori, the father of Akaruio Borogo, Baitogogo's companion, demanded that the heroes (who seem here to have increased from being only two to being a whole band) should give him all their ornaments. The myth ends with an episode that at first appears puzzling: "He did not kill those who brought him many, but killed those who had brought him few." (Colb. 3, pp. 201–6.)

d. INTERLUDE IN A DISCRETE MODE[3]

I propose to dwell on this episode for a moment, although it does not immediately concern my thesis. It is, however, worthy of study since it emphasizes the central position that these two myths occupy in Bororo philosophy, and thus justifies my choice.

In both the key myth and the myth I have just summarized, the hero belongs to the Tugare moiety. Now the two myths are presented by Colbacchini as being etiological narratives: the first explains "the origin of wind and rain" (Colb. 3, p. 221); the second, "the origin of water and ornaments" (*ibid.*, p. 201). Both functions correspond accurately to the role ascribed to the heroes of the Tugare moiety—that is, to the "strong" (?). Whether as creators or as demiurges, they were more often than not responsible for the *existence* of things: rivers, lakes, rain, fish, vegetation, and manufactured objects. The Cera heroes (*Cera* is a word that is sometimes taken to mean "the weak"[4]), being priests rather than sorcerers, intervene after the event as *organizers* and *administrators* of a creation of which the Tugare were the *originators:* they destroy monsters, provide animals with their specific foods, and organize the village and society.

From this point of view, then, there already exists a certain parallel between the two myths. Each one has a Tugare hero who creates water either of celestial origin after moving in an upward direction (by climbing up a hanging creeper) or water of terrestrial origin, after being forced in a downward direction (bowed down by a growing tree whose weight he is supporting). On the other hand, the celestial water is harmful, since it comes from the storms called *badogebague* (which the Bororos distinguish from the gentle, beneficent *butaudogue* rains; cf. Colb. 3, pp. 229–30; I shall come back to this contrast, which is not mentioned in the *Enciclopédia Boróro;* cf. below

---

[3] TRANSLATORS' NOTE: *Interlude du discret:* The author is no doubt playing on the double meaning of *discret,* "discrete" and "discreet." However, the literal meaning requires "discrete" in English.

[4] The meanings "strong" and "weak" were arrived at independently by Colbacchini and myself, in the field. Yet one of Colbacchini's informants disputes their accuracy (Colb. 3, p. 30); and EB (Vol. I, p. 444) rejects them entirely. Nevertheless there is a puzzling phrase in the oldest version of the myth of the twins (M_{46}): if you kill the cannibal eagle, the jaguar says to the heroes, you will be strong and will command "*a muitos tugaregedos (servos*)." (Colb. 1, p. 118); or according to another version: "a great people will be under your sway" (Colb. 3, p. 194).

pp. 213 ff.), whereas terrestrial water is beneficent. The contrast is to be explained by the symmetrically opposed circumstances of their respective creations: the first hero was, through no wish of his own, separated from his village by his father's malevolence; the second was also separated from his village, but he chose to be so and was prompted by a kindly feeling toward his father, to whom he delegated his duties.[5]

After these preliminary remarks, let us now return to the episode of the massacre committed by a certain Akario Bokodori. We come across this personage again, playing a similar part under the name of Acaruio Bokodori (the transcription is different, but such uncertainties are frequent in the source material); he is also a member of the clan of the "upper chiefs" (cf. Colb. 3, glossary of proper names, p. 442: Akkaruio *bokkodori* [*sic*], masculine and feminine, "famous for his adornments made from the [claws] of the great armadillo"). Here is the myth:

M₃. *Bororo. "After the flood"*

After a flood the earth became reinhabited; but previously men had been increasing to such an extent that Meri, the sun, was afraid and looked round for a way to reduce their numbers.

He therefore ordered the entire population of a village to cross a wide river by means of a bridge made from a tree trunk, which he had specially chosen because it was not very strong. It did, in fact, snap under the load; and all the people perished, with the exception of one man called Akaruio Bokodori, who could only walk slowly because his legs were deformed.

The hair of those who were sucked into the whirlpools turned wavy or curly; the hair of those who drowned in calm waters was fine and smooth. This became clear after Akaruio Bokodori had brought them all back to life by incantations with a drum accompaniment. He brought back first the Buremoddodogue, then the Rarudogue, the Bitodudogue, the Pugaguegeugue, the Rokuddudogue, the Codogue, and finally the Boiugue, who were his favorites. But of all these newly returned people, he welcomed only those whose gifts he approved of. He shot down all the others with his arrows and so was dubbed Mamuiauguexeba "killer" or Evidoxeba "cause-death." (Colb. 3, pp. 231, 241–2.)

The same personage appears in another myth: again he murders his companions, but this time it is to punish them for not treating him with the respect due to a leader and for having quarreled among themselves (Colb. 3, p. 30). Unfortunately this story is too disconnected to be of any use.

---

[5] Following Colbacchini, some people may see this as a twofold mystery, since in fact the chieftainship was handed down from one generation to the next and from maternal uncle to nephew. But it can already be understood, from this example, that a myth derives its significance not from contemporary or archaic institutions of which it is a reflection, but from its relation to other myths within a transformation group.

THE RAW AND THE COOKED

We know therefore of at least two myths in which a hero of the Cera moiety, similarly named, kills off a population of "ghosts," who are bearing gifts, because he considered these gifts to be inadequate.[6] In one instance the nature of the gifts is not specified; in the other we know that they consisted of adornments and ritual ornaments, shared out unequally among the clans, but of which each clan—whether or not it was held to be "rich" or "poor" in this respect—had the exclusive ownership. Adornments and ornaments thus introduced divergences within the society.

But let us examine M_3 more carefully. It is not very clear on the subject of presents but is quite definite on two other points. First, the myth claims to account for divergences in physical appearance (instead of social appearance), as in the episode of the hair. Next, through giving a list of names, which remain somewhat puzzling in the present state of our knowledge— apart from the fact that the flexional ending /-gue/ indicates the plural form[7]—the myth suggests distinct and separate human groups, in all probability communities or tribes: these are groups endowed with different values operating not *below* the level of society, like physical differences, but *above* it. In the first case they may be differences among individuals within the group; and in the second, differences among groups. Whereas M_3 has the dual aspect, M_2 occupies an intermediary position and deals with social differences among subgroups within the group.

It would therefore seem that the two myths, taken together, refer to three domains, each of which was originally continuous, but into which discontinuity had to be introduced in order that each might be conceptualized. In each case, discontinuity is achieved by the radical elimination of certain fractions of the continuum. Once the latter has been reduced, a smaller number of elements are free to spread out in the same space, while the distance between them is now sufficient to prevent them overlapping or merging into one another.

Men had to become less numerous for the most closely related physical types to be clearly distinguishable. For if we admit the existence of clans or tribes bearing *insignificant* gifts—that is whose distinctive originality is as weak as one cares to imagine—we should run the risk of finding that between any two given clans or communities there was an unlimited number of

[6] In the *Enciclopédia Boróro* (Vol. I, pp. 58–59) we are told that whenever an unknown Bororo arrived at a village, he was subjected to a thorough inspection, the aim of which was to find out whether he was carrying any object of interest. If he was, he was warmly welcomed; otherwise he was murdered. The little rattle (which is mentioned in M_1) is supposed to have been originally obtained in this way from an Indian woman who had at first been received with hostile demonstrations.

[7] They can be compared with similar or identical forms: *ragudu-dogé, rarai-dogé,* the names of legendary tribes (Colb. I, p. 5); *buremoddu-dogé* "the people with beautiful feet" (nickname of the Ki clan); *raru-dogé,* "a name which the Bororo apply to themselves in several legends"; *codagé* "ants of the *Eciton* genus; *boiwugé* "the last to arrive" (EB, Vol. I, pp. 529, 895, 544, 504).

other clans or other tribes, each one of which would differ so slightly from its immediate neighbors that they all would ultimately merge into each other; whereas in any field a system of significances can be constructed only on the basis of discrete quantities.

If limited purely to the Bororo, this interpretation may seem flimsy. It appears more convincing, however, when it is compared to the similar interpretation I have put forward for myths originating in different communities, but with a formal structure analagous to the one just outlined. For the five great clans from which the Ojibwa believe their society to have sprung to be established, six supernatural personages had to be reduced to five, through the elimination of one. The four "totemic" plants of Tikopia are the only ones that the ancestors succeeded in hanging on to, when a strange god stole the feast that the local divinities had prepared in his honor (L.-S. 8, pp. 27–9, 36–7; 9, p. 302).

In all these instances, therefore, a discrete system is produced by the destruction of certain elements or their removal from the original whole. In all these cases, too, the originator of the reduction is himself in a sense reduced: the six Ojibwa gods were blind from choice and exiled their companion who had been guilty of removing the bandage over his eyes. Tikarau, the thieving Tikopia god, pretended to limp in order to be better able to get possession of the banquet. Akaruio Bokodori also limped. Mythological figures who are blind or lame, one-eyed or one-armed, are familiar the world over; and we find them disturbing, because we believe their condition to be one of deficiency. But just as a system that has been made discrete through the removal of certain elements becomes logically richer, although numerically poorer, so myths often confer a positive significance on the disabled and the sick, who embody modes of mediation. We imagine infirmity and sickness to be deprivations of being and therefore evil. However, if death is as real as life, and if therefore everything is being, all states, even pathological ones, are positive in their own way. "Negativized being" is entitled to occupy a whole place within the system, since it is the only conceivable means of transition between two "full" states.

At the same time, it is clear that the myths I am comparing all offer an original solution to the problem of the change-over from continuous quantity to discrete quantity. According to the Ojibwa way of thinking, it would seem to be enough to take away one unit from the first in order to obtain the second. One belongs to grade 6, the other to grade 5. An increase of a fifth in the distance between each element and the next puts all the elements into a state of discontinuity. The Tikopia solution is more costly: originally foodstuffs were indeterminate in number, and it was necessary to jump from this state of indetermination—that is, from a high and even theoretically limitless figure, since there was no list of the original foodstuffs—to four, in order to ensure the discrete character of the system. We can guess the reason for this difference: the Tikopia clans are in fact four in number, and the myth has, at great cost, to jump the gap between the imaginary and the actual. The Ojibwas' problem was not so difficult, so they could solve it at the cheapest rate, simply by reducing the total by one unit. The five original clans are no more real than the six supernatural beings who founded them, since Ojibwa society is in fact composed of several dozen clans whose relation to the five "great" clans of mythology is purely theoretical. In one instance, therefore, there is movement from mythology to reality; in the other the process remains within the realm of myth.

Although the Tikopia and the Ojibwa may have different evaluations of the cost of the transition from the continuous to the discontinuous, the two categories nevertheless remain strictly homogeneous. In each case they are composed of similar and equal quantities. The only difference is that these

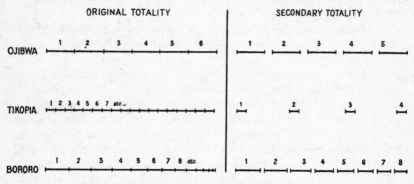

Figure 4. Three examples of the mythological transition
from continuous to discrete quantity.

quantities are more or less numerous—very little more in the case of the Ojibwa, with whom the two figures differ by only one unit; considerably more in Tikopia, since from n, an undetermined but high figure, there is a sudden drop to four.

The Bororo solution is an original one, in relation to those just described. It looks upon continuity as a sum of quantities, at once very numerous and all unequal, beginning with the smallest and extending to the largest. The main point, however, is that the discontinuity, instead of resulting from the subtraction of one or another of the totalized quantities (the Ojibwa solution) or from the subtraction of a considerable number of equal and interchangeable totalized quantities (the Tikopia solution), is achieved, in the case of the Bororo, by making the smallest quantities bear the brunt of the operation. Bororo discontinuity consists therefore of quantities unequal among themselves, but chosen from among the largest, and separated by intervals that have been created in the original continuum by using the space previously occupied by the smallest quantities (Figure 4).

This logical model admirably corresponds to Bororo society[8] as it is shown to be by empirical observation: the clans are rich or poor, each one jealously guards such privileges as it has, and the better off ostentatiously enjoy their worldly possessions—costumes, adornments, ornaments, and jewels. Not only does the myth account for these divergences; it both consoles and cows the humble clans. It consoles them by stating that they were not always poor: as survivors of a massacre in which poorer people than they perished, they can count themselves among the chosen. But it cows them, too, by proclaiming that poverty offends the gods.

It is possible that there were once differences of status between the Ojibwa clans; and it is certain that there existed an order of precedence among the four Tikopia clans and also among their lineages. If my analysis is correct, it should however be possible to prove that in these cases the social differences were not of the same nature as among the Bororo; that they were more ideological and less realistic; in other words, that they were not expressed, as among the Bororo, by unequal rights in respect to the appropriation of valuables. In the case of the Ojibwa we cannot settle the point because of inadequate documentation. In the case of Tikopia the theory is made plausible by Firth's remark (p. 358) that the social hierarchy did not reflect distribution of wealth. Without carrying supposition further, I have merely tried, in the course of this digression, to stress the central position occupied by the Bororo myths and the way they conform to the main outlines of social and political organization.[9]

e. CONTINUATION OF THE FIRST VARIATION

In the myth of Baitogogo (M_2), as in the key myth (M_1), the person who committed incest appeared less guilty than the wronged husband who sought to avenge himself. In each instance it was vengeance, and not incest, that prompted supernatural sanctions.

Now the myth to which I have given second place not only confirms this attitude toward incest; it also points the way to an interpretation. The hero is called Baitogogo, a nickname signifying "the secluded man" (Colb. 3, p. 29). I shall leave aside for the moment the obvious parallel with a synonymous nickname, which is found at the other end of the continent in the myths of the Klamath and the Modoc. I shall return to the problem in another context and shall try to establish then that the two occurrences are open to the same kind of interpretation.

[8] And perhaps also to that of the Arua of the Rio Branco, since one of their myths tells of the destruction of humanity by a flood; the only survivors were two pairs of children from the "best families" who were saved by a god (L.-S. 1, Vol. III, p. 379).

[9] As we shall see later, the corresponding Gran Chaco and Ge myths (M_{29-32}, M_{139}) are intended to account for a kind of discontinuity that is both social and natural: it characterizes women as pretty ones and ugly ones; or, by metonymical extension, family huts.

Nor shall I take it for granted that there is nothing else behind the nickname apart from what is obvious merely from the syntagmatic context. It is possible, and even probable, that the term refers back to a paradigmatic totality in which the Bororo were the counterpart of the Caraja, who were perhaps less definitely matrilineal. Lipkind (2, p. 186) and Dietschy (pp. 170–74) mention an ancient Caraja custom: the segregation or imprisonment of a girl, an heiress of noble birth, who was subject to various taboos. However obscure the information on this point may be, it suggests in turn the Iroquois institution of "the down-fended child." But the method I am following excludes, for the moment, the possibility of attributing to mythological functions any absolute meanings to be looked for at this stage outside the myth. Such a practice, which is only too widespread in mythography, leads almost inevitably to Jungian interpretations. I am not primarily concerned with finding the significance of the nickname Baitogogo on a level that transcends that of mythology, nor with discovering to which extrinsic institutions it might be linked. My aim is to reveal, through the context, its relative significance in a system of contrasts endowed with an operational value. The symbols have no intrinsic and invariable significance; they are not independent in relation to the context. Their significance is primarily *positional*.

What, then, have the heroes of the two myths in common? The hero of M_1 (whose name raises so special a problem that it would be better to postpone its study; see p. 228) commits incest with his mother, because, in the first place, he had refused to be separated from her when she was setting off on a strictly feminine expedition, which—according to the oldest version —consisted in gathering palm fronds in the forest for the making of penis sheaths which were to be given to the boys at the initiation ceremony and symbolized their break with feminine society. We have seen (p. 45) that the arbitrarily corrected version tones down this aspect but does not eliminate it. In raping his mother, the hero acts in contradiction to the sociological situation. Perhaps he himself is as yet too young for initiation; on the other hand, he is no longer young enough to take part in the women's palm-gathering expedition, whether or not this is a preliminary to the initiation. The term *ipareddu*, which is consistently applied to him in the myth, "usually means a boy who has reached a certain degree of physical development, even before puberty and before being given the penis sheath. . . . When they reach the state of *ippare* (plural), the boys begin to leave the maternal hut and go to the men's house" (EB, Vol. I, p. 623). Now, far from resigning himself to this gradual loosening of the maternal bonds, the hero tightens them by an action that, by its sexual nature, is beyond initiation, although he himself is still on the hither side of initiation. So in a doubly paradoxical way he returns to his mother's bosom at a time when other sons are about to be weaned for good.

No doubt Baitogogo, the hero of M_2, is in all respects at the opposite pole from the hero of M_1: he is an initiated adult and a husband and father.

Yet in feeling the incest too keenly, he, too, is guilty of overpossessiveness. Moreover, he strangles his wife and buries her secretly: that is, he denies her the double interment that makes the provisional burial (in the village plaza, a public and holy place, as opposed to the family hut, which is private and profane) a preliminary stage before the final immersion of the bones in a lake or a river (after being stripped of their flesh, painted, and adorned with a mosaic of gummed feathers, and finally assembled in a basket); for water is the abode of souls and the medium necessary for their survival. Finally, Baitogogo's misdeed is the symmetrical opposite of that committed by Geriguiguiatugo; the latter is a child who "goes too far" with his mother when he no longer has the right to do so: Baitogogo is a husband who "goes too far" with his wife, thus depriving his son of his mother while the son is still entitled to have a mother.

If we agree, as a working hypothesis, to interpret the nickname of the second of the two heroes by the common denominator of their respective semantic functions, the term "secluded" can be taken as indicating a particular attitude toward female society, from which the bearer of the nickname —or his homologue—refuses to be separated; on the contrary, he tries to take refuge in it or to dominate it to a greater extent or for a longer time than is permissible. The secluded character, the recluse, is in this case the sort of boy who, as we say, "clings to his mother's apron-strings," the man who cannot break away from the feminine society in which he was born and grew up (since the society is matrilocal), in order to take his place in male society which is different in two respects: physically, since the men have their abode in the men's house in the center of the village, while the women's huts are situated around the outer edge; and mystically, since male society is the earthly embodiment of the society of souls (*aroé*) and corresponds to what is sacred, whereas female society is profane.

Although I have stated my intention of avoiding arguments of a paradigmatic nature at this stage, it is impossible not to mention a Mundurucu myth (M_4), which describes a practice astonishingly similar to the one I have just recounted, except that among the patrilineal Mundurucu (recently converted, it appears, to matrilocal residence) the seclusion of an adolescent boy (whether an actual custom or a mythological assumption) is intended to protect him from female advances. After his son (M_{16}) had been killed by the wild pigs, in spite of being covered with starch to make him look sick and incapable of getting up, the culture hero Karusakaibö created a son for himself without the intervention of a mother, by bringing to life a statue he had carved out of a tree trunk. As he was anxious to keep the handsome lad beyond the reach of covetous desires (M_{150}), he shut him up in a tiny cell, specially built inside the hut and guarded by an old woman so that no other woman might come near and look inside (Murphy 1, pp. 71, 74).

The Apinaye and the Timbira, who were just a little further away from the Bororo and like them were matrilineal and matrilocal, used to seclude their novices during the second stage of the initiation ceremony, isolating them in a corner of the maternal hut by means of mats stretched across poles. Their seclusion lasted from five to six months, during which time they were allowed neither to appear nor to speak (Nim. 5, p. 59; 8, p. 184 and Figure 13). According to the source, this rite was closely related to the marriage rules: "formerly, most of the *pepyé* (the initiated) married soon after the festival and moved into the houses of their mothers-in-law" (Nim, 8, p. 185). "The terminal ceremony, in which their prospective mothers-in-law lead the initiates by a rope, drastically represents the impending union" (*ibid.,* p. 171).

Let us now take up the Baitogogo myth (M₂) again where we left it.

Punishment comes to the hero through his son, whom he had tried to put off the scent. The son changes into a bird and, by means of his excrement, turns his father into a tree-bearing personage.

The Bororo divide the vegetable kingdom into three classes. According to the myth, the first plants appeared in the following order: creepers, the jatoba tree, and marsh plants (Colb. 3, p. 202). The triple division obviously corresponds to the three elements, heaven, earth, and water. By changing into a bird, the child polarizes himself as a celestial personage; by turning his father into a tree-bearer, and a bearer of the jatoba tree (the chief tree in the forest), he polarizes his father as a terrestrial personage, since the earth acts as a support for ligneous plants. Baitogogo succeeds in getting rid of his tree, and therefore in freeing himself from his terrestrial nature, only by creating water, the element that mediates between the two poles: the very water that (since it did not yet exist) he had denied his wife's mortal remains, thus preventing communication between the social world and the supernatural world, between the dead and the living.

After using water to re-establish, on the cosmic level, the mediation he had rejected on the mystic level, he becomes the culture hero to whom men are indebted for adornments and ornaments: that is for cultural mediators that turn man from a biological individual into a personage (all ornaments have a prescribed shape and design, according to the clan of the bearer); and that, by replacing the flesh on the dead man's previously washed skeleton, give him a spiritual body and turn him into a spirit—that is, a mediator between physical death and social life.

Let us agree then to summarize the myth as follows:

A violation of the bonds of marriage (the murder of the incestuous wife, which deprives a child of his mother), aggravated by a sacrilegious act— another form of excess—(the interment of the woman, thus denying her an aquatic burial, the precondition of reincarnation) leads to the disjunction of the two poles: heaven (child) and earth (father). The agent, whose double misdeed banishes him from the society of men (which is an "aquatic" society, like the society of souls whose name it bears), re-establishes communication between heaven and earth by creating water; and having established his abode in the land of souls (since he and his companion became the heroes Bakororo and Itubore, the chiefs of the two villages of the beyond), he re-establishes communication between the dead and the living by making the latter acquainted with bodily ornaments and adornments, which are both emblems of the society of men and spiritual flesh in the community of souls.

f. Second Variation

Colbacchini and Albisetti's study contains another myth, whose hero seems, by his behavior, to illustrate the meaning we adopted for the name Baitogogo as a working hypothesis. Moreover, he is called Birimoddo, which is, as we have seen, Baitogogo's real name. There is, however, one difficulty: Birimoddo is a name of the Arore clan, in the Tugare moiety (Colb. 3, pp. 201, 206, 445; EB, Vol. I, p. 277; Rondon, p. 8), whereas the new hero belongs to the Bokodori clan in the Cera moiety; and yet his sister and himself have the name Birimoddo (Colb. 3, pp. 220–21). There is little point, therefore, in trying to use similarity of names as a basis for argument.

M₅. *Bororo. "The origin of diseases"*

In the days when diseases were still unknown and human beings were unacquainted with suffering, an adolescent boy obstinately refused to frequent the men's house and remained shut up in the family hut.

Irritated by this behavior, his grandmother came every night while he was asleep and, crouching above her grandson's face, poisoned him by emissions of intestinal gas. The boy heard the noise and smelled the stench, but did not understand where it was coming from. Having become sick, emaciated, and suspicious, he feigned sleep and finally discovered the old woman's trick. He killed her with a sharp-pointed arrow which he plunged so deeply into her anus that the intestines spurted out.

With the help of armadillos—*okwaru, ennokuri, gerego,* and *bokodori* (the reverse order from M₂, cf. above, p. 49)—he secretly dug a grave in which he buried the body, just where the old woman used to sleep, and covered the newly dug earth with a mat.

That same day the Indians organized an expedition to "poison" fish and so obtained food for their dinner.[10] The day after the murder the women returned to the fishing ground in order to gather the remaining dead fish. Before leaving, Birimoddo's sister wanted to put her young son in the grandmother's care: the grandmother did not answer her call and for good

---

[10] That is, they threw into the water pieces of a creeper whose sap dissolves and changes the surface tension of the water, thus causing the fish to die of suffocation. Cf. below, pp. 256 ff.

reason. So she set her child on the branch of a tree and told him to wait there until she came back. The child, having been left alone, changed into an anthill.

The river was full of dead fish, but instead of making several trips back and forth in order to transport them as her companions did, she ate them voraciously. Her stomach started to swell, and she began to feel acute pains.

So she moaned, and as she uttered her moans, diseases were released from her body: all the diseases, with which she infected the village, sowed death among men. This is how diseases originated.

The guilty woman's two brothers, who were called Birimoddo and Kaboreu, decided to kill her with spikes. One cut off her head and threw it into a lake to the east; the other cut off her legs and threw them into a lake to the west. And both drove their spikes into the ground. (Colb. 3, pp. 220–21; cf. EB, Vol. I, p. 573, for the beginning of a different version.)

Because of its unusual pattern, this myth poses problems of such complexity that it will have to be analyzed piecemeal and more than once in the course of this book. Here I shall restrict myself to pointing out characteristics that link it to the same group as the myths already discussed.

First of all, the hero is a "Baitogogo," a voluntary recluse shut up in the family hut, that is with the women, because he was reluctant to take his place in the men's house.[11]

---

[11] A half-legendary, half-mythological tale (M_6)—but can one draw a dividing line between myth and legend?—describes the doings of a "Tugare" Birimoddo, his fellow chief Aroia Kurireu, and Kaboreu, who is the brother of the "Cera" Birimoddo in the myth describing the origin of diseases, although, according to the *Enciclopédia Boróro* (Vol. I, pp. 207, 277, 698), he seems to be confused with the other.

The two chiefs imprudently organize and lead a warlike expedition, whose purpose is to steal urucu (*Bixa orellana,* a seed used for dyeing), which is cultivated by their enemies, the Kaiamodogue. In fact, Birimoddo is responsible, having refused to listen to the wise counsels reiterated by his companion. After being surprised by the Kaiamodogue, the entire band is exterminated, except for the two chiefs, who succeed in escaping more dead than alive.

They reach the village: "The two chiefs were worn out with fatigue and their wounds, and could hardly stand on their feet. So their wives made a kind of bed in their hut, by means of stakes driven into the ground and over which was stretched a network of woven bark fibers. There the chiefs lay, hardly able to give a sign of life; they did not even get up to relieve themselves" (Colb. 3, p. 209).

The two prostrate personages, shut up in the women's hut and covered with excrement, are certainly "Baitogogos" in the sense in which I am using the term.

Gradually, however, their strength returned, and eventually they organized a punitive expedition. This time, however, they carried it out with a wariness on which the narrative dwells at length. In approaching their objective, the two chiefs reconnoitered the terrain by skirting around it, one to the right, the other to the left, and only after they had met again in the middle did Kaboreu order his warriors to advance.

When they arrived in sight of the Kaiamodogue, Birimoddo posted his warriors round the village, so that it was encircled by six concentric rings. He stationed Aroia Kurireu and his men to the west, where they could cut off the enemy's retreat, and Kaboreu with the strongest warriors to the east, in preparation for the offensive. He himself

We may wonder whether at one time the Bororo practiced a socioreligious custom that is preserved in their myths as the theme of "the secluded boy." Comparisons with the Caraja, the Apinaye, the Timbira, and the Mundurucu might lead us to think so. Two comments are called for, however. First, the myth appears to refer not to a custom, but rather to an individual attitude that infringes the principles underlying the social and moral order. A second, and more important, point is that empirical observation of Bororo society inclines us to expect symmetrical, although opposite, practices. As has already been noted, at the time of the initiation it is the women who complain of being permanently parted from their sons; the complaint does not come from the sons. On the other hand, there is certainly a Bororo custom involving "a secluded boy" or "bashful fiancé." The wife's female relations had to bring pressure to bear on the young husband and forcibly remove his personal belongings. The young man himself would take a long time to make up his mind to go and live with his wife; for several months he would go on living in the men's house, "until he was cured of the shame of having become a husband" (Colb. 3, p. 40).[12]

Thus the young man would remain shut up in the men's house because he was reluctant to enter female society, as defined by the married state, to which initiation had given him access. The situation described by the myths is the reverse, since it concerns an adolescent boy who shuts himself away in the female domestic society, which he would normally leave at the time of initiation.

Like M_1 and M_2, M_5 has an obviously etiological character: it explains the origin of diseases, whereas the Baitogogo myth gives first an explanation of the origin of terrestrial water, then of ornaments on the one hand and of funeral rites on the other. Now, just as these rites mark the passage from life to death (whereas ornaments indicate the reverse), so diseases, which are an intermediary state between life and death, are sometimes considered in America as being like a garment (this is especially true of their common manifestation, a high temperature).[13]

Third, in this instance, too, the hero deprives his victim of funeral rites by refusing to give her an aquatic burial place. Taking the grandmother's place,

---

moved toward the men's house with a few companions. And when at daybreak an old Kaiamo came out to urinate, he struck him down and gave the signal for the attack. Not a single enemy escaped (Colb. 3, pp. 206–11).

[12] Among the Sherente, at the time of the wedding celebrations the fiancé appeared ashamed, sad, and shy (J. F. de Oliveira, p. 393); his new relatives took him away by force, and for several weeks or months he would make no attempt to go near his wife, in case she spurned him. During this period a prostitute shared the husband's bed (Nim. 6, pp. 29–30).

[13] Cf. for instance Holmer and Wassen. They are also compared to fire: in Bororo, *eru* "fire," *erubbo* "fever" (Colb. 3, p. 297); or in Magalhães' transcription: *djôru* "fire," *djorúbo* "disease," *djôru-buto* "beginning of the dry season" (p. 35).

the other woman polarizes her child in a terrestrial form (the anthill) and then puts to evil use the water that had been withheld. The diseases arise as a form of mediation between earth and water—that is, between life here below and death beyond.

Finally, the denial of the mediatory agent has its origin, as in other myths, in an improper, nonmediatized identification of the male adolescent with female society, for which behavior the grandmother, as a punishment, infects her grandson.

If we remember that, according to a short myth published by Colbacchini (3, p. 211) after the one about Baitogogo, the creation of fish completes and perfects that of water, we shall be still more convinced of the underlying unity of M_2 and M_5, whose hero (or heroine) is called Birimoddo (there are three of them: (1) the one nicknamed Baitogogo; (2) the young man who was infected; (3) his sister, who was responsible for the origin of diseases). If we were to run all these myths together, we would obtain a complete cycle, starting with incest between brother and sister (in the classificatory sense), continuing with the exteriorization of water (without the fish), and going on to incest reversed (grandmother-grandson), which is immediately succeeded by the opposite of incest (abandonment of a son by his mother) and ends with the interiorization of the fish (without water). In the first myth (M_2) one of the victims bleeds (therefore dies through the shedding of blood), whereas the other was strangled (that is, died without bloodshed). In the second myth (M_5) two victims were killed (without bloodshed): one through an external action (impaling), the other through an internal action (bursting through overeating); and they both spread filth, either metonymically (the breaking of wind) or metaphorically (the emission of diseases as groans): this is the same as the filth that in M_2 was dropped on the guilty man in the form of excrement, and that in M_5 is forced upon the guilty man (whose crime is, again, that he has "wronged" female society) in the form of intestinal gases.

If we agree that

1. M_2 = origin of adornments (a) and funeral rites (r)
   M_5 = origin of diseases (d),

and that

2. $a, r = {}^f(\text{death} \rightarrow \text{life})$
   $d = {}^f(\text{life} \rightarrow \text{death})$,

we are justified in deducing the following pattern of relations from M_2:

Father/son: father $\equiv$ earth; son $\equiv$ heaven,

which in M_5 becomes:

Mother/son: son $\equiv$ earth; mother $\equiv$ water.

3. A partial view of the Bororo village of Kejara, on the Rio Vermelho. The men's house stands out against the huts of the Tugare moiety. In the distance can be seen the lower slopes of the *chapada*.

4. A Bororo Indian wearing the special festive penis sheath—that is, a sheath decorated with gummed feathers and provided with a pennant made of stiff straw, painted with the clan colors (*ki* clan).

We have proved that the Bororo myths concerning a hero called Birimoddo, although superficially heterogeneous, can be ascribed to one and the same group, which is characterized by the following fundamental structure: an excessive conception of family relations leads to the disjunction of elements that are normally linked. The conjunction is re-established thanks to the introduction of a mediatory agent, whose origin it is the purpose of the myth to explain: water (between heaven and earth); bodily adornments (between nature and culture); funeral rites (between the living and the dead); and diseases (between life and death).

g. CODA

The bird-nester was not called Birimoddo, nor did he have Baitogogo as a nickname. But:

1. His name also has an aesthetic connotation, since it includes the word *atugo* which means "decorated, painted," while the meaning of the name Birimoddo is "pretty skin."

2. He behaves like "a recluse" because, through his incest with his mother, he reveals his desire to remain shut away in the feminine world.

3. Like the other heroes, the hero of M_1 nearly dies as a result of defilement: this is caused by the rotting lizards attached to his person. And in other respects, too, his experiences can appear as transformations of those undergone by the heroes of M_2 and M_5.

4. Only by superimposing M_1 and M_2 can we obtain triangular classification of the plants to which we have already referred. In the central episode of M_2, the hero is associated with ligneous plants (the jatoba tree); in an early episode and in the final episode of M_1, the hero is associated with aerial plants (the creeper that saves his life), then with aquatic plants (which are created from his drowned father's internal organs).

5. In three distinct myths three masculine heroes defined as sons (M_1, M_2) or as a grandson (M_5) began to waste away, a fact that is stressed in the text. Now the causes of this loss of flesh, although different in each myth, are nonetheless in a transformational relation with each other:

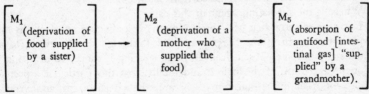

6. Similarly, M_1 and M_5 represent inverted forms of repletion:

$$\left[\begin{array}{l} M_1 \\ \text{(inability to retain} \\ \text{the food consumed)} \end{array} \right] \longrightarrow \left[\begin{array}{l} M_5 \\ \text{(inability to evacuate} \\ \text{the food consumed).} \end{array} \right]$$

7. M_1, M_2, and M_5, have in common only certain features of a central core which can be syncretically reconstituted as follows: at the start, incest— that is, an improper conjunction; at the conclusion, a disjunction that takes place thanks to the appearance of an agent that acts as mediator between the two poles. Nevertheless, incest would appear to be lacking in M_5, and the mediating agent in M_1:

	M_1	M_2	M_5
Incest	+	+	?
Mediating agent	?	+	+

But is this really the case? Let us look at the data more closely.

Although apparently absent from M_5, incest is present in two forms. The first is direct, even if symbolic, since it is represented by a boy who persists in remaining shut away in his mother's hut. Incest also appears in another form—a real form this time, although indirect. It is represented by the grandmother's behavior, which consists of a triply inverted incestuous promiscuity: with a grandmother, instead of a mother; through the back passage, instead of the front; and initiated by an aggressive woman, instead of an aggressive male. So true is this if we compare the two diametrically opposed acts of incest—the one in M_2 which is "normal" and "horizontal" and takes place between collaterals (brother and sister) as a result of male initiative, outside the village; and the incest in M_5, which is "vertical," between less closely related members of the family (grandmother and grandson), and occurs, as we have just seen, in a negative and inverted form, and is furthermore the result of female initiative and takes place not in the village, but in the hut, at night and not during the daytime—we discover, as we pass from M_2 to M_5, a total inversion of the one sequence they have in common— namely that of the four *tatus,* which are listed in M_2 from the largest to the smallest, and in M_5 from the smallest to the largest.[14]

It will be readily accepted that the sin committed by the hero in M_1 leads to a disjunction: in order to be avenged, the father sends him first to the kingdom of the dead, and then abandons him on the cliff face—between heaven and earth; lastly, the hero is forced to remain on the summit for a long time, and then he is separated from his people.

Where is the mediating agent in this case?

I propose to show that M_1 (the key myth) belongs to a set of myths that explain the origin of the *cooking of food* (although this theme is, to all intents and purposes, absent from it); that cooking is conceived of in native thought as a form of mediation; and finally, that this particular aspect remains concealed in the Bororo myth, because the latter is in fact an inversion, or a reversal, of myths originating in neighboring communities which view

[14] The sequences are, however, identical if we look at the native text of M_2 given in Colb. 2, p. 73, which has: "*okwaru, ennokuri, gerego, bokodori.*"

culinary operations as mediatory activities between heaven and earth, life and death, nature and society.

In order to establish these three points, I shall begin by analyzing myths deriving from various tribes of the Ge linguistic group. These tribes occupy a vast region which borders on Bororo territory to the north and the east. There are, moreover, some grounds for believing that the Bororo language might be a distant branch of the linguistic family to which the Ge languages also belong.

2

Ge Variations

(Six Arias Followed by a Recitative)

The story of the bird-nester, which forms the central part of the key myth, occurs in an initial position in the case of the Ge, in the myth about the origin of fire, which is found in all the central and eastern Ge tribes that have been studied up to the present.

I shall begin with the versions peculiar to the northern group, the Kayapo, who may be the Kaiamodogue previously mentioned (p. 60 n. 11; cf. Colb. 2, p. 125, n. 2), although the tendency nowadays is to identify the latter with the Shavante (EB, Vol. I, p. 702).

a. First Variation

M₇. Kayapo-Gorotire. "The origin of fire"

Noticing that a pair of macaws had built their nest on top of a steep rock, an Indian took his young brother-in-law, Botoque, with him to help him to capture the nestlings. He made Botoque climb up an improvised ladder; but when the boy got up to the nest, he said that he could find only two eggs. (It is not clear whether he was lying or telling the truth.) His brother-in-law insisted that he should take them; but as the eggs fell down, they changed into stones which hurt the older man's hand. This made him furious, with the result that he dismantled the ladder and went away, not realizing that the birds were enchanted (*oaianga*) (?).

Botoque remained caught on top of the rock for several days. He grew thin: hunger and thirst obliged him to eat his own excrement. Eventually he noticed a spotted jaguar carrying a bow and arrow and all kinds of game. He would have liked to call out to it for help, but fear kept him silent.

The jaguar saw the hero's shadow on the ground and, after trying in vain to catch it, looked up, asked what had happened, repaired the ladder, and invited Botoque to come down. The latter was afraid and hesitated a long time; in the end he made up his mind, and the jaguar, in friendly fashion, suggested that if he would sit astride its back, it would take him to its home to have a meal of grilled meat. But the young man did not understand the meaning of the word "grilled" because in those days, the Indians were unacquainted with fire and ate their meat raw.

At the jaguar's home the hero saw a big jatoba trunk burning; beside it was a pile of stones such as the Indians now use to build their earth ovens (*ki*). He ate his first meal of cooked meat.

But the jaguar's wife, who was an Indian, disliked the young man and referred to him as *me-on-kra-tum* "foreign, or abandoned, son"; in spite of this, the jaguar, being childless, decided to adopt him.

Each day the jaguar went off to hunt, leaving the adopted son with the wife whose aversion for him steadily increased; she gave him only old wizened pieces of meat to eat, and leaves. When the boy complained, she scratched his face, and the poor child had to take refuge in the forest.

The jaguar scolded the wife, but in vain. One day it gave Botoque a brand new bow and some arrows, taught him how to use them, and advised him to use them against the woman, should the need arise. Botoque killed her by shooting an arrow into her breast. He fled in terror, taking with him the weapons and a piece of grilled meat.

He reached his village in the middle of the night, groped his way to his mother's bed, and had some difficulty in making his identity known (because he was thought to be dead); he told his tale and shared the meat. The Indians decided to get possession of the fire.

When they arrived at the jaguar's home, there was no one there; and since the wife was dead, the game caught the day before had not been cooked. The Indians roasted it and took away the fire. For the very first time it was possible to have light in the village at night, to eat cooked meat, and to warm oneself at a hearth.

But the jaguar, incensed by the ingratitude of his adopted son, who had stolen "fire and the secret of the bow and arrow," was to remain full of hatred for all living creatures, especially human beings. Now only the reflection of fire could be seen in its eyes. It used its fangs for hunting and ate its meat raw, having solemnly renounced grilled meat. (Banner 1, pp. 42–4.)

b. Second Variation

M8. Kayapo-Kubenkranken. "The origin of fire"

Formerly, men did not know how to make fire. When they killed game, they cut the flesh into thin strips, which they laid out on stones to dry in the sun. They also ate rotten wood.

One day a man noticed two macaws coming out of a hole in a cliff. To get at their nest, he made his young brother-in-law (his wife's brother) climb a tree trunk in which he had cut foot holds. But there were nothing but round stones in the nest. An argument ensued, degenerating into a quarrel, which ended as in the previous version. In this case, however, it seems that the lad, annoyed by his brother-in-law's taunts, threw the stones deliberately and wounded him.

In response to his wife's anxious inquiries, the man said the boy must have got lost, and to allay suspicion, he pretended to go and look for him. Meanwhile, suffering extreme hunger and thirst, the hero was reduced to eating his excrement and drinking his urine. He was nothing but skin and bone when a jaguar came along carrying a caititu pig on his shoulders; the animal noticed the boy's shadow and tried to catch it. On each occasion the hero moved back and the shadow disappeared. "The jaguar looked all round, then covering its mouth, looked up and saw the lad on the rock." They entered into conversation.

Explanations and discussions took place as in the preceding version. The hero was too frightened to sit directly on the jaguar but agreed to bestride the caititu, which the latter was carrying on his back. They reached the jaguar's home, where his wife was busy spinning. She reproached her husband, saying "you have brought home another's son." Unperturbed, the jaguar announced that he was going to adopt the boy as his companion, and intended to feed him and fatten him up.

But the jaguar's wife refused to give the lad any tapir meat and allowed him only venison and threatened to scratch him at the slightest opportunity. Acting on the jaguar's advice, the boy killed the woman with the bow and arrow given him by his protector.

He went off with the jaguar's belongings: the spun cotton, the meat, and the burning ash. When he reached his village, he made himself known first to his sister, then to his mother.

He was summoned to the *ngobe* "men's house," where he related his adventures. The Indians decided to change themselves into animals to take possession of the fire: the tapir would carry the trunk, the yao bird would put out the burning ash that might be dropped on the way, while the deer would take charge of the meat, and the peccary of the spun cotton. The expedition was a success, and the men shared the fire between them. (Métraux 8, pp. 8–10.)

c. THIRD VARIATION

M9. *Apinaye. "The origin of fire"*

A man found a macaw's nest with two young birds in a high and vertical cliff. He took his little brother-in-law along, chopped down a tree, leaned it against the wall of rock, and bade the boy climb. The boy went up, but the parent birds rushed at him with fierce screams; so he got frightened. Then the man got angry, knocked the tree aside, and left.

The boy, unable to descend, remained sitting by the nest for five days. He nearly died of thirst and hunger. He was completely covered by the droppings of the macaws and swallows that flew above him. Then a jaguar came past, saw the boy's shadow, and tried in vain to catch it. Then the boy spat down, and now the jaguar raised his head and saw him. They entered into conversation. The jaguar demanded to have the two young macaws, which the hero flung down to him one after the other, and which he immediately devoured. Then the jaguar brought up the tree and asked the boy to step down, promising him that he would not eat him, and that he would give him water to quench his thirst. Somewhat hesitantly, the hero complied. The jaguar took him on his back and carried him to a creek. The boy drank his fill and fell asleep. At last the jaguar pinched his arm and awakened him. He washed the dirt off him and said that, having no children, he would take him home as his son.

In the jaguar's home a huge jatoba trunk was lying on the floor and burning at one end. In those days the Indians were unacquainted with fire and ate only flesh dried in the sun. "What is smoking there?" asked the boy. "That is fire," answered the jaguar. "You will find out at night when it warms you." Then he gave the roast meat to the boy, who ate till he fell asleep. At midnight he woke up, ate again, and then again fell asleep.

Before daybreak the jaguar went hunting. The boy climbed a tree to await his return. But toward noon he got hungry, returned to the jaguar's house, and begged his wife for food. "What!" she shouted, baring her teeth. "Look here!" The hero cried out from fear and ran to meet the jaguar and told him of the occurrence. The jaguar scolded his wife, who excused herself, saying that she was merely jesting. But the same scene occurred again the next day.

Following the advice of the jaguar (who had made him a bow and arrow and told him to shoot at a termite's nest), the boy killed the aggressive wife. His adopted father said, "That does not matter," gave him a lot of roast meat, and explained to him how to return to his village by following along the creek. But he was to be on guard: if a rock or the aroeira tree called him, he should answer; but was to keep still if he heard "the gentle call of a rotten tree."

The hero moved along the brook, replied to the first two calls and, forgetting the jaguar's warnings, to the third as well. That is why men are short-lived: if the boy had answered only the first two, they would enjoy as long life as the rock and the aroeira tree.

After a while the boy again heard a call and replied to it. It was Magalon kamduré, an ogre, who tried unsuccessfully to pass himself off as the hero's father by means of various disguises (long hair, ear ornaments). When the hero finally discovered the ogre's identity, the latter wrestled with him until he was quite worn out, whereupon he put the boy in his big carrying basket.

On his way home the ogre stopped to hunt coatis. Speaking from inside the basket, the hero called to him to make a trail through the woods first, so he could carry the load better. While the ogre was doing this, the hero escaped, after weighting the basket with a heavy stone.

When the ogre reached home, he promised his children a choice morsel, even better than the coatis. But all he found in the bottom of the basket was a stone.

Meanwhile the boy had found his way back to his village, where he related his adventures. All the Indians set off to look for the fire. Various animals offered their help: the jaó was to extinguish the fallen embers; the jacu was spurned, but the tapir was considered strong enough to carry the tree. The jaguar gave them the fire. "I have adopted your son," he said to the boy's father. (Nim. 5, pp. 154–58.)

Another version (M_{9a}) differs in several respects from this one. The two men are a father-in-law and his son-in-law. The jaguar's wife, who is an expert spinner (cf. M_8), welcomes the boy first of all; and when she starts to threaten him, he kills her on his own initiative. His action is disapproved of by the jaguar, who does not believe in his wife's wickedness. The three calls that are then mentioned in the story are uttered, the first by the jaguar himself who from afar guides the hero back to his village; the others by stone and rotten wood; but we are not told how the hero reacts to the last two calls. When the Indians arrive in search of the fire, the jaguar is even more friendly than in the previous version, since it is he who engages the services of the helpful animals. He objects to the caititus and the queixadas but agrees that the tapirs should transport the log, while the birds pick up the fallen embers. (C. E. de Oliveira, pp. 75–80.)

As can be seen, the version above maintains the bond of affinity and age difference between the two men; and these, as will subsequently appear, are the invariant features of the set. But at first glance we have here such an unexpected inversion of the functions of the "wife-giver" and the "taker" that we are tempted to suppose that there must be some linguistic error. As a matter of fact, the narrative was given directly in Portuguese by an Apinaye Indian who, together with three companions, had come to Belem to see the authorities. In every case where it is possible to make a comparison with texts that Nimuendaju collected in the field about the same time, it is noticeable that the versions by the Belem Apinaye, although more long-winded, contain less information (cf. p. 174). It is significant, however, that the jaguar's wife appears less hostile in M_{9a} than in all the other versions, and that the jaguar is even more friendly than in M_9, where he was already extremely friendly: although he does not believe his wife to be guilty, he bears the hero no grudge for having killed her; he shows great eagerness to give the Indians fire and organizes its transport himself.

Once this has been noted, the anomaly pointed out in the preceding paragraph becomes clearer. Among the Apinaye, as among other matrilineal and matrilocal communities, the wife's father is not, properly speaking, a "giver." This role falls rather to the young girl's brothers, who furthermore do not so much "give" their sister to her future husband as "take" the latter and compel him to accept, simultaneously, marriage and matrilocal residence (Nim. 5, p. 80). In these conditions the father-in-law/son-in-law relation in M_{9a} appears less like an inverted form of affinity than as a distended form, since it occurs, as it were, at two removes. This aspect of the situation clearly emerges from a comparison between M_{9a} and the key myth, in which the matrilineal line of descent and matrilocal residence are also relevant factors:

In M$_{9a}$ we have, therefore, a variant in which all family relations, as well as the corresponding moral attitudes, are equally relaxed. In all respects this version is probably the weakest known to us.

d. Fourth Variation

M$_{10}$. Eastern Timbira. "The origin of fire"

Formerly men were unacquainted with fire and dried their meat by laying it out in the sun on a flat stone, so that it was not completely raw.

In those days a man once took his young brother-in-law on an expedition to rob macaws' nests in a cleft of a vertical cliff. But the fledglings made such an outcry that the boy did not dare take hold of them. The man grew angry, knocked down the ladder, and went off. The hero remained sitting by the nest, suffering from thirst, his head covered with birds' droppings, "so that maggots grew there; and the young birds soon lost all fear of him."

What follows is identical with the Apinaye version. It is explained, however, that the jaguar's wife was *pregnant* and could not bear the slightest noise; she therefore flew into a rage whenever the hero made a noise as he chewed the grilled meat his adopted father had given him. But try as he might, he could not eat silently, since the meat was too crisp. With the weapons given him by the jaguar, he wounded the wife in the paw and fled. The wife, hampered by her pregnancy, was unable to follow him.

The hero recounted his adventure to his father, who summoned all his companions. They placed runners at intervals all the way to the jaguar's house and organized a relay system: the burning log was passed from hand to hand and finally reached the village. The jaguar's wife begged them in vain to leave her a burning ember; the toad spat on all those that remained, and put them out (Nim. 8, p. 243).

e. Fifth Variation

M$_{11}$. Eastern Timbira (Kraho group). "The origin of fire"

The two civilizing heroes, Pud and Pudlere, formerly lived with men and put fire at their disposal. But when the heroes went away, they took the fire with them, and men were reduced to eating their meat raw, sun-dried, and accompanied by *pau puba*.

It was during this period that the brothers-in-law undertook their expedition. The younger of the two men was abandoned on the cliff face, where he wept among the angry birds: "After two days the birds became used to him. The macaw deposited its droppings on his head, which swarmed with vermin. He was hungry."

The end is similar to the other versions. The jaguar's wife was pregnant and liked to frighten the boy by threatening to eat him. The jaguar showed the boy the secret of the bow and arrows; and, following his advice, the boy wounded the wife in the paw and ran away. The Indians, after being informed of what had happened, organized a system of runners to get possession of the fire. "But for the jaguar, they would still be eating their meat raw." (Schultz, pp. 72-4.)

In a different context, a Kraho myth, which deals with a visit by a human hero to the jaguar's home, contains the following remark which forms a direct link between the fire theme and the pregnancy theme: "The jaguar's wife was very pregnant [sic] and on the point of giving birth. Everything was ready for the confinement, and in particular a good fire was burning, because the jaguar is master of fire." (Pompeu Sobrinho, p. 196.)

f. SIXTH VARIATION

M₁₂. Sherente. "The origin of fire"

One day a man went into the woods with his little brother-in-law in order to take young macaws out of a nest in the hollow of a tree. The man made his brother-in-law climb a pole; but when he got up there, the young man declared that there were only eggs there. When the man said he knew there were young in the nest, the hero took a white stone in his mouth and threw it down. The stone turned into an egg that was smashed against the ground. The man was angry, pulled away the ladder, and went home, leaving the hero in the tree where he was forced to remain for five days.

Then a jaguar passed by and asked what he was doing up there, made him first throw down the two young macaws (which were in fact in the nest), told him to jump after them, and, growling, caught the boy between his front paws. Then the boy was very much afraid, but nothing happened to him.

The jaguar carried the hero on his shoulders until they came to a creek. Although the boy was suffering greatly from thirst, he was not allowed to drink, because, as the jaguar explained, the water belonged to the camon vulture (urubu). The same thing happened at the second creek, because the water there belonged to "the little birds." Finally, at the third creek, the hero drank so much as to drain the whole creek, in spite of the entreaties of the alligator,[15] the owner of the creek.

The hero was given a chilly welcome by the jaguar's wife, who reproached her husband for having brought back "a lean and ugly boy." She called the boy to delouse her, but when she had him between her paws, she frightened him with her growls. He complained to the jaguar, who made him a bow and arrows and ornaments, gave him two basketfuls of roast meat, and helped him back to his village, after advising him to aim for the wife's carotid, should she try to pursue him. Everything happened as had been foreseen, and the wife was killed.

---

[15] TRANSLATORS' NOTE: In the myths "alligator" is the term commonly used as an equivalent for the Portuguese jacaré. The animal referred to is a cayman (Caiman niger), except perhaps along the northern and northeastern coasts where crocodiles proper exist. To avoid confusion, the usual tradition of using the word "alligator" has been followed throughout the text wherever Lévi-Strauss has crocodile.

Shortly afterward the young man heard people coming. It was his two brothers, to whom he revealed his identity, and who ran home to tell their mother. "You lie," said their mother. "He's been dead long since." But the boy concealed himself again. He came out of hiding on the occasion of the Aikman funeral festival.

Everybody was amazed when they saw the roast meat he had brought back. "Why, how is it roasted?" "In the sunshine," the boy kept repeating, although he finally revealed the truth to his uncle.

An expedition was organized to capture fire from the jaguar. The mutum and the water fowl, both good runners, seized the trunk, but the jacu, following them, picked up the scattered embers. (Nim. 7, pp. 181–2.)

g. RECITATIVE

1. Like the Bororo, the Kayapo, the Apinaye, and the Timbira are matrilocal. The Sherente are patrilocal and patrilineal. In the other Ge groups, the principle of descent is not clear, and different writers have interpreted it in various ways.

Up to a point these aspects of the social structure are reflected in the myth. The Bororo hero in M_1 discloses his identity first of all to his grandmother and his younger brother; the hero in two Kayapo versions (M_7, M_8) discloses his identity only to his mother, or to his mother in the first place, then to his sister; there is no comparable indication in the Apinaye version (M_9) or the Kraho version (M_{11}); in the Timbira version (M_{10}) he discloses his identity to his father; and in the Sherente version (M_{12}), to his brothers. The correspondence therefore reflects only a partial opposition between paternal and maternal; but it is between the Bororo and the Sherente that the contrast between the two types of social structure is most clearly marked.

2. The hero of M_7 is called Botoque. The word refers to the disks made of pottery, wood, or shell which the majority of Ge wore inserted in the lobes of their ears and sometimes in holes pierced in their lower lips.

3. The stone oven, called *ki*, mentioned in M_7, relates to a culinary technique peculiar to the Ge and unknown to either their neighbors, the Bororo, or to the Tupi-speaking tribes. Its place in the myths will be studied separately.

4. Helpful creatures occur in several versions:

M_8	M_9	M_{10}	M_{12}
tapir	tapir		mutum
yao bird	jaó		
	jacu		jacu
deer			
pig			
		toad	
			waterfowl

Their function was to

(a) carry the log: tapir (M_8, M_9), mutum, and waterfowl (M_{12});
(b) carry the meat: deer (M_8);
(c) carry the spun cotton: pig (M_8);
(d) pick up the fallen embers: yao, jaó (M_8, M_9), jacu (M_9, M_{12});
(e) extinguish the remaining embers: toad (M_{10}).

Yao, jaó: a tinamou, (*Grypturus* species); jacu orguan (*Penelope* species, another of the Gallinaceae)—its breast is red through its having swallowed the embers; mutum (*Crax* species). The peccary pig, often distinguished from the caititu in the myths, is in all probability the white-lipped peccary, also called a queixada (*Dicotyles labiatus, Tayassu peccari*). The caititu must therefore be the collared peccary (*Dicotyles torquatus, Tayassu tajacu*). The latter species is smaller, solitary, or only slightly gregarious; the former lives in groups (cf. below, p. 86 ff.).

5. The aroeira tree: M_9 does not specify whether this is the white aroeira (*Lythraea* species), the soft aroeira (the California pepper tree, *Schinus molle*), or the red aroeira (the Brazil pepper tree, *Schinus terebinthifolius*). The context suggests that it is a hardwood tree.

6. Magalonkamduré (M_9). Nimuendaju (5, p. 156) gives the etymology: *me-galon* "image, phantom, shade, soul of dead, bull-roarers." We can compare, in M_{11}, the name of the hero's shadow which the jaguar tries in vain to catch—*mepa/garon* "shadow, spirit, terrifying apparition" (Schultz, p. 72, n. 59; cf. Pompeu Sobrinho: *megahon* "spirit, soul, genius," pp. 195-6); and the Kayapo term, *men karon*: "After death people become *men karon*, hostile and troublesome phantoms, through sorrow at having lost life and through jealousy of those who remain among the living" (Banner 2, p. 36; cf. also pp. 38-40 and Lukesch 2, *me-karon* "human soul, phantom").

7. The episode of the coati hunt (*Nasua socialis*) in M_9 is found over a wide area and even as far away as North America, where raccoons take the place of the coati. Nearer the area we are dealing with here, the episode exists in a scarcely modified form among the Guarani-Mbya of Paraguay:

M_{13}. Guarani-Mbya. "The ogre Charia"

The ogre Charia found some coati and killed one of them. The hero Kuaray (Sun) climbed up a tree, and Charia shot an arrow at him. Sun feigned death and defecated. Charia gathered up the excrement, wrapped it up in lily leaves, and put it into his basket along with the corpse, under the coati. Then he went off to fish, leaving his basket on the river bank. Sun took advantage of the situation and fled, after putting a stone in the bottom of the basket.

Charia arrived at his hut, and his daughters looked in the basket: "Here is Niakanrachichan and here is his excrement!" The daughters brought out the coati: "Here are the coati . . . and that . . . that is a stone." There was nothing but a stone underneath the coati. (Cadgoan, pp. 80–1; there is another version in Borba, pp. 67–8.)

8. The relay system (M_{10}, M_{11}). This is a Ge custom, well attested from other sources. The runners do in fact carry "logs," which are carved and painted pieces of wood. Among the Kraho such relay races took place after a collective hunt. Among other tribes they are sometimes ceremonial in character, sometimes recreational; occasionally the log races were followed by relay races, or the same race had the double character. There is no indication that they are specially linked with the myths we are dealing with.

9. *Pau puba* (M_{11}). Schultz comments: "In Kraho, *pi(n)yapok*; the informant says that there is a lot of it in the forest, but that nobody eats it today! It is impossible to know what is being referred to" (*ibid.*, p. 72, n. 56). In Sherente, Nimuendaju (6, p. 39) gives *puba* as "a fermented manioc paste."[16]

Compare Kayapo: *bero* "a puba, a mandioca amolecida na agua" (Banner 2, p. 49). Among the Tenetehara, *puba* means the soft pulpy consistency of the manioc, which is put to soak (the verb is *pubar*) until it ferments (Wagley and Galvão, p. 39). The word is known in Portuguese: "Puba is softened and fermented manioc which has been buried in mud for several days" (Valdez, "Puba" entry). Later (pp.   ? ff.) I shall give other reasons for supposing that, as in M_8, the reference is really to rotten wood (*pau* "wood").

10. The Sherente village is divided into two patrilineal, patrilocal, and exogamous moieties, each one comprising three clans plus one "foreign" clan, which gives a total of eight clans whose huts are arranged in a horse-shoe pattern, with the opening to the west. The northern half is called Sdakran; the southern half, Shiptato. The first is associated with the moon; the second with the sun.

In M_{12}, the wicked brother-in-law is Sdakran and his victim Shiptato, as is clear from the commentary given by Nimuendaju:

> When the burning tree trunk had to be snatched from the jaguar's dwelling, the mutum and the waterfowl were the first to take hold of it. The mutum, whose head feathers were frizzled by the heat, belonged to the (Shiptato)

---

[16] The same author describes the making, by the Tucuna, of an alcoholic beverage based on manioc dough which has been allowed to ferment for two or three days, after which "it is crusted over with a thick layer of white mold." And he adds later: "To me *paiauarú* has a disagreeable taste of fermentation and rot . . . the Indians, however, drink it with enormous satisfaction" (Nim. 13, p. 34; cf. also Ahlbrinck, "woku" entry). A short Taurepan myth describes how the dog, the first creature to possess hammocks and cotton seed, gave them to men in exchange for their excrement which it called *sakura*—that is a masticated and fermented purée of manioc used in the making of beer. (K.G. 1, pp. 76–7). A similar myth exists in the Gran Chaco (Métraux 3, p. 74).

clan now called Kuze, "fire," whence the occasionally curly reddish-brown hair of its members. The Kuze and the Krenprehi (belonging to the Sdakran clan and facing the Kuze, at the eastern tip of the village circle, somewhere along the axis separating the two moieties) were, and in some instances remain, the makers of most ornaments peculiar to the other clans of their respective moieties. . . The Krenprehi put on all their decorative articles, pendants of red ara tail feathers . . . and in return received girdles of the width of three fingers from black or spotted jaguar skin. (Nim. 6, pp. 21–2.)

It is therefore normal in the myth that the Sdakran should look for aras, and that the Shiptato should allow himself to be adopted by the jaguar. On the other hand, we can link the name of the Kayapo here in M_7 with this commentary connected with ornaments, as well as the Bororo myths analyzed in the previous chapter. These, too, as we have seen, describe the origin of the adornments peculiar to each clan, and their heroes have names meaning "painted" or "pretty skin."

The Aikman funeral celebration was held to honor certain eminent men soon after their interment. All the villages were invited, and during the feast each camp was arranged by moieties and clans like a village. (Nim. 6, pp. 100–2.)

On the whole, the six versions I have summarized are so alike as to be in some ways indistinguishable. It will be noted, for instance, that (except in the case of M_{9a} which has already been discussed) the relation between the two men remains constant: they are, respectively, a sister's husband and a wife's brother, and the first is older than the second. However, we can detect differences that concern certain details but are no less significant for that.

1. The origin of the quarrel lies either in the hero's lack of courage, because he dare not take hold of the fledglings (M_9, M_{10}, M_{11}), or in his spiteful behavior: he deliberately deceives his brother-in-law (M_{12}). In this respect M_7 and M_8 occupy an intermediary position, perhaps only by reason of the vagueness of the text.

2. The hero's defilement varies in degree according to the different versions: in M_9, M_{10}, M_{11} he is covered with bird droppings, and in M_7 and M_8 he is forced to eat his own excrement.

3. The jaguar's attention is aroused spontaneously in M_7, M_8, M_{9a}, and $M_{12}(?)$, but deliberately solicited in M_9, M_{10}, and M_{11}.

4. In M_8 the jaguar climbs the tree to reach the prisoner, whereas in the other versions he waits for him on the ground. On the other hand, the jaguar receives no reward in M_7 and M_8; in all the other versions he demands and is given the fledglings.

5. In M_7, M_8, M_9, M_{9a}, and M_{12} the jaguar's wife is killed, but in M_{11} and M_{10} she is only wounded.

6. The jaguar treats men in a kindly fashion in M_9 and M_{9a}; in M_7 he is ill disposed toward them. Elsewhere there is no indication of his attitude.

If, in each instance, we distinguish between a strong attitude (+) and a weak attitude (−), we arrive at the following table:

	M_7	M_8	M_{9a}	M_9	M_{10}	M_{11}	M_{12}
Hero's behavior	(+)	(+)	−	−	−	(−)	+
Hero's defilement	+	+	−	−	−	−	0
Jaguar's attention	+	+	+	−	−	−	0
Jaguar's initiative	−	+	−	−	−	−	−
Jaguar's unselfishness	+	+	−	−	−	−	−
The woman's fate	+	+	+	+	−	−	+
Antagonism between jaguar and humans	+	0	−	−	0	0	0

In the light of the principles above, then, the Kayapo versions appear both coherent and strong, the Apinaye and Timbira-Kraho versions coherent and relatively weak. The Sherente version seems, from this point of view, to possess less internal coherence, but in certain other respects it is stronger than all the others (cf. the hero's ill-will toward his own people, manifested on two occasions: he deceives his brother-in-law, then the villagers; furthermore, his disappearance is virtually a death, and he causes the jaguar's wife to bleed to death by shooting her in the throat with an arrow); however, from other standpoints it is closer to the weak versions. Finally, we can note one striking inversion: in M_7, the eggs were changed into stones; in M_{12}, a stone is changed into an egg. The structure of the Sherente myth (M_{12}), therefore, contrasts with that of the other versions—a fact that is perhaps to be explained in part by the social structure of the Sherente which, as we have seen, differs sharply from that of the other Ge tribes. I shall return to this point later.

Over and above these common elements, which vary only in their modes of realization, several myths contain themes that do not appear at first glance to be found in the other versions. These are:

1. The episode of the caititu, which acts as an intermediary for the hero who at first refuses to climb on to the jaguar's back (M_8).
2. The origin of man's mortality and the adventure with the ogre (M_9).
3. The pregnancy of the jaguar's wife (M_{10}, M_{11}) and her inability to stand noise (M_{10}).
4. The stealing of the water from the alligator (M_{12}).
5. The trap of the invitation to delouse, which replaces that of food (M_{12}).

A comment: Points 3 and 5 are linked. The various attitudes adopted by the jaguar's wife form a pattern, which can be provisionally demonstrated in the following diagram:

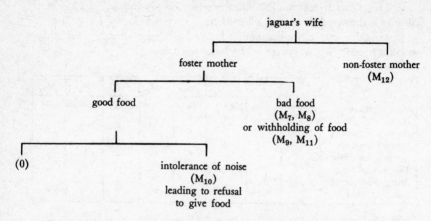

The significance of the other details will become clear only gradually. Each implies that the myth in which it occurs is linked, in this respect, with one or several other transformation groups of which the total—and pluridimensional—pattern must, in the first place, be reconstituted.

PART TWO

1

The "Good Manners" Sonata

a. THE PROFESSION OF INDIFFERENCE

We have seen that the Bororo myths display a remarkable indifference toward incest: the incestuous person is looked upon as the victim, while the person offended against is punished for having taken revenge or for having planned to do so.

A comparable indifference is to be found, in the Ge myths, in the jaguar's relations with its wife. The only thing that seems important to it is the safety of its adopted son (nephew in M_{11}); it sides with him against the scolding wife, encourages him to resist, and supplies him with the means to do so. And when the hero finally makes up his mind to kill her, he acts on the advice of the jaguar, which receives the news of its loss very philosophically. "It's a matter of no importance!" is the reply it makes to the embarrassed killer.

A remarkable symmetry can be discerned in these attitudes of indifference:

1. In each instance, the person concerned is a husband. Yet the Bororo husbands (the father of the bird-nester, and Baitogogo) are not indifferent —far from it; and they are men punished for not being indifferent. Whereas the Ge husbands (the jaguars) really are indifferent, and the myth gives them credit for adopting this attitude.

2. In one case, therefore, the husbands are *objects* of indifference: they suffer because the myth is indifferent to an act that they alone judge to be criminal; in the other case, indifference is a subjective attitude on their part. We might say that when we move from the Bororo Indians to the Ge, the relation between "form" and "background" is, as it were, reversed: among the Bororo the background (the mythic context) expresses the indifference that among the Ge is expressed by the form (that of the jaguar).

3. The nonindifference of the Bororo husbands is displayed in connection with incest. The indifference of the Ge husbands is displayed in connection with an act which, while excessive, is the opposite of incest: the killing of a mother by a "son."

4. In the Bororo myths, family relations (which are relevant here) are

based on true kinship and affiliation; in the Ge myths they are based on adoptive kinship and relations of affinity.

The reasons behind the indifference will appear more clearly if we now look at a myth of the Opaye-Shavante Indians belonging to the south of the Matto Grosso. Until recently they were considered to be part of the Ge linguistic group, but they are now looked upon as a separate family.

M₁₄. Opaye. "The jaguar's wife"

The women were busy collecting wood in a part of the forest that had been burned. One of them, who was still a girl, spotted the carcass of a queixada that a jaguar had left there. "How I should love to be the jaguar's daughter!" she exclaimed. "I should get all the meat I wanted." "Nothing could be easier," replied the jaguar, appearing at that moment. "Come with me. I will not hurt you."

The others looked for the girl in vain, and it was supposed that she had been devoured by the jaguar.

But one day she came back and revealed her identity to her younger sister and her parents. She explained that with her husband the jaguar she wanted for nothing, and that he would be delighted to supply food to the Indians. "What kind of game do you prefer?" "Anything!" "But state a preference. The jaguar will want to know." "All right. Tapir!" "Agreed," said the woman. "But take care to see that the hut posts are strong. The jaguar will leave the meat on the roof."

The next day the father discovered that the roof was covered with well-grilled meat. They made a feast of it. Two days later the supply was renewed.

After a time the jaguar wearied of carrying the meat and, through his wife, proposed that he should settle in the village. The father agreed. (He was afraid of the jaguar, but he was fond of meat.) Besides, the woman explained that the jaguar would not set up his hut too close to that of his parents-in-law; he would build it some distance away, so as not to be seen.

The woman went away; she was beginning to know how to hunt as well as the jaguar. The next day the hut roof was covered with all kinds of meat: caititu, queixada, armadillo, and paca.

The jaguar came to live with the Indians. His brother-in-law became friendly with the new couple who supplied him with choice game: jaó, mutum, inhambu, and macuco. But the grandmother felt mistrust. The young woman was gradually turning into a beast of prey; black spots appeared on her body, and she grew claws on her hands and feet. Only her face remained human, although fangs were beginning to show in her mouth. The old woman therefore resorted to witchcraft and killed her granddaughter.

The father was not very upset, but the whole family was afraid of the jaguar. His brother-in-law went to tell him that his wife was dead, and to ask him if he would take revenge or would agree to accept one of the dead woman's sisters in her place. "No," replied the jaguar. "There is no need for that. I shall leave. I do not wish you any harm. Perhaps you will remember me in years to come. . . ."

And the jaguar went off, incensed by the murder and spreading fear by his roaring; but the sound came from farther and farther away. (Ribeiro 2, pp. 129–31.)

Although this myth lays stress on already grilled meat rather than on fire for cooking, it is obviously very close to the Ge myths; and it develops the same theme: the jaguar provides culinary satisfaction, but the human beings can enjoy it without risk only if the jaguar's wife is removed; and in both cases the jaguar accepts this necessity with good grace and a declaration of indifference.

No doubt the Opaye myth could be called "the jaguar among men," in contrast to the Ge myths about "man among the jaguars." In spite of this inversion, it is explicitly stated in both the Opaye and the Ge versions that the jaguar's wife is a human being (cf. M7, "the jaguar's wife, who was an Indian"); and in spite of this, the humans have more reasons to be afraid of her than of the animal. Although she is the jaguar's wife, he is not deeply attached to her. She is human, yet her fellow human beings kill her in preference to him.

Thanks to the transformation illustrated in the Opaye myth, we can resolve the apparent contradiction by isolating those features that remain invariable at the level of the set.

The jaguar and the man are polar opposites, and the contrast between them is doubly formulated in ordinary language: one eats raw meat, the other cooked meat; in particular, the jaguar eats man, but man does not eat the jaguar. The contrast is not merely absolute: it implies that between the two opposite poles there exists a relation based on a total absence of reciprocity.

In order that all man's present possessions (which the jaguar has now lost) may come to him from the jaguar (who enjoyed them formerly when man was without them), there must be some agent capable of establishing a relation between them: this is where the jaguar's (human) wife fits in.

But once the transfer has been accomplished (through the agency of the wife):

a) The woman becomes useless, because she has served her purpose as a preliminary condition, which was the only purpose she had.

b) Her survival would contradict the fundamental situation, which is characterized by a total absence of reciprocity.

The jaguar's wife must therefore be eliminated.

b. CAITITU RONDO

The preceding demonstration will help to solve another problem along the same lines: the problem of the use of the caititu as intermediary mount in

M8. The body of the animal, which has presumably been hunted and killed by the jaguar, provides a meeting ground, as it were, for man and the beast of prey. In a slightly different context the Opaye version attributes the same role to the queixada (cf. p. 82), whose carcass whets the human heroine's appetite and so brings her into contact with the jaguar. Lastly, a Tucuna myth (M53), which will be dealt with later, mentions the caititu (or collared peccary) as the first game presented by the jaguar to the man whom its daughters want to marry (Nim. 13, p. 150). We have, therefore, a set with a triple transformation:

	Jaguars	Intermediary	Human beings
Opaye (M14)	male	queixada	female, friendly
Tucuna (M53)	female, friendly	caititu	male
Kayapo (M8)	female, hostile	caititu	male

In two of the myths the queixada, alone or accompanied by the caititu, appears at the end instead of at the beginning. In M8 the function of the queixada—that is, the peccary—is to bring back to the village the hanks of cotton, which, given the division of labor between the sexes, have presumably been spun by the jaguar's wife; this is confirmed moreover by M9a. This mediatory function reduplicates that performed by the caititu at the beginning of the same myth. In M9a the jaguar rejects a pair of caititus and another of queixadas as bearers of fire. The mention of these animals, purely for the purpose of stressing their rejection, is all the more remarkable in that it occurs in a variant in which—as I have emphasized (p. 70)—the jaguar's wife is noticeably less hostile, and her husband still more friendly, than in the other myths of the group. In this instance the recourse to an intermediary would appear superfluous.

To justify the part played by the caititu, it is not enough to say that it is eaten both by jaguars and by men, since several kinds of game fulfill this condition. The solution is suggested by other myths.

M15. Tenetehara. "The origin of wild pigs"

Tupan (the culture hero) traveled on this earth accompanied by his young godchild. One day they came to a large village where several relatives of his godchild lived; and Tupan left the child with these relatives, instructing them to treat him well. They did not, however, care for the boy; and on Tupan's return the boy complained of the bad treatment he had received.

Tupan was angry. He told the boy to gather all the feathers he could find and to spread them around the edge of the village. Then Tupan set fire to the feathers, and the entire village was surrounded by the walls of fire. The inhabitants ran from side to side, but they were unable to escape. Little by little their cries became lower until they were transformed into the grunts of pigs; at the same time the people began to take on the form of peccaries and wild pigs. A few of them escaped into the dense forest, and the wild pigs that inhabit the forest today are their descendants. Tupan made his godchild, Marana ywa, the owner of wild pigs. (Wagley and Galvão, p. 134.)

M_{16}. Mundurucu. "The origin of wild pigs"

It was the dry season, and everyone was hunting in the forest. Karusakaibö, the demiurge, with his son Korumtau, had taken up his abode in a shelter some distance from the main encampment. In those days there was only one kind of four-footed game, the caititu; and this was the only creature that was being hunted, apart from the fact that Karusakaibö went after the inhambu bird.[1] And every day he sent his son to his sisters' encampment ("to the neighbors": Coudreau) to exchange the inhambus for the caititus killed by their husbands. Dissatisfied with this procedure, the boy's aunts eventually became angry and heaped reproaches on him (threw him nothing but the feathers and skins: Tocantins, p. 86, and Coudreau; Kruse 3). He came back weeping and told his father what had happened.

Karusakaibö instructed his son to surround the encampment with a wall of feathers, whose top would overhang like a roof (during the operation, the boy changed first into a bird and then into a toad: Kruse 3). Then Karusakaibö puffed clouds of tobacco smoke into the interior. The occupants became dizzy, and when the demiurge cried out to them, "Eat your food!" they thought he was ordering them to copulate. "They proceeded to have coitus and made the usual grunting sounds while doing so." They were all changed into wild pigs. The husks they used to stuff their nostrils as a protection against the smoke became snouts, and their bodies were covered with bristles that Karusakaibö took from the anteater and threw at them.

The other Indians, who had remained behind in the village proper, were completely ignorant of the fate that had befallen their companions. Each day Karusakaibö went secretly to the pighouse made of feathers ("the pig mountain": Kruse 3), and set down food in front of the partly open door in such a way as to attract a single pig. He would then kill it with an arrow, close the door, and return to the village with the animal.

In the hero's absence Daïïru ("the trickster") wrested the secret of the enclosure from Korumtau; but through his clumsiness he allowed the pigs to escape. . . . (Murphy 1, pp. 70–3.)[2]

[1] One of the tinamous of the genus *Grypturus* (cf. p. 74); according to another Mundurucu myth (M_{143}), this is an inferior kind of game which produces a bitter stew.

[2] Other Mundurucu versions are to be found in Tocantins, pp. 86–7 (quoted by Coudreau); Strömer, pp. 137–44; Kruse 3, Vol. XLVI, pp. 923–5; there is an Apiaca version in Kruse 3, Vol XLVII, pp. 1011–12. A myth of the Warao of Guiana (M_{17}) seems to be an inverted version: in this a supernatural spirit, married to a human woman, makes a present of wild pigs to his brothers-in-law, who hunted only birds (which they called

M₁₈. Kayapo-Kubenkranken. "The origin of wild pigs"

While camping on the outskirts of a village with his son, the culture hero O'oimbre sent the boy to ask for food from his mother's relatives. The boy was badly received, and as a revenge, O'oimbre made a charm with feathers and thorns and used it to change all the villagers into peccaries. They remained shut up in their huts as if they were pigsties; Takake, the brother-in-law and rival of O'oimbre, drew one of them out (by the means described in the preceding myth) and killed it. O'oimbre forced a confession from Takake's son, went to the pigsty and set the peccaries free. . . . (Métraux 8, pp. 28–9.)

This version (of which I have quoted only certain features) is particularly interesting since it comes from a Ge tribe, and its meaning can be made more precise with the help of myths belonging to the Tenetehara and the Mundurucu (who are outlying Tupi). The Mundurucu and Kayapo myths agree in restricting the metamorphosis to peccaries or wild pigs ≠ caititu. According to the Kayapo version, the peccaries' snouts are "much longer"; the Mundurucu version adds that the caititu have short black bristles, interspersed with white, whereas wild pigs have much longer bristles and are entirely black. Moreover, in the Timbira language, the word for queixada is *klu*, and the term for the caititu is formed by simply adding the diminutive suffix *ré* (Vauzolini, p. 161). This gives the pattern:

1. Caititu: shorter snout, short bristles interspersed with white.
2. "Peccary" or "wild pig": longer snout, long black bristles, which confirms the identification suggested above:

1. Collared peccary (*Dicotyles torquatus*).
2. White-lipped peccary (*D. labiatus*). The latter species, to which the myths attribute a human origin, is "truculent, noisy, gregarious with communal defense, and is a formidable opponent" (Gilmore, p. 382).

The three myths allow us to understand the semantic position of the two species: they are associated and contrasted as a pair, which is particularly suited to convey mediation between humanness and animality; since one member of the pair represents, as it were, the pure animal which is nothing but animal, whereas the other has become an animal through the loss of its original human nature, to which it was untrue through asocial behavior: the ancestors of the peccaries were human beings who showed themselves to be "inhuman." The caititus and peccaries are therefore semihuman: the former synchronically, since they constitute the animal half of a pair whose other member is human; and the latter diachronically, since they were human beings before they changed into animals.

"wild pigs"); but the untutored brothers-in-law confuse the timid creatures and the fierce, and the latter devour the spirit's child. Since then wild pigs have been scattered and difficult to hunt (Roth 1, pp. 186–7). For a closely connected form of the same myth among the Shipaya and Mura, see Nim. 3, pp. 1013 ff., and 10, pp. 265–6.

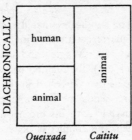

If, as may be the case, the Mundurucu and Kayapo myths preserved the memory of a technique of hunting that was no longer practiced and consisted of driving peccaries into enclosures[3] where they were kept and fed before being killed according to need, the first contrast is reduplicated by a second: semihuman on the mythic level, the peccaries could be semidomesticated on the level of techno-economic activity. If so, it would have to be admitted that the second aspect explains, and is the basis of, the first.

But it is not part of my purpose to inquire into the reasons for the special position attributed to the *tayassuidae* by the natives of central Brazil: it is enough to have followed the use of the term through a sufficient number of contexts for its semantic content to become clear. I am trying to determine its meaning, not to discover its etymology. It is wise to keep the two operations separate, except on those rare and unforeseeable occasions when, through some fluke, they happen to coincide.

On the other hand, it can be seen why the caititu episode figures in a Kayapo version (M_8) rather than in those of the other tribes: we know that the Kayapo versions are "strong" in comparison with the others. They bring out with unequaled force the contrast between the two opposite terms—man and jaguar: the jaguar's final attitude, when it is "full of hatred for all creatures and especially for human beings," implies that from the outset it was already remote from man. A pair predestined to so radical a separation could not have been formed, even tentatively, without the operation of a mediator. The Opaye myth (M_{14}), in which the same mediator is seen at work, is just as "strong" a version; but the final disruption involves both the human wife, who is transformed into a jaguar and then killed, and her animal husband who disappears for good, after taking on a terrifying appearance.

At the same time, if the preceding analyses are correct, particular at-

[3] And which is also suggested by other Mundurucu myths (Murphy 1, p. 36; Kruse 3, Vol. XLVII, p. 1006) and evidence from the Amazon region (Barbosa Rodrigues, pp. 47–8).

tention must be paid to the description of human relations referred to in the myths about the origins of the peccaries. The Tenetehara myth (M_{15}) is not very explicit, since it merely indicates that the culture hero has a godson (*afilhado*), and that he quarrels with the latter's relatives. However, if, as is suggested in the source text (Wagley and Galvão, p. 103), the godson is also a "nephew" (sister's son), the relation between the demiurge and the boy's relatives is the same as that described in the Mundurucu myth (M_{16}) where the hero, O'oimbre, sends his son to beg food from the mother's relatives, and he later quarrels with his brother-in-law, Takake, his sister's husband. Here again, then, the conflict is between affines, but the resemblance goes no further.

The pattern of kinship and affinity suggested by the Tenetehara and Mundurucu myths:

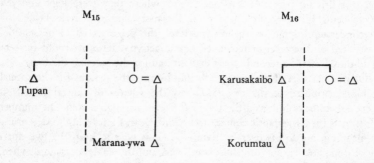

would be hardly conceivable among the Kayapo, where the closest links are between brother and sister, and there is a latent antagonism between husband and wife, which is extended to the latter's maternal relatives (Banner 2, p. 16). This seems to have been the situation among the Bororo, too, when the first missionaries went among them, as is testified by an important passage in Colbacchini's first book:

The men of one dynasty (moiety) are strictly forbidden to speak or laugh with the women of the other dynasty, and even to look at them or to seem to notice their presence. This rule is meticulously and scrupulously observed. Men of any age who happen to meet with one or several women on a path or in any other place, not only walk on again if they are standing still, but also avoid looking at the women or turn their gaze in the opposite direction, as if they wished to signify their desire to avoid any risk or possibility of an exchange of looks. Any violation of this traditional principle is considered an extremely grave matter: the guilty party would arouse public indignation and be universally blamed; since, generally speaking, any exchange of looks or smiles between people of opposite sexes belonging to different dynasties is considered an immoral and harmful act.

The women of one dynasty never allow themselves to be seen in the act of eating or drinking by the men of the other dynasty, and vice versa. But there is no comparable prohibition in regard to individuals belonging to the same dynasty, whether male or female. Consequently if a man and a woman are seen talking together, it can be immediately concluded that they spring from the same dynastic root, since the rules above are observed in public even by husbands and wives, though rather less scrupulously; however, it is almost inconceivable that a man should speak or jest in public with his wife or should put her next to himself, or that they should even be together, except when they go off jointly to look for fruit, tubers, or other products of the forest. This latter activity is looked upon as being of a private nature. (Colb. *1*, pp. 49–50.)

It can thus be stated as a rule that in societies such as these the theoretical break occurs not between blood relatives but between relatives by marriage:

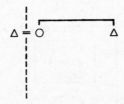

This is the case in M_{18}, but it is conditional on another, remarkable transformation.

A general similarity is noticeable between the Mundurucu pair of culture heroes and the Kayapo pair: Karusakaibö of the Mundurucu corresponds to the Takake of the Kayapo. A comparable relation is observable between the Mundurucu Daïïru and the Kayapo O'oimbre: both are tricksters in the guise of armadillos; both make the same mistakes and are responsible for the same accidents.

But the roles are reversed in the case of the conflict between affines which is the cause of the changing of one of the two groups into pigs. At the same time as:

$$M_{16} \left[\triangle \overset{\#}{\rule{1.5cm}{0.4pt}} \bigcirc = \triangle \right] \rightarrow M_{18} \left[\triangle \rule{1.5cm}{0.4pt} \bigcirc \# \triangle \right]$$

the demiurge gives way to the trickster. In the Mundurucu legends Karusakaibö, when insulted by his sister's husbands, changes them into pigs. He is therefore responsible for the *creation* of wild pigs, whereas Daïïru, the hero in the guise of an armadillo, is responsible for the dwindling of their numbers or their *loss*. In the Kayapo myth O'oimbre, the hero in the guise of an armadillo, replaces the demiurge Takake as the being responsible for the creation of wild pigs, and the latter are represented by the other group of relatives by marriage.

Subsequently, however, the functions remain unchanged, so that, in an apparently illogical fashion, the Kayapo myth makes O'oimbre responsible first for the creation of the pigs, then for their loss. This is achieved by means of a strange story according to which O'oimbre changes the villagers into pigs and behaves immediately afterward as if he had forgotten all about the incident, whereas Takake—who has had no share in it—acts as if he were the only person to know about it. This internal contradiction in the Kayapo version shows that it must be a secondary working of the Mundurucu version. In comparison with the latter, which is a "straight" version, the Kayapo one contains a double twist, the second part of which is intended to cancel out the first part and so restore the parallel with the continuation of the Mundurucu story (Figure 5).

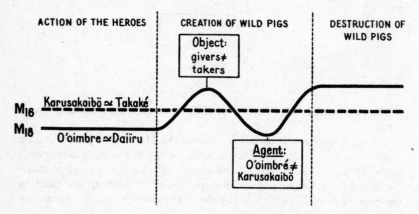

Figure 5. The relation between the Kayapo and the Mundurucu myths.

It is thus possible to reduce the Kayapo version to the Mundurucu version through reciprocal cancellation of the two parts of the twist, and to consider as fundamental only the relation of affinity, which is referred to in the latter version in connection with the illtreatment inflicted on a brother of their wives by the husbands of his sisters: in other words, a "wife-giver" is wronged by "takers."[4]

---

[4] I am leaving aside a Mataco version, which is too elliptical (Métraux 3, p. 61). The Cariri version will be discussed further on pp. 102-3. Of three remaining versions, a Cashinawa one (M_{19}, Abreu, pp. 187-96) and a Bororo one (M_{21}, Colb. 3, p. 260) refer to a conflict, not between brothers-in-law, but between actual or potential spouses, with a correlative transformation of abuse of coitus (in the Mundurucu version) into re-

Here again the Opaye myth (M₁₄) provides the missing link that allows us to connect the set of myths about the origins of wild pigs with that concerning the origins of the use of fire for cooking. M₁₄ stresses the fact that, like the future peccaries, the jaguar is in the position of a wife-taker with regard to a human group. But he is a benevolent brother-in-law who provides men with fire for cooking—or with grilled meat—in exchange for the wife he has received, whereas the wild pigs are the animal embodiment of the malevolent brothers-in-law, who refuse food, or offer it on certain conditions, or give it in an insolent manner.

This being so, it now appears that the internal coherence of the Ge series about the bird-nester is even greater than I supposed it to be. We can see that all the myths of this set present not simply one pair, but two pairs of brothers-in-law: first, the bird-nester (who is a wife-giver) and his sister's husband to whom he refuses (deliberately or not) to hand over the nestlings; then, the same bird-nester (but acting now as an ambassador of the human race) and the jaguar, who has been given a wife by the humans and, in exchange, presents the humans with fire and cooked food:

First pair   *Second pair*

(wicked   △ = ○   (jaguar: △ = ○   (△)
human   good
brother-   brother-
in-law)   in-law)

              △   △
              ↑   ↑
              ¦ ——————— (bird-nester) ——— ——————————— ¦

The jaguar's human wife must therefore be irrevocably lost to humanity (changed into a jaguar, in the Opaye myth), since experience shows that the jaguar, for his part, has no less irrevocably lost the use of fire and the habit of eating cooked meat.

In the Bororo myth about the bird-nester (M₁), this pattern merely undergoes a transformation: a son refuses to give his mother to his father (this is the meaning of his incestuous behavior), and the father takes revenge just as, in the Ge myths, the older brother-in-law takes revenge on the younger, who refuses to hand over the nestlings:

---

fusal of coitus (Cashinawa) or anti-amorous behavior (Bororo). I shall deal with this transformation again later (p. 95). Only the third and last version (Guiana Carib., in Ahlbrinck, "wireimo" entry) does not refer expressly to a relation by marriage: it simply gives the voraciousness of a group of hunters as the reason for their being changed into wild pigs.

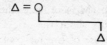

If it is remembered that among the Bororo the line of descent is frankly matrilineal, it can be seen that the basic situation remains unchanged: the son belongs not to his father's group, but to the group of his in-laws. By its implicit reference to the matrilineal principle, the key myth therefore involves the transformation:

$$\left[\begin{array}{c} \triangle \quad \# \quad (\bigcirc) = \triangle \end{array}\right] \quad \left[\begin{array}{c} (\triangle) \qquad \bigcirc \neq \triangle \end{array}\right]$$

this is congruous with the transformation noted in the case of the myth about the origin of wild pigs when the Kayapo and the Bororo versions are considered in relation to the Mundurucu version.

In the case of the Bororo, whose social institutions seem, generally speaking, to be more completely in harmony with the underlying principle of matrilineity than is the case elsewhere, the transformation arises, as has already been pointed out, from the fact that the key myth makes it essential to refer to the rule of matrilineal descent; this is not so with the Ge myths, M_8 to $_{12}$, in which the connection between the two masculine protagonists is purely that of affinity. With the Kayapo-Kubenkranken, who are just as firmly matrilocal as the Bororo but do not have exogamic moieties and perhaps do not even recognize the unilineal principle of descent (Dreyfus), the transformation is determined by the concept of matrilocal residence, as is shown by M_{18}, which refers to two successive quarrels instead of to a single one: the first is between the son of O'oimbre and the men of the *ngobe* (Métraux 8, p. 28) and explains why the son and the father (who identified with each other while in the men's house) should have gone to live outside the village—in other words, should have also escaped from matrilocal residence; and the second, between the son and his "maternal relatives," which is more easily conceivable when he is already separated from them. In a no less logical manner, and in one which is linked with the confusion between the functions of the demiurge and those of the trickster, the character of the child is also reduplicated in M_{18}.

It follows that there is nothing surprising in the fact that the Bororo should deal with the theme of the relations between affines by a process of systematic inversion of its contents:

M_{20}. *Bororo. "The origin of manufactures"*

Once upon a time the men of the Bokodori clan (the Cera moiety) were supernatural spirits who lived happily in huts made of down and feathers, which were called "macaws' nests." When they wanted something, they would send one of their young brothers to their sister to ask her to obtain it for them from her husband.

They expressed a desire for honey; the honey their brother-in-law invited them to eat in his hut was thick, sticky, and full of scum, because he had copulated with his wife while he was busy collecting it.

The wife's brothers went away offended and decided to look on the river bed for the stone with which to pierce holes in palm-nut shells or the shells of shellfish—that is, for the technical means for the production of ornaments such as pendants and necklaces. They eventually discovered the stone and, with it, successfully carried out the work of piercing the holes. Success caused them to give a triumphant laugh, different from the laugh that expresses profane gaiety. This "forced laugh" or "sacrificial laugh" is called the "soul laugh." The expression also refers to a ritual chant peculiar to the Bokodori clan (cf. EB, Vol. I, p. 114).

Being curious to know the cause of the cries that she could hear from afar, the wife spied on her brothers and thus broke the rule forbidding her to look inside the feather hut. Because they had been insulted in this way, the Bokodori decided to put an end to their lives. First they solemnly shared out the ornaments between the various lineages, each ornament becoming an attribute of a particular lineage. Then they threw themselves simultaneously into a blazing fire (with the exception of their already married relatives, who were left to carry on the race).

No sooner were they consumed by the fire than they changed into birds: red and yellow macaws, falcons, hawks, egrets. . . . The other inhabitants of the village decided to leave so somber a place. Only the sister would return regularly to the scene of the sacrifice to collect the plants growing among the ashes: urucu, cotton, and calabashes, which she shared out among her relatives. (Cruz 2, pp. 159–64.)

It is clear that this myth, like those about the origins of wild pigs refers to relations between affines. It develops in the same way, using the same syntax, but with different "words." The two types of brothers-in-law are also resident some distance away from each other; this time, however, the wife-givers are identified with birds (and not with hunters of birds); they are bachelors, and they themselves inhabit feather huts where they lead a paradisal existence, instead of imprisoning married people—their sisters and brothers-in-law—in a comparable hut to suffer the effects of a curse.

In this myth, as in the myths about wild pigs, the wife-givers expect presents of food—meat or honey—from the takers. But—whereas in M_{16}, for instance, the refusal of such presents (or their unwilling concession) produces first wild sexual activity on the part of the guilty, followed by their transformation into pigs—in this case the opposite occurs: sexual activity, which is forbidden during the collecting of honey, involves what is tantamount to a refusal of a gift (since the latter consists of inedible honey), followed by the transformation of the victims (not the guilty) first of all into culture heroes who invent ornaments and the technique of producing them; then, through an auto-da-fé, into birds of brighter and more beautiful colors (and therefore more suitable as raw material for ornaments). It will be remembered that in the set of myths about wild pigs the wife-givers retained their human nature and transformed their brothers-in-law—who were imprisoned in the smoke-filled hut—into pigs with a natural, noncultural function: to serve as food. Only the framework remains unchanged and is expressed in the formula:

$$\text{(givers : takers)} \ :: \ M^{20} \text{(birds : men)} \ :: \ M^{16} \text{(men : pigs)}$$

It will also be noted that relationship of affinity is conceptualized in the form of a contrast: nature/culture, but always from the point of view of the wife-givers: the takers have the status of men only when the givers are themselves spirits. Otherwise they are animals: jaguars or wild pigs: jaguars, when nature is tending in the direction of culture, since the jaguar is a brother-in-law who behaves with civility and presents man with the arts of civilization; pigs, when culture is degenerating into nature, the wild pigs being former human beings who behaved coarsely, and who, instead of improving the daily diet of their brothers-in-law (in exchange for the wives received from them), promptly settled down to sexual enjoyment—in other words, were takers on the natural level instead of being givers on the cultural level.

Analysis of M_{20} confirms that, as we supposed, the Bororo myth respects the code of the corresponding Ge and Tupi myths (M_{15}, M_{16}, and M_{18}), but at the cost of a distortion of the message, which is concerned with cultural achievements peculiar to a particular clan, instead of with a source of food, represented by a particular natural species. It will likewise be confirmed that, to transmit the same message, a Bororo myth about the origin of wild pigs has to resort to a modification of the code:

M₂₁. Bororo. "The origin of wild pigs"

Day after day the men would go fishing and catch nothing. They would return to the village in a sad state of mind, not only because they were empty-handed, but also because their wives were sulking and gave them a poor welcome. The women even got to the point of challenging the men.

They declared that they would do the fishing. But in actual fact all they did was to call on otters, who dived and fished in their stead. The women returned laden with fish, and each time the men tried to get their own back, they caught nothing.

After a time the men suspected some sort of trick. They had the women spied on by a bird who revealed the truth. The next day, the men went to the river, called the otters, and strangled them one after another. Only one escaped.

It was now the men's turn to jeer at the women, who caught nothing. The latter therefore determined to be avenged. They offered the men a drink made with piqui fruits (*Caryocar* species), whose kernels they had left covered with spikes.[5] Choked by these spikes which stuck in their throats, the men grunted, "u, u, u, u," and were changed into wild pigs that give this cry. (Colb. 3, pp. 259–60.)

Thus we have confirmation of the following general pattern of features:

1. With the Bororo, the origin of wild pigs (M_{21}) occurs as a function of the disjunction:

$$(\bigcirc \# \triangle).$$

2. The opposite disjunction:

$$\left(\triangle \overset{\ulcorner \# \urcorner}{} \bigcirc = \triangle \right),$$

which governed the origin of wild pigs in the Mundurucu myths, in the case of the Bororo (M_{20}) also involves the origins of cultural achievements (wild pig, a natural resource).

3. In the case of:

$$M_{16}\left[\; (\triangle \overset{\ulcorner \# \urcorner}{} \bigcirc) \rightarrow (\text{origin of wild pigs}) \quad \right],$$

the sociological contrast between the opposite terms—wife-givers and wife-takers—was presented in the form:

poor hunter (of birds)/good hunters (of caititu).

In the case of:

$$M_{21}\left[(\bigcirc \# \triangle) \rightarrow (\text{origin of wild pigs}) \; \right],$$

the sociological contrast—between husbands and wives in this instance—is presented in the form:

poor fishermen/good fisherwomen.

Hence:

$$a)\begin{bmatrix} M_{16} \\ (</>) \end{bmatrix} \rightarrow \begin{bmatrix} M_{21} \\ (0/1) \end{bmatrix}$$

[5] "The pikia . . . bears a large edible fruit, curious in having a hollow chamber between the pulp and the kernel, beset with hard spines, which produce serious wounds if they enter the skin" (Bates, p. 203). I am leaving aside a version noted in 1917 (Rondon, pp. 167–70), which in some respects is more explicit, because, like the other myths in the same work, it presents lacunae that make it practically unusable without a critical and philological study of the native text.

which emphasizes the contrast, since the wife-giver of M_{16} manages even so to kill some game (although it is inferior to that caught by his brothers-in-law), whereas the husbands of M_{21} catch no fish at all; and:

$$b) \left[\begin{array}{c} M_{16} \\ (\text{game} \equiv \text{air} \cup \text{earth}) \end{array} \right] \rightarrow \left[\begin{array}{c} M_{21} \\ (\text{game} \equiv \text{water}) \end{array} \right].$$

Just as, for

$$\left[\begin{array}{c} \text{Mundurucu} \\ (\triangle \overset{\#}{\frown} \bigcirc = \triangle) \end{array} \right] \Big/ \left[\begin{array}{c} \text{Bororo} \\ (\bigcirc \# \triangle) \end{array} \right],$$

we have:

$$\left[\begin{array}{c} M_{16} \\ \left(\begin{array}{c} \text{wife-givers} = \text{hunters} \\ \text{of birds} \end{array} \right) \end{array} \right] \Big/ \left[\begin{array}{c} M_{21} \\ \left(\begin{array}{c} \text{women} = \text{catchers} \\ \text{of fish} \end{array} \right) \end{array} \right],$$

it will be confirmed later (pp. 266–9) that, correspondingly, for

$$\left[\begin{array}{c} \text{Bororo} \\ (\triangle \overset{\#}{\frown} \bigcirc = \triangle) \end{array} \right] \Big/ \left[\begin{array}{c} \text{Mundurucu, etc.} \\ (\bigcirc \# \triangle) \end{array} \right]$$

we have:

$$\left[\begin{array}{c} M_{20} \\ (\text{wife-givers} = \text{birds}) \end{array} \right] \Big/ \left[\begin{array}{c} M_{150} \\ (\text{women} = \text{fish}) \end{array} \right].$$

4. The transformation given above:

$$\left[\begin{array}{c} M_{16} \\ \text{game} \equiv \text{air} \cup \text{earth}) \end{array} \right] \rightarrow \left[\begin{array}{c} M_{21} \\ (\text{game} \equiv \text{water}) \end{array} \right]$$

can be developed:

$$\left[\begin{array}{c} M_{16} \\ (\text{natural resources} \equiv \text{air} \cup \text{earth}) \end{array} \right] \rightarrow$$
$$\left[\begin{array}{c} M_{20} \\ (\text{manufactures} \equiv \text{water} \cup \text{air}) \end{array} \right] \rightarrow$$
$$\left[\begin{array}{c} M_{21} \\ (\text{natural resources} \equiv \text{water} \cup \text{earth}) \end{array} \right];$$

In other words, in M_{20} the men "fish" the cultural tool (the stone borer) from the river and then are transformed into birds supplying ornamental plumes, just as in M_{21} the women catch the fish, then change the men into pigs.

Moreover, the "fishers" of M_{20} act in the capacity of supernatural spirits (the "souls," whose "laughter" they initiate), whereas the fisherwomen of M_{21} act through the agency of natural beings, the otters.

5. Finally, the general pattern of these operations has equivalents at the level of the acoustic code:

a) M_{16} : (origin of wild pigs) $= {}^f$(amorous cries $\cup$ animal grunts);
b) M_{20} : (origin of manufactures) $= {}^f$(sacred laughter//profane laughter);
c) M_{21} : (origin of wild pigs) $= {}^f$(animal grunts//amorous cries);

since, contrary to what happens in M_{16}, the changing of men into pigs in M_{21} results from the disjunction of spouses who come into conflict, and not from their carnal union.

Let us pause awhile to consider the ground that has been covered. I began by raising a question of detail: the role of the caititu in M_8, which is corroborated by a reference to a queixada at the beginning of M_{14}, both these myths being about the origins of cooking. After discussing the semantic position of wild pigs, I was led to examine the myths about the origins of these animals. The analysis of these myths suggests two conclusions: on the one hand, from a certain point of view—that of marriage relations— there is an isomorphism between the myths of the first set (about the origin of cooking) and those of the second (about the origin of pigs); on the other hand, at the same time as they are isomorphic and therefore supplementary, the two groups complete each other and form what one might call, to emphasize its ideal nature, a meta-system (Figure 6).

This meta-system relates to the condition of the wife-giver—that is, of the man who possesses a sister or a daughter and is doomed to enter into relations with beings whose nature appears irreducible to his own. These beings, who are always identifiable with animals, divide up into two categories: the first is that of the jaguar, a benevolent and helpful brother-in-law, a dispenser of the arts of civilization; the second is that of the pig, a malevolent brother-in-law, only usable *sub specie naturae* as game (since it has even been impossible to domesticate him).[6]

[6] The native folklore of Brazil and of the peasants of the interior shows that herds of wild pig (queixada) are much more feared, and indeed much more fearsome, than the jaguar is. The latter can rarely be considered responsible for any accidents other than those provoked by a hunter's foolhardiness (Ihering, Vol. XXXVII, p. 346).

A Colombian specialist writes: "Contrary to popular belief, the jaguar . . . is not really dangerous to man, since it never attacks first. The Indians know this by direct experience, being much better acquainted with forest animals than we are." To explain the importance of the jaguar in mythology, the same writer goes on to stress its nocturnal habits, which link it with the owl and the bat. Also, the jaguar is big and strong; it works its will on other animals, which it eats. Moreover, it eats the same animals as man—tapirs, deer, wild pigs, small rodents, and cattle. The jaguar is a competitor

The interest of these results is, in the first place, theoretical. The detail I started from related to content, but as I have proceeded with the demonstration, the content has been, as it were, reversed and has become a form. This leads us to see that, in structural analysis, content and form are not separate entities, but complementary points of view essential for the deep understanding of one and the same object of study. Moreover, the content has not simply changed into a form; from being a mere detail at the beginning, it has expanded into a system of the same type and the same kind of dimensions as the initial system in which it figured as an element.

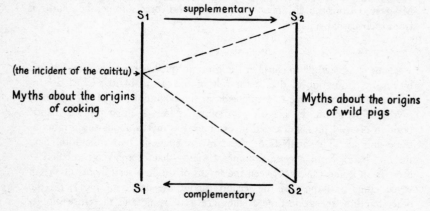

Figure 6. Myths about cooking (cooked food)
and myths about meat (raw food).

Lastly, the two sets of myths—those relating to the bird-nester on the one hand, and those about the origins of wild pigs on the other—are linked by two types of relation: they are partially isomorphic and supplementary, since they raise the problem of affinal relations; and they are also partially heteromorphic and complementary, since each of them is concerned with only one aspect of affinity.

Let us now go one step further and look at the matter at the level of the meta-system which integrates the two systems S_1 and S_2 so that they form a diptych in which the wife-giver (the term common to both) considers his two possible types of brothers-in-law alternatively: on his left is the good jaguar; on his right the wicked pig. In the preceding pages I have elucidated the rules that enable us to transform a given scene into a

---

much feared by man because of its strength, its agility, its acute sight and sense of smell (Reichel-Dolmatoff, Vol. I, pp. 266–7). The jaguar is seen, then, as being much more a "rival" than a "devourer" of man. When the latter function is attributed to it in the myths, either as a fact or as a potentiality, this is mainly a way of giving metaphorical expression to the first function.

different scene—or, if you like, S₁ (myths which have a bird-nester as their hero) into S₂ (myths about the origin of pigs). This procedure would be decisively confirmed if it were possible to repeat the process, but in the opposite direction, and starting this time from myths about the origin of the jaguar to work back to the bird-nester. This is what I shall attempt to do now.

M₂₂. Mataco. "The origin of the jaguar"

A man went fishing with his wife. He climbed a tree to catch parrots, which he threw down to his wife. But the wife devoured them. "Why are you eating the parrots?" he asked. As soon as he came down from the tree, she killed him by breaking his neck with her teeth. When she returned to the village, her children ran toward her to see what she was bringing. She showed them their father's head, saying that it was the head of an armadillo. During the night she ate her children and ran away to the bush. She changed herself into a jaguar. Jaguars are women. (Métraux 3, pp. 60–1.)

M₂₃. Toba-Pilaga. "The origin of tobacco"

One day a woman and her husband went to catch parakeets (*Myopsitta monachus*). The man climbed a tree containing several nests and threw down thirty or so fledglings to his wife. He noticed that she gobbled them up. Seized with fear, he caught hold of a larger bird and, as he threw it down, called out, "Here comes a fledgling, but look out, it can fly."

The woman ran after the bird, and the man took advantage of the situation to climb down and run away: he was afraid she might eat him, too. But his wife went after him, caught up with him, and killed him. Then she cut off his head, which she put in a bag, and feasted on the rest of the body until her stomach was full.

She had scarcely returned to the village when she felt thirsty. Before going to the drinking pool, which was some distance away, she forbade her five children to touch the bag. But the youngest immediately looked inside and called the others, who recognized their father. The whole village was now informed, and everybody took fright and ran away, except the children. When the mother, on her return, was surprised to find the village empty, they explained that the villagers had left after insulting them, having fled through shame at their own spitefulness.

The woman was indignant and, wishing to avenge her children, went after the villagers. She caught up with them, killed a number of them, and devoured the bodies there and then. The same process was repeated several times. Terrified by these bloody comings and goings, the children wanted to escape. "Do not try to run away," said the mother, "lest I eat you, too." The children implored her. "No, don't be afraid," she replied. No one was able to kill her, and the rumor soon spread that she was a jaguar-woman.

The children secretly dug a pit, which they covered with branches. They took flight when their mother announced to them that their turn had now come to be eaten. She rushed after them and fell into the trap. The children went to ask for help from Carancho (the culture hero, a species of falcon, *Polyborus plancus,* simultaneously a bird of prey and a carrion-eater, cf. Ihering), who advised them to hollow out a tree trunk (*Chorisia insignis*) and hide inside with him. The jaguar-woman tried to tear the tree with her claws, but they remained caught in the wood, so that Carancho was able to come out and kill her. Her corpse was burned on a woodpile. Four or five days later a plant sprang up from the ashes. This was the first appearance of tobacco.

The claws were used to make collars for dogs, which were sent to all the villages, so that no one would be in doubt about the death of the jaguar-woman. (Métraux 5, pp. 60–2.)

Another version adds the point that the jaguar-woman had seduced a friend's husband (Métraux 5, pp. 62–4).

M₂₄. *Tereno. "The origin of tobacco"*

There was a woman who was a sorceress. She defiled caraguata plants (a Bromeliacex, the central leaves of which are specked with red at the base) with menstrual blood and then served the plants to her husband as food. The husband, having been told about this by his son, announced that he was going into the bush to look for honey.

After knocking the soles of his leather sandals together "to find honey more easily," he discovered a hive at the bottom of a tree and a snake near by. He kept the pure honey for his son, and for his wife prepared a mixture composed of honey and the flesh of snake embryos taken from the belly of the one he had killed.

No sooner had the woman begun to eat her portion than her body started to itch. As she scratched herself, she announced to her husband that she was about to devour him. He ran away and climbed to the top of a tree where there was a parrot's nest. He kept the ogress quiet temporarily by throwing to her the three nestlings, one after the other. While she was chasing the largest which was trying to flutter away from her, the husband ran off in the direction of a pit that he himself had dug for the purpose of catching game. He avoided the pit, but the woman fell into it and was killed.

The man filled in the hole and kept watch over it. An unknown plant eventually sprouted there. Out of curiosity the man dried the leaves in the sun; at nightfall he smoked in great secret. His companions caught him at it and asked what he was doing. Thus it was that men came to have tobacco. (Baldus 3, pp. 220–21; 4, p. 133.)

This set of Chaco myths raises very complex questions that we shall meet on several occasions in the course of this study. I shall restrict myself for the time being to those that have a direct bearing on this particular demonstration.

It will be noted in the first place that the group is concerned sometimes with the origin of the jaguar, sometimes with the origin of tobacco, and sometimes with both at once. Tobacco, considered separately, establishes a link with the myths about the origin of wild pigs, in which tobacco plays a decisive part and which, in this respect, can be laid out as follows:

$$^T(\text{humans} \rightarrow \text{pigs}) = f^1 \text{ (tobacco smoke, } M_{16}), \; f^2 \text{ (smoke from feathers, } M_{15}),$$
$$f^3 \text{ (feather charm, } M_{18}).$$

That tobacco smoke plays the fully significant part in the series is shown, in the first place, by this method—the only logically satisfactory one—of organizing the series, and then by the derivative character of M_{18} in relation to M_{16}, which has already been established independently; it is also clear from the Cariri version, which I have reserved for quotation in this context.

M_{25}. Cariri. "The origin of wild pigs and tobacco"

In the days when the demiurge lived with men, the latter asked him to let them taste wild pigs, which as yet did not exist. The Grandfather (as the demiurge was called) took advantage of the fact that all the Indians were away and had left only children under ten behind in the village, to change the latter into wild piglets. When the Indians returned, he advised them to go hunting, but at the same time sent all the piglets up into the sky by way of a big tree. The men, seeing this, followed the piglets into the sky and began killing them there. The demiurge thereupon ordered the ants to fell the tree, which the toads defended with their bodies. This is why today toads have swollen backs as a result of the stings.

The ants succeeded in bringing down the tree. The Indians, being unable to get back to earth, put their belts end to end to make a rope. But as it was too short, they fell down one after another and broke their bones: "This is why our fingers and toes are broken in so many places and why our bodies bend according to the breaks inflicted on our parents by their fall."

On returning to the village, the Indians feasted on the flesh of their children, who had been changed into piglets. They begged the Grandfather to come down from the sky (whither he had followed the children) and to return to the village: "but he would not hear of it and gave them tobacco in his stead; they call it Badze and this is why, at certain times, they make offerings of tobacco." (Martin de Nantes, pp. 228–31.)

However distorted this myth may have been in the account left us by a missionary of the late seventeenth century who took every opportunity to show his contempt for native beliefs, we can easily see that it is closely related to the other myths about the origins of wild pigs and especially to the Mundurucu myth (M_{16}). In both cases the splitting of the human family into men on one side and pigs on the other is brought about by tobacco, or the old man Tobacco. But there are also some significant differences.

In the case of the Mundurucu, as in the other Ge and Tupi myths on the same theme, the cleavage cuts through a relation of affinity; it respects the human quality of wives' brothers but pushes their sisters and the latter's husbands into animality. In the Cariri myth, on the other hand, the cleavage cuts through a line of descent, since it separates parents and children from each other.

I have already noted the same type of transformation in certain Bororo myths (p. 92). An ambiguous sentence in Martin de Nantes' account (p. 8)—"Usually the wives dominated their husbands"—may mean that the Cariri, like the Bororo, were matrilineal and matrilocal. But the problem raised by their myth is more complex than that.

In the first place, the breaking of a line of descent also occurs in the Mundurucu (M_{16}), Warao (M_{17}), and Kayapo (M_{18}) versions, but only in the background of the story. All three relate that the scattering of the wild pigs—carelessly or maliciously set free (or herded together) by a trickster—caused the physical disappearance of the hero's son. The disappearance can be explained by considerations of the same order as those already used in the interpretation of the disappearance of the jaguar's human wife (p. 83). The child, who is both a product and a symbol of the marriage relation, loses his semantic function when the relation is dissolved through the transformation of the wife-takers into pigs. The myths emphasize this function, which consists in acting as an intermediary between the brothers-in-law.

No doubt in practice every giver is also a taker. But in this respect the Mundurucu myths (M_4 and M_{16}) are very careful to spare Karusakaibö, the culture hero, the disadvantages of an ambiguous situation. Karusakaibö, having "neither a father nor a mother" and being sole possessor of a child (Tocantins, p. 86), is, as it were, outside the system from the start. The same thing happens in another version (M_{109c}), in which he is a bastard who has been abandoned by his mother and suckled by an animal (Kruse 3, Vol. XLVI, p. 920; cf. p. 181 n. 21). He is sometimes said to be the father of two children not born of women. Or he is married to Sikrida (Shikirida), who was called Aybaman, before she changed temporarily into a fish. This Sikrida is sometimes the mother of the demiurge's elder son, Korumtau (Korumtawbe, Carutau, or Caru-Taru, in different versions); but if so, she conceived him at a distance and was fertilized only by Karusakaibö's speech, since, according to this version, the demiurge "never had sexual relations with a woman" (Kruse 3, Vol. XLVI, p. 920). Sometimes Sikrida appears only after the synthetic birth of the demiurge's second son, and the demiurge marries her solely to have someone to look after the child. When she is a real mother, Sikrida seduces her own son (Strömer, pp. 133–6). When the second son is entrusted to her care, she seduces him, too (Kruse 3, Vol. XLVII, p. 993), or cannot prevent his being seduced by the village women (Tocantins, pp. 87–8).

It can be seen, then, that the spouse theoretically obtained from the "wife-givers" behaves as a taker and, in two extreme ways, as a seductress, and an incestuous one into the bargain. Moreover, after losing his elder son, who is killed by the wild pigs, the demiurge provides himself with another, carved out of a tree trunk—i.e., without putting himself into the position of a wife-taker, since by now he has already changed the givers into game.

The Cashinawa myth (M_{19}) presents us with a striking inversion of this pattern: a girl refuses to be given in marriage and thus causes her fathers and brothers to be changed into wild pigs. She, too, solves the problem by discovering a fatherless and brotherless son in a box (the feminine counterpart of the tree trunk carved by the Mundurucu demiurge) and taking him as her husband (Abreu, pp. 187–96).

In the second place, the Cariri myth is found among the Bororo in a practically unmodified form: it is the myth about the origin of the stars (M_{34}), which will be discussed later (p. 116). Let me simply mention for the time being that in this myth the children are sent up into the sky because they have been greedy (in the Cariri version, because their parents behave greedily). Their mothers try in vain to follow them and, falling back onto the ground, are changed into animals (Cariri version: their parents, who have followed them up into the sky, try to come down again and, through falling, acquire an articulated skeleton and thus become real human beings).

The relations among M_{25}, M_{15}, M_{16}, and M_{18} (origin of wild pigs) can thus be established, thanks to tobacco and providing the following transformations are accepted: horizontal axis → vertical axis; affinity → descent. And the relation between M_{25} and M_{34} (which is concerned with the origin not only of the stars but also of wild animals) can be established in respect of the (vertical) axis and of kinship (through descent), given the acceptance of the transformations: women→men and regression to the animal state → achievement of the human state.

This being so, it is interesting to inquire into the Bororo conception of the origin of tobacco. It is dealt with in two myths. Here is the first:

M_{26}. Bororo. *"The origin of tobacco"* (*1*)

The men were returning from the hunt, and, as is customary, they whistled to their wives to come to meet them and help them to transport the game.

It so happened that a woman called Aturuaroddo picked up a piece of a boa that her husband had killed; the blood coming from the snake's flesh penetrated into her and fertilized her.

While still in the womb, the "son of the blood" conversed with his mother and suggested that he should help her to gather wild fruit. He emerged in the form of a snake, climbed a tree, picked the fruit, and threw it down for his mother to collect. She tried to run away from him, but he caught up with her and returned to the shelter of the womb.

The woman was horrified and confided in her elder brothers who organized an ambush. As soon as the snake emerged and climbed the tree, the mother ran away; when he came down to go after her, the brothers killed him.

The body was burned on a woodpile, and from the ashes sprouted the urucu bush, the resin tree, tobacco, maize, and cotton. (Colb. 3, pp. 197-9.)

This myth is strictly symmetrical with the Toba and the Tereno myths about the origin of tobacco (M_{23}, M_{24}):

M_{23} M_{24} { A husband ($\triangle$, affinal relationship)	has a wife jaguar	destructive through the mouth	of a husband who has climbed a tree
M_{26} { A mother ($\bigcirc$, blood relationship)	has a son snake	protective through the vagina	of a son who has climbed a tree

≡

M_{23} M_{24} { looking for animals (birds)	that the wife ought not to eat (but does);	disjunction through the agency of the husband
M_{26} { looking for vegetable food (fruit)	that the mother ought to eat (but does not);	disjunction through the agency of the mother

≡

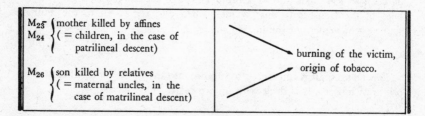

M_{23} M_{24} { mother killed by affines (= children, in the case of patrilineal descent)	
M_{26} { son killed by relatives (= maternal uncles, in the case of matrilineal descent)	burning of the victim, origin of tobacco.

The second Bororo myth about the origin of tobacco takes us back to the hero, Baitogogo (M_2), who, after settling into his aquatic abode, placed "tobacco of souls" in the belly of a fish:

M_{27}. Bororo. "The origin of tobacco" (2)

Fishermen had settled themselves at the water's edge to grill their fish. One of them, with his knife, slit open the belly of a huddogo (an unidentified fish; Portuguese *abotoado*, EB, Vol. I, p. 748) and discovered tobacco inside.

He hid the fish and smoked only at night, without telling his companions. The latter smelled the aroma and caught him at it. He then decided to share the tobacco with them. But the Indians swallowed the smoke instead of blowing it out. "That is not the way to smoke," said the supernatural spirit who appeared in the guise of a vampire. "First, puff, saying, 'Grandfather, receive the smoke and keep evil away from me!' Otherwise, you will be punished, because this tobacco belongs to me." The Indians did not obey; therefore, by the following morning they had become almost blind and had been changed into ariranhas.[7] This is why these animals have such small eyes. (Colb. 3, pp. 211–12.)

In this instance the relation of symmetry is with the Cariri myth about the origin of tobacco, since it presented tobacco as playing a mediating role between earth and heaven; here the mediation is between earth and water (because of the Bororo belief that souls have a dwelling place in water). According to the Cariri myth, through acquiring an articulated skeleton men became truly human, and they can ensure that they are not cast off completely from the sky by making offerings *accompanied by* tobacco. The Bororo myth explains that because men refused to make offerings *of* tobacco, they ceased to be truly human and were changed into animals doomed to live "on the surface of the water," and moreover blind: they were deprived of any "opening" onto the external world, because of their excessive "continence," which was expressed by the refusal to exhale tobacco smoke ("because they have not seen tobacco"; Colb. 2, p. 211).

Finally, to complete the demonstration of the unity of the set, we may note the recurrence of the theme of the clandestine smoker in M_{24} and M_{27}, as well as in an Ashluslay variant quoted by Métraux (5, p. 64), of the Toba myths about the origin of tobacco, which includes an owl, rather reminiscent of the vampire in M_{27}, since it acts as an adviser to humans. The surreptitious nature of the smoking reinforces—or, in the Ashluslay myth, replaces—excessive continence, since in South America the act of smoking is essentially social; while at the same time it establishes communication between mankind and the supernatural world.

---

[7] *Ippié, ipié,* in Bororo; in his translation of M_{21}, Colbacchini renders the term as *lontra* "otter," and he gives a curious definition of it in his glossary (p. 422): "ariranha": *um bichinho que fica a flor d'agua.*" Cf. Magalhães, p. 39, and EB, Vol. I, p. 643: *ipié* "ariranha." "Ariranha" is the usual name for the giant otter (*Pteroneura brasiliensis*), which may be more than six feet in length; but in central and southern Brazil the term refers to the common otter (Ihering, Vol. XXXVI, p. 379).

An older version (Colb. 2, pp. 210–11) lacks the episode of the vampire. In this version Baitogogo himself is annoyed on seeing his subjects put tobacco to a bad use, and he causes them to be changed into "ariranhas."

It should be made clear that the Bororo term *méa* refers not only to tobacco proper and neighboring species of the genus *Nicotiana*, but also to various kinds of aromatic leaves that are smoked in the same way. According to the sources I have used, M_{26} is concerned with *Nicotiana tabacum*, which is connected with the Bokodori clan, and M_{27} with an anonacea controlled by the Paiwe clan (Colb. 2, p. 212; 3, p. 213; EB, Vol. I, pp. 787, 959).

I am not forgetting that my attention was chiefly drawn to the myths about the origin of tobacco by the fact that some of them are also concerned with the origin of the jaguar, and because I was hoping that the myths about the origin of the jaguar would bring me back to the theme of the bird-nester. This is precisely what has happened: the husband of the jaguar-woman is a bird-nester (cf. M_{22}, M_{23}, and M_{24}), related to the heroes of the key myth (M_1) and of the Ge myths about the origin of fire (M_7 to M_{12}).

In all these myths the hero climbs to the top of a tree, or a rock, to get at a parrot's nest. In all of them his intention is to hand over the birds to a partner below: this is either a brother-in-law who is *first* a human brother-in-law, *then* an animal one, or a wife who is *first* human, *then* animal.

The human brother-in-law, who does not intend to eat the nestlings, is refused them by the hero of M_7 to M_{12}, who hands them over to the animal brother-in-law so that he can eat them.

On the other hand, the hero of M_{22} to M_{24} hands the nestlings over to his human wife; but when he sees that she is eating them (and is thus made aware of her animal nature), he refuses to continue, since he replaces the small birds by larger ones able to fly and therefore more difficult to catch (M_{23} and M_{24}). These larger birds represent, as it were, a degree beyond the nestlings, whereas the eggs thrown by the hero of M_7 and M_{12} represent a degree before.

In the Ge myths the hero, by giving the nestlings to the male jaguar, managed to get on good terms with him and so to draw closer to him; in the Toba, Mataco, and Tereno myths, they enable the hero to keep the female jaguar at a distance.

Lastly, fire has a part to play in each instance: it may be "constructive" fire, as in the Ge myths about the origin of fire as a means of cooking; or a destructive fire, as in the Chaco myths about the origin of the jaguar and tobacco, where it is a funeral pyre, from the ashes of which springs tobacco, a plant that, before being consumed, is exposed to the sun instead of being cooked on a hearth—and is therefore treated in an anticulinary manner, just as men dealt with meat before they were acquainted with fire (M_7 to M_{12})—and that is burned as it is ingested, which is another anticulinary manner of dealing with a foodstuff.

Everything is therefore interrelated: tobacco smoke engenders wild pigs, which supply meat. In order that this meat may be roasted, a bird-nester has to obtain cooking fire from the jaguar; finally, to get rid of the jaguar, another bird-nester has to burn its corpse on a fire, thus causing the birth of tobacco. The relations among the three sets of myths can be represented by the following diagram, which both illustrates and justifies the title "rondo" that I have given to this section:

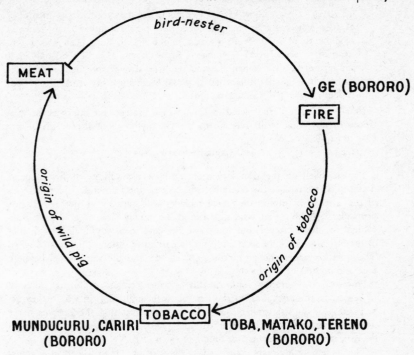

Figure 7. Myths about meat, fire, and tobacco.

NOTE. To obtain the Bororo transformations, the following rules may be applied:

1.   fire → water

since: *a*) the bird-nester of M_1 is a master of heavenly water, which extinguishes cooking fire; *b*) tobacco originates in earthly water, the dwelling place of fish (M_{27}).

Alternatively:

2.   fire → fire;

but in this case, according to M_{26}, we have:

2.1   jaguar (≡ fire) → snake (≡ water)

In case 1 the transformations will be:

1.1   exhaled tobacco → ingested tobacco (according to M_{27});
1.2   wild pigs → ariranhas (according to M_{27}).

Then:

1.2.1   meat → fish

by virtue of M_{21}, in which the ariranhas are presented as the mistresses of fish, whereas men are changed into pigs because of their greedy swallowing of spiky fruits (which ought not to have been spiky), instead of tobacco (in M_{27}); tobacco, according to M_{26}, is good only if it stings the throat: "When the tobacco was strong, the men said: 'It is strong! It is good!' But when it was not strong, they said: 'It is bad! It does not sting!'" Colb. 3, p. 199).

Finally the cycle is completed in M_{121} which presents the otters as the mistresses of fire—that is, in relation to the Ge myths about the origin of fire (M_7 to M_{12}):

1.2.2   jaguar $\rightarrow$ ariranhas

I must dwell on the transformation 1.2.1, whose validity at first appears doubtful. If we replace the otters by fish, because the former are the mistresses of the latter, this implies that meat replaces wild pigs by virtue of the same principle: it follows that wild pigs cannot be simply "meat," as I have been content to suggest so far, but must also be—and in a way analogous to that of the otters—masters of food and, in this particular instance, masters of meat. The question arises: how can the pigs, at one and the same time, be both food and masters of that food?

However, ethnography confirms this *a priori* demand of formal analysis. In respect to the ariranhas, in the first place through M_{21}, in which they act as masters of the fish, and secondly through the fact that the Bororos make use of a magic plant called "the ariranha plant"—*ipie uiorubo*—with which the nets are rubbed to ensure an abundant catch (EB, Vol. I, pp. 643-4).

The corresponding plant controlled by the wild pig (jugo, *Dicotyles labiatus*; *Dicotyles torquatus* is called *jui*) in Bororo is called *jugo-doge eimejera uiorubo,* "the plant which guides or directs a herd of wild pigs." It is the acuri palm (*Attalea speciosa*), the fruit of which is much appreciated by wild pigs: the Indian chiefs scatter its leaves in their villages "so that their people may obey them as the wild pigs obey their chief" (EB, Vol. I, p. 692). Whereas the otter is heteronomous, master of a species other than its own, the pig is autonomous, since it commands its own species. It is therefore understandable that the natives should conceive of it as being both meat and master of meat.

In support of the contrasting couple, ariranha/wild pig, it may also be noted that in M_{21} the men are changed into pigs because they have swallowed the fruit pulp and thorns together; whereas the ariranhas are reputed to eat only the flesh of large fish, leaving aside the heads and the bones (Ihering, Vol. XXXII, p. 373). A Guianian myth explains at length why the otter consumes the crab's body but leaves its claws (K.G. 1, pp. 101-2).

c. CHILDISH CIVILITY

I have established the existence of a symmetrical relation between the brothers-in-law among the Ge set. It shows itself in still another way.

A man asks his wife's young brother to climb up to a nest to catch birds for him. Instead of fulfilling the request, the boy gives his brother-in-law *the shadow for the substance.* According to the various versions, either he dare not take hold of his prey; or he throws down eggs instead of birds, and they break on reaching the ground; or again, instead of eggs, he throws stones which hurt his brother-in-law.

When his second "brother-in-law", the jaguar, appears, the hero's behavior toward him shows a double inversion. First, he does not allow the jaguar to waste time on his shadow on the ground; instead of making fun of the beast's ridiculous efforts, he declares himself. And when the jaguar asks him what is in the nest, he replies truthfully, and on two occasions (since there are two birds) he hands over the prey.

I propose to prove that it is because the hero refrains from mocking or deceiving the jaguar—and, more precisely because he refrains from laughing —that the jaguar does not eat him but *instructs* him in the arts of civilization.

As several American myths testify, there is no more laughable situation, none more likely to cover the central figure with ridicule, than that of someone who sacrifices the substance to the shadow or struggles to grasp the shadow of his prey rather than the prey itself. This is illustrated in the following myth which belongs to the Warao of Guiana and is sufficiently explicit to suffice as evidence, especially since the other elements of this myth will be linked later with those that I am giving now:

M_{28}. Warao. "The origin of the stars"

Once upon a time there were two brothers, the elder of whom was a celebrated hunter. Each day he went a little farther afield in search of game, with the result that finally he came to a creek he had never seen before. He climbed into a tree standing at its edge so as to watch for the animals that came to drink. Suddenly he saw a woman wading through the water toward him, and he thought her behavior very curious. Each time she put her hand into the creek she brought out two fish, and each time she ate one of them and put the other into her basket. She was a very big woman, a supernatural being. On her head she was wearing a calabash, which she occasionally took off and threw into the water in such a way as to make it spin like a top. When she did this, she would stop to watch it, and afterward she would walk on again.

The hunter spent the night up the tree and returned to the village the next day. He told the story to his young brother, who begged to go with him in order to see "such a woman who can catch so many fish and can eat them as well." "No," was the reply, "because you are always laughing at everything, and you might laugh at her." But the young man promised to keep a straight face, and the elder brother allowed himself to be persuaded.

When they reached the stream, the elder brother climbed into his tree, which stood a little way back from the edge; the younger one insisted on taking up his position in a better-placed tree, so as to miss nothing, and he sat on a branch overhanging the water. The woman soon arrived and began behaving as before.

When she reached the spot directly beneath the young brother, she noticed the reflection of his shadow in the water. She tried to catch hold of it, and when she failed, kept on trying: "She put her hand in quickly, first to this side and then that, but of course she did not succeed, and what with all her queer gesticulations and funny capers made so ridiculous an appearance that the brother up above could not resist laughing at her vain attempts to seize the substance for the shadow. He laughed and laughed and could not stop laughing."

Thereupon the woman looked up and spied the two brothers. Furious at having been laughed at, she launched an attack with poisonous ants (*Eciton* species); they bit and stung the boy so badly that, to escape from them, he had to throw himself into the water, where the woman caught him and ate him.

Afterward she captured the other brother and put him in her well-secured basket. On returning to her hut, she put the basket down and forbade her two daughters to touch it.

But as soon as her back was turned, her daughters lost no time in opening it. They were delighted with the hero's physical appearance and his talents as a hunter. Both of them, indeed, fell in love with him, and the younger one hid him in her hammock.

When the time came for the ogress to kill and eat her prisoner, the daughters confessed their misdeeds. Their mother agreed to spare her unexpected son-in-law, on condition that he go fishing on her behalf. But however big the catch he brought back, the ogress would devour it all, apart from two fish. Eventually the hero was so worn out that he fell ill.

The younger daughter, who was by now his wife, agreed to run away with him. One day he told his mother-in-law that he had left his catch in his canoe, and that she should go and fetch it (a fisherman was not supposed to carry the fish himself, since this would spoil his luck). However, he had arranged for a shark, or an alligator, to be under the canoe, and the ogress was devoured.

The elder daughter discovered the murder, sharpened her knife, and pursued the culprit. When she was about to catch up with him, he ordered his wife to climb a tree, and followed after her. But he was not quick enough to prevent his sister-in-law cutting off one of his legs. The detached member sprang to life and became the mother of birds (*Tinamus* species). You can still see, in the night sky, the hero's wife (the Pleiades); lower down, the hero himself (the Hyades) and, lower still, his severed leg—Orion's belt. (Roth I, pp. 263–5; there is a remote variant, cf. Verissimo in: Coutinho de Oliveira, pp. 51–3.)

This myth has many remarkable features worthy of study.

First, it is closely linked with other myths already mentioned: for instance, with the Bororo one about the origin of diseases (M_5) in which the heroine, who is also a glutton for fish and an ogress in her way, is dismembered in a manner comparable to the dismembering of this hero, who is responsible for the death of the ogress. There are three common elements—the ogress, the fish, and the dismembering—but they are differently distributed. The Warao ogress is also connected with the ogre in the Apinaye (M_9) and the

Mbya-Guarani (M_{13}) myths, who captures a hero up a tree (Mbya version) and puts him into his basket with the intention of eating him in the company of his two daughters. Other myths, too, on the theme of the relations of affinity between jaguars and humans refer to a hidden prisoner, with whom the "ogre's" daughters fall in love.

From the formal point of view, the Warao myth illustrates a feature of mythic thought to which I shall often have occasion to draw attention in putting forward my interpretations. It will be remembered that the procedure attributed to the ogress at the beginning of the myth consisted in simultaneously catching two fish, one of which she ate and one of which she kept. It would appear that the only purpose of this remarkable behavior is to prefigure the behavior that the ogress later adopts toward her two human victims, when she devours one and throws the other into her basket. It follows that the first episode is not self-sufficient. It is introduced as a mold to shape the substance of the succeeding episode which might otherwise have remained too fluid. The different treatment meted out to the discreet brother and the impertinent one is dictated by the myth, not by the ogress; either brother would be equally suitable for satisfying an ogre's appetite, unless—as is precisely the case—the behavior of the ogress is nervously obsessive and its peculiarities have been invented by the myth with the express purpose of bestowing a meaning on it retrospectively. This example brings out clearly that every myth is an organized totality; the development of the narrative throws light on an underlying structure which is independent of the relation between what comes before and what comes after.

Finally—and this is the most important point—the initial situation described in the myth is identical with that of the bird-nester: the hero finds himself cornered in an elevated position, up a tree or on top of a rock, and he is discovered by a real or presumed "ogre" through being given away by his shadow below. Once this is granted, the differences can be formulated as follows: in one instance the hero's elevated position is voluntary; he makes fun of the ogre when the latter attacks his shadow; lastly, he is eaten by the ogre or, if he has not made fun of it, must provide it with fish, an aquatic food. In the other instance his elevated position is involuntary; he is careful not to poke fun; and the ogre supplies him with game, a land food, after he has supplied the ogre with birds—that is, food from the air.

The Warao myth, therefore, presents us with a feminine character, who is a glutton and is in an "aquatic" position (at the beginning of the myth she is wading through water and eating fish; at the end she ventures too far into the water and is eaten by a fish); and, on the other hand, with a masculine character, who is temperate by nature (at the beginning of the myth he refrains from laughter, and at the end he supplies the ogress with food, of which he himself eats little or none) and is in a "heavenly" position (sitting on a branch of a high tree at the beginning of the myth; changed into a constellation at the end).

This threefold contrast between male and female, high and low, moderate and immoderate is also the basic framework of another set of myths which must be introduced now, before we proceed further. They deal with the origin of women.

M₂₉. Sherente. "The origin of women"

In the beginning there were no women, and men practiced homosexuality. One of them became pregnant but was unable to give birth, and died.

Once several men, reaching a spring, saw in it the reflection of a woman who was sitting high up in the branches of a tree. For two days they tried to catch the reflection. At last one of them looked up and spied the woman; they brought her down, but since each wanted to have her, they cut her into little pieces which were shared out. Each man wrapped his piece in a leaf and put the bundle in the grass wall of his hut (which is where things to be kept are normally put). Then all went hunting.

On their way back they sent ahead a messenger who discovered that the pieces had all changed into women. The puma (*Fleis concolor*), who had been given a piece from the chest, found himself with a very pretty wife; the semema (*Cariama cristata, Microdactylus cristatus*), who had twisted his slice too tight, found himself with a very lean woman. But each man now had a wife; and when they went hunting, they took their wives along. (Nim. 7, p. 186.)

This myth belongs to one of the Ge tribes, which provided the set of myths about the origin of fire. But all sorts of variants are to be found in the Gran Chaco; the Chamacoco version is surprisingly close to the Sherente narrative, in spite of the distance separating the two tribes:

M₃₀. Chamacoco. "The origin of women"

Once when a young Chamacoco boy was ill and lying in his hammock, he caught a glimpse of his mother's vagina as she climbed over the roof of the hut to repair it. Inflamed with desire, he waited until she came down again, and then made love to her. Then he was indiscreet enough to reveal to her the secret of the masks, which women are not supposed to know about, and she told it to the other women.

When the men realized what had happened, they killed all the women but one, who changed into a deer and managed to escape. But though they performed all the women's work, they were sad and depressed because they lacked women.

One day a man walked under the tree in which the surviving woman happened to be. She spat to attract his attention. The man tried to climb the tree but was hampered in the ascent by the fact that he had an erection; he gave up but not before he had spilled sperm all over the trunk. The other men came on the scene and managed to reach the woman from the neighboring trees. They raped her and then cut her into pieces which became soaked with sperm as they fell to the ground. Each man picked up a piece and took it home. Then they all went fishing.

Two shamans, who were sent ahead as scouts, both claimed that vultures had devoured the pieces of female flesh. The Indians then came back to the village which they found inhabited by women and children. Each man found himself with a wife corresponding to his piece of flesh. The pieces of thigh provided fat women; the fingers, lean ones. (Métraux 4, pp. 113–19.)

Here now are two other versions from the Gran Chaco:

M_{31}. Toba-Pilaga. "The origin of women"

Formerly men used to hunt and store their supply of game on the thatched roofs of their huts. One day, in their absence, a group of women came down from the sky and stole all the meat. The same thing happened the next day, and the men, who did not know that women existed, set Rabbit to watch.

But Rabbit slept all the time, and the grilled meat was stolen. The next day Parrot stood guard, hidden in a quebracho tree, and he saw the women, who had toothed vaginas. After remaining quiet and motionless at first, Parrot threw a fruit down from the tree onto the women who were feasting below. The women began by accusing each other; then they discovered Parrot and began to fight about whose husband he should be. They threw things at each other, and one of the sticks went astray and broke the bone under the parrot's tongue. Being now struck dumb and compelled to express himself through gestures, he could not make the men understand what had happened.

It was now Hawk's turn to mount guard, and he took care to arm himself with two throwing sticks. The first missed its target and enabled the women to discover him; but although they fought with each other about who should have him as husband and then tried in vain to kill him by throwing things at him, with his second stick Hawk succeeded in cutting one of the two ropes used by the women to travel up and down from the sky (one rope was for pretty women with fair complexions, the other for old, ugly ones). Several women fell down and sank into the earth, but not before Hawk had captured two for his own use.

He then called to his companions. Only Iguana could hear him, but since Iguana had very small ears, the other men refused to admit that his hearing could be keener than theirs. Eventually Hawk managed to make himself audible to them. . . .

Armadillo extracted the women from the earth and distributed them among his companions. (Métraux 5, pp. 100–3.)

In the last part, which I have considerably shortened, the myth explains how the men got the better of the toothed vaginas, and how several animal species acquired their distinctive characteristics. It is important to remember that in mythical terms there was no distinction between men and animals. At the same time the myths of this group are intended to explain not only the origin of women, but also the diversity of types: why they are young or old, fat or thin, pretty or ugly, and even why some of them have only one eye. This assertion of isomorphism between the (external) diversity of the animal species and the (internal) diversity of the feminine section of a particular species is not without savor and significance.

Lastly it should be noted that the preceding myth refers twice to the dangers threatening human life, in the form of poisonous snakes and infant mortality. The latter arises from the fact that Dove was the first to be pregnant, because of her husband's amorous propensities; and it so happens that pigeons have delicate health. We shall meet this kind of problem again when we come to discuss the question of human mortality in connection with the Apinaye myth about the origin of fire (M₉; cf. below, pp. 148–9).

M₃₂. Mataco. "The origin of women"

Once upon a time, men were animals who could speak. They had no women, and they lived on fish which they caught in great quantities.

One day they noticed that their supplies of food had been stolen, so they left a parrot on guard. The bird, from its perch at the top of a tree, saw women coming down from the sky by the means of a rope. They ate as much as they could and went to sleep in the shade of the tree.

Instead of giving the alarm as he had been instructed to do, the parrot began to throw pieces of wood at the women, who woke up and discovered him. They bombarded him with seeds, one of which hit the bird's tongue, which has been black ever since.

The iguana heard the sound of the fight and informed his companions; but believing him to be deaf, they refused to pay any attention. The parrot meanwhile had been struck dumb.

The next day the lizard mounted guard, but the women captured him and tore out his tongue, so that he, too, was struck dumb. The men, after a discussion, entrusted the village to the care of the hawk, which could not be seen by the women because the color of its plumage was indistinguishable from that of the trunk of the tree in which it was perched. The hawk gave the alarm; although the women threw things at him, he nevertheless managed to cut the rope. Henceforth the men were provided with women. (Métraux 3, p. 51.)

The end of the Mataco myth, like that of the Toba myth, explains why some women lost an eye as a result of a wrong movement by the armadillo when he was digging at the soil to extract the women who had sunk into it on falling from the sky, and how the men removed the women's toothed vaginas. Métraux (5, pp. 103–7) gives a brief study of the distribution of this myth, which is found from the Argentine to Guiana. To the north of the Sherente, whose version I have summarized, it occurs among the Cariri and the Arawak in Guiana (Martin de Nantes, p. 232; Farabee 1, p. 146).

The Cariri version does not contain the "heavenly" woman element, but it is similar to the Sherente version in that it presents women as having sprung from the pieces of a sacrificed victim. The Taruma version given by Farabee is inverted in comparison with the preceding ones, since the women are in a low position, being fished for by the men (and so have their origin in water instead of in the sky); on the other hand, it shares with the Argentine versions the theme of the unreliable or negligent guardians.

The Caduveo, who were once the southern neighbors of the Bororo, tell the story (M_{33}) of how the demiurge drew primitive humanity from the bottom of a lake, from which men used to emerge surreptitiously to steal his fish, until a bird, which had been instructed to act as sentinel, gave the alarm, after several of the men had fallen asleep (Ribeiro I, p. 144-5). This aberrant version looks like evidence of a mythological "fault" running between the tribes of the Gran Chaco and the Bororo, with whom the myth is found again intact with all its structural features, although the content is different and the position of the women is inverted (cf. above, pp. 112-13).

M_{34}. Bororo. *"The origin of the stars"*

The women had gone to gather maize, but they did not succeed in finding very much, so they took a little boy with them who found a great many corncobs. They pounded the maize there and then to make different sorts of cakes for the men when they returned from hunting. The little boy stole enormous quantities of the corn which he hid in bamboo tubes and brought to his grandmother, with the request that she would make a corncake for himself and his friends.

The grandmother did as she was asked, and the children had a feast, after which, to keep the theft secret, they cut out the tongues of the old woman and of a tame macaw and set free all the macaws that were being raised in the village.

Fearing their parents' anger, they fled into the sky by climbing up a knotty creeper that the hummingbird had agreed to fasten in position.

Meanwhile the women came back to the village and looked for the children. They questioned the tongueless old woman and macaw to no purpose. One of them caught sight of the creeper with the children climbing up it. When pressed to come down, the children turned a deaf ear and even climbed still faster. The distraught mothers went up after them, but the thief, who was the last child, cut the creeper as soon as he reached the sky; the women fell and crashed onto the ground, where they were changed into animals and wild beasts. As a punishment for their heartlessness, the children, now transformed into stars, look down every night on the sad plight of their mothers. It is the children's eyes that can be seen shining. (Colb. 3, pp. 218-19.)

We started, with the Warao myth, from the theme of the origin of the stars, and we have now returned to it. At the same time, and as in the myths of the Gran Chaco, the person on guard in the village—in this case, the grandmother—is made dumb (like the macaw which, among the Bororo, is a domestic creature). This dumbness is correlated with the deafness, either of intermediary animals (guardians of the village or scouts) or of polar opposites, who are also in an intermediary situation (the children halfway between earth and sky, who turn a deaf ear). In both cases there is disjunction of male and female individuals; but in one case the individuals concerned are potential husbands and women who have not yet given birth,

	High/Low	△	High/Low	○	△/○	Age	Conjunc./ Disjunc.	Food	Sentinel/Scout	Provocation (1) Reserved behavior (2)	Salutary or faulty reserve	Human/ non-human
M_{28}	H	sky	L	water	relatives by marriage	○ > △	C→D	animal, aquatic	sentinel	1. laughter 2. silence	+	H→NH
M_{29}	L	earth	H	sky	husband/ wife	△ = ○	D→C	animal, land	scout	silence	–	H→H
M_{30}	L	earth (water?)	H	sky	husband/ wife	△ = ○	C→D D→C	animal, aquatic	scout	1. provocation 2. lie; blindness	–	(H→NH) H→H
M_{31}	L	earth	H	sky	husband/ wife	△ = ○	D→C	animal, land	sentinel	1. provocation 2. silence: sleep; dumbness; deafness		NH→H
M_{32}	L	earth (water?)	H	sky	husband/ wife	△ = ○	D→C	animal, aquatic	sentinel	1. provocation 2. silence: dumbness; deafness	–	NH→H
M_{34}	H	sky	L	earth	parents	○ > △	C→D	vegetable, land	sentinel	2. silence: dumbness; deafness	–	H→NH H→NH

whereas in the other they are mothers and sons (the fathers are mentioned, but only incidentally, in the myth of the matrilineal Bororo). In the Gran Chaco the disjunction represents the initial situation and it resolves into a conjunction at the end. Among the Bororo the conjunction represents the initial situation, and it is finally resolved into a disjunction—of an extreme nature, since there are stars on one side and animals on the other. In all instances one of the polar opposites is gluttony (the women from the sky in the Gran Chaco myths, the star children in the Bororo myth), and the other is temperance (the men are deliberately moderate consumers of meat or fish; the women are involuntarily sparing with the maize). A table of transformations is shown on the facing page.

It would be interesting to study this set for its own sake, or to use it as the starting point for a more general study, which would bring us back to certain other myths, already approached from a different angle. We have seen that the Bororo myth about the origin of the stars (M_{34}) is closely related in structure to the Cariri myth about the origin of wild pigs (M_{25}) which, given the perspective in which it was then being considered, seemed to occupy a marginal position. There is also a directly symmetrical relation between M_{34} and M_{28}, because of their characteristic contrast between the "peopling" of the sky (by the constellations) and of the earth by animal species. On the other hand, the Toba and the Mataco myths (M_{31}, M_{32}) refer back to the Mundurucu myth about the origin of wild pigs (M_{16}), through the element of the clumsy armadillo, which also occurs in the Kayapo myth on the same theme (M_{18}) in the person of O'oimbre; and lastly to the Bororo myths discussed in Part One (M_2, M_5), in which armadillos play a part that balances the one they have in the Gran Chaco and Mundurucu myths, acting as gravediggers for women instead of extracting them from the earth.

These transformations have a counterpart in others, whose basic framework consists of a conjunction/disjunction system operating on two levels: one of propinquity (men and women); the other of remoteness (high and low):

Warao (M_{28})	Sherente-Chamacoco (M_{29}-M_{30})	Toba-Mataco (M_{30}-M_{31})	Bororo (M_{34})
Sky (stars) ↗		Sky ↗	Sky (stars) ↗
	O ↘ / Δ ↗	O ↘ / Δ ↗	Δ ↗ / O ↘
Water . . . ↘		Earth ↘	Earth . . . ↘

This table raises two problem: (1) Is there a conjunction in the Warao myth and a disjunction in the Sherente myth; and if so, what are they? (2) Although the Bororo myth appears to be doubly disjunctive, is it conjunctive on another level?

I shall venture to argue that, in spite of appearances, there is conjunction in the Warao and Bororo myths and disjunction in the Sherente myth.

The conjunction is not immediately perceptible in the Warao myth because it is interiorized, so to speak, within the heavenly pole, in which husband and wife are brought together by the natural contiguity of the constellations mentioned—the Pleiades, the Hyades, and Orion.

Disjunction seems to be completely absent from the Sherente myth, in which the relation between sky and earth is not directly referred to. But the disjunction between these two poles, which is engineered in other myths, is replaced here by the avoidance of a disjunction, along an axis that, instead of being vertical, is horizontal; in other words, there would be disjunction if the husbands were separated from their wives, but the text of the myth states explicitly that they were careful to take their wives with them when they went hunting.

This last interpretation may appear farfetched, yet it is made plausible by the mere fact that the pattern only has to be inverted to reveal the conjunction missing in the Bororo myth: it is an implicit conjunction but balances the disjunction explicitly rejected by the Sherente myth. It consists, in this case, in the transformation of the women into game (instead of hunting companions); they thus remain in a comparable relation of solidarity with the hunters, their husbands; but the relation is one of antagonism instead of collaboration. We have already met other examples of this transformation, which seems typical of Bororo mythology.

I do not propose to take the analysis of these myths any further, because I have been using them to fulfill an accessory function in the demonstration. Myth transformations are multidimensional, and the various dimensions cannot all be explored simultaneously. Whatever angle of vision one adopts, some transformations are thrust into the background or become lost in the distance. They become confused and blurred or are glimpsed only intermittently. In spite of their fascination, if one does not wish to lose one's bearings, one has to stick to the methodological rule of pursuing the line of study that was first decided upon, without deviating from it for any length of time.

I introduced this set of myths about the origin of women with a deliberate purpose: to obtain a series of transformations that would make it possible to elucidate the behavior of a hero, who has already been defined in respect to his relation to the high and the low, when faced by the same danger coming from the opposite pole to the one where he is stationed.

The hero therefore finds himself in the position of being a potential prey, and the lines of conduct open to him can be classified as follows:

1. The hero allows himself to be discovered, passively or actively; in the latter case he makes a sign to his antagonist. This is what the bird-nester does.

2. The hero refuses to cooperate and carefully refrains from making any sign: such was the behavior of the first woman in the Sherente myth. The behavior of her Chamacoco counterpart, whose spitting was meant as a form of mockery rather than as an invitation, is different; but the contrast is only apparent, since this woman, too, refuses to cooperate with the men who are trying in vain to reach her; she does not even allow herself to be influenced by their physiological state.

3. The hero acts in a provocative manner, perhaps deliberately, perhaps not: he bursts out laughing, like the impudent brother in the Warao myth; he teases his antagonist by throwing down fruit or twigs, as the parrot does in the Toba and the Mataco myths; he arouses desire in the antagonist and refuses to satisfy it, as is the case with the Chamacoco woman.

Almost all the myths refer to at least two of these possible forms of behavior. If the birds in the Gran Chaco myths are discovered, this is no doubt because of their indiscreet behavior which arouses the women who are asleep or drowsy after eating. Once aroused, the women invite the parrot to play with them, or they attack it and cut its tongue out. On the other hand, those birds that know how to keep watch properly are careful not to start a conversation: the vulture whistles, and the eagle knows when to keep quiet.

In contrast to these, the inefficient sentinels—the parrot and iguana—do not succeed in warning their companions, either because they are deaf (they are not believed, because how could they have heard anything?), or because they are dumb (and therefore incapable of making themselves understood). Or again, as in the case of the shamans sent ahead as scouts by the Chamacoco ancestors, because they are deceitful or untrustworthy as witnesses.

According to a little Bororo story (M_{35}), the parrot that cries "Kra, kra, kra" is a human child who was changed into a bird for having swallowed whole fruit that had been roasted in ash and was still scorching hot (Colb. 3, p. 214). In this case, too, speechlessness is a result of intemperance.

What, then, is the sanction entailed by the hero's behavior in all these myths? As a matter of fact, there are two. On the one hand, men obtain women, with whom they had not previously been provided. On the other, communication between sky and earth is broken off, because of the action of the creature that refrains from communication, or—to put it more accurately—that refrains from those abusive forms of communication, mockery or teasing; or again—as is shown by the Sherente and Chamacoco heroines who are cut to pieces—from those forms that consist, unlike the behavior of the bird-nester, in taking the shadow for the substance.

The basic framework can thus be reduced to a double contrast, on the one hand between communication and noncommunication and, on the other, between the moderate or immoderate character attributed to the one or the other:

	M_{28} (Warao, origin of the stars)	M_{30}–M_{32} (Chaco, origin of women)	M_{34} Bororo, origin of the stars)
Communication (+) Noncommuniciation (−)	+	+ −	−
Moderate (+) Immoderate (−)	−	−	−

We are now in a position to define the behavior of the bird-nester. It lies halfway between two forms of conduct that are disastrous through their (positive or negative) immoderate character: provoking or mocking at the ogre who takes the shadow for the substance; refusing to communicate with him by being deaf or blind—that is, insensitive.

What significance does mythic thought attach to these two contrasting forms of behavior?

d. SUPPRESSED LAUGHTER

The Warao myth (M_{28}) suggests that the adventures of the bird-nester (M_7–M_{12}) might have taken a different turn. He, too, is a child; what would have happened if, like his Warao counterpart who was faced by the ogress, he had laughed uncontrollably at the sight of the jaguar trying in vain to catch his shadow?

A whole series of myths, connected with laughter and its fatal consequences, confirm that this was a plausible development and allow us to glimpse what might have been the results.

M_{36}. Toba-Pilaga. "The origin of animals"

The demiurge Nedamik subjected the first humans to an ordeal by tickling. Those who laughed were changed into land or water animals: the former were preyed upon by the jaguar; the latter were able to escape from him by taking refuge in the water. Those humans who maintained self-control became jaguars or men who hunted jaguars and got the better of them. (Métraux 5, pp. 78–84.)

M_{37}. Mundurucu. "The jaguar's son-in-law"

A deer married the daughter of a jaguar, without realizing who she was, because at that time all animals were in human form. One day he decided to pay a call on his parents-in-law. His wife warned him that they were vicious and would want to tickle him. If the deer could not refrain from laughter, he would be devoured.

The deer withstood the ordeal successfully, but he realized that his parents-in-law were jaguars when they brought back a deer they had killed while out hunting, and sat down to eat it.

The next day the deer announced that he would go hunting, and he brought back a dead jaguar. It was now the jaguars' turn to be frightened:

From then on the deer and the jaguars kept a mutual watch on each other. "How do you sleep?" the jaguar asked his son-in-law. "With my eyes open," was the reply, "and when I am awake I keep my eyes closed. What about you?" "I do just the opposite." Consequently the jaguars dared not run away while the deer was asleep, but as soon as he woke up, they thought he was asleep and took flight, while the deer ran off in the opposite direction. (Murphy 1, p. 120.)

M₃₈. Munduruçu. "The monkey's son-in-law"

A man married a howler monkey-woman (*Alouatta* species) of human form. When she was pregnant, they decided to visit her parents. But the woman warned her husband about their viciousness: on no account must he laugh at them.

The monkeys invited the man to a meal of cupiuba leaves (*Goupia glabra*), which have an intoxicating effect. When the father monkey was completely drunk, he began to sing, and his monkeylike expressions made the man laugh. This enraged the monkey who waited until his son-in-law was drunk and then abandoned him in a hammock at the top of a tree.

When the man woke up, he found he was alone and unable to climb down. The bees and the wasps came to his aid and advised him to take revenge. The man took his bow and arrows, pursued the monkeys, and killed them all, apart from his pregnant wife. Later the wife had an incestuous relation with her son, from which sprang the howler monkeys. (Murphy 1, p. 118.)

M₃₉. Guiana Arawak. "Forbidden laughter"

Various myth episodes tell about visits to monkeys who must not be laughed at on pain of death, and about the danger connected with laughing at supernatural spirits or imitating their voices. (Roth 1, pp. 146, 194, 222.)

I shall come back later to the jaguar→monkey transformation. For the moment the question is the importance of laughter and its significance. Several myths provide an answer:

M₄₀. Kayapo-Gorotire. "The origin of laughter"

A man stayed behind to tend his garden while his companions went hunting. Feeling thirsty, he went to a spring that he knew of in the forest near by, and as he was about to drink, he noticed a strange murmuring sound coming from above. He looked up and saw an unknown creature hanging from a branch by its feet. It was a Kuben-niepre, a creature with a human body and the wings and feet of a bat.

The creature came down from the tree. It was ignorant of human language and began to caress the man to show its friendliness toward him. But its enthusiastic tenderness was expressed by means of cold hands and pointed nails, the tickling effect of which caused the man to break into an initial burst of laughter.

After being led to the cave where the bats lived and which looked like a lofty stone house, the man noticed that there were no objects or utensils on the floor, which was covered with the droppings of the bats hanging from the vaulted ceiling. The walls were adorned with paintings and drawings which filled their whole area.

The man was welcomed with renewed caresses. He was tickled so much and he laughed so hard that he became quite exhausted, and eventually fainted. Much later he recovered consciousness, succeeded in escaping, and found his way back to his village.

The Indians were indignant when they heard of the treatment he had suffered. They organized a punitive expedition and tried to choke all the bats with smoke while they were asleep by burning a heap of dead leaves in the cave, after the entrance had been sealed off. But the bats escaped through a hole in the roof—all except a young one which was caught.

The villagers had great difficulty in rearing it. It learned to walk, but they had to make a perch for it to sleep on upside down. It was not long in dying.

The Indian warrior despises laughter and tickling, which are barely suitable even for women and children. (Banner 1, pp. 60–1.)

The same theme is to be found in the cosmology of the Bolivian Guarayu; along the road leading to the Great Forefather, the dead have to undergo various ordeals, which include tickling by a sharp-nailed marimondo monkey (*Ateles paniseus,* a type of spider monkey). If the victim laughs, he is devoured (M₄₁). For this reason perhaps, and like the Kayapo, Guarayu men despise laughter, which is looked upon as effeminate (Pierini, p. 709 and n. 1).

This parallel between the mythologies of eastern Brazil and Bolivia is confirmed by a myth (M₄₂) belonging to the Tacana, another Bolivian tribe. It tells of a woman who is married, although she is unaware of the fact, to a bat-man, afraid of light. He remains absent during daytime and pretends he is busy in his garden. In the evenings he announces his return by playing the flute. He is eventually killed by his wife, who is irritated by a bat laughing at her and does not recognize it as her husband (Hissink-Hahn, pp. 289–290).

The Apinaye have a myth similar to that of the Kayapo, although it does not contain the laughter theme (M₄₃). However, it has the same cave as the bats' dwelling place, with an opening in the roof; the conclusion, which relates the sad end of the young captured bat is also the same. In the Apinaye version the bats are the enemies of men, whom they attack, and whose skulls they break open with ceremonial axes shaped like anchors. They succeed in escaping from the smoke but leave behind ceremonial axes and large quantities of adornments, which fall into the men's hands (Nim. 5, pp. 179–80; C. E. de Oliveira, pp. 91–2).

According to another Apinaye myth (M₄₄), these axes had been taken away by the women, when they left the men after the men had killed the alligator, which the women had taken as their lover. One of these axes was seriously lacking in the men's village, and the two brothers obtained it from their sister (Nim. 5, pp. 177–9).

Let us concentrate on the bats for a moment. It is a striking fact that their role, in the two Ge myths where they occur, consists in "opening" the hero or heroes, either by making them "burst out" laughing or by splitting their skulls. Although they have undoubtedly sinister associations, the bats are in all instances the masters of manufactured goods, like the jaguar in the other Ge myths. These achievements take two forms: rock paintings[8] or ceremonial axes (cf. Ryden); in the Tacana myth they perhaps also take the form of musical instruments.

M₄₅. Tereno. *"The origin of language"*

After bringing men forth from the bowels of the earth, the demiurge Orekajuvakai wished to make them speak. He ordered them to stand in single file one behind the other, and sent for the little wolf to make them laugh. The wolf performed all sorts of monkey tricks (*sic*); he bit his tail, but all in vain. Whereupon Orekajuvakai sent for the little red toad, whose comic gait amused everybody. After the toad had passed in front of the row for the third time, all the men began to speak and laugh heartily. (Baldus 3, p. 219.)

M₄₆. Bororo. *"The jaguar's wife"* (*partial version; cf. below, p. 172, n. 14*)

In exchange for being allowed to escape with his life, an Indian had to agree to give his daughter to the jaguar. When she became pregnant and was almost ready to give birth, the jaguar warned her on no account to laugh, and then left to go hunting. Shortly afterward the young woman heard the unpleasant, ridiculous voice of a fat grub (the jaguar's mother, in some versions), which was trying to provoke her into merriment. The woman managed not to laugh, but in spite of herself she smiled. She was immediately

---

[8] The souls of the Gorotire go to the Stone House: "We had the opportunity of visiting this interesting spot which is situated in the savannahs of Rio Vermelho. After spending many long, painful hours climbing a high, loose-surfaced mountain, we sighted, beyond the tree tops, the pinnacles of a veritable forest temple, all white and shining in the midday sun. But, far from being a work of magic, the "Stone House" (*Ken kikre*) is a natural artifact, hollowed out of an enormous white rock. Four rows of columns support the roof, which is haunted by squealing swarms of bats, creatures who are always associated in native thought with the *men karon* [in connection with this term, see above, p. 74]. The walls of the maze of naves and transepts have a number of drawings on them which are supposed to be the work of the *men karon* but can be explained more simply as the patient effort of some primitive sculptor. Among them can be recognized representations of toads, rheas' feet, or quasi-heraldic patterns divided by a crosslike motif" (Banner 2, pp. 41–2).

seized with terrible pains and died. The jaguar returned in time to carry out a Caesarian operation with his claws. He thus brought forth twins, who later became the culture heroes, Bakororo and Itubore. (Colb. 3, p. 193.)

An analogous myth (M_{47}) belonging to the Kalapalo of the Upper Xingu replaces the laughter by a fart that is emitted by the mother-in-law, but for which she makes her daughter-in-law responsible (Baldus 4, p. 45). Thus we have the pattern:

	M_{46}	M_{47}
Imputed/Prohibited	−	+
High/Low	+	−
Internal/External	+	−

In a Guiana myth (M_{48}) a woman is carried up into the sky for being unable to prevent herself from laughing at the sight of little tortoises performing a dance (Van Coll, p. 486).

M_{49}. Mundurucu. "The snake's wife"

A woman had a snake as her lover. Pretending to be going to gather the fruit of the sorveira tree (*Couma utilis*), she went into the forest every day to see the snake, who lived in one of these trees. They would make love until the evening, and when the time came to part, the snake would shake down enough fruit to fill the woman's basket.

Becoming suspicious, her brother kept watch on the pregnant woman. Although he could not see her lover, he could hear her exclaiming in his embrace: "Don't make me laugh so much, Tupasherebo [the name of the snake]! You are making me laugh so hard, I am urinating!" In the end the brother saw the snake and killed it. . . .

Later the son that the woman bore the snake avenged his father. (Murphy 1, pp. 125–6.)

M_{50}. Toba-Pilaga. "The snake's wife"

There was a girl who had a continual flow of menstrual blood. "Does your period never finish?" she was asked. The girl would answer, "Only when my husband is here." But nobody knew who her husband was. Moreover the girl laughed incessantly.

It was eventually discovered that she spent all her time sitting in her hut just above a hole occupied by her husband, the python. A trap was laid for the latter, and he was killed. And when the girl gave birth to six little snakes, all spotted, they too were killed. The girl changed into an iguana. (Métraux 5, pp. 65–6.)

I should like to comment on this last myth. The flow of menstrual blood is interrupted, the heroine says, only when her husband is present—that is, when she is, as it were, stopped up. The "snake women" of South America have the notable characteristic of being normally open. The heroine of a Bororo myth that has already been summarized (M_{26}) is accidentally fertilized by the blood of a snake, which her husband had killed while out hunting. And the snake son that she conceives as a result converses with her and goes in and out of her womb at will (cf. above, p. 103). The same detail occurs in a Tenetehara myth (M₅₁): the son of the snake's mistress emerges from her womb every morning and returns there in the evening. The woman's brother advises her to go into hiding, and the child transforms himself into a ray of lightning (Wagley and Galvão, p. 149). In a Warao myth (M₅₂) the woman carries her lover about inside her body, and he emerges only intermittently to climb fruit trees and obtain provisions for her (Roth I, pp. 143-4).

It follows that the series of myths just considered allows us to establish a link between laughter and various forms of bodily opening. Laughter is an opening; it can cause opening; or the opening itself is presented as a combinative variant of laughter. It is therefore not surprising that tickling, the physical cause of laughter (M₃₆, M₃₇, M₄₀, M₄₁), may be replaced by other, similarly physical, causes of bodily opening:

M₅₃. Tucuna. *"The jaguar's son-in-law"*

A hunter lost his way and found himself at the jaguar's house. The jaguar's daughters invited him in after explaining that the monkey he had been pursuing was their pet. When the jaguar came home and smelled human flesh, his wife hid the hunter in the loft. The jaguar had brought back a caititu for dinner (cf. above, p. 82). After the terror-stricken man had been introduced to him and licked from head to foot, the jaguar took off his skin, assumed human form, and chatted familiarly with his guest while they waited for dinner.

Meanwhile the jaguar's wife secretly warned the hunter that the meat would be highly seasoned, and that when he came to eat it, he should show no sign of being put out by this. Although the food was very peppery, the man succeeded in hiding his discomfort, although not without difficulty. The jaguar was delighted, congratulated him, and set him on the road leading back to his village.

But the hunter went astray, returned to the jaguar's house, and the jaguar showed him another road; he again got lost and came back. The jaguar's daughters suggested marriage; the man accepted, and the jaguar gave his consent.

One day, a long time afterward, he went back to visit his family. His mother noticed that he had become wild and that his body was beginning to be covered with spots like the jaguar's hide. She painted him all over with powdered charcoal. He ran off into the forest where his human wives looked for him in vain. He was never seen again. (Nim. 13, pp. 151-2.)

This myth links up—along two different axes of symmetry—on the one hand, with the Opaye myth (M₁₄) about the jaguar's wife (the sexes are inverted) and, on the other, with the Mundurucu myth (M₃₇) which, like this one, deals with a stranger who becomes the jaguar's son-in-law. In the latter instance the sexes remain unchanged, but a double transformation can be observed: after being a deer (M_{37}), the hero becomes a man (M_{53}), and the ordeal he is put through is not tickling intended to make him laugh (M_{37}), but the eating of a peppery stew that could cause him to cry out with pain (M_{53}). Moreover, the deer is careful not to eat the jaguar's food (deer's meat: homologous with himself), whereas the man eats the jaguar's food, although it is heterologous (inedible, through being too highly seasoned). The result of this is that the man is definitively identified with the jaguar, whereas the deer is definitively distinguished from it.

It follows, from the isomorphism between the two myths, which is worthy of separate study, that laughter caused by tickling and groans provoked by peppery seasoning can be treated as combinative variants of bodily opening and, more precisely in this case, of oral opening.

Lastly, to conclude the subject of laughter, it should be noted that in South America (as in other areas of the world) certain myths establish a connection between laughter and the origin of cooking fire, and this supplies us with supplementary proof of the fact that, in dwelling on the theme of laughter, we are remaining within our stated subject:

M_{54}. *Tucuna. "The origin of fire and of cultivated plants" (partial version, cf. below p. 171)*

Once upon a time men had neither sweet manioc nor fire. An old woman was given the secret of the first by the ants; and her friend, the nocturnal swallow (a goatsucker, *Caprimulgus* species), would obtain fire for her (keeping it hidden in his beak), so that she could cook the manioc, instead of heating it by exposure to the sun or by putting it under her armpits.

The Indians found the old woman's manioc cakes excellent and asked how she prepared them. She replied that she simply baked them in the heat of the sun. The swallow, amused by this falsehood, burst out laughing, and the Indians saw flames coming from her mouth. They forced it open and took possession of the fire. Since then nocturnal swallows have had gaping beaks.[9] (Nim. 13, p. 131.)

A Bororo myth about the origin of fire can be introduced with advantage at this point, although the laughter theme is not explicitly mentioned in it; it will enable me to link the preceding remarks with the body of my argument.

M_{55}. *Bororo. "The origin of fire"*

Formerly the monkey was like a man; he had no hair on his body, sailed a canoe, ate maize, and slept in a hammock.

One day when the monkey was sailing back with the prea (*Cavia aperea*)

[9] In *lingua geral*, the *Caprimulgus (Mãe de lua)* is called *urutau, yurutahy*, etc., "big mouth." An Amazonian version compares this mouth to a vagina (Barbosa Rodrigues, pp. 151–2), which gives the key to the equivalence with certain Guiana myths about the origin of fire, which state that an old woman kept it in her vagina.

from their plantation, he was alarmed to see the animal hungrily gnawing at the maize that was piled loose in the bottom of the canoe: "Stop," he said, "or you'll make a hole in the side, we'll spring a leak, we shall be drowned, and you won't escape because the piranha fish will eat you."

But the prea went on gnawing, and the monkey's forecast came true. As he was a very good swimmer, he managed to slip his hand inside the gills of a piranha fish, and he reached the bank alone, waving his catch.

Shortly afterward he met the jaguar who marveled at the sight of the fish and managed to get himself invited to dinner. "But," he asked, "where is the fire?" The monkey pointed to the sun which was sinking toward the horizon and bathing the distant landscape in a ruddy glow. "Yonder," he said. "Can't you see it? Go and fetch it."

The jaguar went a long way, then came back to say he had not been successful. "But there it is," went on the monkey, "all flaming red! Run after it, and this time catch up with the fire so that we can cook our fish!" So off went the jaguar again.

Whereupon the monkey invented the method of producing fire by rubbing two sticks together, which men were to copy from him later. He kindled a good fire, grilled his fish, and ate it all up, leaving only the bones. After which, he climbed up a tree—some people say it was a jatoba—and settled himself at the top.

When the jaguar came back exhausted, he realized that a trick had been played upon him, and he was indignant: "I'll bite that cursed monkey to death, but where is he?"

The jaguar ate what was left of the fish and tried in vain to trace the monkey's whereabouts. The monkey whistled, once, twice. Eventually the jaguar caught sight of him and asked him to come down, but the monkey refused, being afraid that the jaguar, in spite of his assurances to the contrary, would kill him. The jaguar then stirred up a strong wind, which caused the tree top to sway; the monkey clung to the tree as best he could, but soon his strength was exhausted, and he was hanging on by only one hand. "I'm going to let go," he cried to the jaguar. "Open your mouth." The jaguar opened his mouth wide, and the monkey dropped into it and disappeared into the jaguar's belly. The jaguar, growling and licking his chops, ran off into the forest.

But he was soon in a bad way, because the monkey jumped about so much inside him. He begged the monkey to keep still, but to no purpose. In the end the monkey took his knife, cut open the jaguar's belly, and came out. He removed the dying jaguar's skin and cut it into strips, with which he adorned his head. He fell in with another jaguar, who had hostile intentions. He pointed out the nature of his headgear to this jaguar, who realized he was dealing with a jaguar-killer, and fled in terror. (Colb. 3, pp. 215-17.)

Before broaching the analysis of this very important myth,[10] let me make a few preliminary remarks. In this instance, the prea behaves as the monkey's

[10] It is also found in Guiana, but in a vestigial form, as one episode among many that go to make up the epic tale, rather than the myth, of the hero Konewo. He was sitting on the bank of a river at sunset. A jaguar appeared and asked him what he

imprudent, stubborn, and unfortunate companion. He perishes because of his *gluttony*, which causes the *piercing* of the *canoe*—that is, the opening of a cultural artifact, as opposed (cf. M₅) to a physical body, which is a product of nature. The prea stands, therefore, halfway between the careless watchmen of the Toba-Mataco myths (M₃₁ and M₃₂), who are *stopped up*—asleep, deaf, or dumb—and the imprudent hero of the Warao myth (M₂₈), who *bursts out* laughing; but at the same time it is in an eccentric position: culture instead of nature; and vegetable food, which it eats itself, thus affecting an external object, instead of animal food—fish or meat—eaten by someone else and thus affecting the subject's body.

Among the Opaye, who were once the neighbors of the Bororo to the south, the prea figures in a myth as the agent who introduced humans to fire and cooking (this is the role attributed to the monkey, the prea's companion in the Bororo myth):

M₅₆. Opaye. "The origin of fire"

Formerly the jaguar's mother was the mistress of fire. The animals plotted together to steal a firebrand from her. The armadillo was the first to try: he went to the old woman's hut, asked if he could warm himself because he was feeling cold, and was given permission to do so. He tickled the old woman under the arms to send her to sleep, and when he felt her muscles relax, he seized a burning brand and ran off. But the woman woke up and whistled a signal to her son, the jaguar, who caught up with the armadillo and took back the firebrand.

The agouti, then the tapir, the capuchin monkey, and the howler monkey —in short, all the animals—were equally unfortunate. It was left to that insignificant animal, the prea, to succeed where the others had failed.

The prea adopted a different method. When he arrived at the jaguar's hut, he did not mince his words: "Good day, grandmother, how are you? I have come to fetch fire." Whereupon he seized a burning brand, hung it around his neck, and went off (cf. Mataco in Métraux 3, pp. 52–4; and 5, pp. 109–110).

Having been alerted by his mother's whistle, the jaguar tried to intercept the prea, but the latter managed to avoid him. The jaguar went in pursuit, but the prea had several days' lead. The jaguar eventually caught up with him on the far bank of the Parana. "Let us talk," said the prea to the jaguar. "Now that you have lost possession of the fire, you will have to find some other means of subsistence." Meanwhile the firebrand (what follows suggests that it was more like a log) went on burning, "thus becoming so much the lighter to carry."

The prea is a trickster. He was so even at that time, and tricked the jaguar by telling him that there was no healthier food than raw, bloody flesh. "All right," said the jaguar. "Let me try it," and he hit out with his paw at the

---

was doing. "I am breaking wood for the fire," replied Konewo, pointing to a star shining above the top of a dead tree. And he added the injunction: "Go and fetch that fire to set ours alight!" The jaguar set off, but he journeyed in vain, never coming across fire. Meanwhile Konewo took to his heels (K.G. 1, p. 141).

prea's muzzle, shortening it to the length at which it has remained. Finally, having been persuaded by the prea that there were other kinds of prey (which means that the prea is responsible for the danger that the jaguar represents for man), the jaguar gave him a lesson in cooking: "If you are in a hurry, light a fire, put the meat on a spit, and grill it; if you have time, cook it in an oven that has been hollowed out in the ground and previously heated; put foliage around the meat to protect it, and earth and hot ashes on top." While he was giving these explanations, the firebrand finally burned out.

The jaguar then taught the prea how to make fire by rotating sticks, and the prea went all over the place, lighting fires everywhere. The fire spread even to his own village, where his father and the other inhabitants gave him a triumphal welcome. The charred remains of the fires lit by the prea can still be seen in the bush. (Ribeiro 2, pp. 123–4.)

This Opaye myth, as can be seen, provides a transition between the Bororo myth about the invention of fire by the monkey, the prea's companion, and the Ge myths about the stealing of fire from the jaguar by men, with the help of animals or after having been themselves changed into animals. The prea steals fire from the jaguar (like the animals in the Ge myths) and, after losing it, teaches men how to produce it, like the monkey in the Bororo myth.

It will also have been noted in connection with the prea that the myth explains in passing why the animal has a short snout. This is an important point, because, as we saw earlier (M_{18}), the Kayapo distinguish between the caititu and the· queixada by the length of their snouts. A remark by Vanzolini (p. 160) suggests that the Timbira, in distinguishing among the kinds of rodents, are guided by the presence or the absence of a tail. Two species of rodent figure in the myths we have examined so far. The prea (*Cavia aperea*) is the monkey's little companion (M_{55}) or the animals' "little brother" (M_{56}); the cutia or agouti (*Dasyprocta* species) is the younger brother of the hero in the key myth (M_1). On the other hand, a Kayapo myth (M_{57}; Métraux 8, pp. 10–12) tells of two sisters, one of whom is changed into a monkey, while the other is changed into a paca (*Coelogenys paca*). A zoologist refers to the *Dasyprocta* species as "the species which is probably the most important year-round food animal," and to *Coelogenys paca* as "one of the most desirable of food animals" (Gilmore, p. 372). The agouti (*Dasyprocta*) weighs between 2 and 4 kilogram's, and the paca up to 10 kilograms. We know from the Opaye myth (M_{56}) that the prea is considered a very small animal, and as the most insignificant of them all. It is closely related to the guinea pig and is between 25 and 30 centimeters long; the natives of southern Brazil do not even consider it worth hunting (Ihering, "Préa" entry).

When all these elements are brought together, one is tempted to establish between two species of rodents, or between one species of rodent and a species of monkey, a relation analogous to the one that was established in the myths between two kinds of pigs. The contrast between long and short (applied to pigs' snouts and bristles, cf. M_{16} and M_{18} and p. 86) would also characterize two groups which are, in other respects, associated: the monkey and the prea (M_{55}), and the monkey and the paca (M_{57}), not to mention the agouti and the prea, because of the similar positions they occupy in M_1, M_{55}, and M_{134}. But we cannot be sure whether the contrast is based on relative sizes, lengths of snout, or the presence or absence of a tail. Yet the contrast exists, since a Mundurucu myth (M_{58}) explains how the animals provided women with vaginas, in the days when they had none. The vaginas made by the agouti were long and thin; those made by the paca were round in shape (Murphy 1, p. 78).

If the hypothesis (which I am putting forward here only tentatively) were confirmed, it would be possible to establish an equivalence with the myths about the origin of wild pigs according to the following pattern:

a) Ungulates:

queixada (110 cms.) $>$	caititu (90 cms.)
snout: long	short
bristles: long	short

b) Rodents:

paca (70 cms.) $>$ agouti (60 cms.) $>$ prea (30 cms.) $>$ rat (*Cercomys*)

		"short snout" (Opaye)	
"tailless"[11]		"tailless . . .	. . . long-tailed" (Timbira)
"rounded vagina . . .	. . . long vagina" (Mundurucu)		

a) Large animals : (queixada : caititu) :: (long : short).
b) Small animals : (monkey : rodents *x, y*) :: (rodent *x* : rodent *y*) :: (long : short).

[11] As is explained in a Yurukare myth (Barbosa Rodrigues, p. 253). Cf. also the name given to the paca in the Tunebo language: *batara* "the tailless one" (Rochereau, p. 70). Ihering points out ("Cutia" entry), with reference to the agouti's tail, that it is very rudimentary and scarcely visible in the case of *Dasyprocta aguti* and *D. azarae*. On the other hand, a smaller Amazonian species, *D. acouchy,* has "a more developed tail, about 8 cms. long and with a bunch of bristles at the end." But even in the case of one of the first species, the early observers of Brazilian life noted that the tail was

In this connection, it might then be possible to treat the set just examined as a weaker transformation of the one that includes the myths about the origin of wild pigs: this would enable us to link the latter, by means of an additional connection, to the set of myths about the origin of fire. Besides, the contrast between small and large game is directly given in these myths. The Mundurucu say of Karusakaibö, who is responsible for the creation of wild pigs, that "before his time, there was only small game and he produced large game" (Tocantins, p. 86). The conceptualization of the queixada/ caititu couple in the form of a pair of contrasts is confirmed by a comment by Cardus (pp. 364–5), obviously inspired by some native source.

This line of inquiry would take us beyond the limits I have set myself, and I therefore prefer to demonstrate the connection between the two sets of myths about the origin of fire (stolen from the jaguar or produced by a technique taught by the monkey or the prea)[12] by using a more direct method.

It is clear that the Bororo myth about the origin of fire (M_{55}) and Ge myths on the same theme (M_7 to M_{12}) are strictly symmetrical (see diagram on p. 133).

If the monkey/prea contrast could be interpreted, as we have suggested, as a weak form of the queixada/caititu contrast, this would provide us with an additional dimension, since the latter contrast refers back to the relation between the two heroes of the Ge myths: sister's husband/wife's brother. But there is a still more convincing proof of the validity of my reconstruction.

The Kayapo-Kubenkranken version (M_8) contains a detail that in itself is unintelligible and that can only be elucidated by means of the Bororo myth, M_{55}. According to the Kayapo, when the jaguar raised his head and saw the hero on the rock, he took care to cover his mouth. Now when the monkey in the Bororo myth felt he was about to let go, he asked the jaguar to open his mouth, which the latter did. Thus, in one case we have a

"very short" (Léry, chap. 10) or "only an inch long" (Thevet, chap. 10). An Amazonian narrative divides animals into two groups: those with tails (monkey, agouti) and those, such as the toad and the prea, without (Santa-Anna Nery, p. 209). The Bororo word *aki pio* refers to "all quadrupeds without tails, such as the capybara and the agouti (EB, Vol. I, p. 44).

[12] This distinction is typical of the two groups. The jaguar is in possession of fire *sub specie naturae:* he is purely and simply stated to be in possession of it. In M_{55} the monkey acquires it *sub specie culturae:* he invents a technique for producing it. The prea occupies an intermediary position, since in its case the fire is lost and found again. In this connection it may be noted that there is a parallel between M_{56} and a short Mataco myth (M_{59}). The jaguar was the master of fire and would not give any away. One day the guinea pig went to see the jaguar, ostensibly to take him a fish but really to steal a little fire from him, so that the Indians, who were fishing, would be able to cook their meal. When the Indians went off, the hot ash they left behind set fire to the grass, and the jaguars made haste to put out the flames with water. They did not know that the Indians had taken fire away with them (Nordenskiöld 1, p. 110). Consequently here, too, there are two fires, one that is lost and the other that is preserved.

mediatized (therefore beneficial) conjunction operating upward from below; and in the other case, a nonmediatized (therefore disastrous) conjunction operating downward from above. It follows that the Bororo myth throws light on the Kayapo one: if the Kayapo jaguar had not covered his mouth with his paw, the hero would have fallen into it and would have been swallowed up, exactly in the same way as the Bororo monkey. In one instance the jaguar closes up; in the other he opens, thus behaving either like the deaf and dumb watchers in the Toba-Mataco myths (M_{31}, M_{32}) or like the laughing (and not devouring) brother of the Warao myth (M_{28}), the one who is himself devoured because he has "opened."

On the other hand, the Bororo myth about the origin of fire allows us to give a more precise definition of the semantic situation of the monkey, which lies between the jaguar's and man's. Like man, the monkey stands in opposition to the jaguar; like the jaguar, he is master of fire, with which men are as yet unacquainted. The jaguar is the reverse of man, whereas the monkey is more like his counterpart. The monkey's character is therefore made up of elements that are borrowed now from one of the polar opposites, now from the other. Certain myths show a commutation between the monkey and the jaguar (M_{38}); others, like the one just analyzed, show a commutation with man. Finally, the triangular pattern is sometimes found in its complete form: according to a Tucuna myth (M_{60}), the "lord of the monkeys" had a human shape, although he belonged to a race of jaguars (Nim. 13, p. 149).

When we consider the whole range of myths relating to laughter, we are struck by an apparent contradiction. Almost all of them attribute disastrous consequences to laughter, and the most frequent consequence is death. Only a few associate it with positive events, such as the acquisition of cooking fire (M_{54}) or the origin of language (M_{45}). It should be recalled at this point that the Bororo distinguish two kinds of laughter: that which results from a mere physical or mental titillation, and the triumphant laughter marking cultural invention (M_{20}). As a matter of fact, the nature/culture contrast underlies all these myths, as I have already indicated in connection with those in which bats play a part (M_{40}, M_{43}). These animals embody a radical disjunction between nature and culture, which is well illustrated by the fact that their cave is devoid of furniture and thus consists solely of richly decorated walls contrasting with the floor strewn with droppings (M_{40}). Moreover, the bats have a monopoly of cultural symbols: rock paintings and ceremonial axes. By their tickling and their caresses, they prompt a natural form of laughter, which is purely physical and, as it were, "empty." This laughter is therefore, strictly speaking, deadly, and it functions in effect as a combinative variant of the splitting-open of the skulls with axes in M_{43}. The situation is exactly the reverse of that in M_{45}, where a civilizing hero "opens" men by presenting them with a comic display, so that they are able to express themselves by this articulate speech, which is unknown to the bats (M_{40}); the latter have no choice but to opt for "anti-communication."

M_{55} {two animals	monkey > prea	in water animal (<) too bold	animal (<) leaves the scene (dead)
M_7^- M_{12} {two men	man a > man b	on land man (<) too timid	man (>) leaves the scene (alive)

M_{55} {isolated animal (>)	meeting with the jaguar	*negative mediation, monkey-jaguar* (1) aquatic game (fish) offered and refused by the monkey	(2) the jaguar swallows the monkey
M_7^- M_{12} {isolated man (<)		*positive mediation, jaguar-man* (1) aerial game (birds) demanded by jaguar and given to him	(2) the jaguar avoids swallowing the man

---

M_{55} {the monkey causes the jaguar to take the reflection (=*shadow of the fire*) for the fire	monkey, virtual master of fire	monkey, master of cultural objects (canoe, fire sticks, knife)
M_7^- M_{12} {the man does not cause the jaguar to take the shadow for the substance	jaguar, actual master of fire	jaguar, master of cultural objects (bow, burning log, cotton thread)

M_{55} {monkey above, jaguar below	the jaguar as ogre	imposed conjunction	monkey *in the belly* of the jaguar
M_7^- M_{12} {man above, jaguar below	the jaguar as supplier of food	negotiated conjunction	man *on the back* of the jaguar

---

M_{55} {two jaguars (sex not indicated)	one jaguar killed, the other leaves	skin torn from the jaguar (natural object)
M_7^- M_{12} {two jaguars (one male, one female)	one jaguar killed, the other is left	fire snatched from the jaguar (cultural object)

2

A Short Symphony

The work accomplished so far has made it possible to bring together a great many myths. But in my haste to strengthen and consolidate the most obvious connections, I have left a number of loose threads hanging here and there; and these must be tidied up before I can assert my belief that all the myths so far examined are part of a coherent whole.

Let us try, then, to take an over-all look at the tapestry I have been putting together piecemeal, and let us behave as if it were already complete, without bothering for the moment about the gaps that still exist in it. All the myths with which we are here concerned divide into four big sets, which subdivide into pairs characterized by antithetical forms of behavior on the part of the hero.

The first set presents us with a continent hero: he refrains from complaining when he is made to eat obnoxious food (M_{53}); he refrains from laughing when he is tickled (M_{37}) or is made to watch something funny (M_7 to M_{12}).

The hero of the second group, on the other hand, is incontinent: he does not refrain from laughter when dealing with someone who makes ridiculous gestures (M_{28}, M_{38}, M_{48}) or speaks in a ridiculous tone (M_{46}). He cannot control himself when tickled (M_{40}). Alternatively, he cannot avoid opening his mouth when eating and so chews his food noisily (M_{10}); or he opens his ears when listening and so hears the ghosts call (M_9); or again, he cannot refrain from releasing his sphincter muscles, either because he laughs too hard (M_{49}, M_{50}), or because, as in the key myth, his fundament has been eaten up (M_1); or lastly, because he breaks wind with deadly effect (M_5).

Continence and incontinence, closing and opening are therefore contrasted, in the first place, as manifestations of due control and excess. But we immediately note two further sets, complementary to the preceding ones: in these, continence takes on the character of excess, since it is carried too far, and incontinence (if not carried too far) seems, on the contrary, to be a controlled form of behavior.

Excessive continence is characteristic of insensitive or taciturn heroes (M_{29}, M_{30}); and of gluttonous heroes who are incapable of evacuating the food they "contain" normally, and therefore remain closed (M_{35}) or doomed to a lethal form of evacuation (M_5); or again of imprudent or indiscreet heroes who fall asleep, are (thought to be) deaf, or (become) dumb (M_{31}, M_{32}). Huxley (pp. 149–50) suggests that, on the level of myth, the digestive process can be likened to a cultural procedure, and that consequently the reverse process—that is, vomiting—corresponds to a regression from culture to nature. There is undoubtedly some truth in this interpretation, but, as is the rule in the analysis of myths, it cannot be generalized beyond a particular context. We know of many instances, in South America and elsewhere, in which vomiting has an exactly opposite semantic function and is a means of transcending culture rather than a sign of a return to nature. At the same time it must be added that, in this respect, digestion stands in opposition not only to vomiting but also to intestinal stoppage, since the former is inverted assimilation and the latter impeded excretion. The woman in the Bororo myth (M_5) exudes the fish in the form of illnesses, as she is unable to evacuate them; the greedy little boy in another Bororo myth (M_{35}) loses language, because he is unable to vomit up the burning fruit he has swallowed. The Tereno ancestors (M_{45}) acquire language because their lips are opened by laughter.

Duly controlled incontinence is a feature of those heroes who know how to communicate with the adversary discreetly and—I am tempted to say— below the level of linguistic communication: allowing themselves to be silently unmasked (M_7, M_8, M_{12}), spitting on the ground (M_9, M_{10}), or whistling (M_{32}, M_{55}).

Therefore, whether it is a question of not giving in to a comic illusion, not laughing (through physical or mental causes), or not making a noise while eating (either through chewing audibly or crying out because the food is too highly seasoned), all the myths mentioned belong to the same dialectic of opening and shutting, which operates on two levels: that of the upper orifices (mouth, ear), and that of the lower (anus, urinary canal, vagina).[13]

We arrive, therefore, at the following tentative system:

	M_1	M_5	M_9	M_{10}	M_{46}	M_{49}, M_{50}	M_{53}
Upper			hearing too much	chewing noisily	laughing	laughing	groaning
Lower	evacuation with digesting	exuding farting				urination, menstruation	

[13] And switches freely from one to the other; cf. the Arecuna myth (M_{126}) in which Makunaima covets his elder brother's chaste wife. He changes first into a *bicho de pe* (small parasite *Tunga penetrans*) to make her laugh, but in vain; he then takes on the appearance of a man whose body is covered with wounds, and she laughs. He throws himself upon her at once and rapes her (K.G. 1, p. 44; cf. also M_{95}).

If the upper/lower contrast is combined with the second contrast between front and back, and if we take it that:

$$\text{mouth} : \text{ear} :: \text{vagina} : \text{anus},$$

the above diagram can be simplified:

	M_1	M_5	M_9	M_{10}	M_{46}	M_{49}, M_{50}	M_{53}
Upper (+)/lower (−)	−	−	+	+	+	+, −	+
Front (+)/back (−)	+	−	−	+	+	+	+
Emission (+)/reception (−)	+	+	−	+	−	−, +	+

(Although M_{10} and M_{53} pose the problem in identical terms from the formal point of view, they differ in regard to the solution, since in M_{53} the hero manages to remain silent although the jaguar's food burns his mouth, whereas in M_{10} the hero makes a noise while eating, because the jaguar's food is crisp.)

b. SECOND MOVEMENT: BORORO

Let us now return to the myths assembled in Part One. What has the key myth (M_1) in common with the Ge set about the origin of fire (M_7–M_{12})? At first sight, only the episode of the bird-nester. Otherwise, the Bororo myth begins with the story of incest which does not occur explicitly in the Ge myths. The latter are constructed around the visit to the jaguar, who is master of fire; and this visit is taken as explaining the origin of the practice of cooking food; there is nothing comparable in the Bororo myth. Hasty analysis would lead one to suppose that the bird-nester episode had been borrowed either by the Bororo or the Ge and introduced by either group into an entirely different context from the original one. If so, the myths are made up of odds and ends.

I propose to establish, on the contrary, that in all these instances we are dealing with the same myth, and that the apparent divergences between the versions are to be treated as the result of transformations occurring within a set.

In the first place, all versions (Bororo: M_1; and Ge: M_7–M_{12}) refer to the use of a bow and arrows made out of branches. Some imply that this explains the origin of hunting weapons which, like fire, were unknown to men, and the secret of which was also in the jaguar's possession. The Bororo myth does not contain the jaguar episode, but the lost and famished hero at the top of the cliff face makes a bow and arrows with the material to hand;

and this creation or re-creation of hunting weapons is a theme common to the whole series of myths under consideration. It will be noted, moreover, that the invention of the bow and arrows in the jaguar's absence (he is absent from the myth) is perfectly congruous with the invention of fire by the monkey in the (momentary) absence of the jaguar in M_{55}; whereas, according to the Ge myths, the hero receives the bow and arrows directly from the jaguar (instead of inventing them), and the fire is already kindled.

We now come to the most serious disparity. All the Ge myths (M_7–M_{12}) are patently myths about the origin of fire, a theme that seems to be completely absent from the Bororo myth. But is this certain?

The authors of *Os Bororos orientais* make an important comment on this myth, in two different places. According to them, it deals with "the origin of wind and rain" (Colb. 3, pp. 221, 343), and they go into such geological questions as erosion by rain, laterization of soil, and the formation of steep rock faces with potholes at their base, through the dripping of water. During the rainy season these potholes, which are normally full of earth, fill up with water and look like receptacles. This remark, which has no reference to any incident in the myth (although it occurs as a preliminary statement), is particularly significant if, by any chance, it comes direct from the informant, as is often the case in the work in question. The Ge myths, which I am trying to link with the key myth, refer expressly to the origin of cooking.

But the Bororo myth refers to only one storm and nothing in the text indicates that it was the first. It will be remembered that the hero returns to his village, and that a violent storm occurs during his first night there and puts out all the fires except one. However, the conclusion of the first published version of M_1 plainly suggested its etiological character (cf. above, p. 37), and although the sentence has disappeared from the second version, the commentary confirms that the natives interpret the myth in this way. It follows that the Bororo myth, too, is about origins: the origin not of fire but of rain and wind which (as the text clearly states) are the opposite of fire, since they put it out. They are, as it were, "anti-fire."

The analysis can be carried further. Since the storm has put out all the fires in the village, apart from the one in the hut where the hero[14] has taken refuge, the latter finds himself temporarily in the position of the jaguar: he is master of fire, and all the inhabitants of the village must apply to him to obtain firebrands with which to rekindle the lost fire. In this sense the Bororo myth also relates to the origin of fire, but by a procedure of omission. The difference between it and the Ge myths therefore lies in the weaker treatment of the common theme. The occurrence is situated within the

[14] His grandmother's hut; his paternal grandmother presumably; otherwise his father would be living in the same hut, which is not the case; the version in the Bororo language uses the term *imarugo* (Colb. 3, p. 344), which denotes the father's mother. The word for maternal grandmother is *imuga* (E.B., Vol. I, p. 455).

known history of village life, instead of in mythical times to mark the introduction of the arts of civilization. In the first case the fire is lost by a limited community which had previously been in possession of it; in the second it is bestowed on humanity as a whole, after being totally unknown. However, the Kraho version (M_{11}) provides an intermediary formula, since in it mankind (as a whole) is deprived of fire by the culture heroes, who carry it away with them.[15]

The preceding demonstration would be still further strengthened if it were possible to interpret the name of the hero in the key myth, Geriguiguiatugo, as a compound of *gerigigi* "firewood" and *atugo* "jaguar." This would give "the firewood jaguar," with whom we are acquainted as a Ge hero, and who is obviously absent from the Bororo myths, but whose existence would be indicated by the etymology of the name attributed to a character who, as we have seen, performs his precise function. However, it would be dangerous to pursue this idea, since the available transcriptions are doubtful from the phonological point of view. On the other hand, the accuracy of the etymology put forward by Colbacchini and Albisetti will be confirmed below, without its being necessary for us to exclude *a priori* the possibility that the same name may admit of several interpretations.

Be that as it may, we do not need any further proof in order to accept the fact that the Bororo myth belongs to the same set as the Ge myths and constitutes a transformation of the same themes. The transformation appears in the following points: (1) a weakening of the polar opposites, in regard to the origin of fire; (2) an inversion of the explicit etiological content, which in this instance is the origin of wind and rain: anti-fire; (3) the mutation of the hero who occupies the position attributed to the jaguar in the Ge myths: master of fire; (4) a correlative inversion of the relations of kinship: the Ge jaguar is the (adopted) father of the hero, whereas the Bororo hero, who is congruous with the jaguar, is a (real) son of a human father; (5) a mutation of family attitudes (equivalent to an inversion): in the Bororo myth the mother is "close" (incestuous), the father "remote" (murderous);

[15] It is curious that a form intermediary between the Ge and the Bororo myths (which by its mere existence, confirms the possibility of the transition from one type to another) should be found among the Cuna of Panama, a very long way from central and eastern Brazil. The Cuna myth about the origin of fire (M_{61}) presents the jaguar as the master of fire; the other animals get possession of fire by causing a downpour which puts out all the fires except the one beneath the jaguar's hammock. A little iguana manages to get hold of a burning stick from it and urinates on the remaining ones to put them out. Then he crosses the river with his booty, and the jaguar, unable to swim, cannot catch up with him (Wassen 2, pp. 8–9). This form shares with the Ge myths the presentation of the jaguar as the master of fire. The features it has in common with the Bororo myths are, first, the negative conquest of fire, through the elimination by rain of all sources of fire except one, which is in the hero's hut (in this case, the jaguar's); and, second, the lizard (iguana) as the faster of this last source of fire. In the Choco myths, too, the lizard is the master of fire (Wassen I, pp. 109–10). The jaguar's inability to swim is mentioned in a Cayua myth (M_{119}).

in the Ge versions, on the contrary, it is the adopted father who is "close": he protects the child *like* a mother—he carries it, cleans it, satisfies its thirst, feeds it—and *against* the mother—whom he encourages his son to wound or kill—whereas the adopted mother is "remote," since her intentions are murderous.

Lastly, the Bororo hero is not a jaguar (although he discreetly performs the jaguar's function), but we are told that, to kill his father, he turns himself into a deer. The problems raised by the semantic position of the Cervidae in South American mythology will be discussed elsewhere; here I shall restrict myself to formulating the rule that allows us to transform this episode into a corresponding episode of the Ge set. The latter presents us with a real jaguar, who does not kill his "false" (adopted) son, although such an act would have been in keeping both with the nature of the jaguar (a flesh-eater) and with that of the hero (who is in the position of the jaguar's prey). The Bororo myth reverses the situation: a false deer (the hero in disguise) kills his real father, although this act is contrary to the nature of the deer (a herbivorous animal) and to that of the victim (a hunter stalking his prey). It will be remembered that the killing takes place during a hunt directed by the father.

Several North and South American myths present the jaguar and the deer as a linked and contrasting couple. To mention for the moment only tales that are comparatively close to the Bororo, it is significant that the Cayua of the southern part of the Mato Grosso, whose linguistic connections are doubtful, consider the jaguar and the deer as the first masters of fire (M_{62}: Schaden pp. 107–23). In this case the two species are associated (but in very early times), whereas they are contrasted in a Mundurucu myth (M_{37}). And, according to Tucuna myths (M_{63}), which have equivalents in North America (among the Menomini, for instance), deer were once man-eating jaguars; or heroes, having been changed into deer, became capable of playing the part of either the victim or the killer (Nim. 13, pp. 120, 127, 133).

c. Third Movement: Tupi

There are further reasons for supposing that the Bororo myth relates to the origin of fire, in spite of its extreme discretion on this point. Certain details, which must be attentively examined, seem to be echoes of other myths relative to the origin of fire which, at first sight, offer no resemblance to those of the Ge group and in fact come from another linguistic family, the Guarani group.

According to the Apapocuva (M_{64}), who lived in the extreme south of the Mato Grosso in the middle of the nineteenth century:

> The civilizing hero, Nianderyquey, one day pretended to die, so realistically that his body began to decay. The urubus, who were the masters of fire at

the time, gathered around the corpse and lit a fire in order to cook it. No sooner had they put the body among the hot ash than Nianderyquey began to move, put the birds to flight, took possession of the fire, and gave it to men. (Nim. I, p. 326 ff.; Schaden 2, pp. 221–2.)

The Paraguayan version of the same myth is richer in detail:

M₆₅. Mbya. "The origin of fire"

After the first earth had been destroyed by a flood, which had been sent as a punishment for an incestuous union, the gods created another and placed on it their son, Nianderu Pa-pa Miri. He created new men and set about obtaining fire for them; at the time it was in the sole possession of vulture-sorcerers.

Nianderu explained to his son, the toad, that he would simulate death, and that the toad must seize the burning embers as soon as Nianderu, having recovered consciousness, scattered them.

The sorcerers approached the corpse, which they found suitably plump. Pretending that they wished to revive it, they lit a fire. The hero moved about and shammed death alternately, until the sorcerers had brought together enough embers; the hero and his son then took possession of the latter and put them inside the two pieces of wood that would henceforth be used by men to produce fire by a process of rotation. As a punishment for their attempted cannibalism, the sorcerers were doomed to remain carrion-eating vultures "with no respect for the big thing" (the corpse) and never to achieve the perfect life. (Cadogan, pp. 57–66.)

Although the old authors do not mention this myth as existing among the Tupinamba, it occurs among several tribes who speak the Tupi language or are known to have come under Tupi influence. Several versions of it are found in the Amazonian basin, among the Tembe, the Tenetehara, the Tapirape, and the Shipaya. Others occur in the Gran Chaco and in northeastern Bolivia, among the Choroti, the Tapiete, the Ashluslay, and the Guarayu. It also exists among the Botocudo (Nim. 9, pp. 111–12) and among immediate neighbors of the Bororo, the Bacairi and the Tereno. From Guiana right up to the northern areas of North America, it occurs frequently, but in a modified form; the fire-stealing theme is missing and is replaced by the capture of a daughter of the vultures, by a hero who outwits them by taking on the appearance of a piece of carrion (cf., for instance, G. G. Simpson, pp. 268–9, and Koch-Grünberg's general discussion, 1, p. 278 ff.). Here, for example, are three Tupi versions of the myth about the origin of fire:

M₆₆. Tembe. "The origin of fire"

In the old days the king vulture was the master of fire, and men had to dry their meat in the sun. One day they decided to get possession of fire. They killed a tapir; and when the body was full of worms, the king vulture and his relatives came down from the sky. They took off their feather tunics and appeared in human form. After lighting a big fire, they wrapped the worms in leaves and put them to roast (cf. M_{105}). The men had gone into hiding not far from the dead body, and after a first unsuccessful attempt, they managed to obtain possession of fire. (Nim. 2, p. 289.)

M_{67}. Shipaya. "The origin of fire"

To get fire from the bird of prey who was master of it, the demiurge Kumaphari pretended to die and to decay. The urubus devoured his body, but the eagle had put the fire in a safe place. The demiurge then pretended to die in the form of a roebuck, but the bird was not taken in. Finally Kumaphari took the form of two shrubs in which the eagle decided to put his fire. The demiurge got possession of it, and the eagle agreed to teach him the art of producing fire by friction. (Nim. 3, p. 1015.)

M_{68}. Guarayu. "The origin of fire"

A man who did not possess fire bathed in putrid water, then lay down on the ground as if he were dead. The black vultures, the masters of fire, settled on him in order to cook and eat him, but the man got up suddenly and scattered the embers. His ally, the toad, who was waiting for the opportunity, swallowed some. He was caught by the birds and forced to cough it up again. The man and the toad then repeated their attempt, and this time they were successful. Since then men have had fire. (Nordenskiöld 2, p. 155.)

The Bororo myth does not explicitly mention the origin of fire, but one might say that *it knows* so well that this is its real subject (prefacing it, moreover, with a flood, as in the Guarani myth) that it almost literally reconstitutes the episode of the hero who is changed into carrion (in this case he is dressed as carrion, being covered with putrefied lizards) and arouses the greedy appetites of the urubus.

We can confirm the link by pointing out that one detail of the Bororo myth is incomprehensible until it is interpreted as a transformation of a corresponding detail in the Guarani myth. How are we to explain the fact that in the key myth the urubus, instead of completely devouring their victim, interrupt their feast to save him (see p. 36)? In the Guarani myth, as we know, the vultures claim to be healers, who cook their victim while pretending to revive him, and do not succeed in eating him. The sequence is simply reversed in the Bororo myth, in which the vultures consume (part of) their victim—raw—and afterward behave like genuine healers (lifesavers).

It is a well-known fact that the Bororo way of thinking was greatly influenced by Tupi mythology. In both groups the same myth—the one about the jaguar's human wife, who is the mother of the two civilizing heroes—occupies an essential position. And the modern Bororo versions (Colb. 1, pp. 114–21; 2, pp. 179–85; 3, pp. 190–96) remain astonishingly close to the one that Thevet recorded as existing among the Tupinamba in the sixteenth century (M_{96}; Métraux 1, p. 235 ff.).

But how must we interpret those peculiar features that distinguish the key myth from the myths about the origin of fire, with which we have compared it? They may be a result of the historical and geographical position of the Bororo, who—being caught, as it were, between Guarani and Ge[16] groups— have borrowed from both and fused certain themes, thus reducing or even destroying their etiological significance.

The hypothesis is plausible enough, but inadequate. It does not explain why each mythology, or each separate set of myths, should form a coherent system, as my discussion of the question has shown to be the case. The problem must therefore also be studied from the formal point of view, and we must ask whether both the Ge and the Tupi sets of myths are not part of some larger set, within which they exist as different subordinate subsets.

It is immediately obvious that these subsets have some features in common. To begin with, they attribute the origin of fire to an animal, who gave it to man or from whom man stole it: in one instance it is a vulture; in the other, a jaguar. Secondly, each species is defined in terms of the food it eats: the jaguar is a beast of prey who feeds on raw meat; the vulture is a carrion-eater, who consumes rotten meat. And yet all the myths take into account the element of decay. The Ge set does so very faintly and almost allusively, in the episode about the hero covered with feces and vermin. The Bororo set, which we studied first, is rather more explicit (M_1: the hero dressed in carrion; M_2: the hero defiled by the droppings of his son who has been changed into a bird; M_5: the hero "putrefied" by his grandmother breaking wind; M_6: the heroine exudes illnesses as if they were an intestinal evacuation). And, as we have just seen, the Tupi-Guarani set is quite clear on this point.

It is thus confirmed that the Ge myths about the origin of fire, like the Tupi-Guarani on the same theme, function in terms of a double contrast: on the one hand, between what is raw and what is cooked, and on the other, between the fresh and the decayed. The raw/cooked axis is characteristic of culture; the fresh/decayed one of nature, since cooking brings about the cultural transformation of the raw, just as putrefaction is its natural transformation.

In the total system thus restored, the Tupi-Guarani myths illustrate a more radical procedure than the Ge myths: according to the Tupi-Guarani way of thinking, the significant contrast is between cooking (the secret of which was in the possession of the vultures) and putrefaction (which is a

[16] The presentation of the jaguar as master of fire is typical of the Ge myths; it occurs only sporadically in other parts of South America, and always in an attenuated form—for example, among the Toba, the Mataco, and the Vapidiana. The incident of the hero who is caught in a crevice in a cliff occurs in the myth about the origin of fire belonging to the Caingang of southern Brazil, whose relation with the Ge group is now disputed.

characteristic of their present diet); whereas, in the Ge myths the significant contrast is between the cooking of foodstuffs and eating them raw (the jaguar's present procedure).

The Bororo myth may therefore express a refusal, or an inability, to choose between the two formulas; and the refusal or the inability needs to be explained. The theme of decay is more strongly emphasized among the Bororo than among the Ge, while that of the carnivorous beast of prey is almost entirely absent. On the other hand, the Bororo myth sees things from the point of view of victorious man—that is, from the point of view of culture (the hero of M_1 invents the bow and arrow, just as the monkey in M_{55}—who is a counterpart of man—invents fire, which is unknown to the jaguar). The Ge and the Tupi-Guarani myths (which are closer in this respect) are more concerned with the despoiling of animals, which is an aspect of nature. But the dividing line between nature and culture is different, according to whether we are considering the Ge or the Tupi myths: in the former it separates the cooked from the raw; in the latter it separates the raw from the rotten. For the Ge, then, the raw + rotten relation is a natural category, whereas for the Tupi the raw + cooked relation is a cultural category.

PART THREE

1

Fugue of the Five Senses

Because of its incomplete and provisional nature, the synthesis that emerged tentatively from Part Two is not absolutely convincing, since it fails to deal with important sections of the key myth, and the fact has not been established that these elements also occur in the Ge set. The method I am following is legitimate only if it is exhaustive: if we allowed ourselves to treat apparent divergences among myths, which are at the same time described as belonging to one and the same set, as the outcome either of logical transformations or historical accidents, the door would be thrown wide open to arbitrary interpretations: for it is always possible to choose the most convenient interpretation and to press logic into service whenever history proves elusive, or to fall back on the latter should the former be deficient. Structural analysis would, as a result, rest entirely on a series of begged questions, and would lose its only justification, which lies in the unique and most economical coding system to which it can reduce messages of a most disheartening complexity, and which previously appeared to defeat all attempts to decipher them. Either structural analysis succeeds in exhausting all the concrete modalities of its subject, or we lose the right to apply it to any one of the modalities.

If we take the text literally, the episode of the expedition to the kingdom of the souls, by which a wronged father hopes to ensure his son's death, occurs only in the Bororo myth. This seems all the more evident in that the episode is a direct consequence of the hero's incestuous behavior, which is also absent from the Ge myths.

Let us look at the episode more closely. The hero is sent into the aquatic world of the souls on a precise mission. He is to steal three objects in the following order: the great rattle, the small rattle, and the string of little bells. Three objects, that is, capable of producing a noise, and this explains —the text is absolutely explicit on this point—why the father chose them: he hopes that his son will be unable to gain possession of the three objects without moving them and thus raising the alarm among the souls, who will punish him for his temerity. Once this point has been made clear, certain connections with the Ge myths come to light.

But before venturing on an explanation, I must stress that the Ge myths undoubtedly constitute a set. We already know this to be the case, through the simple fact that the different versions with which we are acquainted, although not all equally elaborate or detailed, are identical in their main outlines. Moreover, the communities in which these myths originated are not all really separate entities, and none is completely distinct: the Kraho and the Canella are two subgroups of the eastern Timbira, who belong to a much broader community, of which the Apinaye—and the Kayapo, too, no doubt—are the western representatives; the separation must have taken place only a few centuries ago at most, as is testified by the legends commemorating it. The separation between the Kubenkranken and the Gorotire is even more recent, since it took place as recently as 1936.[1]

Methodologically speaking, we are in the opposite situation to the one I described a little while ago. When one adopts a structural approach, one has no right to resort to historico-cultural hypotheses whenever principles already enunciated run into difficulties of application. Historico-cultural arguments are in the circumstances no more than conjectures, improvised to meet the needs of the moment. On the other hand, it is certainly our right, even our duty, to take into careful consideration conclusions that ethnographers have arrived at by means of linguistic and historical research, and that they themselves hold to be sound and well founded.

If the present Ge tribes spring from a common historical origin, those of their myths that show resemblances do not merely constitute a set from a logical point of view; empirically they also form a family. It is therefore permissible to use the most detailed versions to testify for the others, provided the poorer versions are distinguished from the former only by what they omit. If the two versions contain different treatments of the same episode, it becomes necessary, within the limits of the subset, to appeal again to the concept of transformation.

After stating these methodological rules, I can now turn to an aspect illustrated by at least two versions (M_9, M_{10}), out of the six summarized, of the Ge myth explaining the origin of fire. Like the Bororo myth, although by means of a different story, the Apinaye and Timbira myths state a problem relating to noise.

This is very clear in the Timbira myth (M_{10}). After being rescued by the jaguar, the hero, like his counterpart in the Bororo myth, finds himself in mortal danger if he ventures to make a noise: by dropping the noisy instruments (Bororo), and by noisily masticating the grilled meat and thus annoying his protector's pregnant wife (Timbira). The problem—we might almost say the ordeal—with which both heroes are faced consists in not making a noise.

Let us now move on to the Apinaye myth (M_9), from which this theme is apparently absent. It is, however, replaced by a different theme which

[1] For the history of the eastern and western Ge, cf. Nim. 8 and Dreyfus, chap. 1.

is not found elsewhere: the origin of man's loss of immortality. Forgetful of the jaguar's advice, the hero replies to more calls than he should; in other words, he allows himself to be affected by noise. He had permission to reply to the echoing calls uttered by the rock and the hardwood; and had he been satisfied to reply only to these, men would have lived as long as those mineral and vegetable entities: but since he also replies "to the gentle call of a rotten tree," the duration of human life is henceforth curtailed.[2]

The three myths (M_1, M_9, M_{10})—Bororo, Apinaye, and Timbira—can therefore, in this connection, be seen to have a common denominator, which is: a cautious attitude toward noise, because the penalty is death. In M_1 and M_{10} the hero must not *provoke others by making a noise*, otherwise *he will die*; in M_9 he must not *let himself be provoked by all the noises he hears*, because, according to the acoustic threshold at which he reacts, men—that is, *others—will die more, or less, rapidly*.

In M_1 and M_{10} the hero is *the subjective producer of noise;* he makes *a little noise* but *not a lot*. In M_9 he is *the objective receiver of noise* and can hear *a lot of noise, not a little*. May we not suppose that, in these three cases, the nature of life on earth, which is—by its limited duration—a kind of mediatization of the contrast between existence and nonexistence, is being thought of as a function of man's inability to define himself, unambiguously, in relation to silence and noise?

The Apinaye version is the only one to formulate this metaphysical proposition explicitly—an unusual feature which is accompanied by another, for the Apinaye myth is also the only one in which the episode of the ogre occurs. The two peculiarities are linked, as a preliminary demonstration will show.

But let me first of all justify the place of "man's loss of immortality" in a myth concerned with the origins of fire. A myth belonging to the Caraja, who are not Ge, but whose territory adjoins that of the Apinaye in the Araguaya valley to the south, makes the link between the two themes very obvious.

M_{70}. *Caraja. "How men lost immortality" (1)*

At the beginning of time men lived with their ancestor, Kaboi, in the bowels of the earth, where the sun shone when it was dark outside, and vice versa. From time to time the cry of a savannah bird, the seriema (*Cariama cristata,*

---

[2] As often happens, the episode is preserved in a Guiana myth (Taurepan, M_{69}) but stripped of its general significance and simply inverted into the account of the hero's exploits: Makunaima dies because he fails to take his brother's advice and replies to the distant cry of Paima, the ogre, or of some ghost (K.G. 1, p. 49). For the complete myth in Guiana, cf. below, p. 184.

With reference to the contrast between rock and decay, and its symbolic relation with the duration of human life, it may be noted that the Caingang of southern Brazil, at the end of the funeral of one of their people, rub their bodies with sand and stones, because these things do not rot. "I am going to be like stones that never die," they say. "I am going to grow old like stones." (Henry, p. 184.)

Microdactylus cristatus), could be heard, and one day Kaboi decided to set off in the direction from which the sound came. Accompanied by a few men, he came to a hole that he was unable to climb through because he was very fat; and his companions emerged without him onto the earth's surface, which they started to explore. There were great quantities of fruit, bees, and honey, and they noticed also dead trees and dry wood. They brought back to Kaboi samples of all they had found. He examined them and concluded that the earth was a beautiful and fertile place, but that the presence of dead wood proved that everything was doomed to perish. They would do better to stay where they were.

For in Kaboi's kingdom, men lived until age made them incapable of moving.

A number of his "children" refused to listen to him, and came to take up their abode on the earth's surface. For this reason, men die much sooner than those of their fellows who chose to remain in the underworld. (Ehrenreich, pp. 79–80.)

According to another version, which does not contain the dead wood theme, the underworld was supposed to be an aquatic region: "there in the depths of the water there was no death." On the other hand, the seriema's cry was heard during a honey-collecting expedition (Lipkind 1, pp. 248–9).

Be that as it may, as in the Apinaye myth, the prime cause of the loss of immortality consists in being rashly receptive to noise: men hear the cry of the bird, set out to look for it, and discover the dead wood. The Apinaye version condenses the two episodes, since the hero hears the call of the rotten tree directly. Consequently, in this respect the myth is more vigorously narrated, and the relevant contrast also stands out more clearly:

$$M_9 : \text{hardwood} \qquad / \qquad \text{rotten wood}$$

$$M_{70}: \qquad \text{living wood/dead wood}[3]$$

The choice of the seriema (sariema, cariama, etc.) confirms the connection. The Shucuru of Pernambuco believe it to be the sun's former mistress, because the bird sings only when it rains, to ask the sun to come back again, as they think (Hohenthal, p. 158). It is therefore normal that it should attract and guide men in the direction of the sun. Furthermore, we have already met an instance in which the seriema is married to a thin ugly woman, because it had given too tight a twist to the piece of flesh from which the latter had been fashioned (M_{29}); and the peasants of the interior of Brazil maintain that the flesh of the seriema, or of its thighs at any rate,

---

[3] The Apinaye myth implicitly divides living wood into hard and soft. But I shall not insist on the contrast between dead wood and rotten wood, because this is by way of being a linguistic problem: the languages of central and eastern Brazil class under the same heading the wood that we call "dead" and wood that is rotten. Thus, in Bororo: *djorighe, gerigue* "firewood" (cf. *djoru* "fire"); *djorighe-arogo* "larva of rotten wood" (B. de Magalhães, p. 34).

is uneatable, being full of worms. There is, consequently, a greater affinity between the call of a bird with tainted flesh and a damaged woman,[4] and the call of a rotten tree, than might at first appear.

The comparison between the Apinaye and the Caraja versions, which tell the story of how men lost immortality, provides an additional interest, in that it establishes a clear link between this theme and that of the origin of cooking. In order to light the fire, dead wood has to be collected, so a positive virtue has to be attributed to it, although it represents absence of life. In this sense, to cook is to "hear the call of rotten wood."

But the matter is more complicated than that: civilized existence requires not only fire but also cultivated plants that can be cooked on the fire. Now the natives of central Brazil practice the "slash and burn" technique of clearing the ground. When they cannot fell the forest trees with their stone axes, they have recourse to fire, which they keep burning for several days at the base of the trunks until the living wood is slowly burned away and yields to their primitive tools. This preculinary "cooking" of the living tree poses a logical and philosophical problem, as is shown by the permanent taboo against felling "living" trees for firewood. In the beginning, so the Mundurucu tell us, there was no wood that could be used for fires, neither dry wood nor rotten wood: there was only living wood (Kruse 2, p. 619). "So far as known, the Yurok never cut growing timber for fuel, nor did any California Indians, nor probably any axless native Americans. Firewood came from dead trees, standing or fallen." (Kroeber, in Elmendorf, p. 220, n. 5). Therefore only dead wood was legitimate fuel. To violate this regulation was tantamount to an act of cannibalism against the vegetable kingdom.[5]

Nevertheless, primitive agriculture obliged men to burn the living tree in order to fell it, and to obtain cultivated plants, which were not to be cooked otherwise than over a fire of dead wood. A Timbira myth (M_{71}) confirms that a vague feeling of guilt attached to this agricultural process, which made a certain form of cannibalism the precondition of civilized nourishment. The hero is an Indian who burns himself accidentally in his garden, by walking on a felled hollow tree trunk which is glowing inside. The wound is considered incurable, and the man would die if kindly ghosts (those of his grandparents) did not come to his aid. But, through having received this wound and having recovered from it, the hero acquires the power to cure the violent abdominal pains that follow the consumption of roast meat, when it is eaten with fingers stained with blood from the hunt (Nim. 8, pp. 246-7): these are internal pains instead of an external

[4] According to the Bakairi, the seriema has "thin, ugly" feathers (Von den Steinen 2, pp. 488–9).

[5] In an interesting study, which appeared after this book had gone to press, Heizer emphasizes (p. 189) how exceptional it was to fell living trees for firewood.

wound, but they, too, result from the conjunction of the dead and the living.[6]

The Apinaye myth (M9) is therefore not making an arbitrary use of "the call of a rotten tree" in order to effect the transition from the obtaining of fire for cooking to the meeting with a cannibalistic ogre. I have already shown that there is an intrinsic link between the theme of man's loss of immortality and the obtaining of fire for cooking purposes. And it is now clear that, for natives who practice the "slash and burn" technique, even vegetarian cooking cannot be dissociated from a kind of "cannibalism," which is also vegetarian. Man's mortality manifests itself in two ways: either through a natural death—old age or disease—as is the case with trees when they "die" and become firewood; or by a violent death at the hands of an enemy, who may be a cannibal—therefore an ogre—and who is always a cannibal, at least in a metaphorical sense, even in the guise of the tree feller attacking the living tree. It is therefore logical that in the Apinaye myth the episode of the meeting with the ogre (who is a "shadow" or a "ghost") should follow immediately on the episode of the call of rotten wood (which is also a ghost). In this way death is introduced in both its aspects.

Nevertheless, the Apinaye myth poses a problem that we have not yet solved. What meaning can be attributed to the strange conception of a call coming from a vegetable or mineral entity that has no power of articulate expression?

The myth lists three calls to which the hero must reply or keep still. In order of diminishing loudness, these are the calls of the rock, the hardwood aroeira tree, and the rotten tree. We have some information about the symbolic value of rotten wood in Ge mythology; it is a vegetable antifood,[7] the only food eaten by men before the introduction of agricultural techniques. Several Ge myths, to which I shall return later, attribute the obtain-

---

[6] The Bororo share this repulsion with regard to blood: "They believe themselves to be polluted whenever, for some reason or other, and even while hunting wild animals, they happen to become stained with blood. They immediately set off in search of water in which they wash and rewash, until all trace of the blood has disappeared. This explains their dislike of food in which the blood is still visible" (Colb. I, p. 28). This attitude is not universal in tropical America, since the Nambikwara eat the small animals that constitute the main part of their meat diet half raw and with the blood still running (L.-S. 3, pp. 303-4).

[7] The same idea also occurs in North America, especially in the northwest area, where the story of the "ogress with the basket" is found in numerous versions, the details of which are remarkably similar to the Ge version. No doubt many American myths are widely diffused throughout the two parts of the continent. However, so many features are common to the northwest area of North America and to central Brazil that we are inevitably faced with a historico-cultural problem; but the time has not yet come to discuss it.

ing of cultivated plants by man to a star-woman who came down to the earth to marry a mortal. Formerly men used to eat their meat accompanied by rotten wood instead of vegetables (Apinaye: Nim. 5, p. 165; Timbira: Nim. 8, p. 245; Kraho: Schultz, p. 75; Kayapo: Banner 1, p. 40, Métraux 8, pp. 17–18). It can be concluded from this that, in the nature versus culture context, rotten wood represents the reverse of cultivated plants.

Now the episode of the ogre shows how the hero tricked his abductor by leaving him a stone to eat instead of a body. Stone, or rock, appears, then, as the symmetrical opposite of human flesh. By filling in the empty space with the only culinary term still available, animal flesh, we arrive at the following table:

$$wood \begin{cases} rock \\ hard\ wood \\ rotten\ wood \end{cases} \qquad \begin{matrix} human\ flesh \\ animal\ flesh \end{matrix} \Big\} meat \\ cultivated\ plants$$

What does this mean? The series of three "calls" corresponds, in reverse order, to a division of the sources of food into three categories: agriculture, hunting, and cannibalism. Furthermore, these three categories, which could be called "gustatory," are coded in terms of a different sensory system: that of hearing. Finally, the auditory symbols used have the remarkable property of immediately suggesting two other sensory coding systems—one olfactory, the other tactile—as can be seen from the following table:

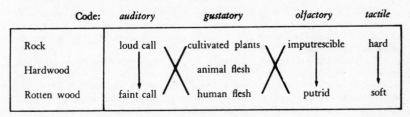

Code:	auditory	gustatory	olfactory	tactile
Rock	loud call	cultivated plants	imputrescible	hard
Hardwood		animal flesh		
Rotten wood	faint call	human flesh	putrid	soft

We can now understand the very precise meaning that must be attributed to the calls uttered by the rock and the wood: the things that emit sounds must be chosen in such a way that they also possess other sensory connotations. They are operators, which make it possible to convey the isomorphic character of all binary systems of contrasts connected with the senses, and therefore to express, as a totality, a set of equivalences connecting life and death, vegetable foods and cannibalism, putrefaction and imputrescibility, softness and hardness, silence and noise.

The point can be proved; for we know of variants of the myths already examined, belonging to the same communities or to more or less neighboring ones, from which the transformation of one sensory coding system into another can be confirmed: the Apinaye, for instance, manifestly code the contrast between life and death by means of auditory symbols; whereas the Kraho use a distinctly olfactory system of coding:

M_{72}. Kraho. "How men lost immortality"

One day the Indians captured a child belonging to the Kokridho, aquatic spirits who are impersonated in ceremonies by masked dancers (according to one of Schultz's informants, they are water bugs).[8] The following night the Kokridho came out of the water and invaded the village in order to recover their child. But they emitted such a stench that everybody died from it. (Schultz, pp. 151–2.)

A Kraho informant restores the auditory coding by adding that the Ko-kridho sang "rrrrrrr" so loudly that they were unpleasant to listen to. This detail reminds us that the Bororo use the same word, aigé, for bull-roarers and an aquatic spirit (EB, Vol. I, pp. 17–26). The Timbira, whose myth about the origin of the Kokrit (= Kokridho) is slightly different (M_{73}), also stress their foul smell (Nim. 8, p. 202). The Jivaro (M_{74}) believe that the smell of decay came into existence at the same time as the demons (Karsten 2, p. 515). An Opaye myth attributes the advent of death to the stench of a skunk-man (jaratataca, one of the Mustelidae) who was subsequently changed into this animal (Nim. 1, p. 378).[9]

[8] They can perhaps be compared with the mru kaok of the Kayapo, an aquatic, snakelike monster which is never seen but can be heard and smelled. It can cause strokes and fainting fits (Banner 2, p. 37). The same term is also supposed to have the meaning "false, counterfeit" (ibid.).

[9] The jaratataca (maritataca, jaritataca) is the cangamba (Conepatus chilensis), the South American equivalent of the North American skunk. It is a nocturnal and carnivorous quadruped, widely distributed throughout central and southern Brazil, and is supposed to have a natural immunity to the poison of the snakes it is fond of hunting. It has an anal gland that secretes a foul-smelling fluid used for spraying its opponents (Ihering, Vol. XXXIV, pp. 543–4). In the state of Pernambuco the word tacáca exists in the colloquial language with the meaning of "rank perspiration, bad smell emanating from the human body" (Ihering, Vol. XXXVI, p. 242). I shall return to the subject of the American skunk in more than one context (pp. 174, 177, 200, 249, n. 22, 271), and here I wish to make only one remark. We are concerned with a member of the Mustelidae family, whose stench spreads death among men (M_{75}). According to M_{27}, the ancestors of the Bororo were changed into Mustelidae (otters) because they refused to exhale the fragrant smoke of tobacco. The Kokridho in M_{72} are water bugs, ani-mals to which Colbacchini's curious definition of the Bororo word ippié (cf. my com-ment on p. 105, n. 7) would be more appropriate than to the otter. It seems that there must have been a kind of ethnozoological equivalence between the Mustelidae and some unidentified aquatic insect. Admittedly there is nothing in the Enciclopédia Boróro to confirm this supposition, except perhaps that the same kind of equivalence is noted with regard to a different animal: the word okiwa refers both to the capybara (Hydro-choerus) and to an aquatic insect that, like its homonym, lives along river banks (EB, Vol. I, p. 829). An aquatic spinning beetle, the y-amai, is one of the most important creatures in the Guarani cosmogony (Cadogan, pp. 30, 35).

The three calls of the Apinaye myth are found, with an olfactory coding, among the Shipaya, whose myth about how men came to die could almost be entitled "the three smells."

M₇₆. Shipaya. *"How men lost immortality"*

The demiurge wished to make men immortal. He told them to take up their position at the water's edge and to allow two canoes to go by; they should, however, stop the third in order to greet and embrace the spirit in it.

The first canoe contained a basket full of rotten meat, which was extremely foul smelling. The men ran toward it but were repelled by the stench. They thought that this canoe was carrying death, whereas death was in the second canoe and had taken human form. As a result, the men greeted death warmly, with embraces. When the demiurge arrived in the third canoe, he had to accept the fact that the men had chosen death—unlike the snakes, the trees, and the stones, who had all awaited the arrival of the spirit of immortality. Had the men done likewise, they would have sloughed off their skins when they grew old, and would have become young again like snakes. (Nim. 3, p. 385.)

The tactile coding was already implicit in the series—rock, hardwood, rotten wood—in the Apinaye myth. It is much more clearly expressed in a Tupi myth:

M₇₇. Tenetehara. *"How men lost immortality"* (1)

The first man, created by the demiurge, lived in innocence, although his penis was always in a state of erection. He tried in vain to induce detumescence by sprinkling it with a manioc beverage. The first woman, having been instructed by the water spirit (who had subsequently been castrated and killed by her husband), taught the man how to soften his penis through copulation. When the demiurge saw the limp penis, he became angry and said: "Henceforth your penis will be soft, you will make children, and then you will die: later when your child grows, he will make another child, and in turn he will die."[10] (Wagley and Galvão, p. 131.)

In connection with the Urubu, a neighboring tribe, Huxley (pp. 72–87) has clearly shown the fundamental role played in native thought by the categories of the "hard" and the "soft." They are used to distinguish modes of speech, types of behavior, ways of life, and even two different aspects of the world.

The visual code has to be dealt with at greater length because of the difficulties of interpretation to which it gives rise. Here, to begin with, is a myth that combines the visual code with others:

[10] Cf. the wax penis which melted in the sun, also a cause of the loss of immortality in an Opaye myth (Ribeiro 2, pp. 121–3).

M₇₈. *Caduveo. "How men lost immortality"*

A famous shaman paid a visit to the creator, in order to discover a means of rejuvenating old men and making dead trees put forth new buds. He approached several inhabitants of the Beyond, thinking them to be the creator, but they explained that they were only his hair, his nail parings, or his urine. . . . Finally he arrived at his destination and presented his request. His guardian spirit had informed him that he must not, on any pretext, smoke the creator's pipe, or accept the cigar the creator would offer—on the contrary, he should snatch it roughly from him—or, lastly, look at his daughter.

After surviving these three ordeals the shaman was given a comb that would bring the dead back to life, and resin (sap) that would make wood put forth green shoots again. He had already started on his way back, when the creator's daughter ran after him to give him a piece of tobacco he had forgotten. She shouted loudly at him to stop. Involuntarily the hero looked back and saw one of the young woman's toes: that one brief glance was enough to make the girl pregnant. So the creator arranged for him to die on his return, and summoned him back to the Beyond to look after his wife and son. From that time on men were no longer able to escape death. (Ribeiro 1, pp. 157–60; Baldus 4, p. 109.)

Using a purely visual coding, a second Tenetehara myth gives what appears to be a different interpretation from that in M₇₇ of the loss of immortality.

M₇₉. *Tenetehara. "How men lost immortality" (2)*

A young Indian woman met a snake in the forest. The latter became her lover, and she bore him a son who was already a youth at birth. Every day the son went into the forest to make arrows for his mother, and every evening he returned to her womb. The wife's brother discovered her secret and persuaded her to hide as soon as the son went off. When the son returned that evening to enter the mother's womb, the woman had disappeared.

The snake son consulted his snake grandfather, who advised him to hunt for his father. But the boy had no desire to do so, so that evening he transformed himself into a ray of lightning and climbed into the sky, taking his bow and arrow with him. When he got there, he broke his weapons in pieces, which became the stars. Everybody was asleep, and no one except the spider saw this take place. For this reason spiders (unlike men) do not die when they grow old, but change their shells. Formerly men and animals also changed skin when they were old, but from this day until now they die when they are old. (Wagley and Galvão, p. 149.)

In this myth we again find the snake's daughter whose vagina is open, thus allowing her husband or her son to take refuge there whenever they want to (cf. above, pp. 124–5). From this point of view, the two Tenetehara myths about the origin of man's loss of immortality are less different from each other than might at first appear; since in the first also the wife owes her initiation into sexual experience to the water spirit, whom she invited to copulate with her by knocking on a gourd placed on the water. According to an Urubu version (M_{80}), the snake was a penis, quite half a mile long, fashioned by the demiurge for the satisfaction of women, for in the beginning men were like children and asexual (Huxley, pp. 128–9). In the first Tenetehara myth the murder of the water spirit deprives the wife of her partner and encourages her to seduce her husband; this leads to the emergence of life, death, and the succession of the generations. In the Urubu myth, after the snake has been killed, the demiurge cuts his body into pieces, which he distributes among men as individual penises. As a result of this, women conceive children in their bellies (and no longer in pots) and suffer pain during childbirth. But how should the second Tenetehara myth be interpreted?

The starting point is the same: conjunction between a woman (or women, M_{80}) and a snake, followed by disjunction; then, in all three cases, by fragmentation: in M_{77} the water spirit's penis is cut up; in M_{80} the snake's head is cut off and his body chopped into pieces; and in M_{81} the snake-son is separated from his mother's body once and for all. But in the first two cases the fragmentation is projected into time in the form of periodicity: the masculine penis is to be alternately hard or soft, one generation is to succeed another, life and death are to alternate, and women experience pain in childbirth. . . . In the third case (M_{79}), the fragmentation is projected into space: the snake-son (who, like the other snakes, is indifferent to his ophidian nature, since he refuses to join his father) breaks his bow and arrow into pieces which, as they scatter throughout the night sky, turn into stars. Because the spider witnessed the fragmentation, for it, and for it alone, periodicity (the sloughing off of skins) means life, whereas for man it means death.

Consequently, the visual code allows M_{79} to use a double contrast. First, between the visible and the nonvisible, since the watching spiders were not just witnesses of a particular spectacle: previously there had been nothing to see; the night sky was uniformly dark, and for it to become "spectacular," the stars had both to fill it and to illuminate it. Secondly, the original spectacle was a qualified one, since it was the result of a contrasting of fragmentation with wholeness.

This analysis is confirmed by a set of Tucuna myths, which also deal with the loss of immortality, although they put it in a rather different perspective, perhaps because of the old Tucuna belief in a rite that was supposed to enable men to obtain immortality (Nim. 13, p. 136):

M_{81}. Tucuna. "How men lost immortality"

This first race of men knew nothing of death. It so happened that a young girl, who was being kept in seclusion for her puberty festival, failed to reply to the call of the immortals (the gods) inviting the humans to follow them. She then committed the additional error of replying to the call of the spirit of old age. The latter burst into her cell and exchanged his skin for hers. The spirit at once was transformed into a youth again, and his victim became a decrepit old woman. . . . Since then humans grow old and die. (Nim. 13, p. 135.)

This myth provides a transition between the Apinaye myth (M₉: the theme of the three calls) and the second Tenetehara myth (M₇₉: change of skin). The latter theme is brought out even more clearly in the following myth:

M₈₂. Tucuna. "How men prolonged life"

A virgin, who was being secluded in her puberty cell, heard the call of the immortals. She at once replied and asked to be granted immortality. Among the guests (at a celebration that was taking place at that time) was a young girl engaged to Tortoise: but she disliked him, because he would eat only tree fungi, and she pursued Falcon with her attentions.

All through the feast she stayed outside the hut with her lover, except for one brief moment, when she went inside to drink manioc beer. Tortoise noticed her hurried exit and uttered a curse: suddenly the tapir hide, on which the virgin and the guests were seated, rose into the air without Tortoise's having time to take his place on it.

The two lovers saw that the hide and its occupants was already high in the sky. The young girl's brothers threw down a thin liana, so that she could pull herself up to join them. But she must on no account open her eyes! She disobeyed and called out: "The liana is going to break!" The liana did in fact snap. As she fell, the young girl turned into a bird.

Tortoise broke the jars full of beer. The beer, which was full of worms, spilled onto the ground and was licked up by ants and other creatures that shed their skin: and that explains why they never grow old. Tortoise changed into a bird and joined his companions in the upper world. The tapir hide and its occupants can still be seen there in the form of the moon's halo—according to another version, the Pleiades. (Nim. 13, pp. 135–6.)

I shall deal later with the astronomical aspect of the visual coding, and confine myself here to a formal analysis. From the formal point of view, there is a striking parallel between the above myth and the second Tenetehara myth about the loss of immortality (M₇₉): there is conjunction of a woman and a forbidden lover (snake or falcon); disjunction follows (caused by the brother in M₇₉, whereas in M₈₂ the two brothers try in vain to rectify it); objects are broken (either in the sky, as in M₇₉, or on the ground, as in M₈₂). Insects that change their skin "take cognizance" of the fragmentation and become immortal. Celestial bodies come into being.

The Tucuna myth is, however, more complex than the Tenetehara myth. This, it seems to me, is due to two reasons. First of all, as has already been indicated, the Tucuna believed that man could attain to immortality. This immortality, which I shall term "absolute," brings with it a supplementary dimension which is added to the "relative" immortality of insects. The Tenetehara myth (M_{79}) merely establishes the contrast between the absolute mortality of humans and the relative immortality of insects, whereas the two Tucuna myths (which are complementary) presuppose a triangular system, whose three tips represent human immortality and mortality, both of them absolute, and the relative immortality of insects. The second Tucuna myth (M_{82}) considers the two forms of immortality, that enjoyed by humans being superior—since it is absolute—to that enjoyed by insects: hence the inversion of the levels of fragmentation and, correlatively, of the objects subjected to fragmentation: masculine weapons or feminine pottery, either in the sky (M_{79}) or on the ground (M_{82}). In this connection the transition from the stars (M_{79}) to the halo around the moon or the Pleiades is particularly significant, since in the second instance we are dealing with celestial phenomena which (as we shall see with regard to the Pleiades, on pp. 218 ff.) are in the category of the continuous, which is also the category of absolute immortality, as opposed to relative or periodic immortality.[11]

Another reason for the complex nature of M_{82} stems perhaps from the fact that the Tucuna seem to be specially sensitive to one particular problem of culinary logic, as a result of the important place occupied by fermented drinks in their ceremonial life. For them, beer is, or can be, the drink of immortality:

M_{84}. Tucuna. *"The drink of immortality"*

A puberty festival was drawing to a close, but the young girl's uncle was so drunk that he could no longer perform the ceremony properly. An immortal god appeared in the form of a tapir, carried off the young girl, and married her.

Much later she reappeared to her mother in the plantations with her baby and asked her mother to prepare an especially strong beer for her younger brother's hair-plucking ceremony. She attended the ceremony with her husband. The latter brought with him a little of the drink of the immortals and offered a sip to each participant. When they were all drunk, they went off with the young couple to take up their abode in the dwelling of the gods. (Nim. 13, p. 137.)

But at the same time this myth, like M_{82}, revolves around a beverage, whose preparation is halfway between fermentation and putrefaction or, to be more accurate, seems, by reason of the native technique employed, inevitably to combine the two processes. (I have already referred to this fact on p. 17, n. 16.) It is tempting to correlate this duality with the duality of the heroines, which at first seems so strange: on the one hand, we have the virgin recluse, who is obliged to fast and who might be said to be in a state

---

[11] The Bororo (M_{83}) believe that men lost immortality as a result of a discussion between stone and bamboo: one is eternal; the other dies and is reborn in its young shoots. The bamboo won the argument on behalf of periodicity (Colb. 3, pp. 260–61).

of "fermentation" on reaching puberty; and on the other, the dissolute girl who despises Tortoise her fiancé, because he "eats rotten matter," and is in love with Falcon who "eats his food raw" (according to a note by Nimuendaju, this type of Falconidae feeds on small birds). Mention is made, then, of three kinds of diet, just as there are three kinds of immortality; or we can say, if we keep within the strict subject matter of the myth, that there are two kinds of immortality—simple immortality (humans becoming immortal) and ambiguous immortality (insects sloughing their skins)—and two types of diet—one simple but nonhuman (raw food), the other human and even sacred, but ambiguous (food that perforce becomes rotten as it ferments).

Be that as it may, my purpose in introducing the Tucuna myths was to obtain a clearer definition of the units of the visual code; and it is obvious that our linguistic categories are ill adapted to this task. The relevant contrast is isomorphic with that between whole objects and broken objects; between the uniformly dark sky and the luminous star-studded sky; finally between a liquid contained within a vessel where it forms a homogeneous mass, and that same liquid spilled and teeming with worms: therefore, between whole and fragmented, smooth and gritty, inert and alive, continuous and discontinuous. These contrasts are in turn isomorphic with other contrasts, which depend on other forms of sensitiveness: fresh and rotten, hard and soft, noisy and silent (hot and cold in a short Arikena version; cf. Kruse 4, p. 409).

These sensory codes are not simple, and they are not the only ones used. For instance, the visual code exists in a crude form as a contrast between visible and invisible. But besides the fact that the contrast is immediately specified, the visual code functions on other levels. In the fourth part I shall deal at length with the astronomical code, and in the fifth, with an aesthetic code which is already in operation in those myths we have studied up till now, and by virtue of which the seriema—a plaintive and ugly bird, the husband of an ugly wife, responsible for death—can be contrasted with the elaborately painted and decorated jaguar,[12] whose fangs and fur are used to make the finest adornments, and with its cousin the puma who, unlike the seriema, has a pretty wife (M_{29}). Finally, in the second section, in dealing with the myths about the origin of wild pigs, I showed the working of what amounts to a veritable sociological coding system exploiting contrasts based on ties of affinity and kinship.

Before I leave the question of sensory codes for the time being, there is a contradiction to be resolved. When we examine the myths dealing with the

---

[12] Vanity caused the jaguar's downfall (Métraux 8, pp. 10–12). In exchange for agility and litheness it gave the lizard "a little beauty, and painted its skin on either side" (Colb. 3, p. 258).

duration of human life, we notice that the poles of each sensory contrast take on different values, according to the example chosen. In M_9, as well as in M_{70} and M_{81}, it is stated that, in order to enjoy prolonged life, or immortality, men must not respond to a faint noise: the "gentle" and "low" call of the rotten tree, the distant cry of the seriema, or the call of the spirit of old age. Let us now look at another myth about the loss of immortality, which, like M_{70}, belongs to the Caraja.

M_{85}. Caraja. "How men lost immortality" (2)

After the fire he refused to give to men had been stolen from him by a toad, the demiurge married a young Indian. Yielding to his father-in-law's entreaties, he agreed to ask the king-vulture for the celestial lights—the stars, the sun, and the moon, which were essential for lighting the earth. The demiurge then asked the vulture to teach men the arts of civilization, using himself, the demiurge, as an intermediary. After which the bird, whom the demiurge had lured down by feigning death, flew off. At that moment the demiurge's mother-in-law was prompted to ask the vulture how old men could be rejuvenated. The reply came from very high up and very far away. The trees and certain animals could hear it, but not men. (Baldus 4, p. 82.)

Here again we find the contrast between death and life, which is the invariant element of the set. But instead of the contrast being coded as hearing/not hearing, the order of the terms is reversed. In order to prolong their lives, the heroes of M_9, M_{70}, and M_{81} ought not to have heard a faint noise. In this myth the condition is reversed.

The same difficulty occurs in connection with the olfactory code. According to the Kraho myth M_{72} and the Opaye M_{75}, death came to men because they smelled its stench. Yet in the Shipaya myth (M_{76}), the fault lies in a lack of olfactory sensitivity: if men had detected the stench of death, they would not have accepted it. Consequently, in one instance a powerful odor ought not to have been perceived, and in the second a faint odor ought to have been detected.

Let us look now at the visual code. A Sherente myth, which will be summarized later (M_{93a}, p. 168), associates the origin of man's loss of immortality with the visual and olfactory perception of a celestial scene. Now the Tenetehara myth (M_{79}) gives the reverse explanation of the origin of man's loss of immortality: men died prematurely because they were asleep and *did not see* the empty night sky suddenly fill with stars. Here we have an invariant feature of the subset to which M_{79} belongs, since it recurs, in an identical form but coded acoustically (M_{86}), in the Amazonian variants: the snake-son, after being abandoned by his mother, goes up into the sky where he becomes the rainbow. Before ascending, he urges men to reply to the calls he will shout down to them from above. But his grandmother is asleep and does not hear him. However, the lizards, the serpents, and the trees do hear; and this is why they are rejuvenated and change their skin.

(Barbosa Rodrigues, pp. 233-35, 239-43). We find the same conclusion in an-other variant (M$_{86a}$), in which the rainbow is curiously referred to as a jag-uar's son; however, this variant was obtained from a detribalized halfbreed (Tastevin 3, pp. 183, 190). A Cashinawa myth (M$_{86b}$) also explains that, unlike trees and reptiles, men became mortal because they failed to reply in their sleep to their ancestor as he soared into the sky and shouted to them: "Slough off your skins!" (Abreu, pp. 481-90).

The old mythographers would have very easily overcome a difficulty such as this. They would have merely assumed that mythological thought was reflecting the loose and always approximate nature of the analyses with which mythography was content. I work on the opposite principle: when a con-tradiction appears, it proves that the analysis has not been taken far enough, and that certain distinctive features must have escaped detection. I can now demonstrate this in the present instance.

In the set of myths dealing with loss of immortality, the mortality of man is viewed from two different angles: it is looked at prospectively and retrospectively. Is it possible to avert death—that is, to prevent men from dying sooner than they want to? And, conversely, is it possible to restore men's youth once they have grown old, or to bring them back to life if they have already died? The solution to the first problem is always formulated in negative terms: do not hear, do not feel, do not touch, do not see, do not taste. . . . The solution to the second problem is always expressed posi-tively: hear, feel, touch, see, taste. On the other hand, the first solution applies only to men, since plants and animals have their own method of avoiding death, which is to become young again by changing their skins. Some myths consider only the human state and can therefore be read in one direction only—prospective continuance of life, negative injunction; others contrast the human state with that of creatures or entities that grow young again, and can be read in both directions—prospectively and retrospectively, negatively and positively.

These transformations are so scrupulously observed that the adoption of a particular point of view implies, in the case of any given myth and any given population, a correlative change in all aspects of the myth belonging to the same community, in which the opposite point of view was expressed. To see this, we have only to compare the two Caraja myths, M$_{70}$ and M$_{85}$. The first deals with the prospective immortality of humans alone; immortality was denied them because they went from below to above and chose to settle on the surface of the earth where they found fruit and honey (natural products) in abundance, as well as the dead wood which allowed them to light a fire (and cook). On the other hand, M$_{85}$ contrasts the human con-dition with that of the animals that slough off their skins. Here the problem is no longer how to prolong life beyond its normal duration, but, as the myth shows, to restore youth to old men. Correlatively there is a descent instead of an ascent (the bird flying earthward); heavenly light is granted instead of earthly fire (which, as the myth is careful to point out, men already possess); and the arts of civilization replace natural resources. As has already been seen, the precondition of prospective immortality in M_{70} is not to hear; that of retrospective youth in M_{85} is to hear.

The apparent contradiction in the sensory codes disappears therefore in the following table, which repeats the demonstration in a condensed form:

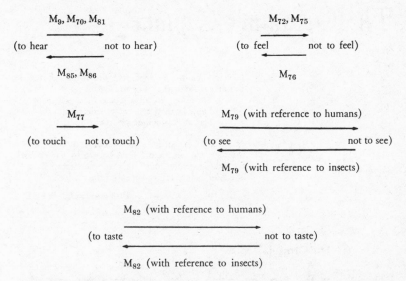

Only the Caduveo myth occupies an intermediary position, which can be explained from three different points of view. In the first place, the myth uses more than one code: the gustatory (do not smoke the pipe); the tactile (seize the creator by the armpit in order to take the proffered cigar by force); the visual (do not look at the girl). Secondly, of the three injunctions, the first and third are negative; the second is positive. Lastly—and this is the most important point—the problem of man's loss of immortality is presented simultaneously from both points of view: the hero sets out to rejuvenate (and resuscitate) old men and trees; but he himself dies sooner than he ought, because, by becoming a father, he has allowed himself to be caught up in the periodic cycle of the generations. In all other contexts the value of the terms of the sensory codes is regularly inverted, according to whether it is a matter of keeping death at bay or making certain of resurrection. The fugue is accompanied by a counterfugue.

2

The Opossum's Cantata

Je veux peindre en mes vers des mères le modèle,
Le sarigue, animal peu connu parmi nous,
　　Mais dont les soins touchants et doux,
　　Dont la tendresse maternelle,
　　Seront de quelque prix pour vous.

(I wish to describe, in my verse, a model mother,
the opossum, an animal little known in our country,
but whose gentle, touching care and maternal
affection cannot fail to appeal to the reader.)

FLORIAN, *Fables*, Book II, I.

a. THE OPOSSUM'S SOLO

I hope that in the preceding section several truths have been established. First of all, when considered from the formal point of view, myths which seem very different but all deal with the origin of man's mortality transmit the same message and can only be distinguished one from another by the code they use. Second, all the codes are similar in type; they use contrasts between tangible qualities, which are thus raised to the point of having a logical existence. Third, since man possesses five senses, there are five basic codes, which shows that all the empirical possibilities have been systematically explored and used. Fourth, one of the codes occupies a privileged position; this is the one connected with eating habits, the gustatory code, whose message is more often transmitted by the others than it is used to translate theirs, since it is through myths explaining the origin of fire, and thus of cooking, that we gain access to myths about man's loss of immortality; among the Apinaye, for instance, the origin of mortality is only one episode of the myth relating to the origin of fire. We thus begin to understand the truly essential place occupied by cooking in native thought: not only does cooking mark the transition from nature to culture, but through it and by means of it, the human state can be defined with all its attributes, even those that, like mortality, might seem to be the most unquestionably natural.

However, I must not conceal the fact that, in order to obtain these results, I have to some extent glossed over two difficulties. Of all the Ge versions, only the Apinaye variant contains the episode about man's loss of immortality. I did, of course, explain at the beginning of the third section why it was legitimate, in the case of the Ge myths, to fill in the gaps in certain versions by referring to more complete versions. It is nevertheless essential to try to discover whether the other Ge groups have a different conception of the origin of man's loss of immortality, and, if so, what exactly that conception is. Furthermore, in order to ensure the reciprocal convertibility of the codes, I have put forward the equation hard wood ≡ animal flesh, and it must be checked. Fortunately all this is feasible, since there exists a set of Ge myths in which the hardwood theme is associated with the theme of man's loss of immortality. Now although these myths—unlike M_9, on which I have chiefly based my argument—do not deal with the origin of fire, they nevertheless have an essentially culinary theme, since they deal with the origin of cultivated plants. Finally, by an unexpected twist, these myths make it possible to obtain decisive confirmation of conclusions I have already put forward.

M_{87}. *Apinaye. "The origin of cultivated plants"*

A young widower, who was sleeping out in the open air, fell in love with a star. The star appeared to him first of all in the form of a frog, then in the form of a beautiful young woman, whom he married. At that time men knew nothing of gardening, and they ate rotten wood with their meat instead of vegetables. Star-woman brought her husband sweet potatoes and yams and taught him to eat them.

The man carefully hid his tiny wife in a gourd, where she was discovered by his younger brother. From then on he lived openly with her.

One day, while Star-woman was bathing with her mother-in-law, she changed into an opossum and jumped on the old woman's shoulder until she drew the latter's attention to a large tree laden with cobs of maize. She explained that "the Indians were to eat this maize instead of rotten wood." As an opossum, she climbed up and threw down quantities of cobs. Then she reassumed human shape and showed her mother-in-law how to make maize cakes.

Delighted with this new food, men decided to chop down the maize tree with a stone axe. But when they stopped for breath, the notch they had cut closed up again. They sent two boys to the village for a better axe. On the way the two discovered a steppe opossum, which they killed and immediately roasted and consumed, though this animal[13] is taboo to boys. Hardly had they finished their meal when they turned into senile, stooping old men. An old magician-doctor succeeded in restoring their youth.

[13] TRANSLATORS' NOTE: The author has a note here stating that he has used the masculine form, *le sarigue,* because in this instance the sex of the opossum is not specified.

When the men had finally felled the tree with great difficulty, Star-woman advised them to make a clearing and plant maize. Star-woman, however, later returned to the sky after her husband's death. (Nim. 5, pp. 165–7.)

Another version of this same Apinaye myth (M_{87a}) contains neither the episode of the opossum nor that of the maize tree. We are simply told that Star-woman brought the cultivated plants from the sky and taught the Indians basket-making. However, her husband was unfaithful to her with a mortal, and she went back to the sky (C. E. de Oliveira, pp. 86–8).

As it is my intention, not to make a thorough analysis of this particular set, but only to use certain aspects of it to complete an argument the essential parts of which have already been put forward, I will shorten the other versions in such a way as to bring out the peculiar features of each.

M_{88}. Timbira. "The origin of cultivated plants"

The hero, enamored of a star-woman, was not a widower but a physically deformed man. After the young woman's hiding place was discovered by her husband's younger brother, Star-woman told her husband about maize (which in this case grew on stalks) and chewed the green seeds, which she spat in his face (into his mouth, according to M_{87a}). Then she taught the Indians how to prepare maize. In clearing part of the forest in order to start a plantation, the men broke their axe and sent a boy to the village to get another one. He came upon an old man busy cooking an opossum. Ignoring the old man's protests, the boy insisted on eating it. Immediately his hair grew white, and he was forced to use a stick to support his faltering steps.

Star-woman would have revealed many other secrets to her husband had he not insisted on her yielding to his amorous demands. She gave in to them but subsequently forced her husband to go with her up into the sky. (Nim. 8, p. 245.)

M_{89}. Kraho. "The origin of cultivated plants" (three versions)

When Star-woman discovered that men fed on *pau puba* (rotten wood: cf. p. 75), she showed her husband a tree covered with every kind of maize, the seeds of which filled the river that washed around the foot of the tree. As in the Timbira version, the brothers were at first afraid to eat maize, thinking it poisonous, but Star-woman succeeded in convincing them that it was not. A young child of the family was caught eating maize by the other villagers, who asked him what he was eating; they were surprised to learn that the maize came from the river in which they were in the habit of bathing. After the news had spread to all the tribes, the maize tree was felled, and the crop shared out. Then Star-woman showed her husband and brothers-in-law how to make use of the bacaba palm (which produces edible fruit: *Oenocarpus bacaba*) and taught them how to hollow out an oven in the ground, fill it with red-hot stones sprinkled with water, and use it to stew fruit. . . . The third and final stage in her teaching dealt with manioc, how to grow it and how to make it into cakes.

During all this time Star-woman and her husband remained strictly chaste.

One day while her husband was away hunting, an Indian raped the young woman, and she bled. She prepared a philter with which she poisoned the entire community. Then she went back up into the sky, leaving cultivated plants to the few survivors.

The second version states clearly that when Star-woman came down from the sky, men were still feeding on rotten wood and the remnants of ant heaps. They grew maize, but only for its decorative quality (the informant is an educated halfbreed). Star-woman taught them how to prepare and eat it, but the quantity of maize available was not enough for their needs. Star-woman, who was already pregnant, taught her husband how to clear the forest and start a plantation. She went back up into the sky and returned with manioc, watermelons, gourds, rice, potatoes, yams, and groundnuts. The story ends with a cookery lesson.

The third version, obtained from a halfbreed, describes Star-woman as being already married, although still a virgin; she becomes the victim of gang rape and punishes the culprits by spitting her poisonous saliva into their mouths. Then she goes back up into the sky. (Schultz, pp. 75–86.)

Among the Kayapo (Gorotire and Kubenkranken), there seems to be no connection between the myth about Star-woman, whether or not she is the donor of cultivated plants, and another myth describing how these plants were revealed to man by a small animal. Only the second of these myths is known among the Gorotire:

M_{90}. Kayapo-Gorotire. "The origin of cultivated plants"

In the days when Indians ate only tree fungi and powdered rotten wood, a woman was told about the existence of maize by a small rat, while she was bathing. The maize grew on an enormous tree where parrots and monkeys were fighting each other for its possession. The trunk was so thick that the Indians had to go to the village to fetch another axe. On the way the young men killed and ate a savannah opossum and were turned into old men. Sorcerers tried to restore their youth, but without success. Since then it has been strictly forbidden to eat the flesh of the opossum.

Thanks to maize, the Indians had plenty to eat. As their numbers increased, tribes with different languages and customs came into existence. (Banner 1, pp. 55–7.)

Among the Kubenkranken (M_{91}: Métraux 8, pp. 17–18), Star-woman is replaced by a woman who is the daughter of a marriage between a man and rain. In order to feed her son, the woman returned to the sky (where she was born) and brought back cultivated plants (potatoes, gourds, and bananas). Here is a summary of the other myth:

M_{92}. Kayapo-Kubenkranken. "The origin of cultivated plants (maize)"

After men had obtained fire from the jaguar (cf. M_8), an old woman was pestered by a rat (*amyuré*) while bathing with her granddaughter. The rat finally succeeded in drawing her attention to the maize tree; so many heads of maize had fallen into the river that it was difficult to bathe there. The villagers enjoyed the old woman's cooking and started to fell the maize tree. But every morning they found that the gash made the previous evening had closed up again. So the men tried to set fire to the tree and sent a youth to the village to get an additional axe. On the way back the youth killed and roasted a long-tailed opossum (*ngina*): his companion warned him about eating "such an ugly animal." He ate it nevertheless and changed into an old man, "so old and so thin and weak that his cotton knee bands hung right down to his ankles."

The men succeeded in cutting down the tree which fell with a crash: they divided the maize among themselves. After this the various communities scattered. (Métraux 8, pp. 17–18.)

Like the Kayapo, the Sherente thought of the two myths as separate, but as might be expected in a definitely patrilineal society, they reversed the semantic valency of the feminine sky (which is here cannibalistic) without changing the significance of the sexual contrast between high and low:

M₉₃. Sherente. "The planet Jupiter"

One night Star (Jupiter) came down from the sky to a young bachelor who had fallen in love with her. The young man hid the star in a gourd, where she was discovered by his brothers. Star told her lover and invited him to accompany her to the sky. Everything was different from its equivalent on earth. Everywhere he saw smoked or roasted human flesh, and when bathing he saw horribly mutilated shapes with open body cavities. He escaped by sliding down the bacaba palm up which he had climbed; and when he got back to earth, he related his adventure. But soon after he died, and his soul went back to Jupiter, and now he is a star beside her in the heavens. (Nim. 7, p. 184.)

An older version (M₉₃ₐ) states that, on opening the gourd, the brothers were terrified at the sight of the young woman, whom they took to be "an animal with fiery eyes." When the man reached the sky, he thought it looked like "a large desolate field." His wife tried in vain to keep him away from her parents' hut, so that he should not see the cannibalistic scene that was being enacted, or smell the putrid stench issuing from it. He escaped and died the instant he set foot on the earth (J. F. de Oliveira, pp. 395–6).

M₉₄. Sherente. "The origin of maize"

A woman was sitting with her child by the village pool and plaiting a trap to catch fish. A rat in human guise came and invited her to come to his house and eat maize, instead of the rotten wood that was the Indians' food in those days. He even allowed her to take away a maize flatcake but had warned her not to disclose where she had obtained it. The child, however, was caught eating his portion. The villagers extracted the truth from the woman and set off for the plantation. When the owner of the maize heard the people coming, he transformed himself into a rat and fled, leaving his plantation for the Sherente. (Nim. 1, pp. 184–5.)

This important set of myths is interesting for two reasons. First of all, it stresses the hardness of the tree on which the first maize grew. This detail might appear to invalidate my hypothesis concerning the congruence between meat and hardwood, in the Apinaye myth about the origin of fire. But on closer examination, it will be seen to confirm it.

The myths summarized above, like those dealing with the origin of fire (they follow immediately upon them, as is stated in M_{92}), contrast nature with culture and even with society: almost all the versions date the development of differences among peoples, languages, and customs from the discovery of maize. While the state of nature still prevailed, humans—earth-dwellers— practiced hunting but knew nothing of agriculture: they fed on meat which, according to several versions, was consumed raw, and on rotten vegetable matter: decayed wood and fungi. On the other hand, the "gods," who dwelt in the sky, were vegetarians, but their maize was not cultivated; it grew naturally and in limitless quantities on a forest tree, whose wood was particularly hard (whereas the stalks of cultivated maize are thin and brittle). So, as far as staple foodstuffs are concerned, maize is analagous with meat, which was man's staple food in the state of nature. This interpretation is confirmed by the Sherente version of the Star-woman myth (M_{93}) which inverts the elements of the other Ge versions of the same set. According to the Sherente version, men already possessed cultivated plants (which they acquired, according to the Sherente, in the days of the civilizing heroes, cf. M_{108}); it was therefore the celestial beings who were carnivorous, and even cannibalistic, since they fed on human flesh, either cooked (roasted or smoked) or rotted (soaked in water).

But the most important of all is that these new myths renew the theme of man's loss of immortality, by including it in an etiological set (the origin of cultivated plants) that is parallel to the one relating to the origin of fire, since both deal with the origin of cooking. The theme of man's mortality is treated in two ways, as different one from the other, it would seem, as each one, taken separately, differs from the way in which the theme is dealt with by the Apinaye myth about the origin of fire (M_9).

In the set we have just discussed, old age (or death) is forced upon humanity as if it were the price that had to be paid by the human race in exchange for cultivated plants; and either as a result of the revenge taken by Star-woman whose brothers-in-law had deprived her of her virginity (for until then she exchanged only chaste smiles with her husband); or because a group of youths ate the flesh of the opossum which was forbidden (or was subsequently forbidden after the fatal meal). Now the myths about man's loss of immortality already analyzed attributed it to quite different causes: positive or negative responses to noise, smells, contacts, sights, or tastes.

In dealing with these myths, I established that, over and above the codes employed, which might vary from one myth to the next while still remaining isomorphic, the point was to express the same relevant contrast, of a culinary nature, between cooked food and raw or rotten food. But now the problem has widened, because the myths that have just been introduced present us with other causes of man's mortality. What link can there be between the response to the call of rotten wood, the olfactory perception of the stench, the acquisition of. a limp penis, the nonperception of a particular scene, the nonconsumption of maggoty beer, on the one hand, and, on the other, the rape of a virgin and the eating of roast opossum? Such is the problem we must now solve, in the first place to validate the connection, affirmed by the myths, between the origin of man's mortality and that of cultivated plants (a demonstration parallel to the one, already given, of the connection between the origin of mortality and of cooking fire); next—and this is the most important consideration—because I shall thus have an additional proof to support my interpretations. Arithmetic uses the rule of "casting out the nines." I propose to establish that proofs also exist in the domain of mythology, and that "the proof by the opossum" can be just as convincing.

b. RONDO

The only zoologist I know of who has carried out research with a Ge tribe observes in regard to the Timbira: "I have never met among the Timbira a concept corresponding to the subdivision *Marsupialia,* and no mention has ever been spontaneously made to me of the marsupial pouch or of the part it plays in the development of the young. I have met with only one species, the gambe or mucura (*Didelphys marsupialia*): *ḳlo-ti*" (Vanzolini, p. 159). It is a fact that the opossum occupies a somewhat modest place in the myths of central Brazil, but only perhaps because of the uncertainty about how to refer to the animal. The old writers sometimes confused it with the fox (Portuguese, *raposa,* one of the Canidae), which the opossum physically resembles. The Indians themselves, it would seem, call some varieties of marsupials "rats." We have seen that, according to the versions of the Ge myth dealing with the origin of cultivated plants, Star (or the master of maize, M_{92}) changes into an animal which is sometimes called an opossum, sometimes a rat. The Timbira name for opossum, *ḳlo-ti*, is equally significant, since it seems to indicate that the natives put the opossum in the same category as the prea (*ḳlo*: cf. above, p. 128), merely adding the augmentative suffix. If the same classification occurs in other languages, we ought to ask ourselves whether the prea, which plays an important part in the Bororo and Opaye myths, is not correlative with, or in contrast to, the opossum. If the myths rarely mention the opossum, this may be because certain tribes put it in the same class as other animals, such as small marsupials, rodents, or Canidae.

Equally puzzling is the almost complete absence of any mythological reference to the marsupial pouch, except in the brief episode in the myth of Apapocuva origin, to which I shall refer later (p. 181). Themes of what might be called a marsupial nature are frequent, and I have already stressed the importance of one of them on more than one occasion: I mean the one about the snake's mistress (or mother), whose lover or ophidian son lives in her womb, which he can leave and return to at will.

The opossum (*sarigue*)—which is called *mucura* in northern Brazil, *timbu* in the northeast, *gamba* in the south, and *comadreja* in the Argentine—is the largest marsupial in South America and the only one of any value as food. Less important are the water opossum (*quica d'agua, Chironectes minimus*), the furry opossum (*mucura-xixica, Caluromys philander*), and dwarf species about the size of a shrewmouse (*catita, Marmosa pusilla, Peramys domestica*) (Guenther, pp. 168, 389; Gilmore, p. 364; Ihering, "Quica" entry). The opossum proper is between 70 and 90 centimeters long. The same word is used to designate four Brazilian species: *Didelphys aurita* (from the north of the Rio Grande do Sul to the Amazon); *D. paraguayensis* (Rio Grande do Sul); *D. marsupialis* (Amazonia); *D. albiventris* (central Brazil) (Ihering, "Gamba" entry). The opossum appears in several types of narrative, which at first might seem to divide into two categories: myths of origin and humorous tales. Let us look at both in turn.

The chief characters in Tucuna mythology are twins called Dyai and Epi. The first was responsible for the creation of humanity, the arts, laws, and customs. The second was a trickster, a muddler, and an impudent fellow; if he wanted to take animal form, he often changed into an opossum. It was he (M_{95}) who discovered his brother's secret wife in the bone flute where Dyai had hidden her (cf. M_{87}–M_{89}, M_{93}); this wife, Tul, was born of the fruit of *Poraqueiba sericea*. He forced her into betraying her presence by making her laugh (cf. M_{46}, M_{47}) at the fish leaping to escape from the heat of the fire, while he himself undid his belt and danced, so that his penis quivered like the fish. He raped his sister-in-law with such violence that the sperm spouted from her mouth and nostrils. She immediately became pregnant and was too big to go back into her hiding place. Dyai punished his brother by forcing him to scrape his own flesh; and he threw the pulp to the fish (Nim. 13, pp. 127-9).

The rape scene confirms Epi's opossumlike nature. The opossum has a forked penis; hence the belief, attested throughout the whole of North America, that the animal copulates through the nostrils, and that the female sneezes its young into its marsupial pouch (Hartman, pp. 321-3).[14]

---

[14] The trickster in Mataco myths possesses a *double penis* (Métraux 3, p. 33), and his Toba equivalent is a "fox."

American beliefs such as these raise a problem of comparative mythology. They occur in the Old World (where there are no marsupials) with reference to weasels. Galanthis was turned into a weasel by Lucina, as a punishment for having helped Alcmena to give birth, and so that she herself would thereafter bring forth her children through

I noted in passing the relation between the myth above and the Ge set about the celestial wife of a mortal. In the Ge myths Star is an opossum who is violated by her brothers-in-law: here the daughter of the *Poraqueiba* tree (the fruit of which has fallen [= descended] to the ground, just as the star came down to earth, first of all in the shape of a frog) is raped by her brother-in-law, who is an opossum. When we move from the Ge to the Tucuna, therefore, the role of the opossum is reversed; and it is interesting to note, at the same time, that among the Tucuna the gift of cultivated plants is attributed to ants and not to the opossum (M54: Nim. 13, p. 130). I shall give my interpretation of this transformation later pp. 180 ff.).

It is clear that the Tucuna myth repeats, in a different context, an incident from one of the most famous Tupi myths (M96), a version of which Thevet noted in the sixteenth century and which is still current: a woman who was pregnant by the civilizing god Maire Ata, was traveling alone, and the child inside her belly conversed with her and guided her on her way. However, because his mother refused "to give him the small vegetables that were growing by the wayside," he decided to sulk and said no more. The woman lost her way and arrived at the house of a man called Sarigoys. During the night he took advantage of her, so that she became pregnant with another son who kept the first company. . . . As a punishment the man was turned into an opossum (Thevet in Métraux 1, pp. 235-6).

The same episode is found among the Urubu, the Tembe, and the Shipaya, who call the seducer Mikur, Mykura, and Mukura, respectively. These names are very close to the word for opossum in lingua geral: *mucura*.

In South America the opossum also appears as the hero of a tragicomic tale. To quote only a few examples, the Mundurucu (M97), the Tenetehara (M98), and the Vapidiana (M99) tell the story of Opossum's disastrous experiences with the sons-in-law he had chosen for himself. Each one had a special gift for fishing, hunting, or cultivating the land. Opossum tried to imitate them and failed, often even hurting himself in the process. Each time he ordered his daughter to take another husband, but with even more disastrous results. Finally Opossum burned or bled to death (Kruse 2, pp. 628-30; Murphy 1, pp. 118-20; Wirth, 2, pp. 205-8; Wagley and Galvão, pp. 151-4).

---

her mouth, whence had come the lie that had deceived the goddess (Ovid *Metamorphoses* L. ix. v. 297 ff.). The weasel was supposed to give birth through the mouth (Plutarch, *Isis and Osiris*, § xxxix); at the same time, wicked women were compared to weasels (Gubernatis II. p. 53). The New World, where weasels are also found, believed that they could facilitate childbirth, because of the ease with which they slipped out of their holes (L.-S. 9, pp. 82-3). Finally, a version of the Bororo myth about the twins (M46), which is a close parallel of the Tupi myth above, refers to one of the Mustelidae (Portuguese *irara*, *Tayra* species) as playing the kind of role that the Tupi attribute to the opossum (Colb. 1, pp. 114-15; 2, pp. 179-80).

The Mundurucu version states that these events took place at a time when opossums were men. On the other hand, the sons-in-law, who were in turn a fisherbird, a bedbug, a pigeon, a honey-eating "fox," a hummingbird, an otter, and a tick, also had human form but "were really animals." This detail—which provides a curious echo of the belief held by the Koasati, a tribe living in the southeastern United States, that the opossums of mythology employed articulate speech (Swanton, p. 200)—makes it possible to see that, over and above the diversity of tone, there exists a basic framework common to all the "opossum stories," whether they are myths of origin or farcical tales. The etiological myths depict gods in human form but with animal names; the tales depict animals in human form. In every case the opossum's function is an ambiguous one. In the Tucuna myth (M_{95}) he is a god who copulates as the opossum is supposed to do in nature. Although he is an animal in the Mundurucu tale (M_{97}), he is nevertheless a man and unlike the other beasts. Finally, according to whether we are considering the myths or the tales, his position seems to be reversed:

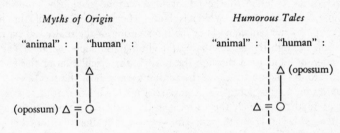

Myths of Origin   *Humorous Tales*

NOTE: The Tucuna myth is careful to state that the girl who was turned into the fruit of the *Poraqueiba* is the daughter of the twins' brother-in-law (the sister's husband). Therefore, in the table on the left, the woman's father is not introduced merely for the sake of symmetry.

Huxley, who has considered the problem of the symbolism of the opossum, claims that two features account for a certain dimly perceived ambiguity: as we have already seen, the opossum has a forked penis, which makes him particularly capable of begetting twins; when he senses danger, he pretends to be dead and therefore seems able to come back to life again (Huxley, p. 195). Apart from the fact that no myth supposes the opossum to have fathered both the twins, but only one, nothing seems so unreliable as conjectures of this sort, which are derived from an eclectic selection of folk tales or even improvised to support a particular argument. It is never possible to postulate an interpretation: it must emerge from the myths themselves or from the ethnographic context, and as far as possible from both. If, in order to understand the semantic function of the opossum, I now propose to take a quick look at the mythology of the southeastern part of the United States, this is not simply because the great mythical themes of the New World are known to be widespread throughout the whole of America, and that it is possible to move, via a series of intermediaries, from one hemisphere to the other: this is a method of research that cannot replace conclusive proof, but at least it will help with the formulation of a hypothesis that the myths we have so far analyzed will confirm in the most cogent manner.

The Creek and the Cherokee Indians believed that the female opossum conceived its young without any help from the male (Swanton, p. 41; Mooney, pp. 265, 449). The Cherokee explain in their myths that the opossum has no wife; and that his tail, which used to be very bushy and of which he was inordinately proud, was shaved off by the grasshopper acting on the rabbit's instructions; and lastly that his paws never become frostbitten (Mooney, pp. 266, 269, 273, 431, 439). The story of the too beautiful tail which was shorn by the grasshopper or lost its fur through the action of fire or water, is also common to the Creek, the Koasati, and the Natchez. It was on this occasion that the skunk acquired the opossum's fine tail (Swanton, pp. 41, 200, 249). Taken together with information we have already given, the characteristics assigned to the opossum or *sarigue* obviously point to an ambiguous sexual nature, which is both deficient (celibacy of the male, procreation by the female without the intervention of the male, and symbolic castration through the loss of the beautiful tail) and superabundant (violent copulation or copulation through the nostrils, the ejaculation of the fetus or sperm through the nostrils, and the constant warmth of the feet).

Having made this point, let us now return to South America to consider a set of myths in which the tortoise is the recurrent figure, with, as his opponent, the jaguar or the alligator—occasionally the two together—and sometimes the opossum.

M₁₀₀. *Kayapo-Gorotire. "The jaguar and the tortoise"*

The jaguar despised the tortoise because it was slow and had a feeble voice. The tortoise challenged the jaguar: let each of them in turn be shut up in a hole, to see which would hold out the longer. Without air, water, or food, the tortoise held out for several days. Then the jaguar submitted to the ordeal, but as the days passed, its voice grew weaker and weaker. When the tortoise unblocked the hole, the jaguar was dead: there was only a swarm of flies hovering over its remains. (Banner 1, p. 46.)

M₁₀₁. *Mundurucu. "The jaguar, the alligator, and the tortoise"*

Some monkeys invited the tortoise to eat fruit with them at the top of a tree. They helped him to climb up and then went off, leaving him stranded at the top.

A jaguar happened to pass by. He advised the tortoise to come down in the hope that he might make a meal of him. The tortoise refused, and the jaguar decided to stay where he was and to keep his eyes fixed on his prey. Eventually he grew weary and lowered his head. The tortoise then let himself fall from the tree, and his hard shell broke the jaguar's skull.[15] "Weh, weh, weh," laughed the tortoise, clapping his hands. He ate the jaguar and out of one of the jaguar's bones made himself a flute, on which he played a song of victory.

Another jaguar heard the music and, anxious to avenge his companion, attacked the tortoise, which however took refuge in a hole. An alligator embarked on a discussion with the tortoise about whether fava beans grow on vines or trees. Annoyed at being contradicted, the alligator stopped up the hole and came back every day to provoke the tortoise: he claimed that a lot of wood fungi (on which tortoises feed) were growing in the forest. But the tortoise was not deceived. He discarded his old shell, secreted another one, and escaped.

Unable to obtain a reply, the alligator opened the hole in order to eat up the tortoise which he thought was dead. The latter, however, suddenly appeared from behind and shut the alligator in the hole, laughing "Weh, weh, weh," and clapping his hands. He came back the next day, and it was now his turn to provoke his enemy: did the alligator not know that there were a lot of fish just spoiling in the river? Soon the alligator began to dry out (cf. M_{12}) and grow weak. His voice became inaudible, then gave out altogether: he was dead. The tortoise laughed "Weh, weh, weh," and clapped his hands. (Murphy 1, pp. 122–3; Kruse 2, pp. 636–7; Tenetehara variant in Wagley and Galvão, pp. 155–6.)

In another Mundurucu version the tortoise triumphs over the jaguar because he can go without drinking for a longer period than the jaguar. He parades in front of the jaguar, after wetting his shell with urine, and sends the animal off to look for the spring that he claims to have discovered (Murphy 1, p. 124).

The same myth exists among the Tenetehara and in various tribes in Amazonia and Guiana, except that the jaguar's (or alligator's) place is often taken by the opossum:

M_{102}. Tenetehara. *"The tortoise and the opossum"*

The tortoise challenged the opossum to a fasting competition. He dug his hole first, and for two months the opossum came every day to inquire how the tortoise was. Each time the tortoise answered with a strong voice that it intended to carry on with the ordeal. Actually he had discovered another entrance to the hole and came out every day to eat. When the opossum's turn came, he could last no more than ten days, and died. The tortoise invited his friends to eat the opossum's remains. (Wagley and Galvão, p. 154; for the almost identical Amazonian versions, cf. Hartt, pp. 28, 61–3; for the Guiana versions, cf. Roth 1, p. 223.)

Certain aspects of the myths above will be studied elsewhere. For the moment I merely wish to note that they present the opossum as inter-

[15] By transformation of the corresponding episode in M_{55} (the jaguar keeps his head raised and opens his jaws) which, as has already been proved (pp. 131–2), belongs to the same set as the reverse episode in M_8.

changeable with the jaguar or the alligator, whom we know to be, respectively, master of fire (M_7 to M_{12}) and master of water (M_{12}).[16] We may therefore wonder what the crucial significance of the contrast is between the tortoise (an invariant term) and the opossum, the jaguar, and the alligator (interchangeable terms). The myths are quite explicit on the subject of the tortoise: either they state that the tortoise can remain underground for a long time and do without food and drink, because it is a hibernating animal; or they describe it as feeding off tree fungi and decayed wood (M_{101}; cf. too M_{82}; and for the same belief among the Urubu, Huxley, p. 149). The tortoise, then, has a twofold claim to be master of decay: it is imputrescible, and it eats decayed matter. The alligator, too, eats decomposed flesh (M_{101}) but only in the water where the decay does not give off a stench (cf. M_{72}: it is only when they come out of the water that the aquatic spirits start to smell). Lastly, we know that the jaguar can be defined in relation to the axis joining the raw and the cooked, thus excluding the rotten.

The fact that in all the myths we are studying, the relevant contrast is between what is foul smelling and what is not foul smelling, what is liable to decay and that which cannot decay, comes out clearly in the repetition of the same detail which is often expressed in identical terms, whoever the opponents of the tortoise happen to be and no matter how remote from each other are the communities in which the myths originate. When the tortoise receives no reply from its rival, he unblocks the hole and, in place of the jaguar or the alligator, finds "a swarm of flies hovering over the remains" (M_{100}, M_{101}); or in place of the opossum; "a swarm of flies" (Amazonia: Hartt, p. 28; Tastevin 1, pp. 283-6); "many flies" (Rio Jurua: Hartt, p. 62); "only flies on his dead body were alive" (Warao, Carib; Roth 1, p. 223).[17]

Let us now go back and discuss the final episode of the stories in the "opossum and his sons-in-law" group (cf. p. 172). An Amazonian version ends with the opossum's misadventure: he is rescued after having been swallowed by a tucuhare fish (*Cichla ocellaris*): "Ever since he has been ugly and foul smelling (*feio et fedorento*) because of the heat in the fish's belly" (Barbosa Rodrigues, pp. 191-4). It should be remembered that the same Portuguese word *feio* is used as an argument for the ban on eating the flesh of the opossum in one of the Kubenkranken myths about the origin of cultivated plants (M_{92}). On the other hand, the Mundurucu and Vapidiana versions of the "opossum and his sons-in-law" end with an episode in which the

---

[16] It sometimes happens that these functions are reversed: cf. Amorim, pp. 371-3; and C. E. de Oliveira, p. 97.

[17] The same detail occurs in an Apinaye tale in which the armadillo is the victim (C. E. de Oliveira, p. 97). The interchangeability of the armadillo and the opossum is also found among the Kayapo; the clumsiness characteristic of Opossum as father-in-law in the "opossum and his sons-in-law" cycle is transferred to the armadillo O'oimbre. Cf. Murphy 1, p. 119 (Mundurucu) and Métraux 8, p. 30 (Kayapo-Kubenkranken). But among the Ge the opossum is called upon to perform different and nobler duties.

opossum burns his tail (Mundurucu) or falls into the water (Vapidiana). So, too, does another Amazonian version (Barbosa Rodrigues, pp. 173–7).[18]

We have seen that, according to the Creek, the hair on the opossum's tail was destroyed through the action of fire or water. In other words: in one instance it was burned; in another it rotted. Does this not mean that there are two kinds of stench: one caused by prolonged exposure to fire; the other by prolonged immersion in water?

Certain myths of the southeastern part of the United States establish a close connection between the opossum and the skunk (*Mephitis mephitica, suffocans*). The Hitchiti tell the story of how the skunk rescued the opossum from the wolves by spraying the latter with its foul liquid (Swanton, p. 158). In this particular myth the wolves play the same kind of part as that played by the jaguars in M101; it is extraordinary that in the southeastern United States, a part elsewhere played by the tortoise should be transferred to the skunk, while at the same time the relations among the opossum, the tortoise, and the jaguar are profoundly modified; the tortoise (terrapin) helps the opossum by giving it back its lost young and by shaping the marsupial pouch so that they are better protected (Swanton, pp. 199–200); the opossum helps the panther to hunt by making the deer believe that the beast of prey is dead, and a mere carcass that they can approach without fear; the panther takes advantage of the trick to kill them (*ibid.*, p. 200). In spite of the geographical remoteness, these are undoubtedly myths belonging to the same set.

The Cherokee have a myth explaining the skunk's stench. To punish it for stealing, the other animals threw it into the fire, and since then it has remained black and had a smell of burning (Mooney, p. 277). Consequently, in North as in South America, the smell of burning and the smell of decay go together: they are the two modes of stench. Sometimes they are associated with the skunk and the opossum; sometimes the opossum alone bears the onus of expressing one or the other modality.

The analysis above leads us to the conclusion that the semantic function of the opossum is to *signify stench*. The Catawba, who used to live in North and South Carolina, referred to the opossum by a term with the approximate meaning of "he who slobbers fluid much" (Speck, p. 7). The Taurepan of Guiana regard the opossum as an animal soiled with faecal matter (K.G. 1, p. 141). In an Amazonian myth of unspecified origin (M103), a young girl escapes from the opossum's amorous advances, because she recognizes the

[18] And also, as Barbosa Rodrigues notes, in the Popol Vuh (cf. Reynaud, p. 49). I have deliberately avoided using the myths of the advanced civilizations of Central America and Mexico because, having been reformulated by educated speakers, they call for prolonged syntagmatic analysis before they can be used as paradigms. I am, however, not unaware of the fact that in many respects they have their place in several of the sets I have defined. For the opossum's place in old Mexico, cf. Sahagun, L. VI, chap. 28, and XI, chap. 4, § 4; and Seler, Vol. IV, pp. 506–13.

animal by its stench (Couto de Magalhães, pp. 253–7; Cavalcanti, pp. 161–77). Another myth from the same region (M_{104}), which in somewhat obscure terms associates the opossum with the aging process—that is, with man's loss of immortality—describes the hut of three old women who have been turned into opossums: "The stench was so powerful that it was impossible to enter the hut" (Amorim, p. 450). The Cayua of southern Brazil relate how the opossum beat the dog in a race by spraying it with urine (Schaden 1, p. 117).[19] The opossum, as we have seen, is variously described in myths as "putrid beast," "putrid tail," and "singed tail." The Tupinamba myth about the twins (M_{96}), to which reference has already been made, expressly draws attention to this same aspect. After he had raped Maire Ata's wife, the seducer "was changed into a beast, which is called by the name of the metamorphosed man, that is, Sarigoys, and whose skin is extremely foul smelling" (Thevet in Métraux 1, p. 236). Travelers, as well as Indians, were struck by this same detail: "The opossum gives off a foul smell" noted the *Encyclopédie* compiled by Diderot and d'Alembert ("Philandre" entry). More recent observers also stress that the opossum "emits a noxious odor" (Guenther, p. 168), "an extremely offensive odor" (Tastevin 1, p. 276); "its glands secrete a most disagreeable odor" (Ihering, "Gamba" entry); "it gives off a dreadful stench," whence the name—derived from that of the opossum—which is given to the waterlily with an unpleasant smell (Ahlbrinck, "aware" entry).

A Bolivian myth brings together most convincingly all the attributes of the opossum, according to the natural philosophy of the South America Indians:

M_{105}. Tacana. *"The origin of the opossum"*

There was once an Indian woman who caught the ticks with which the tapir was infested, while it was asleep. She wrapped them up in a leaf, cooked them in a pot, and ate them (cf. M_{66}).

The "schie" bird (*Crotophaga ani*), which normally fed on the tapir's vermin, complained about this unfair rivalry to the vulture, who promised revenge by changing the woman into an opossum.

The vulture flew over the woman and spattered her with its droppings: there was so much that she was bent double and could only walk with difficulty. The vulture then threw her to the ground, tore out her hair, and with his feces stuck it all over her body. Again using his excrement as glue, he affixed a young snake's tail to the unfortunate woman's rear: the woman shrank to the size of an opossum. The vulture picked up a root, chewed it, and spat it onto the opossum's fur in order to dye it yellow. He made the woman's face into an opossum's snout by sticking on a palm bud.

[19] This south Brazilian myth is illustrated in a ritual dance performed by the eastern Timbira, in which the skunk (instead of the opossum) is represented by a dancer carrying a gourd full of water which he throws over pursuing dogs, personified by women. The latter flee howling, like dogs that have been sprayed with the skunk's fluid (Nim. 8, p. 230).

The vulture told the woman that she would give birth only to ticks, and that those not eaten by the "schie" bird would later be changed into opossums. The opossum eats only the brains and eggs of birds. It sleeps during the day and hunts at night. . . . (Hissink and Hahn, pp. 116–17.)

We can now understand how the Ge myths came to attribute the origin of man's loss of immortality, either to the answering of the call of rotten wood (M_9), or to the inhaling of a smell of decay emanating from the water spirits (M_{73}), or to the eating of the flesh of the opossum (M_{87}, M_{88}, M_{90}, M_{92}). The phenomenon is in each case the same: putrefaction is being accepted through one or other of the sensory channels—the ear, the nose, or the mouth. In this initial connection my interpretations have already been proved valid.

Nevertheless, one difficulty remains. Why, in the Ge myths about the origin of cultivated plants, does Star have to become an opossum in order to reveal the existence of maize to man? We should note, in the first place, that this theme does not recur in all contexts. But wherever it is absent, it is replaced by others: Star *spits out* the maize into her husband's face (M_{88}) or mouth (M_{87a}): like the Catawba opossum, she is therefore a "slobberer"; she *bleeds* after being raped and becomes a murderess (M_{89}); after being raped, she kills her brothers-in-law by *spitting into* their mouths (M_{89}). In all contexts she represents defilement, sometimes in the form of an animal whose skin secretes a foul-smelling fluid, or sometimes in the form of a human creature who is both defiling and defiled. A myth belonging to the same set and current among the Aguaruna of Upper Maranhão (M_{106}) tells how Star changed her urine into food (Guallart, p. 68).

After isolating the above invariant feature, I can bring out the common structure of the myths of origin in which the opossum figures—that is, the Tupi-Tucuna group and the Ge group. In both groups the leading characters are the same: a woman, her husband, and the husband's brother or brothers (sometimes a "false brother"). The pattern of relations through marriage is symmetrical with that which seemed to be the underlying pattern in the myths explaining the origin of wild pigs, and which consisted of a man, his sister or his sisters and their husbands:

(1)	(2)
O = △ △	△ = O △

It is remarkable that among the Ge both these patterns correspond to myths of origin (1) relating to *cultivated/plants/*, (2) relating to *wild/animals/*.

In the Tupi-Tucuna set, however, the part of the opossum is taken by the husband's brother, who rapes his sister-in-law; while in the Ge set it is taken by the sister-in-law. But in each case the food is given a different name. The

Tucuna wife (M₉₅) is a fallen fruit, which has been changed into a woman. A Urubu version (M₉₅ₐ) adds that the fruit, when it fell to earth, was full of worms (Huxley, p. 192).[20] So the divine woman here represents vegetable decay, which is less obvious than animal decay, and this involves a double transformation. First of all, the initial gap separating her from men is lessened, since she falls as fruit from a tree, instead of coming down from the sky as a star. Secondly, whereas in the Ge set she is metonymical—and a real animal during *part* of the story—her opossum function becomes metaphorical in the Tupi group: her child talks in her belly, *as if* he had already been born and were using the maternal womb as a marsupial pouch. Conversely, the Tucuna version, from which this last theme is absent, transforms the brother-in-law who committed rape from a metaphorical opossum (copulation through the nostrils, *like* the opossum), into a metonymical opossum; when he fills his foreskin with a sticky white paste and argues that the presence of this "tallow" proves him to be still a virgin. Now this act of defilement is also vegetable in origin, since the trickster uses the pulp from the fruit of the paxiubinha palm (*Iriartela sebigera* Mart.). I should add that in the Tucuna version, in which the opossum function is assumed by the brother-in-law, the fruit whose form the divine wife takes for a time is that of the umari (spiny andira) tree, the exquisite scent of which is mentioned in several Amazonian myths (Amorim, pp. 13, 379), whereas the opossum is foul smelling. Finally, still in the same version, the woman has sexual relations with her husband—contrary to what happens in the Ge versions—no doubt in order to emphasize, as a Choco myth of the same set does (M₁₀₇), that her husband "needed her solely in her capacity as a cook" (Wassen I, p. 131). Vegetable decay, therefore, denotes normal sexual activity (= conjugal) in the woman, and normal chastity (= puerile) in the man. Animal decay connotes abnormal sexual activity (= rape) in the male, abnormal chastity (= conjugal) in the woman.

Once we have solved the problem of the inversion of the opossum (male or female rapist or raped), we can see what the personifications of the opossum in both the Tupi and Ge sets have in common. In the Tupi myths the opossum, a male, rapes a human, who is already a mother when he makes her pregnant. In the Ge myths the opossum, a female and not a mother (since, although married, she is a virgin), is violated by humans and provides

[20] This is the fruit of the apui tree, which figures frequently in Mundurucu myths under the same name or under the name of *apoi*: "*Apui* or *iwapui*, a parasitic tree which grows on the branches of other trees and throws out suckers, some of which take root in the ground, while others wind round the parent tree and choke it" (Tastevin 1, *Addenda*, p. 1285). It is the tree that holds up the celestial vault, and its roots, like mucus, came out of the nostrils of Daïïru, the trickster. They are also vermin-ridden (Murphy 1, pp. 79, 81, 86). Another version tells how the apui tree's roots came out of the trickster's eyes, ears, nose, and anus (Kruse 3, Vol. XLVII, p. 1000; cf. also Strömer, p. 137). The apui tree has a twofold affinity with fecal matter and decay, and this strengthens a similar connotation in the Urubu myth.

them with food. The Tupi heroine is a mother who refuses to suckle her child (she illtreats her son even while he is still in her womb). The Ge heroine is a wetnurse who refuses to become a mother. That is true of all the Ge versions except the Sherente version (M₉₃) which, as we saw, changes the semantic valencies of sky and earth: the celestial woman is described in negative terms as the daughter of cannibals, and powerless to save her husband. At the same time (M₁₀₈), the role of donors of cultivated plants (manioc in this case) is given to human females—that is, terrestrial women —and furthermore to women who are already mothers and keen to carry out their duty by suckling their young. They become anxious when they leave their babies too long while working in the fields, and come running back so fast that the milk spurts out of their swollen breasts. The drops that fall on the ground germinate in the form of manioc seedlings, both sweet and bitter (Nim. 7, p. 182).²¹ In the last analysis, the contradiction inherent in the personage of the opossum is explained in a brief episode in the myth of the origin of the Apapocuva (M₁₀₉): after their mother's premature death the "elder" of the twins is at a loss to feed his little brother who is still at the breast. He begs the opossum to help him, and the latter, before taking on the task of wetnurse, is careful to lick its chest clean of offensive secretions. As a reward, the god gives it the marsupial pouch and promises that henceforth it will give birth painlessly (Nim. 1, p. 326).²² The Apapocuva

²¹ It will be noticed in passing that this Sherente myth follows an opposite pattern to that of the Bororo myth about the origin of diseases (M₅). In the Bororo myth a mother who had abandoned her child, and who gorges on fish, exudes diseases. In the Sherente myth mothers who come close to their children and produce a generous flow of milk exude certain cultivated plants. The fact that the plant concerned is manioc, including the toxic varieties, will take on its full significance once we have assembled the group of myths dealing with the origin of poison, to which M₅ belongs (cf. p. 179).

²² Cadogan gives another Guarani version (M₁₀₉ₐ), according to which, while the elder of the twins is busy reconstituting his mother's body, the ravenous younger brother rushes at the breast, which is not quite finished, and undoes the whole operation (*id.* in Guarani version M₁₀₉ᵦ; Borba, p. 65). The elder twin loses heart and changes his mother into a paca (*Coelogenys paca, jaicha* in Guarani, but the text also gives *mbyku,* which, in Montoya, is the very word translated by "opossum"). Since that day, the sun delays its rising every time a paca has been caught in a trap during the night (Cadogan, pp. 77-8, 86-7, 197, 202).

The episode contained in the Apapocuva myth reappears in Mundurucu mythology in a slightly modified form:

M₁₀₉c. *Mundurucu. "The childhood of Karusakaibö"*

An adulterous woman tried by every possible means to get rid of her bastard son: she abandoned him on the ground, or in a stream, and even went as far as to bury him alive. But the child survived every kind of illtreatment.

Finally an opossum rescued it and acted as its wetnurse. This explains why the opossum gives birth painlessly. (Kruse 3, Vol. XLVI, p. 920. Cf. M₁₄₄ and M₁₄₅ and p. 271, n. 35.)

myth therefore succeeds in synthetizing the two characteristics of the opossum, which the Tupinamba myth and the Ge myths treated separately. The opossum's stench derives from the Tupinamba myth; its role as foster mother from the Ge myths. However, the synthesis is possible only because the apparently absent function appears in a disguised form in each instance: in the Tupinamba myths, where the opossum is a man, he makes a woman pregnant (which is the masculine way of "suckling" her); in the Ge myths, where the opossum is a woman, she pollutes men who feed on her (literally, when they eat her; metaphorically, when they rape her and she bleeds), by turning them into decrepit old men or corpses.

A Caraja myth clinches the question of the transformation by showing what happens when the "nurse" assumes the masculine sex, thus ceasing to be a female opossum but retaining its function as donor of cultivated plants:

M_{110}. Caraja. "The origin of cultivated plants"

In olden days the Caraja did not know how to clear land for cultivation. They fed on wild berries, fish, and game. One night the elder of two sisters was gazing at the evening star. She told her father that she would like to have it to play with, and he laughed at her. But the following day the star came down from the sky, into the hut, and asked to marry the daughter. He was a bowed, wrinkled old man with completely white hair, and she would have nothing to do with him. Moved by his tears, the younger sister married him.

The following day the man went to talk to the great river and walked in the water. As the water flowed between his legs, he picked up heads of maize, manioc cuttings, and the seeds of all the plants that are grown by the Caraja today. Then he went off into the forest to make a garden, and forbade his wife to follow him. She disobeyed him and saw her husband change into an extremely beautiful young man, richly clad, and with decorative paintings all over his body. The elder daughter claimed him as her husband, but he remained faithful to the younger. The elder sister turned into a nocturnal bird (*Caprimulgus*) with a mournful song. (Baldus 3, pp. 19–21; 4, p. 87; Botelho de Magalhães, pp. 274–6.)

In comparison with the Ge set, several remarkable changes can be noted. The widowed or ill-favored hero, who loves solitude, becomes a young girl with parents with whom she can converse. The man immediately falls in love with the star; the woman merely desires it as a plaything. The meeting, instead of taking place in the bush, occurs in the hut. The Ge hero marries Star, who is raped by his brothers. The Caraja heroine rejects him, and it is her sister who marries him. Cultivated plants are either revealed objectively by a woman in the forest or created symbolically by a man in water. Most important of all, Star in the Ge myths changes humans from young into old men. The Caraja star changes himself from an old man into a youth. His dual personage thus retains the ambiguous nature of the opossum. Yet whereas the Ge myths describe a real situation (the periodicity of human life) through the medium of zoological metaphor, the Caraja myth describes an unreal situation (the rejuvenation of old men) but uses literal terms.

When I first broached the subject of the loss of immortality, I put forward the hypothesis (p. 151) that, in all the myths under discussion, decay was the diametrical opposite of cultivated plants. The "opossum proof" gives definite confirmation of this, for such in fact is the role played by this putrescent (and putrid) animal. Since it cannot be eaten except by old men who have nothing to fear from corruption, and since it belongs to the animal and not to the vegetable kingdom, the opossum personifies a kind of anti-agriculture which is at one at the same time pre- and pro-agriculture. For, in the "upside down" world that was the state of nature before the birth of civilization, all future things had to have their counterpart, even if only in a negative form, which was a kind of guarantee of their future existence. The opossum being, as it were, the reverse pattern of absent agriculture, was an indication of what its future form would be, and at the same time, as we are told in the myths, it is the instrument whereby men obtain agriculture. The introduction of agriculture by the opossum is therefore the result of the transformation of a mode of being into its converse.[23] A logical opposition is projected in time in the form of a relation of cause and effect. What creature could be better suited than the opossum to reconcile the two functions? Its marsupial nature combines antithetical characteristics, which become complementary only in it. For the opossum is the best of wetnurses, and yet it stinks.

c. Second Solo

The Ge myths describing the origin of man's loss of immortality are remarkable in several respects: first of all, their distribution is particularly dense: next, their subject matter shows a corresponding density. These myths arrange into a coherent system themes that, in all other contexts, occur in a state of dissociation: on the one hand, Star's marriage to a mortal and the

[23] The soil of the savannah cannot be cultivated; only that of the forest can be. Now in the Caraja myth about the origin of man's loss of immortality (M_{70}) men became mortal because they replied to the call of the seriema, "the savannah bird." And it seems clear that the Ge myths describing the origin of cultivated plants (and the loss of immortality) distinguish between two kinds of opossum: a forest species, whose form is taken by Star in order to reveal to men the existence of maize *in the forest,* but only on condition that they go off to the forest and look for it; and a *savannah* species which the young men imprudently eat, when they leave the forest in order to look for an axe in the village (cf. M_{87}, M_{90}) and as a result of which they are turned into old men. The existence of the two species analyzes the initial ambiguity by transposing it onto the ecological level. One species brings life, which is—at the present time—outside itself; the other death, which is within it.

As further support for my interpretation of the part played by the opossum, it can be noted that, among the communities of Costa Rica which belong to the Talamanca linguistic group, only professional gravediggers were entitled to go near corpses, carrion-eating vultures, and opossums (Stone, pp. 30, 47).

origin of cultivated plants; on the other hand, the discovery of the food-bearing tree and the origin of death and mortality.

To the southwest of the Ge region, the Mataco and the Ashluslay of the Gran Chaco are familiar with the story of the food-bearing tree (M_{111}); but the tree is described as being full of fish, and its bark is burst open by some foolhardy person, thus releasing water which spreads over the earth and destroys the human race. The story of Star also exists among the Toba and the Chamacoco of the Gran Chaco (M_{112}): out of pity a goddess marries an ugly, despised man whom women laugh at and cover with mucus. During a period of drought the goddess brings forth miraculous harvests, then goes back up into the sky with her husband. But in the sky the man is frozen because he is not allowed to go near the fire, which is cannibalistic. Or alternatively, when Star is discovered in the gourd where her husband has hidden her, she explodes in the face of the prying mortals and burns them. (Métraux 4, *passim*.)

To the north of the Ge region—that is, in Guiana—the story of the star who married a mortal weakens and is reversed: the contrast between the star and the opossum is gradually obliterated in the personage of the vulture's daughter, who comes originally from the atmospheric sky, as opposed to the empyrean sky, and with whom a man falls in love in spite of the fact that she is infested with vermin, foul smelling, and filthy. And, as is indicated by the title "a visit to the sky," by which this particular set is usually known (M_{113}), it deals with the adventures of a mortal man in the celestial kingdom, rather than with an immortal woman on earth. I have already referred to the story (p. 140) and shall come back to it again (pp. 326 ff.).

On the other hand, the myth about the food-bearing tree is found in great abundance among the Arawak and the Carib of Guiana, and even in Colombia; formerly (M_{114}), only the tapir or the agouti knew the secret of this tree, which they refused to share with men. The latter used a squirrel, a bush rat, or an opossum to act as spies. Once they had discovered the whereabouts of the tree, men decided to fell it. Water gushed forth from the stump (K.G. 1, pp. 33–8; Wassen 1, pp. 109–10), turned into a flood, and destroyed the human race (Brett, pp. 106–10, 127–30; Roth 1, pp. 147–8; Gillin, p. 189; Farabee 3, pp. 83–5; Wirth 1, p. 259). The Wapishana and the Taruma of British Guiana tell (M_{115}) how Duid, the creator's brother, fed men with the fruit of the tree of life. But men found out where he was getting the food and resolved to help themselves to it. The creator was furious at this act of insubordination and felled the tree, and the flood waters gushed from the stump (Ogilvie, pp. 64–7).

A version that contrasts the call of the stone with the call of the water makes it quite clear that we are still dealing with a myth that explains man's loss of immortality and is linked with the introduction of cultivated plants and belongs to the same set as the Ge myths. Had men listened only to the call of stone, they would have lived as long as the rocks. They brought about the flood by listening to the spirits that released the waters (Brett, pp. 106–10).[24]

I shall frequently have occasion to refer back to the Ge myths, but for the moment I merely wish to point out two essential features. A Carib version (M_{116}) makes it clear that after men had gained possession of cultivated plants, the bunia bird taught them how to grow and cook them (Roth 1, p. 147). The bunia bird therefore plays, to a certain extent, the part of the opossum in the Ge myths. Now this bird (*Ostinops* species) is referred to as the "stinking bird," because of the nauseating stench emanating from its feathers (Roth 1, p. 371).[25] It therefore clearly represents the "opossum function" coded in ornithological terms. From its excrements, the bunia is supposed to produce the aerial roots of an epiphytic plant called the kofa (*Clusia grandifolia:* Roth 1, pp. 231–2, 371). The Tucuna hero, Epi (M_{117}), who often chose to assume the form of an opossum (M_{95} and Nim. 13, p. 124) sent out a jet of urine from the top of a tree. This solidified and became a spiny-barked creeper (*Philodendron* species),[26] while his brother created a smooth variety by the same method (Nim. 13, p. 124; cf. above p. 180, n. 20 and, below, M_{161}).

The tribes of the Gran Chaco, for their part, describe Star as the mistress of destructive fire and creative water, and they see the fish-filled tree as the master, so to speak, of destructive water. The vegetable-bearing tree of the Guiana myths also controls destructive water.

There is a point about the corresponding Ge myths that I have not yet mentioned, and to which attention should be drawn. In M_{87}, M_{89} (second version), M_{90}, M_{91}, and M_{94}, the propinquity of the first maize heads and water is particularly stressed. A woman is first told about maize while bathing; or it is explained that the fallen grains or heads filled the river. Among

[24] Brett has often been accused of fanciful interpretations because his transcriptions are in verse. But he could not have known of the myths describing the origin of immortality which I noted earlier on. Other variants from Guiana, confirming Brett's evidence, have subsequently been found among the Warao and the Arawak: "People heard that at midnight the spirits Hisi ('stinking') and Kake ('living') were going to pass by; they were to stay awake and call out the names of those spirits. First Hisi passed, but then the people were asleep. Toward morning Kake passed, and the people awoke and called: 'Hisi.' Since then people must die" (Goeje, p. 116). There is evidence to prove that a myth of the same group once existed in Panama (Adrian in Wassen 4, p. 7).

[25] The bunia of Guiana is identical with the japu, which is found in central and southern Brazil. It is a bird of the Icterides family, which also includes the japim (*Cassicus cela,* any common Brazilian oriole), whose unpleasant smell has also been noted (Ihering, Vol. XXXVI, p. 236).

[26] This creeper is the *cipo ambe* or *cipo guembe.* The Cayua who gather and eat the fruit of this species of philodendron (Watson, p. 28) relate that Sun, who had come to beg from the opossum, could obtain nothing from it "for it only possessed the *cipo guaimbe*" (Schaden 1, p. 112).

the Ge and in Guiana, therefore, the food-bearing tree is associated with water that either covers the foot of the tree or is enclosed within its roots. In its interiorized form, water destroys; in its exteriorized form, if it does not actually create (M_{110}), then at least it preserves the seeds or heads.

The twofold transformation (internal → external; destruction → preservation) of the semantic significance attributed to terrestrial water, is accompanied by another kind of transformation that affects the attitude toward food plants. In the myths of Guiana the latter are either generously distributed to men by a bounteous demiurge or cleverly misappropriated for its exclusive use by the tapir (or the agouti), who is the jealous owner of the tree of life. As a punishment (M_{116}), the tapir is deprived of water which he is condemned to draw in a sieve (Roth 1, p. 147; cf. akawai in Brett, p. 128), and of cultivated plants, since the only food he is allowed is the fruit that falls from the wild plum tree (*ibid.;* Amorim, p. 271). Men meet with exactly the opposite fate, since they no longer wish to be treated as children in need of food: they are given cultivated plants but are destroyed by the water that gushes out too profusely from the roots of the felled tree (Ogilvie, pp. 64–7). Egotism and ingratitude receive symmetrical punishment.

The Ge myths manage to remain at an equal distance from both these dangers. In them the misuse of food plants takes on another form. It lies neither in men's decision to embark actively on agricultural tasks (M_{115})— although they could have lived a passive life—nor in their decision to keep the fruit of the tree for themselves (M_{114}, M_{116}). The Ge texts are extremely enlightening on this point. Having been informed by the opossum, who (unlike the tapir) was a generous and disinterested mistress of the tree of life, the villagers could have kept the secret of the tree to themselves and could have continued to enjoy long life. But through the child being seen, other families or other villages learned of the existence of the tree. From then on, the tree was no longer enough for all needs: it had to be felled, and the seeds divided and planted. And it was while men were engaged on this task that the youths tasted the flesh of the opossum, thus allowing mortality (the intermediary state between violent death and prolonged life) to become established.

Consequently the mediatory function of the opossum, which places it at an equal distance from the demiurge acting as imperious foster father and the miserly tapir who figures in the myths of Guiana, offers a midway solution to the philosophical problems arising from the introduction of an agricultural mode of life. The solution consists, on the synchronic level, in the fair division of resources among peoples who have been encouraged to increase their numbers and become more diversified, because of a plentiful supply of food; and on the diachronic level, in the periodicity of agricultural tasks. At the same time, water becomes a preserver of life: it is neither creative nor destructive, since it does not endow the tree with life from within and does not destroy men outside the tree, but remains stagnant at the foot of the tree for all eternity.

From the methodological point of view, two lessons can be drawn from the foregoing analysis. In the first place, it confirms a point I have already stressed—namely that as far as structural analysis is concerned, etymological problems must be kept separate from problems of meaning. I have not at any moment suggested that water might be an archetypal symbol: indeed, I have been careful to leave this problem on one side. I have been satisfied to show that in two particular mythological contexts, a variation of the semantic significance of water is a function of other variations, and that, in the course of these transformations, the rules of formal isomorphism are constantly respected.

Secondly, I can provide an answer to the question raised by the absence, among the ancient Tupinamba, of the Guarani version of the myth about the origin of fire, according to which fire was stolen from the vulture by a demiurge who feigned death and putrefaction (we have evidence that this myth was known to almost all the Tupi tribes of Brazil). I have drawn attention to the fact that the Ge tribes have two strictly parallel mythological series to account for the transition from nature to culture. In one series, culture begins with the theft of fire from the jaguar; in the other, with the introduction of cultivated plants. But in all contexts the origin of man's loss of immortality is linked with the advent of civilized life, which is thought of as culture whenever the question at issue is the origin of fire (the conquest of "the jaguar's belongings"; M_8: fire for cooking purposes, bows and arrows, spun cotton), and as society whenever the question at issue is the origin of cultivated plants (M_{90}: the increase in the number of separate peoples, the diversification of languages and customs). Finally, depending on the particular group, man's loss of immortality is linked either with the origin of fire and culture (Apinaye) or with the origin of cultivated plants and society (other Ge groups); lastly, in Guiana and the Gran Chaco it is linked with the origin of water and (the destruction of) society.

If we limit ourselves here to a consideration of the Ge and the Tupi, it is clear that among the Apinaye, the origin of man's mortality ("the call of the rotten tree") is a function of the origin of fire (M_9); while among the other Ge groups the origin of man's mortality ("the call of the opossum," a putrid animal) is a function of the origin of cultivated plants. We thus arrive at the following hypothesis: since the theme of decay (god-decaying carcass) exists among the present-day Guarani and Tupi as a function of the myth explaining the origin of fire, may not the absence of a similar myth among the ancient Tupinamba be explained by the fact that the theme of decay has been transferred to the myth describing the origin of cultivated plants? Now according to Thevet (M_{118}; Métraux 7), the Tupinamba believed that cultivated plants originated in a miraculous child who, when beaten, released cultivated plants from his body—that is, a child who, although not dead, was at least "mortified" and putrescent because of the blows he had received. An Amazonian legend of Tupi origin tells how the first manioc grew on the tomb of a young child, who had been conceived by a virgin (Couto de Magalhães, p. 167).[27] It would therefore seem that the Tupinamba differed from the Guarani and the majority of the other Tupi groups in the same way as the other Ge groups differed from the Apinaye: that is, they regarded the problem of man's loss of immortality from a sociological, rather than a cultural, standpoint.

d. CONCLUDING ARIA: FIRE AND WATER

I have on several occasions more or less explicitly accepted the fact that in the mythological thought of South America there are two distinct kinds of water: creative water of celestial origin and destructive water of terrestrial origin. Similarly, there seem to be two kinds of fire: one celestial and destructive, the other terrestrial and creative, that is, fire for cooking purposes. We shall see presently that the situation is rather more complex than this. But first of all we must go more deeply into the significance of the basic contrast between water and fire.

For this purpose we must return to the key myth, which, as I showed (on pp. 137 ff.), is a myth about the origin of fire in the guise of a myth about the origin of water, and restore it to its place among the series of Ge myths dealing with the origin of fire (M_7–M_{12}). Although, because of their matrilineal and matrilocal social structure, the Bororo form a more complete contrast with the patrilineal and patrilocal Sherente than with any of the other Ge tribes (and perhaps precisely for this reason), an extraordinary symmetry can be observed among the myths of these two groups, the hero of which is a bird-nester (M_1 and M_{12} respectively).

In the first place, and only in the set of myths 1 to 12, the myths deal simultaneously with fire and water. The Bororo myth creates water in order to destroy fire or, more precisely, to allow the hero to become the master of fire. The Sherente myth states that, in order to become the master of fire, the hero had first of all to behave as master of water: we might say that he obliterated it by drinking it all. It will be remembered that, after being rescued by the jaguar, the hero complained of acute thirst which he succeeded in satisfying only by drinking the stream dry, without leaving a single drop for the alligator (*Caiman niger*) who owned it. Light is thrown on this incident by a Cayua myth (M_{62}), which states emphatically that the alligator was the master of water, and that it was his task to prevent the earth from

[27] The pattern is found fairly widely in tropical America, among the Caingang (a victim's corpse is dragged across the plantations and creates the first maize; Borba, p. 23); in Guiana (cultivated plants were exuded, excreted, or procreated by an old woman); among the Bororo and the Paressi (cultivated plants arose from the ashes of young people who may or may not have been incestuous, and who died at the stake).

drying up: *Jacaré é capitão de agua, para não secar todo a mundo* (Schaden 1, p. 113).[28]

Secondly, the hero of both myths is shown as a trickster, not always at the beginning (where the contrast is chiefly between the Kayapo and Sherente versions: the eggs he throws down become stones, and the stones he throws down are changed into eggs, respectively), but at the end. The Bororo bird-nester deceives his own people for a long time by disguising himself as a lizard. His Sherente counterpart also deceives his own people by claiming that the jaguar's meat was cooked simply through exposure to the sun. In both cases his distrustful attitude is unjustified.

His extreme behavior corresponds to another feature peculiar to the two myths, in which the theme is not, as in the Apinaye version, a human life whose duration is henceforth to be *measured*, but death followed by resurrection. The theme occurs twice in the Bororo myth, where the hero betrays his identity during a "dance of the ancestors," then succeeds in returning safe and sound from his expedition to the kingdom of the souls. The Sherente myth, on the other hand, suggests that the hero remained hidden from his people for a long time because he was dead. He only reappears on the occasion of the Aikman funeral rites which were performed in honor of the illustrious dead (cf. p. 76). By stretching the sense of the texts very slightly, we might say that the timid hero procures a restricted life for men, whereas the brazen hero brings them a promise of resurrection. The contrast between prolonged life and a shortened life, on the one hand, and death and resurrection, on the other, seems isomorphic with that which can be perceived between myths that deal either separately with the origin of cooking ($\equiv$ fire) or cultivated plants ($\equiv$ water), or jointly with the origin of fire and water.

Let us begin by establishing, by means of a lemma, that the following relation is definitely present in native thought:

$$\text{fire} = \text{water}(^{-1}).$$

The theme of one of the most widespread South American myths, for which ample evidence is found among the Ge, is a challenge that the mythological twins, Sun and Moon, or the anteater and the jaguar, address to each other in connection with their respective diets. Depending on the versions, the diets consist, respectively, of ripe fruits and green fruits, meat (raw food)

[28] With regard to the jaguar-alligator couple (one master of fire, the other master of water), it will be recalled that Tupinologists have compared the Tupi name for the jaguar, *iagua,* with the word *jacaré* meaning alligator, which can be split up into *iagua-ré* "the other sort of jaguar." I do not know what value philologists would attach to this etymology, but it is interesting to note that it was rejected as soon as it was put forward, for the sole reason that no possible equivalence could exist between the two species (Chermont de Miranda, pp. 73–4).

and ants (decayed food, cf. M$_{89}$ and M$_{54}$ by reason of the transformation oppossum → ant: cf. above, p. 172), animal foods and vegetable foods, etc.:

(Sun : Moon, anteater : jaguar) :: (rotten : raw, ripe : green, vegetable : animal . . .)

Except for the above difference, the great anteater and the jaguar might be said to be interchangeable. Brazilian folklore has a wealth of stories that treat as equals the two most powerful animals of the *sertão*: one because of its powerful fangs, the other because of the grip of its powerful forepaws. It is said, for instance, that the jaguar never fails to overcome the anteater in the savannah, but that the opposite is true in the forest, where the anteater stands erect by supporting itself against a tree trunk with its tail and suffocates the jaguar between its front legs.

Each animal claimed that the food it ate was the "strongest," and to settle the dispute they decided to defecate, while keeping their eyes shut, and then to compare their excrements. The anteater pretended that it had difficulty in performing, and took advantage of the respite surreptitiously to exchange its excrement for that of the jaguar. A quarrel ensued, during which the anteater tore out the jaguar's eyes. Or sometimes the story goes as follows:

M$_{119}$. *Cayua. "The jaguar's eyes"*

The jaguar learned from the grasshopper that the toad and the rabbit had stolen its fire while it was out hunting, and that they had taken it across the river. While the jaguar was weeping at this, an anteater came along, and the jaguar suggested that they should have an excretory competition. The anteater, however, appropriated the excrement containing raw meat and made the jaguar believe that its own excretions consisted entirely of ants. In order to even things out, the jaguar invited the anteater to a juggling contest, using their eyes removed from the sockets: the anteater's eyes fell back into place, but the jaguar's remained hanging at the top of a tree, and so it became blind.

At the request of the anteater, the macuco bird made the jaguar new eyes out of water, and these allowed it to see in the dark.

Since that time the jaguar only goes out at night. Having lost fire, it eats its meat raw. It never attacks the macuco—in the Apapocuva version, the inhambu bird, also one of the Tinamidae. (Schaden 1, pp. 110–11, 121–2.)

This version is particularly instructive in that it links the rivalry between the jaguar and the anteater with the theme of the jaguar, master of fire, which I have been using as a guideline from the outset. According to Schaden's informant, the link is even stronger than at first appears, since had the jaguar retrieved the fire stolen from it by the animals, it would have used it to set fire to the earth. The fact that the jaguar lost its original eyes ("the reflection of fire could be seen in its eyes": M$_7$) was a final warning to humanity of this danger: henceforth even the jaguar's eyes were to be *pura agua,* only water. . . .

How then are we to interpret the connection between the excretory contest and the eye contest? I have said that, diet apart, the jaguar and the anteater are interchangeable. Now in regard to interchangeability, excretions and eyes are in direct and, one might say, anatomical opposition: excretions constitute an eminently interchangeable part of the body, since it is their function to leave the body, whereas eyes are not removable. The myth therefore assumes simultaneously that:

a) fire $=$ water$(^{-1})$,
b) jaguar $=$ anteater$(^{-1})$,
c) excretions $=$ eyes$(^{-1})$.

If excretions are interchangeable but eyes are not, it follows that an exchange of eyes (unlike an exchange of excrement) cannot involve a change of owner, since the parts of the body remain identical, but involves a change of the parts of the body, since the owner remains identical. In other words, in one instance the jaguar and the anteater exchange excretions; in the other the jaguar exchanges its own eyes with itself. It loses its fiery eyes, which were in keeping with its nature as master of fire, and having lost fire, it replaces them with eyes made of water, which is the opposite of fire.

The fact that in other versions of the same myth, the jaguar's artificial eyes were made of resin, not water, merely leads us to develop the equation given on page 189:

$$:: (. . . \text{ vegetable : animal, water : fire}).$$

This lemma brings us back, then, to the inversion of fire and water which seemed to characterize the contrast between the Bororo myth (M_1) and the Sherente myth (M_{12}): one destroyed fire and created water; the other destroyed water and created fire. But the water in the two myths was not of the same kind: in M_1 it was celestial, maleficent, and exteriorized (tempest); in M_{12} it was terrestrial, beneficent, and interiorized (drinkable). Nor was death introduced into each construct in the same way:

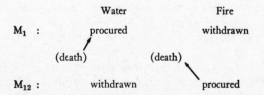

In other words, the Bororo hero's death is the *condition* of the procuring of water, and the death of the Sherente hero is the *consequence* of the procuring of fire.

I have already referred to the fact that the Bororo and the Sherente had entirely different social structures. But to account for the relation of inversion that exists between their etiological myths relating to fire and water, we must refer to other aspects of the culture of the two groups. Unlike the Ge tribes, the Bororo did not live exclusively on the plateau or in the valleys that cut across it. They were settled chiefly along the western edge, or at the foot of the plateau, in the lowlands which slope toward the southwest and eventually become submerged under the waters of one of the largest swamps in the world—the Pantanal. It follows that their mode of life has remained partly that of land dwellers, partly that of marsh dwellers. Water is an element with which they are familiar, and they believe that by chewing certain leaves they can remain under water for several hours to fish (Steinen 2, p. 452). This mode of life is accompanied by religious beliefs in which water plays a big part. The Bororo bury their dead twice: a brief initial burial takes place in the village plaza where for several weeks relatives water the corpse lavishly, in order to hasten the process of decomposition. When decay is sufficiently advanced, the grave is opened, and the skeleton is washed until all trace of flesh has been removed. The bones are painted red, decorated with mosaics made from feathers glued together with resin, placed in a basket, and ceremoniously dropped to the bottom of a river or lake, "the abodes of the souls." Water and death are therefore always connected in native thought. In order to procure the one, it is necessary to undergo the other. This is exactly what the Bororo myth about the bird-nester is, in its peculiar way, trying to convey.

The Sherente, who live in the valley of the Rio Tocantins, would not seem to be particularly exposed to the danger of drought. Nevertheless they are obsessed by a fear of drought to a degree unequaled in any other region. Their great fear is that the sun may become angry and dry up and destroy the earth. In order to appease the sun, in the old days the adult men used to undergo a long fast, lasting for several weeks and ending in a complicated ritual the details of which I shall return to later (pp. 289 ff.).

It is enough for the time being to remember that in Sherente thought the human race lives under the threat of a universal conflagration. Corresponding to this belief in fire as the chief cause of death, there is a myth that, as we have seen, maintains that you must endure death in order to obtain fire.

It is only by taking these ecological and religious factors into account that the inversion of the Bororo and Sherente myths can be understood. The Bororo live—and, above all, think—in terms of water; for them, water connotes death, and many of their myths—which explain cultivated plants or other cultural blessings as emerging from the ashes of heroes who are dying, sometimes voluntarily, on a burning woodpile (cf., for instance, M_{20}, M_{27}; and Colb. 3, pp. 199, 213-14)—testify to their belief in a connection between fire and life. The opposite is true in the case of the Sherente: they think in terms of drought—that is, of negativized water. In their myths, far more emphatically than in any others, fire connotes death; and they contrast it with water, which is not lethal (in the rites performed during the long fast, stale water is offered to the participants only so that they can refuse it) but life-giving. And yet all the water in the world is hardly enough to quench the thirst of a thirsty man.

In support of the contrast between fire and water, it may be noted that, in common with their Bacairi neighbors, the Bororo also possess a myth about destructive fire; but it is significant that their fire myth appears in a secondary form, as if it were the consequence of the loss of water. The danger resulting from it is easily overcome:

M_{120}. *Bororo.* *"Destructive fire"*

Formerly Sun and Moon used to live on the earth. One day when they were thirsty, they went to see the aquatic birds who kept water in huge heavy jars.

Disobeying the birds, Sun tried to lift one jar to his lips, but it slipped out of his hands and broke, and the water spilled. The birds became angry. Sun and Moon ran away, and the birds followed them to the hut where they had taken refuge.

By now Sun had become too hot. Feeling discomfort through being so near to him, the birds flapped their woven straw fans and caused such a powerful wind that Sun and Moon were carried up into the sky, where they have remained. (Colb. 3, pp. 237–8; Bacairi version (M_{120a}) in Steinen 2, pp. 482–3.)

Other myths concerning Sun and Moon show them destroying fire by water: either as in M_{121} by urinating on the otters' fire (Colb. 3, p. 233), or as in M_{122} by pouring water on the fire made by men (*ibid.*, p. 231). Consequently here again water is proved to have primacy over fire.[29]

It is not enough to say that for the Bororo water is the final cause of death, whereas for the Sherente fire is its efficient cause. This difference between

---

[29] A whole series of Bororo myths about the origin of fire describe the latter as being extinguished by rain (M_1), spilled water (M_{122}), and urine (M_{121}). In the set explaining the origin of cultivated plants, the Sherente myth (M_{108}) describes manioc as having germinated from the drops of milk spilled by the mothers. This gives the following transformation:

$$(Fire\ series)\left[\ urine \rightarrow fire\ (\ -\ )\ \right] \longrightarrow (Plant\ series)\left[\ milk \rightarrow plants\ (\ +\ )\ \right]$$

It is interesting to note that a Mexican myth from the Nayarit region (M_{123}) offers a reverse transformation, which makes it possible to arrive at the first term by starting from the second: the iguana having taken the fire to the sky, the crow and the hummingbird failed to get it back. The opossum succeeded by pretending that he only wanted to warm himself at it (return to M_{56}, via the opossum → prea transformation). But he let the fire drop, and the world burst into flames. However, the Earth succeeded in putting out the fire with its milk (Preuss 2, Vol. I, pp. 169–81).

I have already pointed out (p. 138 n. 15) that the Cuna of Panama, like the Bororo, change the origin of fire into the origin of water: in one instance rain puts out all fires except one (cf. M_1, M_{61}); in another urine puts out a single fire (M_{121}, M_{61}).

them is accompanied by another, which can be seen in the parallel series of myths explaining the origin of cultivated plants. The Sherente completely dissociate the origin of plants from that of fire. Unlike the other Ge tribes, they include the myth about cultivated plants in the cosmogonic cycle describing the terrestrial adventures of the two culture heroes, Sun and Moon (M_{108}). Conversely, the Bororo take the origin of cultivated plants as a theme for legendary, rather than mythical, tales. They are concerned less

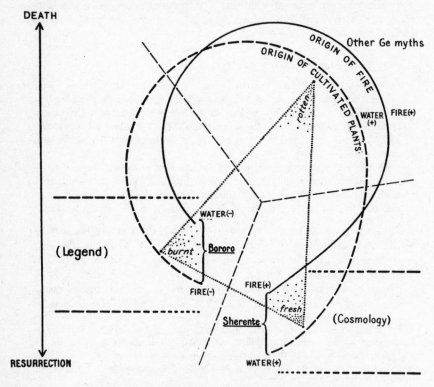

Figure 8. Interrelationship of the Bororo and Ge myths
about the origin of fire or cultivated plants.

with explaining the origin of agriculture as a civilizing art than with establishing to what extent each individual clan can legitimately claim a particular plant, or even a particular variety of a single species, as an eponym. Privileges of this kind go back to the sacrifice made by clan heroes who went voluntarily to a burning woodpile (destructive fire/cooking fire). In all respects, therefore, Bororo and Sherente mythologies relating to the transition from nature to culture occupy extreme positions, whereas the mythology of the other Ge groups is situated in the middle of the scale. Both the Bororo and the Sherente associate fire with water, although they attribute opposite functions to them: water > fire/fire > water; exteriorized water/interiorized water; celestial, maleficent water/terrestrial, beneficent water; culinary fire/funerary woodpile, etc.; and the main events to which they all refer are situated now on a sociological and legendary level, now on a cosmological and mythological level. Finally, both the Bororo and the Sherente stress resurrection, not the shortening of life.

As we have seen elsewhere, the other Ge groups dissociate the origin of cooking (connected with fire) from the origin of cultivated plants (connected with water): the two themes are given parallel and independent treatment, instead of forming an asymmetrical pair within the same mythological series. Furthermore, they associate cultivated plants with decayed matter; and not with the burned, like the Bororo; or with the fresh, like the Sherente.

This pattern of relations can be illustrated by a diagram (Figure 8).

PART FOUR

WELL-TEMPERED ASTRONOMY

1

Three-Part Inventions

I propose to give the name *armature* to a combination of properties that remain invariant in two or several myths: *code* to the pattern of functions ascribed by each myth to these properties; and *message* to the subject matter of an individual myth. Referring back now to the remarks with which I concluded Part Three, I can define the relation between the Bororo myth (M_1) and the Sherente myth (M_{12}) by stating that when we move from one to the other, the armature remains constant, the code is changed, and the message is reversed.

The results of this analysis would be definitively confirmed if it were possible to arrive at the same contrasting structure by a regressive process, which would be a kind of *a contrario* proof. The problem thus posed can be formulated as follows:

Let us suppose two myths, which we will call M_x and M_y, and which happen to be linked by a transformation relation:

$$M_x \rightarrow M_y$$
$$(f)$$

If we agree that $M_y = f M_x$, does there exist a myth $M_z = f M_y$, in connection with which we can prove that it reconstitutes M_x by means of a transformation symmetrical to the one that produced M_y from M_x, but operating in the reverse direction? In other words, after establishing that a Sherente myth about the origin of fire (M_y) is a transformation of a Bororo myth about the origin of water (M_x), can we now find a Sherente myth (M_z) explaining the origin of water which takes us back to the Bororo myth which was our starting point, and at the same time confirms the following isomorphism:

$$\begin{bmatrix} M_z \rightarrow M_x \\ (f) \end{bmatrix} \approx \begin{bmatrix} M_x \rightarrow M_y \\ (f) \end{bmatrix} ?$$

Such a myth does in fact exist among the Sherente:

M_{124}. Sherente. "The story of Asare"

Once there was an Indian who had a wife and many sons, all of them adult except the youngest, Asare. While the father was hunting one day, the brothers sent Asare to fetch their mother and bring her to the bachelors' house, bidding her to cut their hair and decorate them. But when she entered, her own sons seized and ravished her.

Asare revealed what they had done, and the culprits were severely thrashed by their father. They took their revenge by setting fire to the hut where the couple were living. The parents changed into falcons of the kind that like to fly in the smoke, and thus escaped.

Then the sons went far away. On the way Asare suffered from thirst, and the water from tucum nuts (*Astrocaryum tucuma*) knocked down by his brothers was not enough to quench it. Then one of them began digging a well in a hollow, and so much water gushed forth that Asare, however much his brothers urged him to drink, could not exhaust it. The water spread more and more, finally forming the sea.

Then Asare recollected that an arrow he particularly prized had been left on the opposite bank. He swam across, found his arrow, and was swimming back when in the middle of the water he found an alligator (jacare), which had developed out of a swarm of lizards which Asare had killed while traveling, and which the spreading waters had carried away. Asare begged the alligator to let him sit on him, and when the latter refused, Asare called him names, making fun of his ugly nose. The alligator gave chase. Meanwhile the brothers saw the arrow drifting on the water, concluded that their youngest brother had perished, and marched on.

Asare reached land when his pursuer was already close behind. He ran into the woods where the woodpeckers were pecking the bark from the trees in order to eat the insects under it. At his request the birds covered him with strips of bark and sent the alligator off on a false scent. Once the danger was over, Asare went on his way and crossed another river where he met another alligator, with the same consequences. He escaped from it, thanks to partridges who happened to be digging out groundnuts (*Arachis hypogaea*) and who hid him under the straw. The same incidents occurred again when Asare swam across a third river, but this time he hid under the rinds of the jatoba fruits which monkeys were busy eating. One of the monkeys, from inborn talkativeness, came near divulging the secret, but another struck it on the lips, so he kept silent.

Asare finally got to his uncle, the skunk, who was not afraid at all. When the alligator came, the skunk squirted his fluid at him, and the alligator died of the stench. The skunk called the little inhambus (*Tinamus* species) to drag the corpse into the river. Asare, however, stayed with his uncle.[1]

When the sea was formed, Asare's brothers had at once tried to bathe. Even today, toward the close of the rainy season, one hears in the west the sound of their splashing in the water. Then they appear in the heavens, new and clean, as Sururu, the Seven Stars (the Pleiades). (Nim. 7, pp. 185–6.)

There is a great deal to be said about this myth. Let me begin by establishing, in accordance with my stated intention, that, with the help of a

---

[1] The skunk is identified in the text with *Mephitis suffocans*, "cangamba" (Maciel, p. 431). In reality, the South American equivalent of the North American skunk is a member of the Conepatus family (cf. above p. 154, n. 9).

certain number of transformations affecting either content or code, it faithfully reconstitutes the Bororo myth about the bird-nester (M_1).

The initial situation is the same: a mother is raped by her son (or sons). Two differences, however, will be noted: in the Bororo myth the mother was raped in the forest where she had gone to carry out a task only performed by women. Here it is the father who is away in the forest hunting—that is, engaged on a masculine occupation—and the rape is carried out, not just somewhere in the village, but in the men's house, which women are not usually allowed to enter. Secondly, M_1 laid stress on the culprit's youth (he has not yet been initiated), whereas M_{124} describes the culprits as being initiated adolescents, obliged to reside in the men's house (cf. Nim. 6, p. 49).

A third difference follows inevitably from the two I have just noted. The Bororo father is unaware of his misfortune and makes inquiries to confirm his suspicions; once they are confirmed, he tries to kill his son. The Sherente father, on the other hand, is immediately informed of what has taken place, and it is his sons who want to kill him. The Bororo father has recourse to water in order to satisfy his passion for revenge (fire was to appear later); to satisfy their passion for revenge, the Sherente sons use fire (water appears later).

The Sherente parents escape death by changing into falcons, which are fond of kitchen fires: the Bororo son escapes death thanks to rescuers in the form of urubus, who are enemies of kitchen fires (since, according to the myth, they feed on carrion and raw flesh).

The vertical disjunction (low → high) affects both the Bororo son and the Sherente parents. On the other hand, whereas in the first case, the son is separated vertically—by air—from his parents, the Sherente hero is separated horizontally from his brothers by water.

The Bororo hero, far from the village, and after climbing to the top of a rocky cliff, suffers from hunger: also far from his village, and after covering a great distance, the Sherente hero suffers from thirst. Each one tries two remedies, which are contrasted by the two myths. In M_1 there is, in the first place, raw animal food, which decomposes because there is too much of it; then raw vegetable food, which is never adequate because the hero is unable to retain it. In M_{124} there is first a vegetable drink in short supply, then nonvegetable (chthonic) water, of which there is so much that the hero is unable to consume it all. In both cases the quantitatively insufficient remedy is vegetable and beneficent (palm-nut juice, fresh fruit) and the quantitatively sufficient (and even superabundant) remedy is nonvegetable in origin and maleficent (decomposed lizards and sea water, which both threaten to bring about the hero's death).

Both the Bororo and the Sherente myths take the form of myths explaining the origin of water; in the first case the water is rain or celestial water; in the second, it is chthonic: that is, it gushes out from the earth.

The Bororo hero has to cross water in order to bring back the ritual instruments; the Sherente hero crosses the water in order to bring back an arrow —that is, a weapon used in hunting.

On three occasions the Sherente hero meets with an alligator that has sprung from the lizards he killed before the water spread out over the earth. Lizards are also killed by the Bororo hero, in order to appease his hunger and to provide a reserve food supply. It is because this food decomposes very quickly that the vultures attack him.

If we were to keep strictly to the text of M_1, the episode would remain incomprehensible. Or, to be more accurate, the absence of any syntagmatic context would, if we were bent on finding an interpretation, lead us to comb through the whole of American mythology, which would supply us with more answers than we could cope with: for the Kubenkranken, the lizard is a precultural food (Métraux 8, p. 14); for the Warao, the Choco, and the Cuna (cf. above, p. 138, n. 15), a master of fire; elsewhere it is a master of sleep because it has no eyelids; and among populations as far apart as the Jicarilla Apache of North America and the Amuesha of Peru it is a symbol of incest and witchcraft. . . .

But where as research into the etymology—one might almost say the "mythemology"—of the lizard would be a rash undertaking, research into its significance is not. As is indicated in no uncertain terms by the Sherente myth, the lizard is the terrestrial counterpart of the aquatic alligator. M_1 and M_{124} therefore shed light on each other: one takes place on land and makes the hero a hunter of lizards for the same reason that the other, which takes place on water, makes the alligator a "hunter of heroes." The fact that a Bororo myth and a Ge myth present this reciprocal view of things perhaps allows us to derive confirmation for the former from an Apinaye text: "It is said that when an Apinaye male child is born, the urubus rejoice because there will be yet another hunter to leave them dead flesh in the bush. But when a female child is born, the lizards rejoice, because it is the women's duty to prepare berubur—that is, meals—and the fallen scraps provide food for lacertians" (C. E. de Oliveira, p. 67).

If it were legitimate to extrapolate, we could say we were dealing with a twofold contrast: one is an internal contrast, in M_1, between lizards and urubus with the double valency: female/male, cooked/raw;[2] the other is external, covering both M_1 and M_{124}, and opposes the lizards and the alligator, also with a double valency: land/water, cooked/raw.

Finally, we know that the Sherente believe the alligator to be the master of water and the jaguar master of fire (M_{12}). It is therefore perfectly consistent that in their myth about the origin of terrestrial water (M_{124}) the hero should encounter an alligator, just as in their myth about the origin of terrestrial fire (M_{12}) he should encounter a jaguar. And since we have

---

[2] And perhaps vegetable/animal, too, if we follow another indication from the same source, where lizards are grouped with grasshoppers, rats, and rabbits as garden parasites (C. E. de Oliveira, p. 65).

established (pp. 189 ff.) that fire = water $(-^1)$, it is equally consistent that in both myths the respective behavior of the animal and the hero should be inverted. The hero in M_{12} behaves courteously toward the jaguar who offers to help him: the hero of M_{124} behaves insolently toward the alligator who refuses to help him.

Let us pause for a moment and consider the episode of the helpful animals, which occurs at the beginning of the Bororo myth and at the end of the Sherente myth. In descending order of effectiveness, these animals are, in the Bororo myth, the hummingbird, the pigeon, and the grasshopper. Although the Sherente myth does not mention the respective abilities of the wood-peckers and the partridges, it clearly indicates that the monkeys are the least effectual, since they almost betray their protégé. We can therefore take as our starting point the following hypothetical correspondence between the two series:

Bororo		*Sherente*	
hummingbird	(1)	woodpeckers	(1)
pigeon	(2)	partridges	(2)
grasshopper	(3)	monkeys	(3)

But the correspondence seems to be reversed when we try to define the species according to the categories of high and low. In the Sherente series the monkeys eat fruit (high), the woodpeckers attack the bark of trees (medium), the partridges dig up seeds (low). If we take into account the fact that in the Bororo series the grasshopper naturally occupies a lower place than the birds, and that the respective missions assigned to the three animals consist in gaining possession of the large and small rattles (which are held in the hand, therefore more or less in the "high" range, and un-equal in size), then of the ankle bells (low), we should arrive at the follow-ing table:

High   : hummingbird (1)⟍   ⟋monkeys   (3)
Medium : pigeon   (2)⟍⟋woodpeckers (1)
Low   : grasshopper (3)⟋⟍partridges (2)

Let us see if it is possible to overcome the difficulty. It will be remembered that the Sherente myth about the origin of fire (M_{12}) supplied a different series of three animals who played the part of masters of water. These were in the following order:

urubus   (1)
"small birds" (2)
alligator   (3)

We do not know what these "small birds" were, unless we suppose they were inhambus, which in the Asare myth are also described as "small." The inhambus (like the "partridges" in the same myth) are gallinaceans which live on the ground, flying only occasionally and clumsily. In respect of the high and low categories, they could perhaps be placed between the urubus and the alligator. On the other hand, the ancient Tupi along the east coast used white feathers flecked with black taken from these birds to decorate their weapons when they went to war, or when they were getting ready to execute their prisoners (Claude d'Abbeville, p. 237). This custom clearly corresponds to the role of "undertakers" assigned to the small inhambus in the Asare myth (although the *inambu-tin* referred to in the old source may have belonged to a larger species).

The myths already examined refer on several occasions to gallinaceans (Tinamidae or Cracidae) and seem always (apart from M_{14}, in a passage of no great significance) to treat them as beings of little merit, if not downright sinister. The gallinaceans destroy the scattered remnants of fire, being too weak to transport it (M_8, M_9, M_{12}). The inhambu is an inferior fowl which provides a bitter soup (M_{143}) and is not accepted in exchange for the flesh of the caititu, a nobler variety of game (M_{16}): it is the sole diet of a boy who is being kept in seclusion (Murphy 1, p. 74; Strömer, p. 133). A certain constellation in the night sky is the mother of the Tinamidae (M_{28}); the reason the jaguar does not attack birds belonging to this family and has acquired nocturnal habits is that the Tinamidae made him eyes with water to replace the eyes of fire he had lost (M_{119}). The link between stars, night, and gallinaceans can no doubt be explained by the Sherente custom. "The hours are counted during the day by the sun and at night by the stars and by the scream of the inhambu" (J. F. de Oliveira, p. 394).[3]

We possess more definite information about the semantic value of the other animals. According to the Ge myths analyzed below (M_{163}), the woodpeckers are the masters of destructive fire, which means that they are both correlated with, and opposed to, monkeys which, according to a Bororo myth we have already studied (M_{55}), are masters of creative fire (fire for cooking). The dove or pigeon is a master of water, as is attested not only by the key myth but also by a Sherente myth (M_{138}), which shows a whole family escaping from the flood thanks to a pigeon's carcass (*Leptoptila rufaxilla*) which grows miraculously bigger and bigger until it becomes another Noah's ark (Nim. 6, p. 92). In several versions of the "opossum and his sons-in-law" (M_{97}, M_{98}), Pigeon (one of the sons-in-law) catches fish from a lake by drying it up through drinking all the water it contains (Murphy 1, p. 119; Wagley and Galvão, p. 152). The water the pigeon

[3] Evidence of the same belief is given by Ihering ("Inhambu" entry) in connection with *Grypturus stirgulosus,* whence its popular name *"Inhambu relogio"*: the clock-bird. Cf. also Cavalcanti, pp. 159–60: the cujubim bird (one of the Cracidae) announces daybreak, but the inhambu sings at night. Finally, the mutum, which is also a member of the Cracidae family "sings at night at such regular intervals that it can be heard every two hours . . . thus for the natives it is a kind of forest clock" (Orico 2, p. 174).

has to conquer or nullify is defined by its negative properties, like destructive fire. We can therefore establish the principle that the pigeon and the woodpecker are isomorphic, in respect of water and fire.

The Bororo myth (M_1) describes the grasshopper (*mammori*: *Acridium cristatum,* EB, Vol. 1, p. 780) by its slow flight (similar to that of the partridge), which causes it to run the risk of death during its mission. In the Sherente series, it therefore corresponds on the one hand to the monkeys (one of which also almost betrays its mission), on the other to the partridges which, in the form of small inhambus come into—physical, not moral—contact with death, since they play the part of gravediggers. If we postulate that M_{124} is based essentially on the second of these homologies, only the hummingbird, about whose semantic position we have less information, remains to be explained. The Ge myths have very little to say about the hummingbird; we have to look farther afield.

In the mythology of Guiana the hummingbird is presented as being in correlation with, and opposed to, the bunia bird (cf. above, p. 185); together they help a man who is trapped at the top of a tree to get down, then to find his way back to his village. But whereas the bunia bird is a foul-smelling creature whose droppings are transformed into creepers (Roth 1, pp. 209, 371), the hummingbird emits a delightful perfume, although it is occasionally soiled by excrement (*ibid.*, pp. 335, 371). We have therefore a twofold contrast: bad smell/pleasant smell, and defiling/defiled. On the other hand, the role usually assigned to the hummingbird in the myths of Guiana is to look for tobacco and bring it to men. The tobacco grows on an island in the middle of a lake which the hummingbird succeeds in crossing, as in the Bororo myth; the myths make it clear that the tobacco will serve to "call forth" spirits, provided it is used in conjunction with the ceremonial rattles (Roth 1, p. 336), that it is the hummingbird's task to bring back in the Bororo myth. Leaving aside for the time being the problem of tobacco, to which I shall return later (in Volume II), we should note the relation between the hummingbird and water, a point on which some light is shed by the myths of the southeastern United States. These myths, of which we possess several versions—Natchez, Alabama, Koasati, Hitchiti, Creek, and Cherokee—contrast the hummingbird and the crane as diurnal/nocturnal (in Guiana, according to a Warao myth, defiled/defiling, Roth 1, p. 335); on the other hand, they explain how the hummingbird staked water and fish on the result of a race, and lost: for this reason the hummingbird never drinks (Swanton, pp. 202, 273, and *passim*).

In Brazil, the Botocudo and the Caingang tell very similar stories: the hummingbird who was formerly master of all the water in the world had it taken from him by the other creatures (Nim. 9, p. 111: Métraux 6, Vol. I, p. 540; Baldus 1, p. 60). A Kraho myth gives the hummingbird a negative relation to water, since it is the only creature capable of flying through flames (Schultz, p. 127). According to a Surura myth, it causes disjunction between fire and water by making the alligator laugh, so that it can seize fire from inside the jaws of the alligator and bring it to men (Becher, p. 105). In a Toba myth it steals fire (Métraux 5, pp. 107–8, 110).

If we agree, as a working hypothesis, to generalize the above convergent details, the hummingbird can be defined as a function of water but in negative terms, and it can be placed in correlation with, and in contrast to, the pigeon which was a great drinker.[4]

We arrive, then, at the following coherent system:

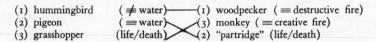

Bororo (M_1)   Sherente (M_{124})

(1) hummingbird   ($\neq$ water)———(1) woodpecker ($\equiv$ destructive fire)
(2) pigeon   ($\equiv$ water)   (3) monkey ($\equiv$ creative fire)
(3) grasshopper   (life/death)   (2) "partridge" (life/death)

in which we again have, on the one hand, the contrast between water and fire and, on the other hand, the linking of one or the other element with the transition from life to death, which struck us as being characteristic of the way problems are posed in the Bororo and Sherente myths respectively.

Let us now look at the matter from a different viewpoint. In the course of their missions the animal helpers come into contact with things: lifesaving musical instruments in the Bororo myth, materials used as lifesaving hiding places in the Sherente myth:

Bororo (M_1)   Sherente (M_{124})

hummingbird : large rattle   woodpeckers : bark of trees
pigeon   : small rattle   "partridges"   : straw
grasshopper : little bells   monkeys   : rinds

The things in the Bororo myth are sonorous objects that "must not be heard." The things in the Sherente myth no doubt prevent the alligator from *seeing* the hero; but at the same time they have the unusual feature of being food refuse—that is, things *that are not to be eaten*. They are therefore antifoods forming a series comparable, in this respect, to the series in the Apinaye myth (M_9): rock, hardwood, and rotten wood, which are also antifoods but, like the Bororo instruments, "consumable" by the ear, if not

---

[4] A myth belonging to the Pima of Arizona associates the hummingbird with a divinity called El Bebedor, "The Drinker," who was responsible for the flood (Russell, p. 226, note). If the negation of water is taken to its extreme limit, the hummingbird may be confused with the woodpecker, the master of destructive fire. This in fact occurs in a Caingang myth (M_{124a}), in which the hummingbird and the woodpecker jointly steal fire from the jaguar (Baldus 4, p. 122). But the remarkable thing is that in this instance it is the woodpecker who undergoes a transformation: first he gets wet, then he becomes a master of cooking fire—not completely, however, since this fire (which becomes destructive) sets the earth alight, and since creative fire (for cooking) is reduced to a secondary factor.

by the mouth. Through the medium, in this instance, of M_9 the symmetry between M_1 and M_{124} can be confirmed once again.

In M_1 as in M_{124}, a person offers assistance in addition to the series of three animals: a human grandmother in one context, an animal uncle (a skunk) in the other. The grandmother saves the hero by lending him a magic wand; the uncle, by releasing his foul-smelling fluid. I shall come back later to the parallel between the two myths, which admits of different interpretations (see pp. 270–1).

Lastly, and to complete the comparison, M_1 refers to the start of the rains—that is, to the end of the dry season; whereas the last few lines of M_{124} refer to its beginning.

The existence of a correlation between M_1 and M_{124} has thus been confirmed down to the smallest details. It has in fact been proved that if $M_y = fM_x$, there exists a myth $M_z = fM_y$ which has the same relation to M_x as M_x has to M_y.

The demonstration can be carried still further. The demonstration I have just given started from a Bororo myth with a dual theme: the appearance of celestial water and the disappearance of cooking fire. I have shown that this myth stands in a transformational relation to a Sherente myth, the theme of which—also a double one—formed a contrast with the other through a double inversion, since this time the subject was the appearance of *fire* and the disappearance of *water*, and the water was *terrestrial*, not *celestial*.

Going one step further, we asked whether there existed a Sherente myth dealing with the appearance of terrestrial water, and whether such a myth would not reproduce the framework of the initial Bororo myth about the appearance of celestial water. After giving an affirmative reply to both these questions, we moved on automatically to a third: was there a Sherente myth about the introduction of celestial water of which a Bororo myth, in return, could be a transformation?

We know of no such myth, perhaps simply because Nimuendaju did not come across it. Perhaps also because its existence among the Sherente would be inconceivable, since in their view the sky is inhabited by cannibalistic divinities (M_{93}) and controlled by a sun that is anxious to dry up rain and destroy the earth (cf. pp. 192 and 289). On the other hand, the myth exists among the other Ge tribes, whose mythology, as we have shown, occupies an intermediary position between the mythologies of the Bororo and the Sherente.

In actual fact the Ge have not one, but two myths relating to celestial water. It would seem that they distinguish between two types of rain—one beneficent, the other maleficent. The Kubenkranken (Métraux 8, p. 17) and the Gorotire (Lukesch 1, p. 983) attribute good rain to the celestial daughter of a mortal, who introduced cultivated plants (M$_{91}$) and whose father is directly responsible for tempests and storms. Since the key myth is also connected with the origin of tempests, it is the father, rather than the daughter, with whom we shall be concerned:

M$_{125}$. Kayapo. "The origin of rain and storms"

Some hunters once killed a tapir. One of them, who was called Bepkororoti, was given the task of gutting and cutting up the animal. While he was busy washing the intestines in the river, the others divided the flesh among themselves, leaving him only two paws (the intestines, Lukesch 1, 2). Bepkororoti's protests were in vain. When he got back to the village, he asked his wife to shave his head and to paint him red and black with urucu paste and genipa juice. Then he told her what had happened and warned her that he intended to withdraw to a mountain top. Finally he told her to take shelter when she saw a black cloud.

Bepkororoti made a bow and arrows and a large, heavy club the end of which he smeared with the blood of a tapir. He took his son with him to the top of the mountain. When he reached the summit, he started to shout like a herd of wild pigs (like men, when they are out hunting pigs; Lukesch 2). When they heard the noise, the Indians came running to hunt the pigs. At that moment, lightning flashed across the sky, there was a rumble of thunder, and Bepkororoti caused a thunderbolt to fall, which killed many people. He and his son went up into the sky. (Kubenkranken version from Métraux 8, pp. 16–17. Gorotire versions: Banner 1; Lukesch 1, 2.)

Some Gorotire versions (M$_{125a}$, M$_{125b}$) link the injustice done the hero with the fact that either previously (through carelessness) or afterward (through anger) he had appeared in the presence of his companions with blood-stained hands. Before withdrawing to the mountain top (or to some other high ground) he invented and introduced among the Indians the practice of shaving the head and painting the body, as well as the use of genipa juice and the custom of anointing clubs with blood before setting off for war. From his retreat the hero hurled insults and defiance at his former companions, whom he struck down with lightning as soon as they attacked him. Then he rose into the sky and disappeared. Shortly afterward there occurred the first storm accompanied by thunder and lightning. Ever since then, each time a storm threatens, the Indians arm themselves and put on their warpaint, and try to ward it off by threats and shouts (Lukesch 1, p. 983; Banner 1, pp. 46–9).[5]

---

[5] Here again (cf. above p. 149, n. 2) a myth, which exists as a complete whole in central Brazil, survives in Guiana merely as an episode devoid of any structural function among the exploits performed by Makunaima (Arecuna: M$_{126}$). The young hero kills a tapir. But his elder brother assumes the right to cut it up and share out the pieces, leaving the hero only the intestines. Makunaima, mad with anger, transports the family hut by magic onto a mountain top, then brings it down again (K.G. 1, p. 43).

I shall have no difficulty in identifying the Bororo myth, of which the Kayapo myth is a transformation; it is obviously the Baitogogo myth (M_2); in other words, a myth about the origin of water, but terrestrial not celestial water, and beneficent, not maleficent.

The following table shows the various operations:

M_2 { gathering female occupation	women + "tapir" man	"tapir" man rapes a woman	the hero bleeds his ("tapir") victim too slowly
M_{125} { hunting male occupation	men + tapir (animal)	male hunters kill a tapir	the hero bleeds his (tapir) victim too quickly

M_2 { son deprived of mother	dissociated from father	who is crushed beneath a tree	shame-ridden hero
M_{125} { son deprived of food	associated with father	who goes up onto a mountain	angry hero

M_2 { creation of terrestrial water	tree disappears under water	ritual music	origin of adorn- ments and funeral rites
M_{125} { creation of celestial water	mountain exalted (to the sky)	cries like those uttered by wild animals	origin of adorn- ments and warlike rites

M_2 {Indians kill	} scattered population
M_{125} {Indians killed	

It will be seen that, keeping faithfully to my method, I accept the fact that even the tiniest detail may be relevant. When the informants to whom we owe M_{125} compared the cries of Bepkororoti to those uttered by wild pigs (or pig hunters), they were not letting their imaginations run away with them. For the Tenetehara, too, associate the wild pig with thunder, whose favorite animal it is: "When the Tapirape have made kills of wild pigs, which are pets of Thunder, he will be angry and send a sudden rain or clouding of the sky" (Wagley, p. 259, n. 23). The fact that the man who raped the woman in the Bororo myth belonged to the tapir clan is no accident either, since the animal is also present in the Kayapo myth. I shall return to this point later (p. 272). Finally, one detail in the Bororo myth that remained incomprehensible when viewed from the angle of syntagmatical relations, becomes clear when compared to a corresponding detail in the Kayapo myth. The careful and elaborate killing of his rival by the hero in M_2, who inflicts a series of wounds of which only the last proves fatal, preserves in an inverted form (since the messages in both myths are inverted) the careless and hurried behavior of the hero in M_{125} who sits down to eat with his hands still blood-stained from his work of butchery (cf. M_{71}).

The only difference between the two myths consists in the progression of the Bororo myth, which divides the hero's misconduct into three successive stages, each one of which corresponds to a single aspect of the one offense committed by the Kayapo hero:

M_2 { the hero disposes too slowly of the "tapir" man	he strangles his wife (without bloodshed)	he is defiled by excrement
M_{125} { the hero disposes too quickly of the tapir (animal)	he dismembers the animal and spills its blood	he remains stained with the animal's blood

We note, then, in M_2 a kind of dialectical pattern of defilement:

$$\overset{1}{\left[\text{blood }(+)\right]} \longrightarrow \overset{2}{\left[\text{blood }(-)\right]} \longrightarrow \overset{3}{\left[\text{dejecta}\right]}$$

which seems to be absent from the Kayapo myth; unless, remembering that the conditions of the murder of the Bororo wife implied the denial of an aquatic burial, we replace the second term of the formula above—avoidance of bloodshed—by a different one—the avoidance of water—which has its equivalent (in the avoidance of ablutions) in the Kayapo myth, thus allowing us to construct the following parallel series:

M_2 = blood (+)	water (−)	bird droppings (animal excrement)
M_{125} = blood (+)	water (−)	genipa dye (vegetable remains)

It is therefore clear that the four myths about the origin of water that have been compared are linked by transformational relations which, by a chiasmus, establish a contrast between the Bororo versions and the Ge versions:

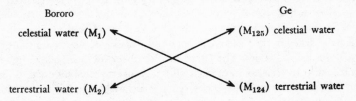

On the other hand, if we remember that while M_1 is simultaneously concerned with water and fire, there also exists M_{12} which is simultaneously concerned with fire and water,[6] we can complete the table above by adding the aforementioned myth to it. We then obtain a group of transformations with a double twist.

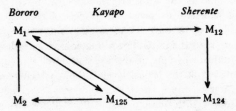

In all cases it is a matter of either the *addition* or the *subtraction* of an element, which may be *water* or *fire*. Each element can be analyzed according to two modalities, one celestial, the other terrestrial: cooking fire, the only kind of fire dealt with in this particular group, is terrestrial, as opposed to celestial fire which is destructive. This point will be established later (cf. p. 291). Lastly, the significant event is the result of a disjunction, which can be either vertical or horizontal:

	M_1	M_{12}	M_{124}	M_2	M_{125}
Addition/subtraction	+/(−)	+/(−)	+	+	+
Fire/water	−/(+)	+/(−)	−	−	−
Terrestrial/celestial	−	+	+	+	−
Horizontal/vertical	−	−	+	+	−

It is worthy of note that if we confine ourselves to the four contrasting sets of elements listed in the table, M_2 and M_{124} appear identical. Yet these two

[6] As is M_{125}, too, if we remember the information provided by Lukesch (1, p. 983; 2, p. 70) that it was from Bepkororoti that the Indians learned the technique of producing fire by twirling sticks.

myths are so different in content that any comparison between them would seem unthinkable, except through the medium of M_{125}, which itself differs from both of them through two transformations: terrestrial → celestial, horizontal → vertical.

The anomaly can be accounted for, if it is made clear that the contrasting elements listed in the table relate only to the messages, which are transmitted with the help of codes. The latter, in their turn, comprise both a grammar and lexical material. I have been able to prove by analysis that the grammatical armature of these codes remains invariable in the case of all the myths we have studied. But the same is not true of either the messages or the lexical material. Compared with those of other myths, the message of any one myth may seem to have been either more or less transformed or to be identical. But these differences affect the lexical material, too. In two myths belonging to one set, the lexical material may remain all the more similar because the corresponding messages have undergone a profound transformation; and if the transformational area is reduced in respect of the message, it will tend to increase in respect of the lexical material. It is therefore possible—as I have done—to combine two partially inverted messages and arrive at the initial lexical material in accordance with the rule that two semitransformations at the message level are equal to one complete transformation at the lexical level; although each semitransformation, considered separately, must affect the composition of the lexical material more than a total transformation would have done. The more partial the transformation of the message, the more blurred the initial lexical material tends to become, so that it is made unrecognizable when the transformation process brings the messages back to a state of identity.

The diagram given on page 211 can therefore be completed by noting that the myths occupying the upper angles of the quadrilateral use the same lexical material to code inverted messages, whereas those in the lower angles transmit the same message by means of different lexical resources.

I have already pointed out that all the tribes under consideration subdivide fire into two categories: celestial and destructive fire, terrestrial (or cooking) and creative fire. The point will become much clearer later; but, on the basis of information already mentioned, we know that the contrast between the two kinds of fire is given very little emphasis in Bororo mythology (cf. M_{120}). Conversely, water seems to be analyzed less thoroughly in the Sherente mythology we have at our disposal than in the mythology of other Ge tribes. In Sherente mythology only one kind of water is recognized—the sea, which is extended by the inland network of lakes and rivers, rather as a tree trunk puts out branches and twigs (the Choco myth explaining the origin of cultivated plants refers explicitly to this image; cf. Wassen 1, p. 109). The myths of the other Ge tribes do not allocate any special place to the lake and river systems; but, on the other hand, they differentiate between two kinds of celestial water: stormy rain and gentle rain, associated respectively with the "father" and "daughter" of rain (M125, M91). As for the Bororo, they subdivide water into three distinct categories: terrestrial water, formed by the lake and river system (M2), and two kinds of celestial water —thunder rain on the one hand, and calm, gentle rain on the other:

M127. Bororo. "The origin of gentle rain"

Because they were illtreated by their mothers and sisters, men of the Bokodori Cera clan changed into xinadatau birds (*galinha do bugre*) and disappeared into the air. The women only just managed to keep back one child. The birds told their little brother that if ever he were thirsty or too hot, he had only to imitate their call: "toká, toká, toká, ká, ká," and they would know that he needed water, and would cause a cloud to appear, which would bring a calm and gentle rain. This kind of rain is associated with the Butaudogue spirits, whereas violent rainstorms accompanied by wind and thunder are associated with the Badogebague spirits. (Colb. 3, pp. 229–30.)

In interpreting this myth, we encounter two difficulties. First of all, what were these birds which were called xinadatau in Bororo and *galinha do bugre* in the Portuguese vernacular? Ihering, who is familiar with the Portuguese term, admits that he is unable to identify the species. He thinks that the bird in question might possibly be the jacamin or the trumpeter bird, *Psophia crepitans*. But the cry of this bird, as he transcribes it: "hu-hu-hu-hû, with the final syllable prolonged as if emitted by a ventriloquist" ("Jacamin" entry), offers no resemblance to the cry described in M127. Under the heading *Činadatáo,* the *Enciclopédia Boróro* (Vol. I, p. 542) gives the following information: "an onomatopoeic word (a bird whose song seems to say *činadatáo*): Cancan (*Nomonyx dominicus*)." In spite of its brevity, this definition raises several difficulties. First of all, as I have just pointed out, the Bororo myth describes the bird's song very exactly, and the phonetic transcription it gives is quite different from the native word, which cannot therefore be an onomatopoeic term. Secondly, in the Portuguese vernacular *cancan* refers also to one of the Falconidae (Ihering, "Cancan" entry); M. Jacques Berlioz, a professor at the Natural History Museum, has been kind enough to explain that *Nomonyx dominicus* is a diving duck of the Erismature group (Anatidae-Oxyurinae). It therefore seems quite impossible that popular taxonomy should be guilty of the solecism of applying the term *galinha* "hen" to a duck. Actually, the vernacular term *galinha do bugre* "the Indians' hen" would seem to apply—by antiphrasis—only to the *cancan*, a carrion-eating bird which does not take fright at the approach of human beings, or perhaps to a bird that is directly associated with a gallinacean in the native mind. In both cases the bird would be the opposite term within the wild-pig/bird couple, either for the reasons previously indicated (p. 203), or because the contrast between them would be reducible to that between a technophilic and a technophobic animal.

Secondly, we do not know what the "gentle rain" referred to in the myth is exactly. We have seen that Colbacchini attributes it to the Butaudogue spirits, but this seems to be contradicted a little earlier by the statement that these same spirits "harassed the Indians with cold, wind, and rain" (Colb. 3, p. 229). In Magalhães' *Vocabulario* (p. 26) the word *butau* is given the meaning of "winter, the rainy season." According to the *Enciclopédia Boróro* (Vol. I, pp. 295-6), the Butao-doge preside over the rainy season, which lasts from the beginning of October to the end of April. The rest of the year is taken up by the dry season: *boe ki* "time of dryness," or *erubutu* "the burning" (of the brush or savannah). Yet in the sacred language these same spirits seem to be associated with gentle rain (EB, Vol. I, p. 975). Lastly, the *Enciclopédia Boróro* contains no reference to the Badogebague spirits, and the term *Baado Jebage* occurs there only in sociopolitical contexts (pp. 190-93).

In spite of these uncertainties, the myth establishes clearly that the Bororo conceived of two kinds of celestial water, which are in correlation with, and in opposition to, each other. One is calm and gentle, the other violent; one is beneficent since it is refreshing and thirst-quenching, the other is malefi-cent. I have shown that there exists a direct transformational relation between the Kayapo and Bororo myths about the origin of water, whether terrestrial (Bororo, M_2) or celestial (Kayapo, M_{125}). We can now see that there is also a direct transformational relation between the Kayapo myth (M_{125}) about the origin of maleficent celestial water and the Bororo myth (M_{127}) about the origin of (beneficent) celestial water. In each case we note vertical disjunction, which is the result of illtreatment inflicted either within a functional monosexual group (male hunters) or within a familial, bisexual group. The victim who has undergone disjunction is transformed either into an enemy (Kayapo) or into a friend (Bororo), according to whether his young doublet (son or brother) goes with him to the sky or remains on earth. The avenging hero lures his former companions by imitating the cries of the wild pigs, which are a superior kind of game; the faithful companions will be drawn toward the hero if he imitates the call of birds, an inferior kind of game. In one instance thunder-rain occurs, bringing death in its wake; in the other instance there is a gentle rainfall, ensuring material well-being and life.

At the same time we know that the Bororo deal with the rainy season in another myth (M_1), which I have shown to be symmetrical with the Sherente myth (M_{124}) dealing with the beginning of the dry season. In M_{127}, therefore, it cannot be the rainy season that is referred to, but possibly one of those rare showers of rain, very good for gardens, which sometimes occur in the middle of the dry season and are called, according to the region, either *chuva de preguiça,* because only this kind of rain is fine enough to penetrate the sloth's coat; *chuva de cigarra,* because they occur just when the cicadas are hatching out (Barbosa Rodrigues, p. 161); or, further south, *chuvas de caju,* because they make the cashew nut swell. If this hypothesis is correct, the Bororo water system can be expressed as follows:

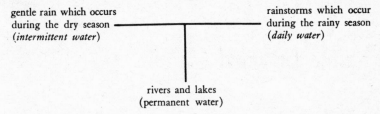

gentle rain which occurs during the dry season *(intermittent water)*

rainstorms which occur during the rainy season *(daily water)*

rivers and lakes (permanent water)

The Mundurucu also seem to have a triple classification of water: (1) rain and wind; (2) thunder rain; (3) fine rain (Murphy 1, p. 21; cf. also Kruse 3, Vol. 47, pp. 1002–5).

We must at this point go back to a detail in M_1. This myth about the origin of wind and rain (and therefore corresponding to the rainy season, as I have shown by a comparison with M_{124}, and as I shall prove directly) ended with the murder of the father, who was drowned in the waters of a lake, or rather a swamp (overgrown with aquatic plants). Anyone who has traveled in the Pantanal knows that it is impassable during the rainy season (the hero of the myth is responsible for the rainy season), but that parts of it dry up during the tropical winter (April to September). Consequently the lake and river system and the swamp form a twofold contrast: running water/stagnant water; nonperiodic (the whole year through)/periodic (for half the year). The same myth adds that the swamp is the abode of cannibal spirits, the buiogoe fish ("piranhas"); whereas another Bororo myth (M_{128}) explains that the creation of lake and river system by the hero Baitogogo was incomplete, because the water contained no fish. So a certain Baiporo ("opening of the hut") of the Paiwe clan took it upon himself to finish the work begun by his predecessor, and created the different species of fish (the myth is careful to exclude the piranhas) by throwing the branches of various floral species into the river (Colb. 3, p. 211).

The three categories of water therefore correspond to three types of diet: cannibalism is associated with the swamp, which itself is a relative function of the rainy season; fishing, which is congruous with hunting in relation to water, is associated with the permanent lake and river system; vegetable foodstuffs with the intermittent rains that occur during the dry season. The triple division of water corresponds to that of the three calls emitted by certain antifoods (M_9)—rock (the reverse of cannibalism), hardwood (the reverse of meat), and rotten wood (the reverse of cultivated plants)—as I showed on page 153 and following. I have also proved that the three kinds of antifood correspond to the triple patterns in the Sherente myth (M_{124}) about the origin of terrestrial water, which is itself homologous with the initial triad of three musical instruments in the key myth (M_1).

2

Double Inverted Canon

There is a third type of *canon*, which is very rare both because of its excessive difficulty and because it is normally not very pleasant to listen to. Its only merit is that it is very difficult to compose. I refer to what might be called a *double inverted canon*, because of the inversion in the part-singing, and the inverted relationship between the various parts themselves as they are sung. There is so much art in this kind of canon that, whether the parts are sung in their natural order or whether the score is turned round and they are sung backward, with the result that the beginning becomes the end and the top line the bass, the harmony remains sound and the canon regular.

J. J. ROUSSEAU, *Dictionary of Music,* "Canon" entry.

Let us now return to the Asare myth (M₁₂₄), an essential element of which I left temporarily unanalyzed. It will be remembered that the myth ends with the episode of the hero's brothers disporting themselves in water to the west, after which "they appear in the heavens, new and clean, as Sururu, the Seven Stars (the Pleiades)." In his monograph on the Sherente, Nimuendaju (6, p. 85) makes it clear that Asare is the star X of the Orion constellation, and that in native thought the X of Orion is in opposition to the Pleiades: the former is associated with the deified sun and with the "foreign" clan Prase belonging to the Shiptato moiety; the Pleiades are associated with the deified moon and the "foreign" clan Krozake belonging to the Sdakran moiety (the same contrast exists between the various clans in the myth about the origin of fire (M₁₂: cf. p. 76). I showed that the elder of the brothers-in-law belonged to the Sdakran clan, the younger to the Shiptato clan. Nevertheless, it is clear from M₁₂₄ that the two constellations both stand in the same relation to the contrast between the rainy season and the dry season, since their return coincides with the beginning of the latter. An unexplained detail in the myth confirms the association: Asare's brothers try in vain to quench his thirst by cracking open nuts of a tucum palm (*Astrocaryum*) so that he can drink the water inside. Now, further to the southwest (latitude 18° to 24°S.), about the middle of the eighteenth century, the Caduveo used to observe important feast days in mid-June, in connection with the return of the Pleiades and, according to an early nineteenth-century source, with the ripening of the palm nuts (*Acrocomia*; Ribeiro 1, p. 68).[7]

[7] The Caduveo have two different myths about the origin of nibetad, the Pleiades. They were said to be either children who had been changed into stars as a punish-

The enormous importance of the Pleiades ritual among the Gran Chaco tribes presents problems that I will not tackle here. I mention it simply as further evidence of the link between the Pleiades and the seasons throughout the whole tropical America (cf. Von den Steinen 1).

In connection with the Sherente, we have extremely detailed information to help understand the text of M$_{124}$ which, from the astronomical point of view, is rather puzzling.

> They count the months by lunar periods, and their year begins in June with the appearance of the Pleiades, when the sun is leaving the constellation of Taurus. They call the Pleiades Sururu, and this constellation is known to all natives of Brazil. About a week later appear the *pluvias Hyades* and Orion's swordbelt, also known to the Sherente. When these stars appear in the morning, it is believed to be a sign of wind. Various legends are related about the Pleiades. Their heliacal rising (before the sun) and also their cosmic rising (with the sun) are observed. Between two such risings of Sururu the Sherente count thirteen moons (thirteen *oá-ité*), and this forms a year = *oá-hú* (*hú* "collection"?).
>
> They divide the year into two parts: (1) four moons of dry weather, more or less, from June to September; (2) nine moons of rain (*á-ké-nan*) from September to May. In the first two dry months the large trees of a piece of forest land are felled, to free it for cultivation. In the following two months the ground is cleared by burning the scrub, and then seeds are sowed to profit by the rains at the end of September and October. (J. F. de Oliveira, pp. 393–4.)

Something similar is observed among the Tapirape who live approximately on the same latitude (10° S.), but a little farther to the west: "The Pleiades . . . are watched anxiously and impatiently as the rains diminish, because their disappearance over the western horizon in May signals the end of the rains. This is the time for the largest ceremonial of the year. The position of the Pleiades is noted to date the many ceremonies of the heavy rainy period (November to April)" (Wagley, pp. 256–7). The Timbira (3° to 9°S.) prepare for the rainy season, which lasts from September to April, when the Pleiades (Krot) are visible on the western horizon after sunset; this is the appropriate time to work in the plantations. And when, toward evening, the Pleiades are no longer visible in the same direction, the period controlled by the so-called rainy season moieties begins (Nim. 8, pp. 62, 84, 163). In the case of the Bororo, the Pleiades appear on

---

ment for having played too noisily after nightfall (cf. in M$_{124}$ the noise made by Asare's brothers as they bathe, and later M$_{171}$, p. 302), or a male star which had come down from the sky to marry a mortal, to whom he gave maize and manioc which, in those days, ripened as soon as they were planted (Ribeiro 1, p. 138). The transformation of Star into a male character, which is typical of North American mythology, is found in South America among the Caraja (M$_{110}$) and the Umotina (Baldus 2, pp. 21–2).

the horizon before dawn, toward the end of June, and are a sign that the dry season is already well advanced (EB, Vol. I, p. 296).

In Amazonia, the Pleiades disappear in May and reappear in June, thus heralding floods, the molting of birds, and the renewal of vegetation (Barbosa Rodrigues, p. 221, n. 2). According to the same author, the natives think that the Pleiades, during their short period of invisibility, hide at the bottom of a well where the thirsty can come to drink. This well is reminiscent of the one dug by Asare's brothers—who were incarnations of the Pleiades—in order to appease the hero's thirst.

Farther to the north (3° to 5°N.) the Taurepan believe that the disappearance of the Pleiades heralds rain and abundant supplies of food, where as their appearance heralds the beginning of the dry season (K.G. 1, p. 12, and Vol. III, pp. 281 ff.). In French Guiana (2° to 5°N.) "the Pleiades are known to all the natives . . . they joyously greet their return on the horizon, because it coincides with the beginning of the dry season. Their disappearance, which occurs about the middle of May, is accompanied by a fresh outbreak of rain which makes navigation impossible" (Crevaux, p. 215). The Pleiades were equally significant for the ancient Tupinamba, who lived along the coast: "They also know," Thevet writes, "that the Pleiades is the constellation which makes their manioc grow, from which they in turn make flour" (Métraux 1, p. 51, n. 3). It is said of the seventeenth-century Tupi: *Annos suos numerant ab exortu Heliaco Pleiadum quos Ceixu vocant atque ideo annum eodem nomine denotant: accidit autem is ortus mense nostro Maio* (Piso, p. 369).[8]

In spite of the fact that all the accounts above stress the importance of the Pleiades, there are divergences between them. We have just seen that among the Taurepan the appearance of the Pleiades is linked with the beginning of the dry season; the Palikur, who live on the same latitude, refer to them in order to forecast the start of the rainy season (Nim. 14a, p. 90). But, apart from the fact that the various texts give hardly any indication of the time of night when the observations are made, or of the precise feature that is held to be significant—cosmic rising or heliacal rising, visibility or nonvisibility on the western horizon after sunset, etc.[9]—we must also take into consideration the various modes of life. The abundance to which the Taurepan refer is a plentiful supply of fish in the rivers, and this does not necessarily coincide with an equal abundance of ground game or

[8] The connection between the first rising of the Pleiades and the burnings undertaken during the dry season no doubt explains why the opossum chose this time to set fire to his tail (Barbosa Rodrigues, pp. 173-7).

[9] It is very rare to find references as detailed as the following: "When in the evening, after the stars have become visible, the Pleiades rise in the east, then for them (the Orinoco Indians) the new year (rainy season) begins . . ." (Gumilla, Vol. 11, p. 281); or "Hence, from east to west of the Guiana area from the Orinoco to Cayenne, the reappearance of the Pleiades, or 'seven sisters,' on the eastern horizon soon after sunset in December constitutes the passing of a year" (Roth 2, p. 715).

vegetable products. In the Guiana area the natives think in terms of four seasons instead of two: there is a "short" and a "long" rainy season, and a "short" and a "long" dry season (Ahlbrinck, "weyu" entry); and these terms have only a relative value, since rain continues to fall throughout the year and varies only in intensity. Finally it must not be forgotten that in Brazil climatic conditions in respect to rain are reversed when one moves from the northeast coast to the central plateau, and from the northern coast to the south (Figure 9).

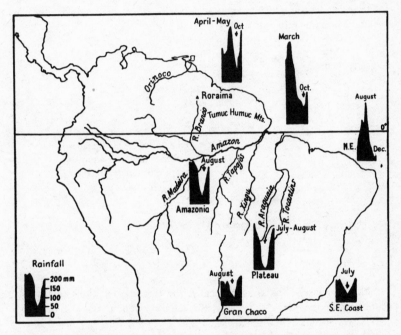

Figure 9. Average total annual rainfall in tropical America (from P. Gourou, *Atlas Classique,* Vol. II, Paris, Hachette, 1956).

Be that as it may, I propose to restrict myself for the moment to the particular problems posed by the Asare myth (M124), which is concerned with one star of the Orion constellation and the Pleiades. In the myth they are simultaneously in correlation with each other—they are brothers—and in opposition to each other—one brother is innocent, the others guilty, and although they are brothers, they belong to different moities. Now this twofold relation can also be found in the Old World, where, however, the appearance of the two constellations cannot have the same meteorological implications, since the seasons are reversed in the northern and southern hemispheres.

For the ancients, Orion was associated with the bad season: *Cum subito adsurgens fluctu nimbosus Orion* (Virgil *Aenead*. I. 535). At the same time, a rapid survey of the adjectives used by the Latin poets in connection with Orion and the Pleiades shows that, from the meteorological point of view, the two constellations were closely associated. Orion is *nimbosus, aquosus, nubilus, pluvius;* the Pleiades are *nimbosae, aquosae, pluviae, udae* "humid," *imbriferae* "causing rain," *procellosae* "stormy." They can even by extension be understood in the sense of storm: *Haec per et Aegaeas hiemes, Pliadumque nivosum Sidus* (Statius *Silvae* I. 3, 95, in Quicherat). In spite of the fact that there appears to be an etymological link between "spring" and the Latin word for the Pleiades—*vergiliae* from *ver* "spring"—sailors believed that the constellation brought rain and storms.

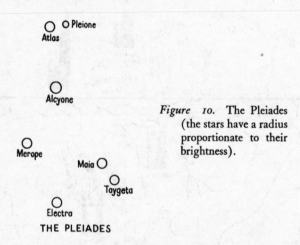

Figure 10. The Pleiades (the stars have a radius proportionate to their brightness).

Although closely linked symbolically, the two constellations often differ in respect to the ideas underlying the names given to them. This is apparent, for instance, in French usage: *Les Pléiades;* formerly *la Pléiade,* is a collective concept embracing several stars that are not differentiated one from another. The same is true of the popular names given to the constellation—*les Chevrettes, la Poussinière* in French; in Italian *Gallinelle*; and in German *Gluckhenne.* The Orion constellation, on the other hand, is split into various parts. The stars, or groups of stars, are differentiated by their connection with certain individuals, parts of the body, or objects: right knee, left foot, left shoulder; and shield, sword, belt, or rake—in German *Jacobsstab;* in Spanish *las tres Marias* or *los tres Magos* (cf. Hoffman-Krayer, pp. 677–89).

It is a remarkable fact that the same contrast is found in many South American languages: "For the Bacairi Indians, this star (Sirius) constitutes a group along with Aldebaran and the Pleiades. Orion is a large wooden frame for drying manioc; the principal stars are the tops of stakes. Thus,

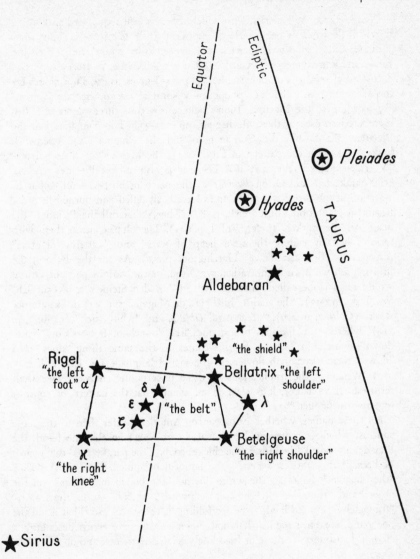

Figure 11. The Orion constellation.

Sirius is the end of a horizontal beam which supports the frame longitudinally. The Pleiades . . . represent a handful of flour spilled on the ground" (Von den Steinen 2, p. 461). The Tupi along the northwestern coast used to associate a constellation that they call *seichujura* ("the bee's scaffolding") with the Pleiades. It was a "constellation of nine stars arranged in the shape of a gridiron and predicted rain.

We have here the Pleiades, with which they are well acquainted and which they call Seychou. It only starts to appear in their hemisphere about mid-January, and as soon as it appears, they expect to have rain: and indeed the rain starts immediately afterward." (Claude d'Abbeville, p. 316.)

Instead of *seichu,* Von den Steinen (1, p. 245) gives, as the Tupi names for the Pleiades, terms that are phonetically similar: *eischu, eiruçu* "swarm."

According to the Macusi, Orion's belt consisted of three pieces of a dismembered corpse (Barbosa Rodrigues, pp. 227-30). The Tamanac call the Pleiades "the bush"; the Cumanagoto and the Chaima, "the openwork basket" (cf. with the pattern in Figure 12); the Mojos, "the little parrots" (Von den Steinen 1, pp. 243-46). The Caraja also call the Pleiades *teraboto* "the parakeets," and Orion *hatedäotä* "the patch of burned land"—that is, a section of the forest where the trees have been felled and burned in order to start a plantation (Ehrenreich, p. 89). The Aztecs call the Pleiades "the heap" or "the market" (Seler, Vol. I, p. 621). The Hopi contrast them with Orion's belt by calling them "a heap of stars" and "a string of stars" respectively (Frigout; Tewa: Harrington, p. 50). As for the Bororo, the information we have is contradictory. Orion, or the various parts of Orion, would seem to be called "tortoise shell" (Von den Steinen 2, p. 650; EB, Vol. I, pp. 612-13), "the wading bird" (B. de Magalhães, p. 44) or "migratory stork" (Colb. 2, p. 220), "great cart" (*ibid.*), and "white stick" (Colb. 3, p. 219); whereas the Pleiades bear names like "bunch of flowers" or "white down"—which, in fact, in Bororo comes to the same thing, since *akiri* "down" means savannah flowers in the sacred language (cf. EB, Vol. I, p. 975). Whatever the implications of these uncertainties may be (we shall return to them later), it is clear at all events that the pattern of contrast remains unchanged.[10]

All these names, whether European or American, refer then to the same contrast which is represented in a variety of ways: on the one hand, the Pleiades are called "the kids," "the chickencoop," "the parakeets," "the swarm of bees,"[11] the "tortoise's nest," "the handful of spilled flour," "the Bush," "the openwork basket," "the white down," "the bunch of flowers": on the other hand, "the rake" or "the belt" ("sword," "shield," etc.), "the frame," "the patch of burned land," "the scaffolding," "the stick," etc. That is, on the one hand, we have names that boil down to collective terms describing a chance distribution of more or less closely related elements: and on the other,

---

[10] Comparisons can be made with several of the names given to Orion in North America: "the hanging cords" (Zuni), and among the Eskimo of the Bering Strait, "posts on which rawhide lines are being stretched"; these contrast with names for the Pleiades, like "the litter of fox cubs" (Nelson, p. 449). The Alaska Eskimo also apply a collective term to the Pleiades: "the hunters" (Spencer, p. 258).

[11] A contemporary astronomer writes in connection with the Pleiades: "The telescope reveals an association numbered at least in the hundreds, looking somewhat like a swarm of bees. If the apparent motions of the stars were speeded up some billions of times, the analogy could be still closer with the individual members darting this way and that while the swarm as a whole retained its coherence."

analytical terms describing a systematic arrangement of clearly individualized elements, which are often manufactured and composite objects. Certain analogies are even more striking. For instance, the Tucuna compare the Pleiades with a group of people who are lifted up to the sky on a tapir hide (M_{82}), while the Ancients used to refer to the constellation as "the merchants' cloth" (the use of the term has, however, been explained by a rationalization: the merchants, so it is said, could tell by the Pleiades whether the winter would be cold, and they would sell a lot of cloth). Similarly, the splitting of the constellation of Orion into "shoulders" and "knees" also has its equivalent among the Tucuna: the word *venkiča* means Orion and the N-shaped hook used for hanging up kitchen utensils on the hut walls. One of the Tucuna myths that mentions Orion (M_{129a}) relates how the knee of the god Venkiča became paralyzed in a bent position (which explains the hook shape) and became Orion, "the celestial hook" (Nim. 13, pp. 15, 142, 149). Another Tucuna myth (M_{129b}) represents Orion as a one-legged hero (Nim. 13, p. 147):[12] and this is reminiscent, on the one hand, of the Guiana

[12] This myth, although obscure, is of special interest. The beginning—which shows two sons, the elder of whom behaves prudently toward an ogre, the younger imprudently—is reminscent of M_{28} which is also about the origin of Orion. But at the same time this particular myth has to do with cooking: the younger brother's offense consists in eating the ogre's cooked sweet potatoes. Informed of the fact by a loquacious sweet potato, the ogre sends the culprit into such a deep sleep that his brother cannot waken him, even by burning him with a blazing firebrand. Then the ogre tears off one of his legs and eats it.

In spite of being thus maimed, the one-legged man proves himself an expert, and even miraculous, hunter, since he only takes small pieces of flesh from the game he kills, and when he gets back to the village, the tiny fragments become large enough completely to cover the hero's wife, who, to begin with, had been disappointed at the sight of such a small quantity.

The hero finally kills a tapir, which he offers to the buzzards, on condition that they take him up into the sky, where he becomes the constellation Orion (Nim. 13, p. 147).

In this particular myth, therefore, everything appears to happen the wrong way round: the ogre is the master of cooked vegetable matter, the meal speaks after it has been eaten, the one-legged man moves more quickly than if he had two legs, the cook is buried under the meat she ought to have been putting into the pot. . . .

Now the final episode is clearly the reverse of the Tupi myth about the origin of fire: the hero offers the buzzards a freshly killed tapir, instead of turning himself into a "well-hung" tapir (although he has not avoided being burned by a firebrand, an anti-culinary and "cannibalistic" use of cooking fire); in return he is transported into the sky in the shape of a star (celestial fire), instead of bringing cooking fire, which until then had been reserved purely for cannibalistic uses, back to earth. We are therefore dealing with a disjunction on the sky-earth axis, the origin of which lies in a culinary paradox (the ogre lives on vegetable tubers, like a civilized human being), whereas in the Tupi myth, the means of cooking is wrested from the cannibalistic vultures as a result of a conjunction on the sky-earth axis. In one instance the hero is actually dismembered in order to be eaten fresh; in the other instance he pretends to offer himself intact in order (not) to be eaten in a state of putrefaction.

When the two myths are looked at from this standpoint, it must be admitted that their transformation can be conceived of in one direction only. It is possible that M_{129b} may have emerged from M_{65} through inversion of all the elements. The contrary

myths, one of which has already been dealt with (M28), and on the other, of the North American practice, especially prevalent among the village tribes of the Upper Missouri (Mandan, Hidatsa), of identifying the three stars of the belt and the stars situated below it, with a severed hand, the story of which is told in certain myths (Beckwith, pp. 41–2).

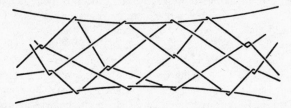

Figure 12. String game played by the Toba Indians representing the constellation of the Pleiades (from Lehmann-Nitsche, 5, p. 183).

I do not claim that the contrast with which I have just been dealing, and which—reduced to its simplest expression—puts the Pleiades in the category of the continuous and Orion in that of the discontinuous, is present every-where. To confine ourselves to South America, it is possible that it still exists

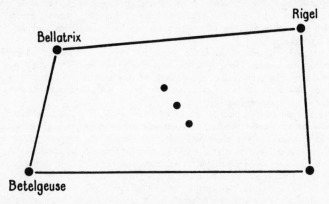

Figure 13. The constellation of Orion according to the Toba Indians (from Lehmann-Nitsche, 4, p. 278).

in a weak form among the Ipurina, who see the Pleiades as a snake and Orion as a beetle. The terminology used by the Urubu is more complicated and corresponds to some extent to my hypothesis, since they call the Pleiades

hypothesis would give rise to insoluble difficulties. We have here then a typical example of the light that structural analysis, even when kept at the most formal level, can throw on the concrete, historical relations among peoples.

"grandfather many things" and Orion "three-eyes"; but contradicts it insofar as they think of each star of the Pleiades as "really a man dressed in his feather ornaments" (Huxley, pp. 184–5). The Toba and other tribes of the Gran Chaco call the Pleiades either "grandfather" or "grandchildren" (Figure 12), and they see Orion as three old women sitting in their house or their garden (Figure 13).

However, there are other, different groupings. The Mataco make a single, large constellation, which they call "great stork," out of the Pleiades (the head), the Hyades (the body), and what we refer to as Orion's belt (the foot).

Figure 14. Australian painting on bark by natives of Groote Eylandt, representing the Pleiades, above, and Orion, below (from *Australia. Aboriginal Paintings-Arnhem Land,* New York Graphic Society-Unesco, 1954, Plate XXX). The complex system of opposites used will be noted: convergent/divergent, rounded/angular, continuous/discontinuous. These correspond to different pairs of opposites on the mythological plane: female/male, passive/active, etc. (cf. Charles P. Mountford, *The Tiwi: Their Art, Myth and Ceremony,* London-Melbourne, 1958, p. 177 and Plate 62 B).

Elsewhere the Big Dipper and Orion are imagined as looking like a one-legged man or animal (Lehmann-Nitsche 3, pp. 103–43).

The Guianian Indians seem to proceed according to a different principle. It is not enough to say that for them Orion's belt represents a severed limb. This detail is part of a complex succession of events: the Pleiades represent a woman trying to catch her husband (the Hyades), one of whose legs has just been cut off (the belt; M_{28}); alternatively, the Pleiades are a woman seduced by a tapir, with the Hyades representing the head and Aldebaran the eye, while the husband (Orion) pursues the guilty lovers (Brett, pp. 199–200). Finally, according to the Taurepan, the Pleiades, the Aldebaran group, and part of Orion form one and the same personage and correspond respectively to the head, the body, and the one remaining leg (K.G. 1, p. 57).[13]

In spite of all the exceptions, all the shades of distinction that should not

[13] The "diachronic" Guianian pattern of the chase is found among the central Eskimo. Cf. Boas 1, pp. 636, 643.

be omitted, and all the necessary corrections, I nevertheless believe that throughout the world Orion and the Pleiades are seen as being both in correlation with, and in opposition to, each other. The relation occurs with sufficient frequency and in regions far enough apart to be credited with significance. And this significance seems to be due to two remarkable characteristics of these particular constellations. Taken together, Orion and the Pleiades can be defined, diachronically, in terms of presence or absence. On the other hand, during the period when they are visible, they form a contrast—synchronically this time—as a well-organized system and as an ill-organized mass, or if another image is preferred, as a clear-cut outline of the field and a blurred form within the field.

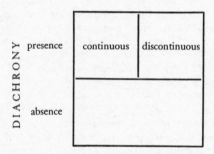

The second contrast, by simultaneously interiorizing and reinforcing the first, turns the Orion-Pleiades couple into a special symbol of the seasonal alternation to which it is empirically linked and which can be conceptualized in a variety of ways, according to the particular region and society: summer and winter, dry season and rainy season, settled or unsettled weather, work and leisure, abundance and famine, meat diet and vegetarian diet, etc. Only the pattern of contrast remains constant, while the ways in which it is interpreted and the subject matter it is supposed to contain vary from group to group and from one hemisphere to the other. In the latter case, and even with respect to a contrast in which the subject matter is identical, the common functions of Orion and the Pleiades will obviously be inverted.

Nevertheless, without the fact being clearly obvious, we find ourselves faced with a curious problem. Classical antiquity associated Orion with rain and storms. Now we have seen that in central Brazil, Orion is also associated with water—but terrestrial, not celestial water. In Greek and Roman mythology Orion caused rain to *fall*. As Asare, the thirsty hero, Orion makes water rise up from the depths of the earth.

It is easy to understand, since it is an obvious cosmographical fact, that the same constellation that causes rain to fall in the northern hemisphere should be a harbinger of drought in the southern hemisphere: in the inland areas between the equator and the Tropic of Capricorn, the rainy season corresponds approximately to our autumn and winter, the dry season to our spring and summer. The Asare myth faithfully presents the "southern" version of this factual truth, since the Pleiades, and Orion which follows closely in their wake, are said to herald the beginning of the dry season. Up to this point there is nothing surprising to note. However, the myth goes much further: it divides the water theme into two parts—celestial water which is made to recede/terrestrial water which is made to gush forth: that is, on the one hand, the advent of the dry season; on the other, the creation of the ocean and the lake and river system. In the latter connection the Asare myth maintains the northern association of Orion with water, but the water is inverted.

How does it happen that in one hemisphere Orion is associated with celestial water in accordance with meteorological experience, while in the other hemisphere, without there being any possibility of establishing a connection with experience, symmetry is preserved by means of an apparently incomprehensible link between Orion and water which is chthonic in origin—that is, celestial water conceived of, as it were, upside down?

A preliminary hypothesis can be put forward and straightway dismissed. Prehistorians believe that the American Indians came from the Ancient World during the middle Paleolithic; and we might suppose that the mythology relating to Orion goes back to that period and was brought to America. The Indians may simply have adapted it to fit the new astronomical and meteorological conditions of the southern hemisphere. The problem posed by the precession of the equinoxes would not give rise to serious difficulties; on the contrary, the global cycle is in the region of twenty-six thousand years, which corresponds roughly to the time when people first appeared in the New World (at least according to the present state of our knowledge). At that period therefore, the position of the constellations on the zodiac was approximately the same as it is today. On the other hand, there is nothing to prove—and a good deal to contradict—the supposition that meteorological conditions were the same in South America at that time as they are now, or that they have remained the same throughout the ages. But the suggested explanation comes up against another, and much more serious, difficulty. In order to associate Orion with the origin of terrestrial water, the distant ancestors of the Sherente would have had to do more than merely reverse the meteorological symbolism of the constellation: they would have had to have known that the earth was round and then—logically, but only on this one condition—to have changed the rain that fell from the sky on the Old World into water that, in the New World, rose up from the depths of the earth.

We are thus forced to come back to the only acceptable explanation. The Sherente myth about Orion, in which the stars fulfill a function whose relation to water is symmetrical with that assigned to them in the northern hemisphere, must be reducible to a transformation of another myth belonging to the southern hemisphere, in which the role assumed by the hero is exactly identical with that played by Orion in the other hemisphere. Now such a myth exists, and we are perfectly familiar with it, since it is the key myth about the Bororo bird-nester who was responsible for creating storms, wind, and rain; he is a hero to whom the epithet *nimbosus* applies perfectly: Orion, too, was called *nimbosus* in the Mediterranean area—and "fearful star" according to Pliny.

The hero of the Bororo myth is called Geriguiguiatugo, a name whose possible etymology I have already discussed (cf. p. 138). I indicated at that point that the etymology put forward by the Salesians would eventually be confirmed. They break down the name into *atugo* "jaguar" (a detail whose significance has been stressed, since the Bororo hero occupies the position of master of fire, like the jaguar in the Ge myths) and *geriguigui* "land tortoise" which is also the name of the southern constellation, Corvus. It is therefore possible that Geriguiguiatugo is Corvus, just as Asare is χ *Orionis*.

Colbacchini himself, writing either alone or in conjunction with Albisetti, quotes the word *geriguigui* on several occasions as meaning "constellation of Corvus, *cágado:* land tortoise" (Colb. I, p. 34; 2, pp. 219, 254, 420). The *Enciclopédia Boróro,* compiled by Albisetti, suddenly abandons the initial meaning in favor of a different constellation, situated in the immediate vicinity of Orion, thus reverting, it would seem, to an old reading *"jaboti* shell," noted in the past by Von den Steinen for part of Orion (Jabuti-Schildkröte 2, p. 399, in the German original). As a matter of fact, in the dialects of the Mato Grosso the terms *jaboti* and *cágado* are used with a certain latitude and occasionally overlap (cf. Ihering, "Cágado" entry; EB, Vol. I, p. 975: in the sacred language, the *jaboti* is called "great *cágado*"). According to the *Enciclopédia Boróro,* the word *jerigigi* means not only "a variety of *cágado*" (pp. 185, 689) but also a small constellation consisting of five stars in the shape of a tortoise, the head of which is represented by Rigel (p. 612). It should be noted in passing that this constellation may be the same as the one described by Koch-Grünberg as "consisting of Rigel and four smaller stars, situated to the north and the south," and which the Guianian Indians call "Zilikawei's bench," Zilikawei being the hero who is represented in their mythology by Orion (K.G., 1, Vol. III, p. 281).

This discrepancy between the Salesian sources calls for one or two further comments. In the first place, Von den Steinen noted eighty years ago that the Bororo "were not always in agreement about the meaning of the constellations" (2, p. 650). I have already quoted (p. 222) significant examples of this lack of stability in the astronomical vocabulary, which is proved by the modern character of certain names: "great cart" for the Big Dipper (Colb. 2, p. 220), "great gun" and "small gun" for two other constellations (EB, Vol. I, pp. 612–13). It follows that one particular appellation does not necessarily exclude others, and consequently the most recent are to be viewed with a certain degree of suspicion. Having made this point, I add that it seems inconceivable that Colbacchini should have persistently confused the southern constellation Corvus with a part of Orion which was more than one hundred degrees removed from it (the right ascensions are twelve hours and five hours, respectively). Even in his first book Colbacchini showed that, in addition to Corvus, he could identify such modest constellations as Telescopium, Argo, and Pavo, whereas his successors are almost always vague and uncertain (1, pp. 33-4). For instance, they place the constellation, which Colbacchini declared was virtually identical with Argo, "in the vicinity of Orion," in spite of the fact that there was three hours difference between the respective right ascensions and sixty degrees betwen the declinations.

For the reasons above, I do not doubt that fifty years ago Colbacchini's informants intended *geriguigui* to mean the southern constellation Corvus. This particular meaning has since disappeared, either as a result of the independently testified confusion among words designating tortoises of different species, or because the original name of Corvus has been transferred to part of Orion. Far from excluding the second hypothesis, the first tends rather to confirm its probable accuracy.

A fresh link now appears between the Geriguiguiatugo myth (M_1) and the Asare myth (M_{124}). I have already shown, independently, that the two myths stand in a transformational relation to each other. It is not simply a matter of extending the demonstration to a different field, since it now includes astronomical equivalences. We also obtain two essential results.

First of all, it becomes clear why the Sherente make Orion the origin or the sign of earthly water. As might be supposed, there is no direct link between the popular astronomy of the Ancient World and that of the New: there is however an indirect link and a perfectly plausible one. The Greek and Latin races associated Orion with the rainy season for empirical reasons. We need only postulate, first, that in their hemisphere the Bororo followed a similar procedure in associating Corvus with the rainy season, and second, that Orion and Corvus dominate the southern sky at different periods, for it to follow that if two myths are as systematically opposed to each other as are M_1 and M_{124}, even though they use the same terminology and one deals with celestial water and the other with chthonic water (cf. the tables on p. 211): then, if one of the myths refers to the constellation of Corvus, the other must inevitably refer to the constellation Orion, always provided that a contrast between the two myths is in fact present in the native mind.

The preceding explanation depends on the fulfillment of certain conditions. But its verification would lead to another result, even more important than the first. For in the last analysis we perceive that the course I have been following from the beginning can be verified objectively, in its entirety (so far as its various parts have formed a logical sequence). The transformational relations I have discovered between the two myths have so far remained a question of interpretation. The proof of their reality now depends on one hypothesis, and one alone: namely that the southern constellation Corvus can fulfill the same function in the southern hemisphere as the Orion constellation does in the northern hemisphere, or as it did in the past. The hypothesis can be proved in two ways. Ethnographically, by establishing that the Indians of Brazil do in fact observe Corvus with this function in mind; or if this is not feasible, by checking whether there exists a time lag between the course of Corvus and that of Orion in the southern sky which would roughly correspond to the difference between the seasons.

As for the first point, it is a pity that South American ethnographic studies do not provide such a wealth of detailed information as is available for several Pacific islands in comparable latitudes where Corvus appears to have had the function postulated in my hypothesis. Thus, in the Caroline Islands, *Sor-a-bol* ("Corvi") means literally "the viewer of the taro patches," because the constellation is visible during the taro season (Christian, pp. 388–9); in the Marquesas *me'e* ("Corvus") has perhaps a connection with *mei,* the fruit of the breadfruit tree, harvested during the rainy season, which is also the time when fish are most plentiful (Handy, pp. 350–52); in Pukapuka *Te Manu* ("Corvus") is a bird whose morning rising heralds the season of collective reef fishing (Beaglehole, p. 350). These details are all the more interesting in that in Polynesia the Pleiades play a part similar to that attributed to them by the South American Indians. In Polynesia, too, we find myths explaining the origin of certain constellations, whose armature is identical with that of the American myths (cf. below, p. 242).

In the case of tropical America we have to be content with less definite information. We shall probably never know whether the heart-shaped constellation, visible during the rainy season in northeastern Brazil, which the ancient Tupi used to call the "vulture" (Claude d'Abbeville, chap. 51), was Corvus or not. As support for the theory that it was, we may note the fact that the tribes along the tributaries on the right bank of the Rio Negro also give this particular constellation the name of a bird: "the flying heron" (K.G. 0, p. 60); they therefore imagine diagonal lines linking the stars at the tips of the trapezium in pairs, instead of linking the sides, as the Bororos do and as Claude d'Abbeville himself does when he talks about a "tortoise shell" or a "heart." We must not jump to conclusions, however, since we have seen earlier (p. 221) that the Tupi who lived along the coast, unlike the Sherente who lived inland, associated the Pleiades with the rainy season, and perhaps Orion, too. The Palikur, another coastal tribe living a few degrees farther north, took the four constellations to be "masters of rain." Two of these constellations were possibly Orion and Scorpio; the other two have not been identified (Nim. 4a, p. 90).

Under the name Pakamu-sula-li, "the pakamu fish barbecue" (*Batrachoides surinamensis*; Ahlbrinck, "pakamu" entry) the constellation Corvus played an important but obscure part in the cosmology of the Caribs of Guiana. Its probable vespertine rising was said to coincide with the "short" dry season of the equatorial zone (mid-February to mid-May), and in certain circumstances that remain rather vague, its diurnal culmination was supposed to herald the end of this world and the birth of a new one (Penard in Goeje, p. 118).[14]

In the inland regions of Guiana the natives give the name Tauna to an evil-minded divinity who is responsible for creating storms and destroying trees by lightning. Tauna can be seen standing in the sky between his two barbecues, *tauna-zualu,* which are formed by the four main stars of the Big Dipper and Corvus respectively (K.G. 1, Vol. III, p. 278 ff.). This item of information has a threefold interest for us. In the first place, it contains an explicit reference to Corvus which is associated, as among the Bororo, with wind, storms, and rain. Second, the male god Tauna, who punishes mankind by means of tornadoes and lightning, immediately calls to mind Bepkororoti in the Ge myth (M_{125}, M_{125a}, M_{125b}), which, as I have already shown, but on different grounds, is in a transformational relation with the key myth (cf. pp. 209–12). If the Guianian divinity corresponding to the Ge hero, like the Bororo hero, represents the constellation of Corvus (or a group of constellations including Corvus), then this fact constitutes an additional argument in support of my reconstruction. Finally, the Guianian legend stresses the fact that the four main stars of the Big Dipper (which are situated at the tips of a trapezium), and those of Corvus which present the same formation, have almost the same right ascensions (the difference is only a few degrees). It is possible therefore that Tauna, who stands between these two constellations, ought to be identified with stars, or a group of stars, having the same right ascension as the constellations and differing from them only in declination, which would be somewhere between that of the Big Dipper ($+60°$) and that of Corvus ($-20°$). Coma Berenices, which satisfies both conditions, consequently seems eminently fitted to play, in mythology, the role of combinatory variant of Corvus. Now it so happens that this small constellation occupies an important place in the beliefs of the Kalina of Guiana, but by a paradox which can very quickly be resolved, it is ostensibly

[14] At first blush, one hesitates to accept the fact that natives can refer to the diurnal culmination of a constellation as if it were an observable phenomenon. Yet, through practice no doubt, their keenness of vision is far superior to ours. The Bororo, for instance, are said to have "a marvelously well-developed sense of sight . . . which allows them to point out to a companion the position of the planet Venus in broad daylight" (EB, Vol. I, p. 285). The astronomers I have consulted have been skeptical about this and completely incredulous about the diurnal culmination of Corvus. However, it is not necessary to accept the fact that the culmination was actually observed (any more than the cosmic rising of the Pleiades, to which I referred on p. 217) in order to understand how myths can refer to concepts of this order. It would be enough if the diurnal position of stars such a Venus (six hundred times brighter than Corvus, according to M. Pecker) were perceptible to more practiced eyes than ours, and the natives thus felt authorized to assume the existence, in the day sky, of events comparable to those that we ourselves can only discern in the night sky.

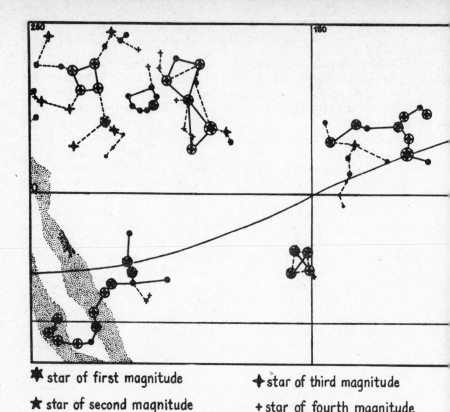

🟊 star of first magnitude   ✦ star of third magnitude

★ star of second magnitude   ✛ star of fourth magnitude

Figure 15. The equatorial sky (according to K.G.o). From left to right: Hercules ("the pacu fish") and Boötes ("the piranha fish") enclosing Corona Australis ("the armadillo"); at the bottom on the left, Scorpio ("the big snake"), followed on the right by Cervus ("the flying heron"); then Leo ("the crab"), then Gemini, Canis Major with Columba below, and moving up along the length of the Milky Way again, Orion and Eridanus ("the dance axe"). For the Indians this group (minus Eridanus) consists of the five otters busy stealing

associated, not with the rainy season as might be expected from its position on the zodiac, but with the "long" dry season, which even bears its name (Ahlbrinck, "Sirito" entry, 5c; "weyu," 8).

To solve the difficulty, we must take a closer look at the situation. The long dry season lasts from mid-August to mid-November, and in the area inhabited by the Kalina, Coma Berenices becomes visible during the month of October (Ahlbrinck, "Sirito" entry)—that is, when the dry season is drawing to a close. In Kalina the constellation is called *ombatapo,* which means "face." The myth of origin (M_{130}) explains how a starving old woman stole a fish from her son-in-law's net. This made the latter very angry, and he told the pataka fish (*Hoplias malabaricus*) to gobble her up. Although only her

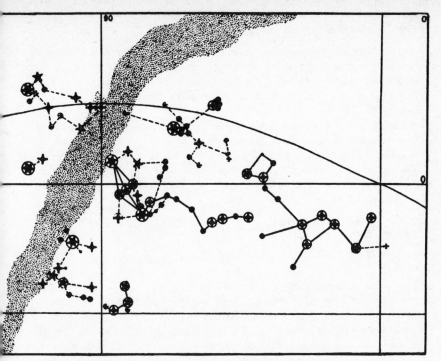

 native constellations   European constellations

the fish placed on a barbecue (Columba), by a fisherman armed with a net (stretched between Rigel, Betelgeuse, and three stars of the constellation Orion). Above and to the right, the Hyades and Pleiades ("the small boys," "the swarm of wasps"); on the extreme right, Cetus ("the jaguar"). The Milky Way is indicated by stippling; the section in the center and on the right is that to which the myths refer.

head and the upper part of her chest remained, the woman succeeded in reaching the bank. She decided to go up into the sky and to change into a star. As a form of revenge, she resolved to exterminate all fish: "When the dry season comes, I shall appear and cause the swamps and holes where fishes live to dry up. The fish will die. . . . May I be the right hand of the sun in order to make them pay for this" (Ahlbrinck, "ombatapo" entry). From these various indications we can conclude (1) that it is at its morning rising that Coma Berenices is associated with the dry season; (2) that the association refers to a period when the dry season is well advanced and therefore causing ponds and swamps to dry up and fish to die; this would be shortly before the start of the rains. It is therefore conceivable that two neighboring communities might have different views of the same constellation. For one, it could be the symbol of prolonged drought wreaking its final havoc; and for the other, the harbinger of the rainy season. It is as a harbinger of rain that Coma Berenices could be a combinatory variant of Corvus.

The preceding analysis is further confirmed by the existence in Guiana of two series of contrasts, which can be defined in fishing terms. We shall see that Orion and the Pleiades herald a glut of fish (M_{134}, M_{135}), and we are already in the process of verifying that in the same region the function of a constellation that replaces Corvus is to signify the disappearance of fish.

Thus we have:

$$\text{Corvus : Orion ::} \quad \overset{\text{(Bororo-Ge)}}{\left[\text{rainy season } (+) : \text{rainy season } (-) \right]} ::$$

$$\overset{\text{(Guiana)}}{\left[\text{fish } (-) : \text{fish } (+) \right]} (=\text{prospective rain : retrospective rain})$$

This is an understandable transformation, since the contrast between the dry season and the rainy season is both less obvious and more complex in the equatorial zone than in central Brazil; and this leads to its being transferred from a purely meteorological axis to an axis dependent on the biological and economic features of the climate, where another contrast, comparable to the first in its simplicity, can be established with a minimum of effort. Moreover, it should not be forgotten that although the arrival of the fish coincides with the floods, fishing is easier in lakes and streams when there is less water. And yet it is clear that certain structural elements survive when we move from the Bororo myth about the origin of Corvus (M_1) to the Kalina myth about the origin of Coma Berenices (M_{130}). In both cases a guilty ally (male or female) is devoured by fish. The man's *internal organs* rise to the surface of the water and remain there; the woman's *head* remains afloat and then rises into the sky. The parallel raises a problem to which I shall return (p. 239).

A certain amount of evidence has thus been assembled to prove that there is a connection, directly or indirectly present in the native mind, between the rainy season and the constellation Corvus. What now remains to be done is to approach the problem according to the other method, by trying to discover what link exists objectively betweeen Corvus and Orion on the one hand, and the alternation of the seasons. This brings us back to a difficulty that has already been mentioned—namely, that raised by the precession of the equinoxes. Roughly speaking, there is a gap of two to three thousand years between the periods when the Greco-Latin and the American traditions were recorded in writing. The gap is probably negligible, since in both cases the myths must have evolved much earlier. Besides, the precession of the equinoxes would raise a real difficulty only if we were examining either the myths of the Ancient World or the myths of the New separately, and if we were proposing, through an attempted correlation of the content of myths with the course of the seasons, to arrive at an approximate idea of the antiquity of the former. As far as the New World is concerned, two variables remain unknown: the climatic evolution of the southern hemisphere during the last ten or twenty thousand years (although geology has thrown some light on the matter) and, more especially, the movement of present-day and preceding communities throughout the length and breadth of the continent. Even during the past three centuries the Ge and Tupi tribes have moved about a good deal.

But there is no need for us to raise such questions. We are not attempting to find out what the correlation might be between the time of rising or the culmination of a constellation and certain meteorological circumstances, at a given period and in a specified area. What we are trying to discover is merely the relation between the course of constellation *a* in one hemisphere and that of constellation *b* in another. The relation remains constant, whatever the period we choose to consider. For our problem to have a meaning, we need only suppose, as seems most likely, that from a very early period, which was approximately the same for all branches of mankind, men had an elementary knowledge of astronomy and used it for the definition of the seasons.

I am extremely grateful to the eminent astronomer M. Jean-Claude Pecker, who has kindly agreed to offer a solution to the problem as it has just been presented, by drawing up the three graphs in Figure 16. We can deduce from them: (1) that about 1000 B.C., the vespertine rising of Orion could no longer be observed toward the end of October, the period that coincided with the beginning of the winter season (subsequently Orion had already risen when the stars became visible after dusk); (2) that at this period, when Orion enjoyed its complete meteorological significance, it was in appreciable phasic opposition to Corvus as it can be observed today. This means that, in the southern hemisphere at the present time, the latter constellation is well qualified to fulfill—but by the morning rising—the role formerly assigned to Orion in the northern hemisphere.

Finally if we take into account the fact that at whatever period it is observed (provided the period is the same), the phasic relation between Orion and Corvus is roughly 120°, and that this relation corresponds in central Brazil to the relative durations of the dry season and the rainy season (five months and seven months respectively, and more often four and eight according to native calculations), it will be seen that astronomy supplies external verification of the internal arguments that prompted me (p. 217) to establish a contrast between M_1 and M_{124}. It follows from this data that if Orion can be associated with the dry season, then Corvus can be associated with the rainy season. Correlatively, if Corvus is associated with celestial water, the relation between Orion and water will inevitably be established with the opposite of celestial water—that is, with water that rises from below.

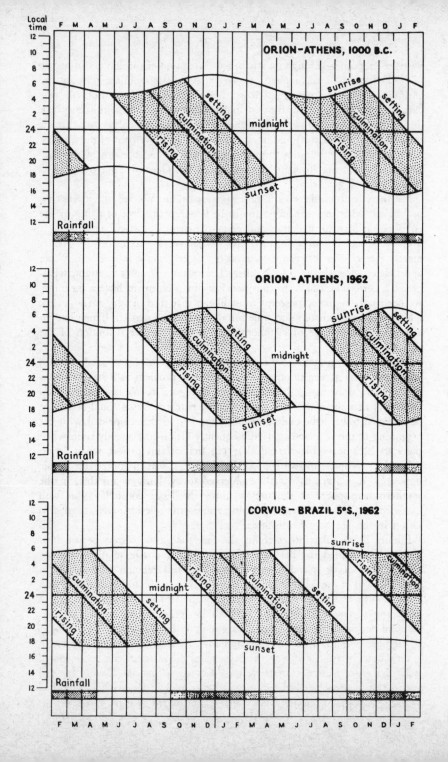

This second consequence can be verified in a different way: by trying to obtain a supplementary reflection to add to all those that have already been caught in our series of reciprocal mirrors. We have recognized the South American Corvus as being symmetrical to Orion. We have also seen that as we move from the northern to the southern hemisphere the functions of Orion were reversed along two axes: the seasonal axis, which the constellation defines as being damp, or dry; and the high/low axis (sky and earth), in relation to which the preceding values are interchangeable, since it is also true that Orion always denotes water—either water from above when the constellation foretells the rainy season, or water from below when it heralds the dry season (M₁₂₄).

Let us now go a step farther in order to formulate a fresh question. If on the mainland of South America Corvus fulfills a reverse function to that of Orion, and if the function assigned to Orion is reversed, too, when we move from one hemisphere to the other, it should also follow that from one hemisphere to the other the respective functions of Orion and Corvus recur.

I started to prove this by comparing the mythology of Orion in the Ancient World with that of Corvus in the New. But can the demonstration be carried to its logical conclusion? Or, to put the question more precisely, does Corvus fulfill in the Ancient World any function that might, in turn, correspond to one assigned to Orion by the Indians of tropical America?

A reference in the *Grande Encyclopédie du XIXe siècle*—"Among the ancients some regarded this constellation as the Crow which Apollo condemned to endure eternal thirst . . ."—prompted me to call upon the erudition of my colleague M. J.-P. Vernant, who has kindly supplied the following information. First, a passage from Aratos' *Phaenomena* links the three neighboring constellations Hydra (watersnake), Crater, and Corvus: "In the center of the convolution (of Hydra) is placed the Crater, and at the end the image of the Crow, which appears to be striking Hydra with its beak" (*Arati Phaenomena,* ed. J. Martin, Biblioteca di studi superiori, Vol. XXV, Firenze, 1956, p. 172). Three variants of a fairly ancient tale (as M. Vernant reminds us, there is an allusion to it in Aristotle, Rose edition, fragment 29) account for the association. The variants are found in: Pseudo-Eratosthenes *Catasterismoi* 41; Elienus *De nat. an.* I. 47; Dionysius *Peri ornithôn* (in A. Cramer, *Anecdota Graeca* e codd. manuscriptis Bibliothecae Regiae Parisiensis, I. 25. 20). Although the details of the story vary, it is mainly about the crow that was asked by Apollo to fetch water but stopped in a field of green wheat or near a fig tree and waited for the corn or the fruit to ripen before carrying out its mission. Apollo punished it by condemning it to remain thirsty throughout the summer. M. Vernant rounds off

Figure 16. Orion's course in the Old World compared with that of Corvus in the New World.

this information with the remark that, in many texts and in certain rites, crows (as well as rooks and jackdaws) were represented as atmospheric birds, weather signs, and more especially as harbingers of rain.

Like Asare the hero of M₁₂₄, whom the Indians recognized as a star in the Orion constellation (I remind the reader of this point for the last time), the crow of the Greek myth, and the prototype of the constellation that was to take its name, is afflicted with *thirst*. Even *ripe* fruits could not quench

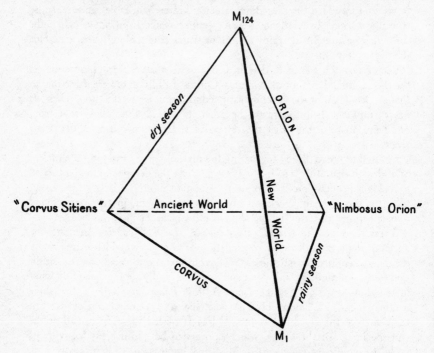

Figure 17. The respective positions of Orion and Corvus
in the myths of the Ancient and the New Worlds.

Asare's thirst; a well had to be dug, which was to become the sea. The Greek crow spurned a fountain from which gushed water that was also earthly in origin, and persisted in waiting for the ears of corn or the fruit to *ripen*; and as a result it was never able to quench its thirst.

In one case the fruit ripen at the end of the rainy season (during which they become swollen and full of water); in the other case they ripen at the end of the dry season, through prolonged exposure to the sun. This helps to explain how in ancient Greece the crow, as a constellation associated with the dry season, could also be a harbinger of rain. The bird calls for the absent celestial water because it is thirsty; and it is thirsty because it has disdained the available earthly water and shown itself too greedy for the fruits of the sunny season. It will be remembered that Asare had disdained the benefits of the rainy season (the water inside the nuts), and that, in order to slake his acute thirst, earthly water had to become not only present but superabundant, so as to allow the hero to satisfy his thirst and refresh his whole body, before the dry season settled in. Because of the dry season, on the other hand, the voice of the crow was to become raucous, and its throat parched. In one of the variants of the Greek myth the crow accuses a snake, who is master of the fountain, of preventing it from reaching the water. This is precisely what an alligator, also master of water, tries to do in the Brazilian myth.

It is therefore clear that the two myths, the one belonging to the Ancient World and the other to the New, are, as I postulated, reflections of each other. The apparent inversions arise simply from the fact that while both are concerned with the dry season, one myth refers to the beginning (after the rains) and the other to the end (before the rains). Consequently, in the Ancient World and in the southern regions of the New World, the myths dealing with Orion and Corvus form contrasting pairs, similarly arranged in relation to the good and the bad seasons:

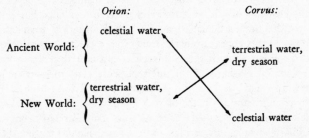

Thus four types of myth form a chiasmus, and each one is defined as a function of three sets of contrasting terms: the Ancient World and New World, the dry and the rainy seasons, Corvus and Orion (Figure 17).

3

Toccata and Fugue

a. THE PLEIADES

In granting that myths have an astronomical significance, I do not propose to revert in any way to the mistaken ideas characteristic of the solar mythography of the nineteenth century. In my view, the astronomical context does not provide any absolute point of reference; we cannot claim to have interpreted the myths simply by relating them to this context. The truth of the myth does not lie in any special content. It consists in logical relations which are devoid of content or, more precisely, whose invariant properties exhaust their operative value, since comparable relations can be established among the elements of a large number of different contents. For instance, I have shown that one particular theme, such as the origin of man's mortality, occurs in myths that appear quite different from each other in subject matter, but that in the last analysis these differences can be reduced to a variety of codes, evolved on the basis of the different sense categories—taste, hearing, smell, feel, and sight. . . . In the preceding pages I have been solely concerned to establish the existence of a different code, also a visual one, but whose lexical material consists of contrasted pairs drawn from a stable spatio-temporal whole, consisting, on the one hand, of the diachronic periodicity of the year and, on the other, of the synchronic arrangement of the stars in the sky. This cosmographic code is no truer than any other; and it is no better, except from the methodological point of view, as far as its operations can be checked from without. But it is not impossible that advances in biochemistry may one day provide objective references of the same degree of accuracy as a check on the precision and coherence of the codes formulated in the language of the senses. Myths are constructed on the basis of a certain logicality of tangible qualities which makes no clear-cut distinction between subjective states and the properties of the cosmos. Nevertheless it must not be forgotten that such a distinction has corresponded, and to a lesser extent still corresponds, to a particular stage in the development of scientific knowledge —a stage that in theory, if not in actual fact, is doomed to disappear. In this respect, mythological thought is not prescientific; it should be seen rather as an anticipation of the future state of science, whose past development and present trend show that it has always been progressing in the same direction.

Be that as it may, the emergence of an astronomical coding in certain of the South American myths encourages me to check whether the same code might not also exist, in either an overt or a latent form, in other myths where it has passed unnoticed. It goes without saying that the Bororo myth explaining the origin of the stars, which has already been analyzed (M_{34}), has an astronomical aspect; but is it not possible to give a more accurate definition of the myth's apparent subject matter—in which the stars are mentioned in general terms—by limiting it more particularly to the origin of the Pleiades? The children who provoke a glut of vegetable food (which they consume greedily) may be the counterparts in vertical disjunction of Asare's brothers (M_{124}) who, in a state of horizontal disjunction, call forth a superabundant "mineral" drink which they dispense generously (insisting that their young brother should not leave a single drop).

The connection is all the more plausible in that a Mataco myth, whose armature very closely resembles that of the Bororo myth about the origin of stars (M_{34}), refers explicitly to the Pleiades:

M_{131a}. *Mataco. "The origin of the Pleiades"*

Formerly the Indians used to climb into the sky by means of a huge tree. There they found an abundance of honey and fish. One day, after they had returned from the sky, they met an old woman at the foot of the tree. She asked for a small share of their provisions, but they refused. In order to be avenged on them for their greed, the old woman set fire to the tree. The Indians who had remained in the sky turned into stars and formed the constellation of the Pleiades. (Campana, pp. 318–19.)

I have already mentioned that, according to other myths of the Gran Chaco area, the Pleiades came into being when children, who had been playing too noisily after dusk, were taken up into the sky. Now in South America there is a very widespread taboo on nocturnal meals. Several tribes in the Upper Amazon explain it by the belief that it is impossible to digest food that has remained in the stomach all night; hence the practice of inducing vomiting in the morning by tickling the back of the throat with a feather. The Arawak of Guiana believe that anyone who eats after sunset will be changed into a beast (Roth 1, p. 295; cf. myth, *ibid.*, pp. 184–5).

The theory that there may be an equivalence between excessive noise and excessive eating is confirmed, in the case of the Pleiades, by a Macusi myth that follows very closely the Bororo myth about the origin of stars, while at the same time repeating the Gran Chaco myths about the origin of the Pleiades by a simple transformation of the noisy children (Bororo = greedy) into insatiable children:

M_{131b}. *Macusi. "The origin of the Pleiades"*

A man had seven sons, who continually wept and asked for food. The mother scolded them saying, "Children, I am always giving you food and you are never satisfied. What gluttons you are!" For the sake of peace and quiet, she took a tapir's jaw[15] from the grid and threw it to them. The hungry children protested that it was not enough and, having shared out the meat between the youngest, they all decided to turn into stars. Holding each other's hands and singing and dancing, they started to climb skyward. When she saw what they were doing, the mother exclaimed, "Where are you going? Here is food for you!" The children explained that they bore no resentment, but that they had made up their minds. And they gradually vanished from sight. (Barbosa Rodrigues, p. 223.)

Now this Guianian myth acts as a kind of link between the Bororo myth (M_{34}) and several North American myths dealing with the origin of the Pleiades which are exactly symmetrical to the Bororo myth, but with semantic inversion (children starved by their parents instead of starving them), as might be expected from the change of hemisphere. Here is the Wyandot version:

M_{132}. Wyandot. "The origin of the Pleiades"

Seven young boys were playing and dancing together in the shade of a tree. After a while they became hungry. One of them went to the house and asked for some bread, but the old woman would not give him any. They went on with their games, and then a little later another child went to the house and asked for some bread. Again the old woman refused. One of the children made a drum, and they began to dance around the tree.

No sooner had they started the dance than they began to be lifted upward. They went on dancing, and still higher into the air they ascended. Looking around, the old woman saw them dancing high above the tree. She now came running with food, but it was too late. They refused to listen. Now she was willing to give them food, but they would not even notice her and continued their dancing while moving upward. Filled with despair, the old woman started to weep.

The seven stars are the same boys dancing together. They were not given anything to eat: that is why they became the Hutinatsija, "the cluster," which we now see in the sky. (Barbeau, pp. 6–7.)[16]

In the Hervey Islands, in Polynesia, there exists an almost identical myth, except that it is concerned with the constellation Scorpio (Andersen, p. 399). In the Amazonian and Guianian regions, Scorpio is associated with the Pleiades in forecasting the November and December rains and the sudden floods of which they are the cause (Tastevin 3, p. 173).

It is also very likely that the key myth (M_1), whose hero, as we have al-

[15] Probably a representation of the Hyades; cf. Roth 1, p. 266; and Goeje, p. 103: "the Hyades were called 'tapir-jaw' or 'tapir-fork' by the Indians. . . ."

[16] Since the transformational relations among the myths of tropical America and those of the central and northern regions of North America are to be the subject of a later book, I merely mention in passing the existence of a Blackfoot myth about the origin of the Pleiades, which provides a transition between myths of the type I have just been dealing with and the Asare myth (Wissler-Duvall, pp. 71–2).

ready noted, bears the same name as the constellation of Corvus, conceals another astronomical reference, this time to the Pleiades. It will be remembered that at the end of the myth the hero, who has turned into a deer, throws his father into the waters of a lake, where he is eaten by the cannibalistic fish, the piranhas. Only his internal organs remain floating on the surface, where they turn into aquatic plants.

This theme is so widely diffused throughout the whole of America that it occurs in almost identical form among the Alaskan Eskimos (M_{133}). The wife of the eldest of five brothers hated the youngest and killed him. When the brothers discovered the body, it was full of worms. They then resolved that the woman should be subjected to the same fate, and dragged her to the edge of a lagoon ostensibly to take part in a race that was to be run around it. But the woman could not run as fast as her husband, and when he overtook her from behind, he pushed her into the water where the other brothers had placed meat as a bait to lure the worms; the worms threw themselves on the woman and devoured her flesh. Soon all that was left was her lungs floating on the surface of the water (Spencer, pp. 73–4).[17]

Among both the Eskimo and the Bororo the theme of the floating internal organs seems devoid of any astronomical significance. This is not so in the intermediary zone. The Zuni believe that the "little stars" originated in the lungs of a dismembered ogre (Parsons 1, p. 30). Conversely, their neighbors, the Navajo, relate that aquatic animals sprang from the submerged entrails of a huge bear (Haile and Wheelwright, pp. 77–8). A Guianian myth juxtaposes both interpretations:

M_{134}. *Acawai. "The origin of the Pleiades"*

A man who coveted his brother's wife killed his brother and presented his sister-in-law with her husband's severed arm, as proof of his death. She agreed to marry him but, having been warned by the ghost's groans, she soon realized the truth and rejected the criminal. The latter thereupon imprisoned the unhappy woman and her little child in a hollow tree and left them there to die. That night the brother's ghost appeared to the man and explained that he bore no resentment for the crimes, because his wife and son had turned

---

[17] It is even more strange to discover that the same association between water, the viscera, and aquatic plants exists in Australia: "As for the waterlilies which normally abound in water holes, the natives eat these flowers because they believe that their growth has been encouraged by the bones of the dead" (Spencer and Gillen, p. 546). On the other hand, in the southwest of the province of Victoria, the natives used to roast the flesh of their relatives' corpses and eat it, apart from the vitals and intestines which were burned along with the bones (Frazer 2, Vol. IV, p. 262). When combined with the American data, these observations suggest the existence of an important contrast, on the anatomical level, between viscera and bones, and a link between them, on the one hand, and water and fire, on the other: fire overcomes the contrast (conjunction of viscera and bones), whereas water actualizes it (disjunction of the bones, which sink to the bottom, and the viscera, which remain on the surface in the form of aquatic plants).

into animals (*acouri* and *adourie* respectively)[18] and were henceforth safe. On the other hand, the ghost demanded that his brother give a proper burial to his maimed corpse and promised him an abundance of fish, on condition that he buried only the body and scattered the entrails.

The murderer did as he had been requested, and he saw the entrails floating through the air and rising into the sky, where they became the Pleiades. Since that time, every year, when the Pleiades appear, the rivers teem with fish. (Roth 1, p. 262.)

The hero of a Taurepan myth about the origin of the Pleiades (M_{135}) likewise exclaims: "When I reach the sky, there will be storms and rain. Then shoals of fish will appear and you will have plenty to eat!" (K.G. 1, p. 57.) The link between the Pleiades and floating viscera is also found in the following myth:

M_{136}. *Arecuna. "Jilijoaibu (the Pleiades) kills his mother-in-law"*

Jilijoaibu's mother-in-law used to feed her son-in-law on fish taken from her uterus. When he discovered her trick, Jilijoaibu broke crystals and threw the fragments onto the bank where his mother-in-law was in the habit of going, but took care to conceal them under banana-tree leaves. The mother-in-law tripped and fell; the stones cut her arms and legs and the whole of her body. She died. The stones leaped into the water and turned into "piranhas," which for this reason have remained cannibalistic. The old woman's liver also fell into the water and floated on the surface. It can still be seen in the form of *mureru brava,* an aquatic plant with red leaves, the seed of which is the old woman's heart. (K.G. 1, p. 60.)

It is hardly necessary to emphasize that this myth, whose hero is the constellation of the Pleiades, exactly corresponds to the final episode of the key myth, whose hero is the constellation Corvus. And, according to the Bororo, Corvus is responsible for rain, a function that the Guianian Indians assign to the Pleiades.

The preceding myths suggest that as a code term the theme of the floating viscera fulfills two distinct functions and is, in a sense, bivalent. In the "aquatic" code the viscera are congruous with fish and marsh plants. In the "celestial" code they are congruous with the stars, and especially the Pleiades. If, in the area which the Bororo occupied two centuries ago and whose central section they still inhabit (15° to 20° S., 51° to 57° W.), the rising of the Pleiades occurs in the middle of the dry season, it is normal that the myth (M_{34}) about the origin of the stars (= the Pleiades) should also be a myth about the origin of wild animals. The manifest reference is to hunting, since the dry season is particularly suitable for this activity in a region where the heavy rain makes traveling difficult. On the other hand

---

[18] *Acouri* is *Dasyprocta agouti; adourie* possibly referred to a small species of Cavidae (Goeje, p. 67) or, according to Roth (2, p. 164), *Dasyprocta acuchy*. Cf. M_1 and M_{55}, and above, p. 129.

the myth dealing with the rainy season makes manifest use of the aquatic code, thanks to the floating viscera theme, but it avoids any direct reference to the Pleiades.

Here we come up against two fundamental characteristics of mythic thought, which are at once complementary to each other and diametrically opposed. First, as I have already proved in a different example (p. 55), the syntax of mythology is never absolutely free within the confines of its own rules. It is inevitably affected by the geographical and technological substructure. Of the various operations that are theoretically possible from a purely formal point of view, some are definitively excluded from the outset, and the gaps, so to speak, punched out of the fabric make a pattern that would otherwise have been regular, and describe the negative outline of a structure within a structure, which must be integrated with the first, if one is to arrive at the true system of operation.

Secondly—and in spite of what has just been said—mythic thought seems to proceed as if the sign system had its own built-in resistance to the buffetings to which the things signified have to submit from without. When objective conditions eliminate certain of these things, the corresponding signs are not automatically abolished. For a certain length of time at least, they continue to mark the outline of the missing elements, which thus appear in hollow relief instead of standing out in bold relief. In the Guiana area the floating viscera theme can have its double meaning, since the appearance of the Pleiades in the sky coincides objectively with the appearance of fish in the rivers. The two features do not necessarily coincide in all other situations.

At the present time, in Bororo country, the predawn rising of the Pleiades occurs in the middle of the dry season, toward the end of June or the beginning of July. The natives celebrate it with a festival called *akiri-dogé e-wuré kowudu* "to burn the feet of the Pleiades," which is intended, so they say, to slow down the course of the constellation and so prolong the dry season, which is suitable for nomadic activities (EB, Vol. I, p. 45). It is therefore clear that the Bororo, like the Sherente, associate the Pleiades with the dry season, although they do not appear to observe the constellation at the same moment—but unlike the Sherente, they assign a negative meaning to its appearance.

Nevertheless, among the Alaskan Eskimo as well as among the Bororo of central Brazil, the feature that ceases to be positively signified (the Pleiades) retains its potential place in the system of signs.[19] What happens is simply that one of the codes disappears, while the other becomes latent, as if to conceal the isomorphic link between them. Finally, both phenomena are accompanied by a change of lexical items: through an identical transformation among the Eskimo, where viscera → viscera; and by a non-

[19] It appears that the same thing occurs among the Shipaye, but in an even weaker form. Cf. Nim. 3, p. 1033.

identical transformation among the Bororo, where viscera → aquatic plants (≠ animals).

b. THE RAINBOW

Let us return now to another Bororo myth, which has already been analyzed (M₅), and from which all astronomical references also appear absent. But first, a brief digression.

In South America the rainbow has a double meaning. On the one hand, as elsewhere, it announces the end of rain; on the other hand, it is considered to be responsible for diseases and various natural disasters. In its first capacity the rainbow effects a disjunction between the sky and the earth which previously were joined through the medium of rain. In the second capacity it replaces the normal beneficent conjunction by an abnormal, maleficent one—the one it brings about itself between sky and earth by taking the place of water.

The first function is clearly demonstrated by the Timbira theory: The rainbow (rain-person) has its two ends resting in the open mouths of two sucuriju snakes, which themselves yield rain. It appears as a sign that the rain has ceased. When the rainbow disappears, two eel-like fish, puppeyre (Port. *muçum*), rise to the sky, where they drop into a water hole. When there is a heavy rain, they again drop back into the terrestrial water. (Nim. 8, p. 234.)

Evidence of the rainbow's second function is found from Guiana to the Gran Chaco: "The rainbow makes the Carib ill when it finds nothing to eat above. . . . When it appears to them while they are on land, they hide in their homes and think that it is a strange and masterless spirit which seeks to kill somebody" (La Borde in Roth 1, p. 268). In the Gran Chaco the Vilela have a myth (M₁₇₃) about a shy, solitary boy who used to hunt birds and who changed into a multicolored and deadly serpent, the rainbow. Lehmann-Nitsche, who has published various versions of this myth, has also shown how often in South America the rainbow is identified with a snake (Lehmann-Nitsche 2, pp. 221–33). Lastly, the same author accepts the theory that the food-bearing tree in the myths of Guiana and the Gran Chaco (cf. above, pp. 184 ff.) can be identified with the Milky Way. This would give the following equivalence:

(a)   Milky Way : rainbow :: life : death.

The equivalence is certainly not valid for the whole mythology of the New World, since there are good reasons to suppose that it is inverted in several mythological systems of North America. Yet its validity seems to be indirectly confirmed, as far as tropical America is concerned, by certain remarks made by Tastevin. In a study of the mythological representations of the rainbow in the Amazonian basin, Tastevin emphasizes that, according to his informants, the Boyusu snake appears during the day in the form of the rainbow and at night as a black spot in the Milky Way (3, pp. 182–3). The nocturnal counterpart of the rainbow would therefore be the non-presence of the Milky Way at a point where it would normally occur, hence the equation:

$$(b) \quad \text{Rainbow} = \text{Milky Way} \; (-1)$$

which confirms the preceding one.

After these preliminary explanations it will be more readily admitted that, even though the text of M₅ does not specifically say so, the mother of diseases may be transformable into a rainbow. In respect to diseases, both are similarly qualified, since both cause them. The myth's final episode strengthens the theory. It will be remembered that the guilty woman's brothers cut her body into two pieces, one of which they threw into a lake in the east, the other into a lake in the west.[20] Now we have seen that the Timbira associate the two ends of the rainbow with two snakes, and this "dual" aspect of the rainbow occupies an important place in South American myths, either in a simple form or in a form that is itself duplicated: "The Katawishi distinguish two rainbows: Mawali in the west, and Tini in the east. Tini and Mawali were twin brothers who brought about the flood that inundated the whole world and killed all living people, except two young girls whom they saved to be their companions. It is not advisable to look either of them straight in the eye: to look at Mawali is to become flabby, lazy, and unlucky at hunting and fishing; to look at Tini makes a man so clumsy that he cannot go any distance without stumbling and lacerating his feet against all the obstacles in his path, or pick up a sharp instrument without cutting himself" (Tastevin 3, pp. 191, 192).[21] The Mura also believed that there were two rainbows, an "upper" and a "lower" (Nim. 10, Vol. III, p. 265). Similarly, the Tucuna differentiated between the eastern and the western rainbows and believed them both to be sub-aquatic demons, the masters of fish and potter's clay respectively (Nim. 12, Vol. III, pp. 723–4). The latter association is commented on by Tastevin (3, pp. 195–6). At the same time the Indians of Guiana establish a direct link between potter's clay and diseases: "The Indians firmly believe that it it only during the first night of commencing full moon that they dare carry on the work. . . . Whole crowds congregate there on that particular evening and return home at day break with a big supply. The Indians are absolutely convinced that the pots made from clay obtained at any other time not only

[20] In Guiana, people used to defend themselves in similar fashion against the mythical *camudi* snake, which killed its victims by asphyxiating them with foul-smelling emissions: "So people never traveled alone—there always had at least to be two of them, so that if the *buio* . . . attacked one, the other could beat and cut the air between his companion and the monster with his hair or with the branch of a tree" (Gumilla, Vol. II, p. 148).

[21] There is also evidence of the existence of this belief in the Gran Chaco (Grubb, p. 141).

possess the defect of readily breaking but also bring a number of diseases to those who eat out of them." (Schomburgk, Vol. I, p. 203; Ahlbrinck, "orino" entry, gives similar information.)

Let us pause for a moment to examine these Amazonian beliefs. The two rainbows are the masters of fish—aquatic animals—and of potter's clay, which lies, too, on the "watery" side, since the Tucuma myths are always careful to specify that it is dug out from river beds (Nim. 13, pp. 78, 134). This is moreover confirmed by ethnographic observation: "In all the *igarapés* "streams") inhabited by the Tucuna, a plastic potter's clay of good quality is found more or less frequently; it almost always occurs in the sloughs at the foot of the high bluffs along the river" (Nim. 13, p. 46; cf. also Schomburgk, Vol. I, pp. 130, 203). Pregnant women are strictly forbidden to dig up the clay.

The Bororo heroine is the opposite of a pregnant woman, since she is the mother of a young child. Like the western rainbow of the Tucuna, she assumes, or rather usurps, the role of mistress of fish. She is a bad mother and leaves her child on a branch (therefore in an external position, whereas a pregnant woman's child is internal) and causes it to turn into an ant heap—that is, into hard, dried earth, the opposite of the supple, moist clay found in the streams. At the same time as she enters into physical conjunction with water in order to feed on the dead fish drifting on the surface, she creates a disjunction between sky and earth, as the myth indicates in two ways. The child who was in a tree, and therefore in a high position, is polarized in an earthy form; and he assumes this earthy function in respect to dryness, since it is by its dryness and hardness that the soil of which ant heaps consist is the reverse of the earth used by the potter. It will be remembered that in the Ge myths, the remains of ant heaps were one of the sources of food available to men when they were still living in a state of nature; potter's clay, on the other hand, constitutes one of the raw materials of culture. Lastly, the two kinds of clay, which are already polar opposites in respect to earth and water, dryness and moisture, nature and culture, are also opposites in respect to rawness and cooking. The ant heap remains which men used as food when they were living in a state of nature were raw, since they had no connection with fire. Potter's clay, on the other hand, has to be baked. In this last respect the Kayapo theory about the rainbow is halfway between the beliefs of the Bororo and those of the Tucuna. The Gorotire see the rainbow as "the great earth-oven" in which the wife of Bepkororoti, the master of storms (M_{125}), cooks her manioc pies. Conversely, the Bororo mother of diseases eats raw fish.

It is strange that all these different threads of the Bororo myth about the origin of diseases should lead to a Toba myth (M_{137}), in which they all come together, but in so tangled a skein that the attempt to unravel it would be too lengthy and hazardous a process. In the Toba myth the culture hero appears as an egotistical master of fish, and Fox claims to be both his rival and his successor. To punish Fox for his overweening conceit, the rainbow causes a flood. Fox takes refuge on the branch of a tree and there turns into a termites' nest, which is destroyed by men. As a result of this, the men are threatened by an epidemic (Métraux 5, pp. 137–8). Diseases, the rainbow, water, and the termites' nest are therefore openly linked in the Toba myth.

I shall confine myself to the Bororo myth, especially since the hypothesis about its latent astronomical coding can be proved in a different way. The heroine in the Bororo myth has two aspects. First, she is a bad mother since she abandons her child in order to be able to stuff herself with fish; next she exudes the fish from her body in the form of diseases which kill large numbers of human beings.

Now in a previous chapter I defined the opossum by means of two modalities comparable to those just referred to. I said that the opossum was a good nursing mother, and that she stank. If we express the two modalities as (1) and (2) respectively, we obtain the transformation of the opossum into the heroine of the Bororo myth on the following, twofold condition:

$$(1) \longrightarrow (-1)$$
$$(2) \longrightarrow (2^n)$$

In other words, the Bororo heroine is an opossum whose positive modality is transformed into its opposite, and whose negative modality is raised to a high, although indeterminate power. She is an opossum whose stench (which has become fatal to the whole of humanity) completely cancels out her qualities as a nursing mother.

This having been established, it is all the more extraordinary that the Guianian Indians should call the rainbow *yawarri* "opossum" (*Didelphys* species) because of "the reddish color of its fur, bearing some fancied resemblance to the coloration of the (rain) bow" (Roth, 1, p. 268). Whatever the origin of this rationalization—it may well be native—the explanation obviously does not go very deep.[22] The opossum is characterized by ambiguity: as a

---

[22] The semantic value attributed to the coloring in this case is all the more curious in that the North American name for the opossum (*Didelphys virginiana*, Kerr) is derived from a dialect of the Indians of Virginia, in which the word *apasum* means "the white animal." The Delaware Indians call the opossum *woap/ink*, which has exactly the same meaning (Mahr, p. 17). One might be tempted to compare this inversion of the chromatic value of the opossum with a similar reversal that sometimes seems to occur, between South and North America, in the respective symbolic functions of the rainbow and the Milky Way, if it were not an established fact that the North American opossum is generally gray, sometimes white, and that genuine albinos have been occasionally found (Carter, p. 209). In support of the theory that some kind of logical necessity is behind the inversion of the chromatic valency of the opossum between South and North America, we can quote the mythology of the Pawnee Indians in which the skunk and not the opossum (I have, however, shown that they form a pair of opposites) is associated with the rainbow. Correspondingly, the Pawnee myths credit the skunk with the exclusive power of resuscitating the dead; this is the reverse of the power of depriving men of immortality which, in the myths of tropical America, belongs to the opossum (cf. Dorsey, pp. 71–3, 342).

nursing mother, it serves life; as a foul-smelling or rotten beast, it anticipates death. We need only switch these two opposite attributes around in order to obtain a kind of maximum significance of the opossum, merging into the normal significance of the rainbow, which can itself be identified with the serpent. I shall return to this aspect of the problem in the next volume.

For the time being, I wish to note that the astronomical coding bestows an additional dimension on certain myths, and that, by looking at them from this angle, we can link them up with other myths, whose overtly astronomical coding thus appears to be no accident. What we obtain by a backward variation of the semantic values of the opossum is its transformation into a rainbow. And we know already that, by switching them around so that each one is reversed, but in different directions, we obtain the transformation of the opossum into a star. The star, who is married to a mortal, is a "super nurse" (the donor of cultivated plants) and not at all foul smelling, because a second opossum—or the same one, after its nature has been changed by rape—takes upon itself the entire burden of the negative function of depriving man of immortality:

Star		*Opossum*		*Rainbow*
(f max.)	⟵———	f nurse	———⟶	(f neg.)
(f neg.)	⟵———	f foul-smelling	———⟶	(f max.)

Now the Sherente, who make no mention of the feminine star (= the planet Jupiter, M_{93}) in her role as wetnurse, lay considerable stress on her other function in a myth constructed according to the same pattern, in which a masculine star (= planet Venus) consequently occupies a position exactly between that of the stellar opossum (all the other Ge myths) and that of the meteoric opossum (Bororo):

M_{138}. *Sherente*. *"The planet Venus"*

Venus (a masculine personage) was living in human shape among men. His body was covered with malodorous ulcers, and behind him was buzzing a swarm of bees. All the people turned up their noses when he passed, and refused him when he asked permission to rest in their houses.

Only the Indian, Wainkaura, made the poor wretch welcome and gave him a new mat on which to sit. He asked his guest whence he came and whither he was bound. Venus explained that he had lost his way.

Wainkaura ordered hot water to be brought to him so that he could wash Venus' ulcers and, ignoring his guest's protests, insisted that this should take place inside the hut, and not outdoors. He even ordered his virgin daughter to let Venus sit on her bare thighs, and washed him in this position. Thus the visitor recovered.

After nightfall the visitor said to Wainkaura, "What would you like to have?" and as Wainkaura did not understand, he explained, "Do you want to live or to die? Waptokwa is angry over the mutual massacring of the

Indians. They have even pierced little children with arrows. So it would be better to destroy all of them at once. But tell no one and quickly pack up your belongings."

He ordered Wainkaura to kill the juruty dove (*Leptoptila rufaxilla*). When Wainkaura returned with the dove, Venus said that he had deflowered his daughter, and offered to pay compensation. However, Wainkaura refused to accept anything.

By means of the dove's carcass, Venus made a large boat in which Wainkaura took his place along with his family. Venus took leave and departed, a whirlwind lifted him up to the sky. At once a distant noise became audible. Then the flood came and carried them all away. Before long, all drowned or died from hunger. Only Wainkaura and his family escaped. (Nim. 6, pp. 91–2.)

This myth can be commented on along two different lines. First, as I indicated above, M_{138} can be compared with M_5, and it magnifies the negative function of the opossum to the extreme limit.[23] But there is a difference. In M_5 the operation of the stench was in an outward direction: it attacked others, in the form of diseases, before attacking the subject himself. The reverse happens in M_{138}, since Venus only inconveniences his fellows by reason of the disease with which he himself is afflicted. Now only the first instance is a metaphorical expression of the zoological reality: the opossum is not bothered by its own stench which, moreover, does not result from a pathogenic state. It follows then that the stench that was external before being internal presupposes a "female" opossum (cf. M_5 and the Ge series on the theme of the star who married a mortal), whereas the stench that was internal before being external implies a transformation: female → male, with a corresponding inversion of all the terms. In place of a virgin, who is a visitor from the sky, M_{138} features a virgin who is an earthly hostess, and whose functions, described with relish in the myth, form a sort of chiasmus with those normally associated with a nursing mother: the feminine star of M_{87}–M_{92} was an active nursing mother; the young Indian girl in M_{138} is a passive nurse. The part played by the first has to be understood in a metaphorical sense; she was "feeding" men by imposing upon them the use of cultivated plants. The role played by the second is one of physical contiguity: she sits the sick man down on her bare thighs.

That is not all. Star, a raped virgin, became a source of defilement and introduced death. In M_{138} the celestial being changes both his sex and his function: he is at first defiled by the ulcers with which he is afflicted, he makes himself out as the raper of a virgin, and saves the lives of the people he has taken under his protection. Finally, the feminine Star kills her relations by means of water, which is internal in regard to its source or destination (it is a poisonous potion which she administers, or a lethal saliva which

---

[23] It will be noted, on the other hand, that the Bororo seem to associate the planet Venus with physical beauty (EB, Vol. I, p. 758).

she spits out), and she spares other men. Masculine Venus kills other men by means of external water (the flood) and spares his relations.

Secondly, we have approached M₁₃₈, which, as we have just seen, belongs to the "marriage of the star" set (M₈₇–M₉₂), through the medium of the Asare myth (M₁₂₄), although at first sight this myth offers few points of similarity with the others. The procedure will be justified retrospectively, if we can prove that there exists a larger set, of which the Asare set on the one hand and the Star-wife set on the other form two subsets. This is possible thanks to a Kraho myth that seems to lie precisely at the point of intersection of the two subsets:

M₁₃₉. Kraho. "The story of Autxepirire"

An Indian whose wife was unfaithful to him decided to leave her and go far away. He took with him his sons and his daughter who was the youngest of all his children. Hardly had they entered the forest when the men turned into deer in order to advance more rapidly, but the little girl was unable to imitate them. They met the ogre Autxepirire, who was fishing with *timbo* (a fish poison), and the men turned into diving birds in order to steal his fish from him. Once again the little girl did not succeed in imitating them and went imprudently up to the ogre, who, on seeing her, fell in love with her and asked for her hand in marriage. Since he wished to be as prettily painted as his fiancée, the men told him that he must allow himself to be roasted in the fire. The ogre agreed to this and was burned to death.

The little girl noticed that she had left a gourd (a bracelet, in another version) behind near the fire, and she came back to get it. She stirred up the embers and took out a piece of the ogre's penis. The ogre, as it happened, was on the point of rising again from its ashes. The girl ran off, pursued by the monster.

Two rivers barred her path. She crossed each one in turn on the back of an alligator, who agreed to play the part of ferryman on condition that the little girl would insult him immediately afterward (*sic*). In spite of his promises, he ran after her in order to eat her. The heroine took refuge first of all with a rhea (*ema*), then with wasps who hid her in their nest. She finally rejoined her family, and with some difficulty all eventually escaped from the Autxepirire cannibal spirits, who attacked them in the tree where they had taken refuge. They succeeded in cutting the rope up which their persecutors were climbing. The latter fell to the ground and changed into crabs.

Again lost and abandoned, the little girl arrived at a village belonging to the seriemas, the urubus, and the vultures. She hid near a spring, and by spitting on the gourds with which the birds came to draw water, she broke them all (cf. M₁₂₀). To take their revenge, the birds formed into a flock and forced her to undergo gang rape, sparing neither her eyes, her ears, her nostrils, or the spaces between her toes. . . . Having thus been made "rotten" with caresses, the young girl died, and the animals dismembered her body. Each one chose a piece of the vulva and hung it on a perch, to the accompaniment of magic words. At once each piece grew and covered the roof of the hut. The hawk, who had been the first to help himself, had a fine house, but the urubu's share remained small, dry, and shriveled (cf. M_{29}, M_{30}). (Schultz, pp. 144–150; Pompeu Sobrinho, pp. 200–203.)

I do not intend to embark on a complete analysis of this myth, of which the narrative I have given here is only a very brief summary. What interests me most about it is that it cuts across other myths already mentioned and confirms them at various points. The first part is an obvious transformation of the Asare myth. Both begin with the horizontal dislocation of a family group, followed by incidents for which water (M_{124}) and fire (M_{139}) provide a pretext. Asare, a masculine hero, meets his downfall when he goes to look for an arrow; his feminine counterpart in M_{139} suffers the same fate when she goes back to look for a gourd or a bracelet. Both cross streams where they meet alligators. I have already given (p. 202) the rule whereby this episode can be transformed into the episode of the meeting with the jaguar in the M_7 to M_{12} group. A fresh transformation accounts for the particular features of this meeting in M_{139}:

M_7– M_{12} } a jaguar	offers to help the hero,	on condition that he is treated with respect	vertical axis: high-low
M_{124} } an alligator	refuses to help the hero;	consequently is shown no consideration	horizontal axis: water-earth
M_{139}	offers to help the heroine,	on condition that he is shown no consideration (!)	

It can be seen that the demands made by the alligator in M_{139}, which are absurd on the syntagmatic level, become coherent from the paradymatic point of view, since they correspond to a permutation of the elements in the third section, and this permutation is, necessarily and by definition, different from the two other permutations.[24]

The second part of M_{139} is a transformation, on the one hand, of the myth about the origin of *women,* as the conclusion proves, corresponding

[24] In an obscure and fragmentary Caraja version, the alligator demands that the heroine yield to his desires, but she succeeds in tricking him (Ehrenreich, pp. 87–8). This group, which occurs again in North America, includes other transformations. To refer for the moment only to tropical America: an alligator asks the hero to hurl abuse at him so that he can devour him (Tembe, Nim. 2, p. 299); he accuses him of having hurled abuse at him in order to have an excuse for devouring him (Kayapo, Métraux 8, p. 31); he is actually insulted by the hero when he is no longer in a position to devour him (Mundurucu, Murphy 1, p. 97), etc. The general problems raised by the "touchy ferryman" group will be dealt with in Volume III in connection with North American examples.

exactly, as it does, to that of M_{29} and M_{30} and, hardly less literally, to that of the other myths in this group (M_{31} and M_{32}); and on the other hand, of the myth about the origin of *woman:* she is either a star that has come down to earth (M_{87} to M_{92}) or a rotten fruit that has undergone a metamorphosis (M_{95}, M_{95a}). But here again the transformation is based on a triple inversion. In M_{139} the woman exists at the outset—and she is so completely and totally human that she cannot, like her father and brothers, assume animal form— and only at the end does she retrogress to the state of rottenness. The myth therefore refers to the disappearance, rather than to the origin, of woman. Furthermore, her disappearance affects animals (birds), whereas elsewhere the appearance of women is beneficial to humans. This being so, it is under-

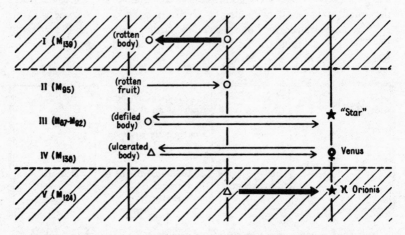

Figure 18. The system of myths concerned with the incarnation of a star.

standable why the myth describing woman's disappearance should respect the laws of logic by proceeding to a third inversion; that of the final episode in M_{29} where the pieces of the first woman, hung up *inside* the huts, pro- duced a wife for each man, a housewife for each home, whereas here, the same pieces hung up *outside* the huts produce nothing more than new roofs—that is, passive guardians of the home.

Consequently, and but for the transformations to which I have drawn attention, M_{139} borrows half its armature from the Asare myth (M_{124})—the young boy saved from water, therefore from decay, and subsequently changed into a star—and the other half from the Tupi-Tucuna myths (M_{95}, M_{95a}) about a rotten fruit that is changed into a woman (who is also saved from decay). And we discover that when the two fragments are put end to end, they reconstitute the armature of the myths about a celestial body being changed into a human (male or female), but only on condition that it yields to decay. This emerges clearly from a cursory examination of the diagram above which demonstrates:

(1) the inverted symmetry of M_{124} and M_{139};

(2) their ability to be added together thanks to sign inversion, since the constructs I and V, added to each other, reconstitute the total field of the constructs II, III, and IV.

4

Chromatic Piece

Myths concerning a supernatural being who, in the guise of an old man, a cripple, or some other poor wretch, puts human generosity to the test are found throughout the length and breadth of the New World. To mention only tropical America for the moment, myths of this nature exist from Colombia and Peru (Davila, pp. 125-7) to the Gran Chaco. We have already encountered one myth (M₁₀₇) of the Choco Indians, whose hero was Moon, covered with incurable sores and caught between a malicious wife and a compassionate daughter (Wassen 1, pp. 110-11). In a corresponding Toba myth the hero is a scabby dog who is given shelter by a charitable family, to whom he shows his thanks by saving them from the flood (Lehmann–Nitsche 5, pp. 197-8). These variants confirm the equivalence introduced on page 251:

$$\overset{\text{(stench)}}{\left[\text{external} : \text{internal} \right]} :: \left[\text{female} : \text{male} \right]$$

Can we find a reason for this?

The mother of diseases in the Bororo myth (M₅) manifests herself during a collective fishing expedition known as *à la nivrée* in French Guiana—that is, fishing with poison. This method consists in suffocating the fish, by throwing into the water the coarsely ground stems of plants of various kinds, usually creepers (*Dahlstedtia, Tephrosia, Serjania, Paullinia*, etc.). The dissolved sap is said to cut off the supply of oxygen to the fishes' respiratory systems. The poisons used in fishing are divided into two categories, called *timbo* and *tingui*, but I propose to use only the first term, since it is the most common.

It has not been established with any certainty that in central Brazil fishing with *timbo* is a purely masculine occupation, the women's task being limited to carrying the fish back to the village, so as to avoid bringing bad luck to the fishermen. This second practice seems to be obligatory in Guiana (cf. M₂₈). As far as the actual fishing is concerned, women may well be forbidden any active participation, as the following details relating to the Mundurucu would suggest: "The men who are to poison the water go upstream, while the rest of the men and the accompanying women and children wait for the stunned fish to swim downstream." And further: "The women use hand nets to scoop up the fish, while the men impale them with fishing arrows or club them" (Murphy 2, p. 58).

On this point, the Bororo myth contains a curious detail. The text makes it clear that the fishing expedition took place the day before the grandmother was murdered, and that on that particular day the men brought back and ate the fish they had caught. It was only on the following day that the women went to the river to look for the remaining dead fish, and it was on this occasion of a conjunction between women and water that the heroine, instead of transporting the fish to the village like her companions, devoured them on the spot and then, on returning to the village, exuded diseases. If my supposition about a sexual division of labor in fishing with *timbo* is correct, it follows that in M₅, the appearance of diseases must be linked with violation of taboos.[25] But before proceeding further, I must digress a little.

The Kayapo-Gorotire have a myth about the origin of diseases which is different from the Bororo myth but contains the fishing with poison theme. This myth (M₁₄₀) refers to an aquatic bird (egret) which has been captured and tamed, and whose mysterious nature is revealed during a storm: lightning strikes the old mortar that has been used to make a pond for the bird, causes the water to boil, and surrounds the bird with smoke, yet without disturbing it. Shortly afterward, women waiting at the water's edge to collect the dead fish the men are poisoning upstream notice the bird perched on a branch. Suddenly it dives toward them, and although it hurts no one, the women die "like the poisoned fish." This is how diseases originated. The akranre bird is especially responsible for the ankylosis which accompanies malaria, and for landslides (Banner 2, p. 137). In Gorotire, the word *kapremp* means both diseases and landslides (Banner 1, pp. 61–2). The Amazonian Indians believe that the rainbow not only causes diseases but also makes cliffs collapse (Tastevin 3, p. 183).

However obscure this myth may be, through both the lack of variants and the absence of any ethnographic context, we can sense that its armature is based on a double equivalence: on the one hand between (boiling) water, in conjunction with fire, and water (foaming because of the frothy sap of the *timbo*) in conjunction with the deadly poison; on the other hand, between the poison, "which kills without injuring," and disease. This interpretation can be supported to some extent by the belief held by the Guarani to the south, that there is a correlation between disease, a substance deposited in the human body, and fire, a substance deposited in wood. The Kaiova-Guarani take fever to be an argument in support of this conception (Schaden 2, p. 223).

[25] Fishing with *timbo,* as practiced by the Bororo, is a very effective method. But the fish must be dressed immediately; otherwise it goes bad and is dangerous to eat. When they are a long way from their village, the natives cure the fish they have caught so skillfully that it remains in a good state of preservation for several days (Colb. 1, p. 26). This is not always the case, since we have the following information relating to the Oayana of French Guiana (it is much more in the spirit of the Bororo myth): "The cured fish does not keep well and can give rise to serious epidemics of poisoning, which occur especially a short while after the large-scale *nivrées*. Such epidemics often take the form of dysentery and can cause deaths" (Hurault, p. 89).

It would be hazardous to analyze the myth further, since it raises a delicate ethnographic problem. The Iroquois also have a myth that echoes word for word the belief that gullied hillsides devoid of vegetation are attributable to the destructive action of a supernatural bird: "The eagle ("Dew-Eagle") is so tremendous that his wings obscure the sun, and in landing his forward-thrust talons plow great furrows in the earth, leaving ravines" (Fenton, p. 114).

Now from the point of view of medical properties, the Iroquois eagle is symmetrical with the Kayapo egret; the eagle cures; the egret kills. It is especially significant that in order to define the exact nature of the diseases to which the Kayapo myth refers, and to establish a closer connection between them and the gullied hillsides, Banner uses the words "convulsions and other such phenomena" (1, p. 62), while among the Iroquois the purpose of the eagle dance is chiefly to cure "convulsions that are symbolic of the eagle's manner of commencing flight" (Fenton, p. 114).

All this might be pure coincidence if we did not know from other sources that the Kayapo myth can be interpreted as a direct and simple transformation of the Iroquois myth from which the eagle dance emerged.[26] The Iroquois myth (M_{141}) deals with a young hunter who took shelter in a hollow tree and was carried by an eagle beyond the mists and clouds into the empyrean. Because he agreed to act as foster father to the eaglets—using his flint knife to cut the game brought back by the eagle into tiny morsels—the eagle finally brought him back among men, to whom the hero taught the rites of the dance (Fenton, pp. 80–91). We thus arrive at the following group of transformations:

M_{140}	egret in conjunction with water	carried away by a man and put in a hollow tree (filled with water)	in the village (disjunction: water→earth)	fire (sky) in conjunction with water through smoke or steam (hot)
M_{141}	eagle, in conjunction with fire (empyrean sky)	carries off a man hiding in a hollow tree (full of air)	far from the village (disjunction: earth→sky)	fire (sky) in disjunction with the earth by mists and clouds (cold)

M_{140}	women at the river, become accomplices of a murder (they pick up fish they have not killed);	women succumb to disease;	egret guilty of murder
M_{141}	man in the sky becomes foster-father (cuts up the game he has not killed);	man conquers disease;	eagle, a healer

[26] This is by no means a solitary example of an Iroquois-style myth occurring in the heart of central Brazil; cf. the Mundurucu myth about the origin of tobacco in Kruse 3, Vol. 46, p. 918.

That is not all. Although no definite variant of the Kayapo myth has been found among the other Ge tribes, it has an undeniable affinity with the Apinaye and Timbira myths about one (or two) supernatural birds of prey which either capture men in order to eat them or decapitate them with a stroke of their wings. In the Apinaye version (M_{142}) the birds are killed by the mythical twins Kenkuta and Akreti after the two brothers have lived in seclusion for a time (this is a myth that determined one phase of the initiation ritual), and in very unusual circumstances: they follow the course of a creek upstream, bathe, then stretch out on a thick log extended across the creek. The next morning their grandfather, who is worried about their disappearance, sets off to look for them, first downstream, then upstream, where he eventually discovers them. The brothers declare that they propose to remain on the tree trunk; and alongside the grandfather builds a grate of poles, with a platform just above water level. Every day he puts food there, and the brothers grow up big and strong (Nim. 5, pp. 171–2). In another version the structure made of branches is replaced by a hut on stilts (C. E. de Oliveira, pp. 74–5); elsewhere, by the prototype of the men's house (Pompeu Sobrinho, p. 192). However this detail is treated, the theme seems to be a transformation of the (Iroquois) hollow-tree theme and the (Kayapo) mortar filled with water theme:

M_{140}	hollow tree / water inside	vertical conjunction: sky $\longrightarrow$ water	ambiguous heroines (mothers guilty of murder)
M_{141}	hollow tree / air inside	vertical disjunction: earth $\#\!\!\rightarrow$ sky	ambiguous hero (man as foster-father)
M_{142}	solid tree / water outside	horizontal disjunction: downstream $\#\!\!\rightarrow$ upstream	ambiguous heroes (heroic foster-children)

M_{140}	horizontal disjunction: upstream $\#\!\!\rightarrow$ downstream	egret as murderer
M_{141}	vertical conjunction: sky $\longrightarrow$ earth	eagle as healer
M_{142}	vertical disjunction: sky $\#\!\!\rightarrow$ earth	eagles (more) guilty of murder

The hollow trunk thus appears as a mediator, either between water and the sky (M_{140}) or between earth and sky (M_{141}), while the solid tree fulfills the same function between earth and water (M_{142}).

Let us return now to the Bororo myth about the origin of diseases (M_5), whose details assume their full significance when this myth is compared with the myths dealing with the origin of *timbo*:

M_{143}. Mundurucu. "The origin of fish poison"

There was once an Indian who never had any luck when he went hunting. He brought back to his wife only inhambu birds (cf. M_{16} and p. 203), which made bitter soup. One day, having overheard his wife make some uncomplimentary remark, he went off into the forest where he met a band of capuchin monkeys (*Cebus* species; children who had been changed into monkeys). He tried to capture first a female, then a male, by catching hold of their tails. But the monkeys threw themselves on the man, killed him, and ate him all up, except for one leg. They then took on human form and went to make the widow a present of her husband's leg. The widow, however, was not deceived by her visitors, who tried to make her believe their basket contained an ordinary piece of game. She recognized the leg but did not betray the fact that she had done so; she ran away, taking her little girl with her.

While the monkeys were pursuing her, she met in turn a poisonous snake, a spider, and all the beasts of the forest, not one of which was willing to come to her aid. Finally, an ant told her to go and see a frog sorcerer (the sorcerer, Uk'uk, so-called because he cries "uk'uk" during the night). The latter made a bulwark for the fugitives with its body and, using a bow and arrows, killed the monkeys and other animals who were about to devour the two unfortunate creatures.

When the slaughter was completed, the frog ordered the woman to skin the victims and start curing the meat, then to burn the skins. There were so many skins to burn that the woman became all blackened with soot. The frog told her to go and wash in the river, but warned her to keep facing upstream and not to look behind her.

The woman did as she was told, and the filth from her body turned the water quite black and produced the same effect as *timbo*. The fish rose to the surface and died, after beating the water three times with their tails. The noise caused the woman to turn around in surprise to see where it was coming from. The fish at once came back to life and swam away. Meanwhile the frog arrived to collect the dead fish. Not seeing any, it questioned the woman, who confessed she was to blame. The frog explained to her that if she had obeyed his instructions, Indians would have been relieved of the arduous task of looking for wild *timbo* in the forest.[27] The fish would have been killed more easily had they been poisoned by the dirt washed off by women bathing. (Murphy 1, pp. 112–113; Kruse 2, p. 618; regarding this last version, cf. below, p. 269, n. 33.)

M_{144}. Vapidiana. "The origin of fish poison"

A woman handed over her child to be brought up by a fox. But as the child cried a great deal, the fox got rid of it by passing it on to a female tapir. When the boy grew up, the tapir married him. She soon became pregnant and

[27] This detail is essential since, in addition to wild lianas, the Mundurucu use a shrub that they grow in their plantations (Murphy 2, pp. 57–8; Frikel 2, p. 12). Tocantins (pp. 122–3) had already pointed out that the Mundurucu cultivated *Paullinia pinnata*.

begged her husband to shoot her with his arrows and remove the child from her corpse. Having obeyed her instructions, the man discovered that every time he washed the child in the river, the fish died. And when the child died, it turned into *timbo-aiyare*, from which fish poison is extracted. (Wirth 1, pp. 260–1.)

A much more detailed version of the same myth comes from another Guianian tribe:

M_{145}. *Arecuna. "The origin of the fish poisons aza and ineg"*

Exasperated by her child's crying, a woman left him to the fox. The latter took him home, fed him, and brought him up, but a female tapir stole him. The child grew up completely covered in ticks, which are the tapir's beads.

When he became a grown man, the female tapir took him as her husband. She taught him the different meanings that beings and things had for tapirs: the poisonous snake was an oven, but the dog was a poisonous snake. . . .

It so happened that the female tapir, who had become pregnant, laid waste the plantation belonging to her husband's parents. Thereupon she urged him to visit his relatives but advised him to keep their marriage secret. The boy was warmly welcomed, but people expressed surprise at the fact that he was covered with ticks. He maintained that this was on account of his losing his way in the forest.

The following morning it was discovered that the plantation had been ruined, and the tapir's tracks were noticed. It was decided to kill the tapir. The young man thereupon confessed that she was his wife, and that she was pregnant. They could kill her, provided they were careful not to wound her in the belly, but only under the arm, in the head, or the legs. And he asked his mother to follow the hunters, in order to remove the child from the animal's body as soon as it was dead.

As the hero had also foretold, the mother discovered that every time she bathed the child in the river (in secret, following her son's injunctions), quantities of fish died. She therefore washed the child each time there was a shortage of food.

But the hero's relatives (sisters' husbands) were curious about the mysterious glut of fish and sent children to spy on their mother-in-law. In this way they discovered the old woman's secret. From then on, the bathing and the collecting of the fish were to take place in public with everyone helping.[28]

In this way the fish-eating birds came to know that when the child was washed in the river, there would be a miraculous glut of fish. The tuyuyu bird (*Mycteria mycteria,* a wood ibis) asked the father to bathe the child for their benefit, and suggested that the operation should take place, not in a stream but in the pool below a waterfall where the fish were more plentiful. The father was frightened and protested, "You will kill my child!" But the

[28] This is the actual wording of the myth, and there is no reason to agree with Koch-Grünberg when he proposes to change the informant's phrasing: "The old woman invited all his relatives to gather up the fish . . ." to "The old woman invited . . . to eat . . ." (K.G. 1, p. 71, n. 1).

bird was so insistent that, for the sake of peace, the father, the child, and the whole family went to inspect the pool.

There they found the birds, who had arranged to assemble at the spot. The pool was found to be full of fish. The father ordered his son to dive in, but the latter was afraid of the deep and threatening water. The father insisted. Furious, the boy plunged into the water and dived over and over again. Then the father said to him, "That is enough, my son! There are a lot of dead fish. Come back now!" But the child was annoyed and refused to listen. The dead fish began to pile up. Finally, the swimmer reached a rock in the middle of the pool and lay there, face downward, without uttering a word. Now he was cold, for when he had dived into the water, he was burning with anger and covered in sweat. And while the men and the birds busied themselves gathering up the fish, he died without speaking. What had happened was that during one of his dives Keyemen—the rainbow in the shape of a huge watersnake—had shot him with an arrow and wounded him. Keyemen was the grandfather of aquatic birds, and the entrance to his subterranean abode was at the bottom of the pool where the fatal fishing expedition was taking place.

Full of bitterness, Kulewente (this was the father's name) blamed the birds for his son's death and asked them to avenge it. The birds took turns in trying to dive down to the bottom of the pool, but without success. Then the terrestrial birds and quadrupeds tried, and they too failed.

Two remaining birds (two diving birds, *Colymbus* species) stayed in the background, for they had made no request to the father and bore no responsibility for the boy's death. Nevertheless they agreed to intervene. They dived to the bottom of the pool and killed Keyemen.

By means of a liana that they fastened round his neck, the men and the animals succeeded in hauling the monster onto dry land. They skinned the body and cut it into pieces, which they shared out among themselves. According to the nature and color of the portion allotted to each one, the animals acquired the cries, the anatomical peculiarities, the coats, or the plumage that were henceforth to be characteristic of each species.

Kulewente put his son's body in a basket and then went off. The grandmother took the basket and walked away with it, singing. Blood oozed from the basket, then pieces of decomposed flesh fell out, creating *timbo,* from which fish poison is extracted. The bones and sexual organs produced the weak variety, and the rest of the body the strong variety. The grandmother finally turned into an ibis which eats the earthworms men use as bait in fishing. (K.G. 1, pp. 68–76.)

Here is another version from Guiana:

M₁₄₆. Arawak. "The origin of fish poisoning"

An old man who was fond of fishing one day took his son with him to the river. Wherever the lad swam, the fish died. And yet he could safely eat them.

The father took the lad with him to bathe day by day till the fish knew of his plans and resolved to defeat him. They made up their minds to slay the boy. They dared not attack him in the water, so they chose an old log as the scene of the slaughter where the boy, after swimming, would bask in the sun.[29] There the fish attacked him, and the stingray fatally wounded him. The father carried his son into the forest. When the dying youth saw his blood drop on the ground, he told his father of the curious plants that would grow wherever his blood took root, and he forecast that the roots of these plants would avenge his death. (Brett, p. 172.)

The theme of fish poison produced by the dirt washed off a child is also found in the mythology of the southern Guarani (Cadogan, p. 81). Conversely, the Tucuna tell the story (M_{146a}) of a virgin who was fertilized by the spirit of *timbo* by means of a *timbo* root, and gave birth to a child who only had to be dipped into water for the fish to die. It would appear that it was an old Tucuna ritual to wash pubescent girls with a solution of *timbo,* so as to ensure profitable fishing expeditions (Nim. 13, pp. 91–2).

The complex nature of these myths makes it necessary to tackle them piecemeal and to postpone the analysis of the third part of M_{145} (the origin of the plumage, the coat, and the cries of the various animal species).

I shall begin by establishing that, in spite of its different story pattern, this myth belongs to the same set as the Mundurucu myth about the origin of *timbo* (M_{143}). The transformation can be made through the medium of a curious Amazonian myth, which probably originated on the left bank of the Rio Negro:

M_{147}. Amazonia. "The story of Amao"

There was once a young virgin girl called Amao. Having been accidentally fertilized by a fish which got inside her vulva, she gave birth to a boy. When the baby was two months old, she happened to lay him down on a stone while she was catching small fish. Toward midday she went to pick him up again, but the child was dead.

She wept all night. In the morning the child started to talk and explained that the animals had killed him by frightening him. If his mother wanted to be safe from their attacks, she should smoke them with a resin fire until they changed into stones.

When evening came, Amao buried her son. At midnight all the animals had turned into stones, except the great snake, the stingray, the wild pig, and the tapir who had gone off in the direction of the spring where the child had died.

Amao went there, killed the wild pig and the tapir, cut them up, and threw all the flesh into the stream, apart from a thigh belonging to each animal, which she laid on the rock where they turned into stone.

Next, by means of a lasso, she captured the great snake and the stingray which were feeding on the bed of the stream. She turned them into stones with the help of resin.

Then she went back to her own people to teach them cooking and the arts

---

[29] Like the rock in M_{145}, the trunk here is comparable with the one in M_{142}.

of civilization. After which she disappeared, and no one knows where she went. (Amorim, pp. 289–90.)

The theme of the child lying on a stone at the water's edge and being killed by hostile animals (one of which is the great snake) links the myth above with the M₁₄₄–M₁₄₆ set. The theme of cooking, which is here subdivided into anticooking (which, however, turns everything black like cooking proper) and real cooking (which had been unknown until then), relates it to M₁₄₃.

We come even closer to M₁₄₃ in a short Amazonian myth (M₁₄₈), which tells how the *curupira,* the spirit of the woods, killed a hunter and removed his liver, then took it to the wife of his victim, whose appearance he had assumed. The wife became suspicious and fled with her son. Mother and child put themselves under the protection of a frog, which smeared a tree with resin extracted from its body. In trying to climb the tree, the *curupira* got stuck and died (Barbosa Rodrigues, pp. 63–74).

The author to whom we owe the above myth also describes the curious habits of the arboreal toad *cunauaru* (in fact, a tree frog: *Hyla venulosa,* according to Schomburgk, Vol. II, pp. 334–5): "In order to make its nest, this batrachian collects *breu-branco* (*Protium heptaphyllum*) resin and forms it into funnel-topped cylinders in which it lays its eggs. Water enters through the lower orifice and protects the eggs. It is believed that the resin comes from the toad's own body, and this is why it is called cunauaru icica, cunauaru resin. It is used as a fumigant to relieve headaches" (Barbosa Rodrigues, p. 197, n. 1).

This explanation is given by way of commentary on a myth (M₁₄₉), which leads straight back to the bird-nester set (M₁, M₇–M₁₂). A bachelor had a guilty relation with his sister-in-law. The husband, who was something of a sorcerer, caught a macaw by its tail and put it inside a hollow tree trunk. Then he persuaded his wife to ask his rival for the bird, so that she could rear it. The man climbed the tree, but a "bad thing"—a specter—seized hold of him. He called in vain to his brother for help and was changed into a *cunauaru* toad (Barbosa Rodrigues, pp. 196–7).

It would be particularly interesting to explore this back-connection, since there exists an Arecuna myth (M₁₄₉ₐ) about man's loss of immortality, the hero of which steals not birds, but frogs. Just when it is being captured at the top of a tree, the frog swims off with the man to an island and abandons him there at the foot of a tree. The poor man cannot move away from the tree, because the island is so small, and the vultures cover him with excrement. Venus and Moon in turn both refuse to come to his aid. Sun agrees to do so, warms him, washes and dresses him, and gives him one of his daughters in marriage. But the Indian is unfaithful to her with one of the vulture's daughters. As a result of this, his youth and beauty are destined to be short-lived (K.G. 1, pp. 51–3).

However, to avoid overburdening the argument, I will say no more at this juncture about the paradoxal frog hunter, who loses eternal youth through having succumbed, like the man looking for macaws in M₉, to the sweet call of decay. I had only one purpose in casting a rapid glance at the set of "frog" myths: to establish the existence of a paraculinary series, the terms of which are resin smoke, sooty smoke from cooking with too much fat, the filth of the human body, and *timbo*. For the series to be complete within itself, we need only accept the possibility that the "frog" in M₁₄₃ is the *cunauaru*. In the myth the frog kills the animals pursuing the mother and child by shooting arrows at them. The *cunauaru* ejects, over a range of a yard or so, a caustic and odorless secretion which, on touching the body, causes blisters and removes the top layer of skin (Chermont de Miranda, "Cunauaru" entry). It is therefore a producer of both resin and poison.[30]

Le us now return to fish poison, whose origin is very rapidly indicated in the Vapidiana myth (M₁₄₄). In spite, or because, of its brevity, the Vapidiana version is valuable in that it provides an intermediary stage between the Mundurucu myth about the origin of *timbo* (M₁₄₃) and another myth of which we possess innumerable versions (Mundurucu, Tenetehara, Tupari, Apinaye, Kayapo, Kraho, Opaye, Toba, Tacana, etc.). I mean the myth about the tapir's mistress, and especially about women who take tapirs as their lovers. Their husband (or husbands), having discovered the secret, kills the tapir and punishes her, either by making her eat the tapir's penis or by using it as an instrument with which to kill the culprit by brutally thrusting the severed member into her vagina.

Now only by referring to the myth above is it possible to interpret the Mundurucu myth about the origin of fish poison. The fact that they are symmetrical is already evident from their respective conclusions. The myth about the origin of fish poison regards the poison as a substitute for—one might almost say an ersatz of—the layer of dirt that covers a woman who is an enthusiast for cooking—and not for wantonness, like the tapir's mistress. As we have seen, the heroine of M₁₄₃ exasperates her husband by grievances of a

[30] ". . . The animal when seized let flow a whitish juice out of its ears which, while brushing away some mosquitoes, got onto the skin of my face where it caused the most scorching pains: next morning the spots had turned a dark color, and after a few days the whole skin peeled off" (Schomburgk, Vol. II, p. 335). De Goeje (pp. 48, 127–8) must be given credit for having seen that the *cunauaru* raises a problem. But he failed to understand the reasons why the mythical animal is a master of hunting, and the real animal is used as a talisman in hunting. These reasons involve the whole problem of the native attitude toward poison. Cf. below, pp. 274 ff., 319 ff. Further confirmation can be obtained by comparing M₁₄₃ with two Guianian *cunauaru* myths in Roth 1, pp. 213–15, which are themselves variants of M₁₇₇, which I shall deal with later (p. 310).

culinary nature, and an immoderate culinary operation is the cause of her filth. In the "tapir as seducer" cycle the adulterous women are alienated from their husbands because of their excessive eroticism, which the animal is better able to satisfy. Their filth is moral, as is conveyed by the naïve Portuguese of a native informant who refers to the tapir's mistress as a *semvergonha muito suja* ("shameless, very dirty"; Ribeiro 2, p. 134). Even today this kind of woman is referred to in popular French as *une saleté*. Now the women who are forcibly fed with tapir (through either the mouth or the vagina, according to the different versions) take their revenge by turning into fish. They are a vegetable means of fishing in certain myths (M_{143}) and the animal object of fishing in others.

Let us now examine the two types of myth in detail: they correspond exactly to each other. The husband in M_{143} is a poor hunter. The tapir's mistresses are poor cooks and neglect their children. In the Mundurucu version of the "tapir as seducer" myth (M_{150}) the heroine is in such a hurry to get back to her lover that she forgets to suckle her baby. The child changes into a bird and flies away.[31]

At the same time the episode in M_{143} of the angry husband who encounters a band of monkeys and climbs a tree to try to grab the tail of a female monkey who cries, "Let go! It will snap!" upon which he seizes the tail of a male monkey who turns round and bites him on the nose, can only be understood by reference to the tapir-seducer, whom the women encounter while bathing (Mundurucu, Kayapo; Apinaye with the transformation: tapir → alligator), at the foot of a tree (Kraho), or by calling him down from the top of a tree (Tupari), and whose enormous penis is emphasized in so many versions. To justify this interpretation, we need only consider the species to which the monkeys in M_{143} belong. According to the myth, they are capuchin monkeys, in Portuguese *macaco prego* (nail monkey): a name that is explained by the almost constant state of erection of the animal's penis, the tip of which is moreover flattened like a nail head. In respect to indecency, the capuchin monkey is on the same level as the tapir, as is confirmed by native comparisons: the Tupari, who do not remove their particularly tight-fitting penis sheaths even when bathing, compare civilized men, who bathe naked and expose their penises, to "tapirs and monkeys" (Caspar 1, p. 209).

The men who kill the tapir make the women and children eat its flesh, or they punish the guilty woman with the penis (M_{150}–M_{155}). The monkeys who kill the husband cut off his leg and present it to his wife as game (M_{143}); and, as if to bring out more clearly the true meaning, this metaphorical transposition is preceded by three others: the female monkey is caught by her tail

---

[31] Compare with M_5:

$\begin{cases} M_{150}\text{: women changed into fish: mother (water)/child (sky).} \\ M_5 \text{ : fish "changed" into woman: mother (water)/child (earth).} \end{cases}$

It will be remembered, too, that in M_5 the seducer of Baitogogo's wife is a man belonging to the Tapir clan.

which will easily snap; the male monkey is subjected to the same treatment and retaliates by biting the hunter's nose. . . . In the "tapir as seducer" cycle the women are in disjunction from the men either because they have become fish in water (M_{150}, M_{151}, M_{153}, M_{154}), or because they start a new village a long way away (M_{155}, M_{156}). In the case of the Mundurucu myth about the origin of *timbo* (M_{143}) they take to flight as a way of achieving terrestrial disjunction from the monkeys and other animals of the forest who are pursuing them. The woman in M_{143} almost becomes fish-killing *timbo*, but through her own fault she reverts to being the woman whose function it is simply to pick up fish she has not killed. The tapir's mistresses want to be fish, but once they have been caught by men, they change back into women.

It is not surprising that a myth about the origin of *timbo* should be based on an inversion of a myth about the origin of fish. Fish are a food, and when they are caught with *timbo,* they are an exceptionally abundant form of food.[32]

As for *timbo* itself, a Mundurucu myth clearly defines its position on the margin of the semantic field which embraces all food products: it is a means of acquiring food, without being in itself a food:

M_{157}. *Mundurucu. "The origin of agriculture"*

Formerly there were neither gardens nor cultivated plants.

An old woman was pestered by her young nephew, who was hungry and was asking for agricultural produce which did not yet exist.

She had a section of the forest cleared and burned and informed men of all that would grow there: maize, sweet potatoes, sugar canes, bananas, sweet manioc, cara, melons, cashew nuts, inga pods, fava and *feijão*. . . . And she explained when each plant should be harvested, and how it should be cooked and flavored.

But she also explained that *timbo* (fish poison) was poisonous and should not be eaten. Men should pull it up, grind it in water, and invite everybody to share the dead fish which, unlike the *timbo*, could be eaten.

She had herself buried in the garden, and from her body sprang all of the plants. . . . (Murphy 1, p. 91; a significantly different version of the same myth in Kruse 2, pp. 619–21, and 3, pp. 919–20 will be discussed in a different context in *Du miel aux cendres* [Vol. II, pp. 45–7]).

Fish poison is included, then, in the category of vegetable foods, although it is what one might call an inedible food. Now it so happens that the Opaye have two variants of the myth about the marriage of a human being and a

[32] "The efficacy of this system of fishing is remarkable. My wife and I took part in one such venture . . . in which more than one hundred people from four different villages participated, and approximately two tons of fish were killed" (Murphy 2, p. 59).

tapir; and they are of special interest, since they provide a much more direct link than the others with alimentary and vegetable themes, and the sex of the respective partners is inverted from one variant to the other.

One (M_{158}) tells the story of a young man who marries a tapir woman by whom he has a daughter (this version therefore closely resembles M_{144}, the Vapidiana version). He comes back to live among his own people and explains to them how, thanks to the tapirs, they, like himself, can enjoy vast quantities of food (this is reminiscent of the Guianian myths, M_{114}–M_{116}, in which the tapir is master of the tree of life). The women, however, being meticulous gardeners, cannot tolerate the presence of the tapirs, which lay waste the gardens and foul the paths. (In the Tacana versions the man is overfastidious about his food; cf. Hissink-Hahn, p. 297.) Discouraged by this, the man and his tapir family disappear. Humanity is thus deprived forever of the vast quantities of food (Ribeiro 2, pp. 128–9).

The second version (M_{159}) depicts a period when men did nothing but hunt, and left farming to the women. However, one Indian woman both neglected her garden and spurned her husband's advances. He kept a watch on her movements and discovered a tapir's lair, full of dung, in the middle of the plantation. There every day the woman came to meet her lover whom, however, she seemed more eager to please with her cooking than with her caresses. With the help of his brother-in-law, the husband killed the tapir. The woman succeeded in keeping the penis in order to derive solitary pleasure from it. She was caught doing so, and while she was bathing, her hut was set alight, and the penis completely destroyed. The woman died of melancholy (Ribeiro 2, pp. 133–5).

The first version ends, therefore, with a refusal of food; the second, with a sexual refusal. Let us look more closely at the alimentary aspect, in those versions where it is most in evidence.

The Vapidiana and Arecuna myths about the origin of fish poison describe how a vegetable substance—inedible although classed as a food—was obtained for man's use.

The first Opaye version relates how men were refused a vast quantity of supremely edible vegetable food.

The myths about the origin of fishes describe how men obtained an edible animal food, itself a function of an inedible, vegetable food (*timbo*), which ensures vast supplies of the other.

How, then, are we to define the Mundurucu myth about the origin of *timbo? Timbo* is not withdrawn but left; the refusal concerns a poison of the most extreme form: female filth which differs from *timbo* through certain special features: it is animal in origin, for it comes from the human body; and at the same time its cause is cultural, since the filth in question is acquired by a woman through her function as cook.

From the alimentary point of view, therefore, the myths I have just compared can be classed according to four contrasting concepts:

	M_{144}, M_{145} origin of *timbo*	M_{158} loss of the abundance of food	M_{143} loss of the abundance of *timbo*	M_{150}, etc. origin of fish
Edible/inedible	−	+	−	+
Animal/vegetable	−	−	+	+
Cultural/natural	−	−	+	−
Obtained/refused	+	−	−	+

In addition to the alimentary aspect, all these myths present a sexual aspect. As is the case the world over, the South American languages bear witness to the fact that the two aspects are closely linked. The Tupari express coitus by locutions whose literal meaning is "to eat the vagina" (*kümä ka*), "to eat the penis" (*ang ka*) (Caspar 1, pp. 233–4). It is the same in Mundurucu (Strömer, p. 133). The Caingang dialects of southern Brazil have a verb that means both to "copulate" and "eat"; in certain contexts it may be necessary to specify "with the penis," in order to avoid ambiguity (Henry, p. 146). A Cashibo myth (M_{160}) relates how man had no sooner been created than he asked for food; and the sun taught him how to sow or plant maize, the banana tree, and other edible plants. Then man asked his penis, "And what would you like to eat?" The penis replied, "The female organ" (Métraux 7, pp. 12–13).

However, it is worthy of note that in the myths just discussed the sexual code should be apparent only in its masculine references: the tapir's penis is explicitly referred to and amply described. When the references are feminine, the sexual code becomes latent and is concealed beneath the alimentary code; the means of catching fish (*timbo*) and the object of fishing (fishes), are obtained; abundance of food, abundance of poison are lost. . . .

In order to understand this lack of parity between the two codes, we must take into account an ethnographic fact. In their sexual life the Brazilian Indians are particularly susceptible to the smells of the female body. The Tupari believe that the vaginal smell of an old woman causes migraine in her masculine partner, and that only the vaginal odor of a young woman has no harmful consequences (Caspar 1, p. 210). Seeing a rotten fruit full of worms, Mair, the Urubu demiurge, exclaimed, "That would make a nice woman!" and straightway the fruit turned into a woman (Huxley, p. 190). In a Tacana myth the jaguar decides not to rape an Indian woman after he has caught the smell of her vulva, which seems to him to reek of worm-ridden meat (Hissink-Hahn, pp. 284–5). A Mundurucu myth, which has already been quoted (M_{58}), relates that after the animals had made vaginas for the first women, the armadillo rubbed each of the organs with a piece of rotten nut, which gave them their characteristic smell (Murphy 1, p. 79).[33] Here again, then, we

[33] For the same reason no doubt, a Warao myth attributes to the bunia, the foul-smelling bird (see above, p. 185), the task of fashioning the vagina of the first woman

are dealing with stench and decay which, as has already been established, signify nature, as opposed to culture, but this time they are expressed in terms of anatomical coding. And woman is everywhere synonymous with nature, even among the matrilineal and matrilocal Bororo, where the men's house, strictly out of bounds to the opposite sex, acts as a sanctuary for the religious life, at the same time as it offers the living a reflection of the kingdom of souls.

Just as mankind in the state of nature fed on rotten wood, and therefore on inedible food, and just as fish poison (which also comes into the category of inedible food) can be the equivalent of a form of infantile filth if the child was born of the direct union between a man and an animal—that is, nature— or of female filth if the latter is culinary in origin and results from a direct conjunction between the woman and culture—so stench is the natural manifestation, in an inedible form, of femininity, of which the other natural manifestation, milk, represents the edible aspect. Vaginal odor is therefore the counterpart of the suckling function: being anterior to it, it offers an inverted image of it and can be considered to be its cause, since it precedes it in time. The anatomical and physiological code thus re-establishes a logical pattern which we first discovered in terms of the alimentary code, and in accordance with which the opossum, being congruous with the rotten wood that men ate before the introduction of agriculture, could be associated with the origin of agriculture (p. 183).[34] But this opossum is a virgin. Only when woman becomes a mother can she be compared to the food-giving opossum. As long as her connotation remains merely sexual, she merely has an unpleasant smell.

The Bororo myth about the origin of diseases (M_5) implicitly affirms what I have just said. We saw that the young heroine, who gorges on fish and introduces death, can be transformed into an opossum whose attributes can be varied by being taken to their extreme limit (p. 246). From this point of view, she is a reduplication of the dead grandmother who infected her grandson with intestinal gases and thus fulfilled the same function as the skunk (cf. above, p. 177). The association with the skunk is indirectly corroborated by the Asare myth (M_{124}) and by the fact that the latter is symmetrical with the bird-nester myth (M_1), which belongs to the same set as M_5. The skunk whose intestinal gases are deadly also figures in the Toba and Mataco myths (Métraux 5, pp. 128–9; 3, pp. 22–3). It is a cause of death in an Opaye myth (M_{75}).

I have proved the existence of a parallel between the animal helpers who intervene in M_1 and M_{124}. In so doing, I noted, too, that in each myth a fourth personage comes onto the scene at the end and is not just an animal but a relative: a grandmother in M_1, who acts positively by giving the hero a magic

---

(Roth 1, p. 131). Conversely, the demiurge, Makunaima, gave flavor to the fruit of the inaja palm tree (*Maximiliana regia*), which at first had no taste, by rubbing it against his penis (K.G. 1, pp. 33 ff.).

[34] It should be noted that in the Kraho versions of the star myth (M_{89}) Star, who had been raped and defiled, poisoned her guilty brothers-in-law, either with her saliva or with an infusion made from bark, a preparation analagous to that of *timbo*.

stick; an uncle in M_{124}, who acts negatively by killing the alligator with his harmful fluid, for this uncle is a skunk. We observe, then, that the following transformation has taken place:

a) (M_1) helpful grandmother (human)→(M_{124}) helpful uncle (animal=skunk).

And since it has also been shown that M_1 and M_5 are symmetrical, it is not at all surprising that, via the medium of M_{124}, the following transformation can now be proved:

b) (M_1) helpful grandmother (human)→(M_5) hostile grandmother (human≡skunk).

This having been established, we come to realize that the myth about the origin of diseases, in its two successive episodes, illustrates the two possible ways for a woman not to behave like a mother: physically, if she is a grandmother or a woman who has got beyond the age of child-bearing; morally, if she is a young mother whose excessive appetite prompts her to abandon her child. The one kills metonymically by breaking wind (the wind is part of the body); the other by the diseases she exudes metaphorically, since she is unable to evacuate the food she has eaten. However different they may be, these two solutions are referable to one and the same principle: if you remove the maternal element from femininity, what is left is stench.

What I have just said is only another way of applying the "proof of the opossum" (pp. 170–83). We shall now return to the Arecuna myth in order to look at it from different angles which, as it happens, will still bring us back, or very nearly, to the same point.

Let us begin by emphasizing a detail that will make it possible to consolidate the "tapir as seducer" set by using a different approach from the one already adopted. It is obvious that such a set would deserve a special study, which I cannot embark upon here, so I shall merely sketch a rough outline of it.[35]

[35] Thus, to elucidate the semantic function of the fox in M_{144}–M_{145}, it would be necessary to construct a set which, in spite of seeming simplicity, would involve contrapuntally a considerable number of opposites, such as seclude/exclude; nourished/antinourished; human/animal; true mother/adoptive mother; nursing mother/ogress; wife/mother; skunk/vixen; *timbo*/fish:

M_5	child (1) in seclusion	antinourished by substitute mother≡skunk	
	child (2)		excluded by human mother —anti-nurse greedy for fish caught with *timbo*
M_{144} M_{145}	child excluded	nourished by substitute mother≡vixen	adopted by animal nurse (tapir)→wife, rich in *timbo* for catching fish

When the Indians in M_{145} decide to kill the female tapir which has laid waste their plantations, the hero—whose pregnant wife the tapir happens to be—solemnly entreats them, saying, "If you want to kill this tapir, shoot an arrow at its armpit, not at its belly.... You may shoot it but not in the belly! You can aim for the head or the paws, but not the belly!" (K.G. 1, p. 70). This attempt to list, with one notable exception, the various parts of the body at which arrows can be aimed, reminds us at once of a similar passage in a Bororo myth, which was summarized at the begining of this book (M_2, pp. 49–50), and to the significance of which I have already drawn attention (p. 210). In order to avenge himself on an Indian who had raped his wife, Baito-gogo aims several arrows at him, crying, "I will wound you in the shoulder, but do not die! I will wound you in the arm, but do not die! I will wound you in the hip, but do not die! I will wound you in the buttocks, but do not die! I will wound you in the leg, but do not die! I will wound you in the face, but do not die! I will wound you in the side—now die!" (Colb., p. 202–3).[36] Now it will be remembered that the victim is a man belonging to the tapir clan, and so he, too, is "a tapir seducer." I used this same argument when correlating and contrasting M_2 (a myth about the origin of terrestrial, beneficial water) with the Kayapo myth about Bepkororoti (M_{125}), which deals with the origin of celestial, maleficent water, and in which the tapir, both as animal and game, is killed, skinned, and cut up in a rough and ready manner which contrasts with the long-drawn-out torture inflicted on the tapir man in M_2. The Arecuna myth completes and enriches the comparison, since it contains an episode of the same type and, like the Bororo myth, depicts a tapir seducer (but female instead of male; and an animal, not a human). In M_{125}, therefore, the tapir which retains its animal nature and—to facilitate the comparison with M_2 and M_{145}—can be said to undergo an identical transformation (identical to itself) is the victim of a botched murder; whereas in M_2 and M_{145} (which are in twofold contrast with each other: male/female, human/animal) the tapir is the victim of a carefully executed murder, but one inspired by a very different purpose, which is either to wound every part of its body before killing it (M_2) or (M_{125}) to aim at any part of its body but not at a specific area (the belly, where the child would be in danger of being killed):

After this it would be necessary to trace the various transformations of the vixen from Amazonia (cf. M_{109c} which is about a female opossum) to the extreme south of the continent, among the Yamana, where the vixen, the adopted mother of twins—created by the division into two parts of a child which had been abandoned because it never stopped crying—plans to eat them; the natives explain this intention by the fox's liking for dead flesh (Gusinde, Vol. II, pp. 1141–3).

[36] In connection with other myths, Koch-Grünberg (1, pp. 270 ff.) had already stressed the characteristic nature of this narrative device. It would be interesting to inquire whether the myths he quotes as examples and the ones we are comparing in the same connection also form a set. Also, in Colbacchini (2, p. [25], n. 2) there are several examples of the use of this same narrative device.

M_{125} (tapir⟶tapir) $= {}^{f}$(botched murder)

M_{2} (tapir⟶human) $= {}^{f}$(carefully executed murder : wound>kill)

M_{145} (human⟶tapir) $= {}^{f}$(— — : kill>wound)

In order to justify this system of equations, it should be made clear that the man belonging to the tapir clan in M_{2} can be reduced to a "tapir function" assumed by a human, whereas the tapir woman in M_{145} can be reduced to a "human function" (mother and wife) assumed by an animal.

Let us now go on to a second aspect of M_{145} (Arecuna version) and M_{144} (Vapidiana): why is the origin of fish poison linked with the theme of the tapir as seducer? Since I propose to show that the link between them presupposes a very special view of the place occupied by vegetable poisons in the system of creation, I will first introduce a new myth dealing with the origin of curare, a poison used in hunting but not in fishing. It comes from a small Carib-speaking tribe living along the middle section of the Trombetas and Cachorro rivers:

M_{161}. *Kachuyana. "The origin of curare"*

There was once a young bachelor who lived a long way from his tribe's people in a lonely hut. On returning from a particularly successful hunt, he cooked all the game and ate it, except for a female howler monkey (*Alouatta* species), which he put on to smoke overnight. Then he went to bed.

On waking up next morning, he resolved to eat the monkey before setting off to hunt, but when he saw the body with the hair all burned off, he experienced a feeling of revulsion, then of anger: "What is this she-monkey to me? I am hungry and cannot eat it!" But he left it to smoke, and went off to hunt.

In the evening he ate the game he had killed during the day and said, "Tomorrow I will eat the she-monkey. . . ." But when the next day came, the same scene occurred; he had only to glance at the she-monkey, and any desire to eat her vanished, so plump and pretty did she seem. After a final glance at the monkey he sighed, "If only she could change into a wife for me!"

When he returned from hunting, the meal was ready—meat, soup, pancakes . . . and the same was true the next day, when he got back from fishing. The Indian was puzzled and started looking everywhere, until finally he discovered a charming woman lying in his hammock; she told him that she was the she-monkey he had wished for as a wife.

After the honeymoon the man brought the woman to the village in order to introduce her to his relatives. Then it was the woman's turn to present her husband to her people—a family of monkeys whose hut was at the top of a tree. The woman helped the man to climb up into it; the next morning she went off with the other monkeys. Neither she nor they ever came back, and the man, who could not climb down unaided, remained marooned at the top of the tree.

One morning, the king vulture happened to be passing by. He questioned the man, who told him his story and explained the difficult situation he was in. "Wait a moment," said the vulture as he forced himself to produce a sneeze. From his nose there spurted (nasal) mucus which stretched to the ground and changed into a creeper. However, the creeper was so slender that the man said it might snap under his weight. The vulture thereupon called upon the harpy eagle (Portuguese *gavião-real*) which also sneezed and whose threads of mucus formed a stronger creeper, down which the hero was able to slide (cf. M_{116}–M_{117}). Before leaving, the harpy eagle told him how to take his revenge. He should cut the liana known as "the harpy eagle's arrow" and make it ready in accordance with its instructions and, having duly invoked his protector, go off and hunt the howler monkeys.

The man did as he was told. All the howler monkeys were killed, except one little one, from which present-day monkeys are descended. (Frikel 1, pp. 267–9.)

There is a good deal to be said about this myth. The poison used in hunting (and formerly perhaps as a weapon of war) by the Kachuyana is extracted from a liana. Its preparation calls for prolonged abstention from any form of contact with the feminine body, and for this reason young bachelors are often entrusted with the task. The natives believe the harpy eagle to be the most powerful sorcerer of the other world.[37] Lastly, and although the poison is used today chiefly in hunting the spider monkeys (whose flesh is considered more tasty and is consumed ritually), the natives put the poison on their arrows with a brush made from the bristles of the bearded howler monkeys (Frikel, pp. 269–274). This particular species would seem to be doubly characterized in respect to poison and putrescence. Like other monkeys, the howler monkeys are usually hunted with poisoned arrows. But "even when it is seriously wounded, the *bugio* (= *guariba*) remains up the tree, hanging on by its tail, with its body dangling in the void. It is said to be able to stay in this position for several days and only falls to the ground when it is half rotten" (Ihering, Vol. 33, p. 261). So the howler monkeys must be rotten to succumb to poison, unlike the opossum of the Ge myths which, whether rotten or defiled, itself becomes poison. Be that as it may, I propose to deal with only a few aspects of this complex problem so that we do not lose sight of our aim, which is to define the common characteristics of the myths of origin dealing with vegetable poisons.

One characteristic is instantly obvious: the poison always comes from a form of bodily filth: female filth (M_{143}), infantile filth (M_{144}–M_{146}), and nasal

---

[37] "In the Beyond is where all the knowledge of the vulture lies," the natives of Surinam say, in order to explain the place occupied by the bird in their myths (Van Coll, p. 482). True eagles (*Aquila*) are not to be found in Brazil, where the term *gavião-real* usually refers to one of the four species of harpy eagle, or two species of the *Spizaëtus* genus (also called *gavião pega-macaco*) and *Morphnus guianensis* and *Thrasaetus harpyia,* which have a wing span of up to 2 meters (Ihering, "Harpia" entry).

mucus (M_{161}, in which two kinds of liana were created from the mucus sneezed out by the bird protectors, although it must be admitted that there was nothing to show that the poisonous sort came from the same source). Furthermore, the ordure is hyperbolical in the principal myths: it is the result of excessive culinary activity (M_{143}); it belongs to a child who is doubly "natural" (born out of wedlock, son of a beast: M_{145}); or to a bird, master of fish, whose mucus is described (in contrast to that produced by another bird) as being particularly copious (M_{161}).

Most important of all, it would seem that, in order to culminate in poison, the myths must all pass through a kind of strait, the narrowness of which considerably lessens the gulf between nature and culture, animality and humanity.

The Mundurucu woman (M_{143}) accepts the protection of a frog and acts as its cook—that is, in the capacity of a cultural agent. The Arecuna hero (M_{145}) allows himself to be seduced by a female tapir; the Kachuyana hero (M_{161}) by a she-monkey. In every instance nature imitates the world of culture, but in reverse. The kind of cooking demanded by the frog is the opposite of human cooking methods, since the frog orders the heroine to skin the game, arrange the meat on the barbecue, and put the skins in the fire; this is to go against common sense, since normally game is cured in its skin over a gentle wood fire.[38] In the Arecuna myth, topsyturvydom is even more pronounced: the female tapir covers her son with ticks which are meant as beads: "She put them round his neck, his legs, his ears, his testicles, under his arms, all over his body" (K.G. 1, p. 69); for her, the poisonous snake is a plate on which to roast manioc cakes, the dog a poisonous snake. . . . The Kachuyana hero is obsessed by the human aspect of the smoked corpse of a she-monkey.

It is therefore not enough to say that in these myths, nature and animality are reversed so as to become culture and humanity. Nature and culture, animality and humanity become mutually interpermeable. It is possible to move freely and without hindrance from one realm to the other: instead of there being a gulf between the two, they are so closely interconnected that any term belonging to one realm immediately conjures up a correlative term in the other, and both terms are capable of mutually signifying each other.

This special sense of a reciprocal transparency between nature and culture—a sense that is given poetic expression in the behavior of the hungry hero in M_{161} who cannot bring himself to eat game whose shape suggests that of the charming wife he would like to have—may well have been inspired by a certain conception of poison. Poison causes a kind of short circuit between nature and culture. It is a natural substance which, as such, is inserted into a

---

[38] This episode is missing from M_{143} in Kruse 2, where all the terms are shifted in the human direction: the monkeys are children who have undergone metamorphosis; the frog is a sorcerer in human form, whose characteristic cry betrays his true nature (cf. above, p. 260).

cultural activity like hunting or fishing and simplifies it to an extreme degree. Poison outclasses man and all the other technical means he has invented; it amplifies his movements and anticipates their effects; it acts more quickly and more effectively. We should not be surprised, then, if in native thought poison were looked upon as an intrusion of nature into culture. The former is probably seen as achieving a temporary invasion of the latter; for a few moments a joint operation is in progress, and it becomes impossible to distinguish the respective part played by each.

If I have interpreted native thought correctly, the use of poison would appear as a cultural act, developing directly from a natural property. As the Indians see the problem, poison no doubt represents a point of isomorphic coincidence between nature and culture, resulting from their interpenetration.

Now this natural entity that manifests itself directly in the cultural process, but to deflect its course, is the very image of the *seducer,* when he is described exclusively as such. The seducer is a being devoid of social status in respect to his behavior—otherwise he would not be exclusively a seducer—acting only in accordance with his natural properties, physical beauty and sexual potency, in order to subvert the social order of marriage. Consequently he, too, represents the violent intrusion of nature into the very heart of culture. This being so, we can understand how fish poison can be the son of a tapir seducer or at least of a tapir seductress. For human society, which is primarily a masculine society, refuses to recognize that the seduction of a woman by a man is on a par with the seduction of a man by a woman. If the contrast between nature and culture corresponds to the contrast between female and male, as is virtually the case the world over and certainly among the communities we are concerned with here, then the seduction of a human female by a male animal must inevitably give rise to a natural product, according to the following equation:

$$\text{a)} \quad \text{nature} + \text{nature} = \text{nature}$$

and consequently the women seduced by a tapir become fish, whereas the seduction of a man by a female animal can be expressed as:

$$\text{b)} \quad \text{culture} + \text{nature} = (\text{nature} \equiv \text{culture})$$

with fish poison as the product: a composite being of ambiguous sexuality, whom the Arecuna myth (M_{145}) describes as a child, obviously a male, but whose testicles have not reached maturity and produce only a weak variety of poison. But that the two operations belong to one and the same set is clear from the fact that, in the first, women do not become just any animal. As fish they re-establish a relation of complementarity with *timbo.* They are the object of its action.[39]

[39] The fact that fish poison is the tapir's child accounts for an extraordinary belief about the habits of the animal: "When the tapir finds a well-stocked pool, he defecates in it. Then he dives in and beats his feces with his feet; the fish, drawn by the smell,

The technique of fishing also respects the mythological complementarity, since men and women have different functions. Men play an active part, prepare and handle the *timbo,* and come into contact with the living fish. Women have a passive part to play; they assemble a little way downstream and wait for the dead fish to float along on the current when all they have to do is pick them up.[40] Thus:

	Mythological Level		Empirical Level	
	(M_{143})	(M_{145})		
a)	$\dfrac{\text{women}}{\text{fish}}$:	$\dfrac{\text{male child}}{timbo}$ ::	$\dfrac{\text{men}}{timbo}$:	$\dfrac{\text{women}}{\text{fish}}$

The chiasmus results from the fact that on the mythological level the transformation of women into fish is actively realized, and that of the child into *timbo* passively submitted to; whereas on the empirical level it is the men who have the active role, and the women the passive one.

Proof of this can be seen in the mistake made by the Mundurucu heroine of M_{143}. She would have retained her valuable physiological toxicity if she had kept her gaze firmly fixed upstream, so that it was impossible for her to see the fish still alive around her—in other words, if she had respected the principle governing the allocation of fishing sites to the two sexes. She violated the principle by looking downstream to watch the fish die; men who remain upstream among the living fish can look downstream, while women look upstream to see the dead fish floating toward them with the current. This usurpation of the male prerogative has a threefold result: the poison is changed from animal to vegetable; from cultural to natural; and from being a feminine possession to being a masculine possession.

It will also be noted that the equation:

Empirical Level

b)   men : women :: upstream : downstream

still holds good, thanks to the intensifying of the two contrasts, in the Arecuna myth (M_{145}), where the two opposite terms are not men and women but humans and fish-eating birds. The latter stand in the same re-

---

come to feed, become intoxicated, float on the surface of the water, and are devoured by the tapir. The Creoles, who know about the trick, wait at the water's edge and carry off what he leaves." It is explained (Pitou, Vol. II, p. 44) "that his dung, which resembles that of the horse, acts as an intoxicant for the fish which are particularly fond of it." This is an astonishing example of the distortion of reality through the misunderstanding of a myth.

[40] Cf. for instance the following episode in a Mundurucu myth: "On the fifth day of travel Perisuat encountered a jaguar couple fishing in a stream with *timbo.* The husband was upstream drugging the water, and the female was farther downstream catching the fish." (Murphy 1, p. 99. Cf. also Kruse 2, pp. 644-5).

lation to humans as, in fishing, the women do to the men; another Guianian myth describes aquatic birds in the following words: "all the birds that live today along the banks of stagnant ponds, in mud, feeding on fish and decomposed flesh" (K.G. 1, p. 262). The tuyuyu bird (the Amazonian name of the genus *Mycteria,* large wading birds, called *jabiru* and *jabwu* farther to the south), which as spokesman of the aquatic birds plays a fatal role in M_{145}, personifies a species whose members swoop down in their thousands after the floods and devour the stranded fish, which lie about in such vast quantities that it is thought that, but for the birds, the atmosphere would become poisoned by organic decay (Ihering, Vol. XXXVI, pp. 208–9). The birds who wait until the fish are dead before eating them are therefore transformable into the women who, during fishing expeditions, wait until the fish are dead (killed by the men's efforts) before picking them up. The episode in which the birds demand that the fishing should be carried out in deep water can be explained by the following transformation:

c) (men/women) : (upstream/downstream) :: (humans/birds) : (river/pool at base of waterfall).

This last equation is important, because it provides proof of the fact that the loss of *timbo* of human origin has the same cause in M_{145} as in M_{143}. In one case the woman who possesses *timbo* loses her power because, through her own fault, she has put herself into the masculine position. In the other the child who possesses *timbo* dies because, through the fault of the birds, which are a transformation of women fishers, he assumes a low position (at the base of the waterfall), and this low position is congruous with downstream—that is, with the feminine position. This inversion of a pattern common to both myths is accompanied by an inversion of their respective conclusions: loss of extraordinary *timbo* (M_{143}), origin of ordinary *timbo* (M_{145}).

Let us come back now to the problems raised by poison. The Arecuna myth attributes its origin to the intervention of the rainbow, and I have put forward the suggestion (pp. 246 ff.) that there might be a link between the heroine of the Bororo myth about the origin of diseases (M_5), who gorged on fish caught with *timbo,* and the rainbow. The Bororo heroine is the mother of diseases, and I have shown that, throughout the whole of tropical America, diseases are generally attributed to the rainbow, at least when they take the form of epidemics. Let us try to analyze this conception more fully.

Unlike old age, accidents, and war, epidemics create enormous gaps in the population. This is a feature they have in common with fish poison which, as we have seen, creates a degree of havoc among the denizens of the river out of all proportion with the results that can be obtained by other means. This connection between disease and fish poison is not pure speculation, since it provides the theme of a Guianian myth:

M₁₆₂. Carib. "The origin of diseases and fish poison"

In ancient times men knew nothing of disease, suffering, and death. There was no quarreling, and everybody was happy. The spirits of the forest lived at that time with men.

One day one of them, who had assumed the form of a woman suckling her baby, paid a visit to the Indians who gave her such a hot and highly seasoned stew that the supernatural woman was burned "to the heart." She at once asked for water, but her malicious hostess claimed she had none left. The spirit therefore ran to the river to quench her thirst, leaving her child in the hut. As soon as she had gone, a wicked woman threw it into the pot that was boiling on the fire.

When she got back to the hut, the spirit hunted everywhere for her child and when, on passing near the pot, she automatically stirred the stew with the ladle, she saw the little corpse rise to the surface. Weeping bitterly, she hurled reproaches at the Indians and told them that henceforth their children would die, so that they should weep as she had been made to weep. Women would also suffer pain in giving birth to their children. As for the men, they would no longer be able simply to drain the streams with their gourd containers in order to pick up fish, then fill the streams again so that there would again be an abundance of fish. Henceforth they would have to work and labor and strive in order to poison the pools with roots. Finally, the spirit of the forest killed the guilty woman and offended the children by rudely insulting their mother's memory. It disappeared only when the word "sweet potato" happened to be pronounced; spirits cannot abide this particular tuber. (Roth 1, p. 179; for an analysis of this myth, cf. below. pp. 308 ff.)

In the Bororo myth (M₅) and the Kayapo myth (M₁₄₀), both of which deal with the origin of diseases, a village engaged in a collective fishing expedition becomes the collective victim of the first epidemic. Two Bororo myths (M₂, M₃) make the advent of culture dependent on the massacre of a community. From a study of these two myths, I inferred (pp. 50–5) that the transition from nature to culture corresponds, in native thought, to the transition from the continuous to the discontinuous.

As I have indicated, the problems raised by fish poison led me to the conclusion that semantically this poison is situated at a point where the transition from nature to culture is effected without—or very nearly without—any solution of continuity. Let us say that in the natives' conception of poison of vegetable origin, the interval between nature and culture, although present as it is in all other contexts, is reduced to a minimum. Consequently poison, whether used for fishing or hunting, can be defined as maximum continuity which brings about maximum discontinuity, or, to use another formula, as a union of nature and culture which brings about their disjunction, since one depends on continuous quantity and the other on discrete quantity. It is not, therefore, an accident that the Arecuna myth (M₁₄₅) about the origin of fish poison should include an episode—which

I mention only briefly here and shall return to later—which presents the fragmentation of the rainbow as the cause of the anatomical discontinuity of living species—that is, of the advent of a zoological order, which, like the creation of the other realms of nature, ensures that culture has some hold over nature (L.-S. 8 and 9, *passim*). Behind the juxtaposition of seemingly incongruous themes, we can dimly perceive the action of a dialectic of short and long intervals or—to borrow convenient musical terms—of the chromatic and the diatonic. It is as if South American thought, being resolutely pessimistic in inspiration and diatonic in orientation, invested chromaticism with a primordial maleficence of such a kind that long intervals, which are necessary in culture for it to exist and in nature for it to be "thinkable" to men, can only be the result of the self-destruction of a primeval continuity, whose power is still to be felt at those rare points where it has survived its own self-destructiveness: either to the advantage of men, in the form of poisons they have learned to handle; or to their disadvantage, in the form of the rainbow over which they have no control.

The chromaticism of poison is ideological in nature, since it depends on the principle that there is a very short interval between nature and culture. The chromaticism of the rainbow is empirical and tangible. But if, following the observations that have just been made, we could accept the fact that chromaticism, so far as it is a category of the human understanding, implies the conscious or unconscious apprehension of a colored pattern, some of Jean-Jacques Rousseau's remarks on the subject of chromaticism, would become still more interesting:

> The word chromaticism comes from the Greek Χρῶμα, which means color, either because the Greeks indicated this particular style by red, or variously colored, signs; or, according to some writers, because the chromatic style is intermediary between the two others, just as color is intermediary between black and white; or, according to other writers, because this particular style adds beauty and variety to the diatonic through its semitones, which produce, in music, the same effect as is produced in painting by the variety of colors. (*Dictionnaire de Musique*, "*Chromatique*" entry.)

It is hardly necessary to emphasize that, like G. Rouget, who in a recent article has given an admirable definition of the problem of primitive chromaticism, I am taking the term in the very general sense of the use of short intervals, which covers both the Greek and the modern senses (although they differ from each other in other ways) and preserves the meaning of the word "chromaticism" common to both music and painting. I shall give a further quotation from Rousseau to show that the South American conception of chromaticism—conceived, in the first place, in terms of the visual code—is neither bizarre nor exotic, since from Plato and Aristotle on, West Europeans have treated it (albeit on the musical level) with the same mistrust and have credited it with the same ambiguity, associating it, as the Indians of Brazil do the rainbow, with suffering and bereavement:

> The chromatic style is well suited to express grief and affliction: as its sounds swell on the ascending scale, they make the heart bleed. It is no less powerful on the descending scale; the sounds then are like actual moanings. . . . Moreover, being especially effective, this style should be used sparingly, like those rich dishes that one soon tires of if given a surfeit of them, whereas they keep their appeal if served with discretion.

To which Littré, who quotes the beginning of Rousseau's article, adds: "In conversation, *le chromatique, du chromatique* means a langorous, soft, or plaintive passage" (*ibid.*).

This is an appropriate point to remind the reader that in Guiana the rainbow is called by the name of the opossum. A very different line of argument from the one I am pursuing at this moment led me to look upon the identification of the rainbow and the opossum as a result of the very short interval separating the logically opposite functions fulfilled by the opossum in the myths: it is a giver of life and a giver of death (p. 249). Consequently the opossum, too, is a "chromatic" being. It administers poison to its seducers in M_{89} and is itself poison in the other myths of the same set.

I will not go so far as to suggest that Isolde can be reduced to an "opossum function." But, since the analysis of South American myths has led us to consider fishing or hunting poison as a combinatory variant of the seducer, who is a poisoner of the social order, and to see both poison and seducer as two modalities between nature and culture of the domain of short intervals, we may conclude that the love philter and the death philter are interchangeable for reasons other than those of simple expedience, and we may thus be prompted to reflect anew on the fundamental causes of the chromaticism in *Tristan*.

PART FIVE

RUSTIC SYMPHONY
IN THREE MOVEMENTS

And yet that these relations are nothing akin to those foppish tales and vain fictions which poets and story-tellers are wont, like spiders, to spin out of their own bowels, without any substantial ground or foundation for them, and then weave and draw them out at their own pleasures, but contain in them certain abstruse questions and rehearsals of events, you yourself are, I suppose, convinced. And as mathematicians do assert the rainbow to be an appearance of the sun so variegated by reflection of its rays in a cloud, so likewise the fable here related is the appearance of some doctrine whose meaning is transferred by reflection to some other matter.

PLUTARCH, "Of Isis and Osiris" *Morals*
(edited by W. W. Goodwin, London 1870).

1

Divertissement on a Folk Theme

Let us now return to the key myth and take stock of our position.

We have proved that the Bororo myths (M_1 and M_5) and the Ge myths (M_7–M_{12}) belong to the same set, and that it is possible to move from one myth to the other through the operation of certain transformations, the chief of which occurs on the etiological level, since certain myths, which all have a bird-nester as their hero, purport to be either about the origin of water (M_1) or about the origin of fire (M_7–M_{12}). The Bororo myths are an example of the former case; the Ge of the latter. We must remember, too, that they are not dealing with any kind of fire or any kind of water. The fire is that used for domestic purposes, and the water is the sort that puts out domestic fires in the form of storms and rain.

The water/fire contrast is accompanied by another. In all the myths the hero's successful accomplishment of an expedition to the kingdom of souls, who are the masters of water (Bororo), or to the house of the jaguar, the master of fire (Ge), is directly or indirectly dependent on certain precautions concerning noise: he must not provoke noise or be provoked by it; or, to express the matter more simply, he must behave as if he were *dumb* or as if he were *deaf*. Even the Sherente myth (M_{12}), from which this theme is apparently absent, refers to it at the end, as if through an afterthought: when he returns to the village with the roasted meat, the hero *turns a deaf ear* to the questions fired at him by his fellow villagers, and claims that the meat has simply been cooked in the sun (p. 73). His deafness is thus the counterpart of the silence maintained by the Bororo hero, whereas the Apinaye hero (M_9) has an overacute sense of hearing (he hears the call of rotten wood), and the hero of the Timbira myth (M_{10}) makes too much noise when he eats. When the myths are approached from this angle, the dividing line is moved, so that it cuts through the Ge set, with the Bororo and Timbira myths on one side (more or less effective abstention from speech) and the Apinaye and Sherente myths on the other (deafness, also more or less effective).

Negatively and positively, all the myths have to do with the origin of the cooking of foodstuffs. They contrast this method of nourishment with others: the eating of raw meat by the carnivorous animals, and the eating of rotten meat by the carrion-eaters. But—and here we have a third difference—the myths refer to various forms of cannibalism: aerial (the vultures) and aquatic (the piranhas) in the Bororo myth; terrestrial in the Ge myths, but in this case it is sometimes natural, when the flesh is raw (carnivorous animals), and sometimes supernatural, when the flesh is cooked (the Apinaye ogress).

Having thus categorized the Bororo and Ge myths, I could consider my task completed, were it not for two remaining difficulties.

In the first place, why do the Bororo connect the origin of storms and rain (anti-fire) with the consequences of incest, when there is no corresponding theme in the Ge myths? No doubt the theme is not completely absent, since the antagonism between father and son (who, in a matrilineal society, are relatives by marriage) is replaced by antagonism between two brothers-in-law, one of whom is an adult, the other a child. But instead of the direct inversion we might expect,[1] there is merely a weakening of the contrast, which is a constant feature of the group, between two males of different generations, who are interlinked through the medium of a woman. This weakening calls for an explanation.

Secondly, how are we to interpret the curious connection, which is common to almost all versions, between the cooking of food and the attitude to noise?

As a matter of fact, the two problems are one and the same; and as soon as this is realized, the solution is in sight. The point is a difficult one to demonstrate; and in order to prove it, I shall have recourse to a somewhat unorthodox method: I propose to leave aside the Brazilian myths for the moment and to make one or two rapid excursions into the realm of general mythology and folklore. This may seem to be a roundabout procedure but it is in fact a shortcut.

If one were to ask an ethnologist *ex abrupto* in what circumstances unrestricted noise is prescribed by custom, it is very likely that he would immediately quote two instances: the traditional charivari of Europe, and the din with which a considerable number of so-called primitive (and also civilized) societies salute, or used to salute, eclipses of the sun or the moon. I propose to consider each instance in turn.

The *Encyclopédie* compiled by Diderot and d'Alembert defines "charivari" as follows:

> The word . . . means and conveys the derisive noise made at night with pans, cauldrons, basins, etc., in front of the houses of people who are marrying for the second or third time or are marrying someone of a very different age from themselves.

[1] It will be seen later, on pp. 295–6, that the inversion does exist, but in an indirect form.

This unseemly custom was at one time so widespread that even queens who remarried were not spared. ("Charivari" entry.)

Van Gennep gives a list of the circumstances and people who provide grounds for charivari: a marriage where there is disparity in the ages of the spouses; the remarriage of a widower; husbands beaten by their wives; girls who turn down a suitor of high repute for another who is richer, too old, or foreign; girls who lead a dissolute life; pregnant fiancées who marry in white; a youth who "sells himself" to a woman for her money; married women who commit adultery; girls who have a married man as their lover; compliant husbands; and marriages that do not respect the prohibited degrees of kinship. According to Du Cange, it was possible to buy exemption from charivari by paying compensation to the "Abbot of Youth." In the majority of cases, according to Van Gennep, it is the man, and not the woman, who is subjected to charivari (Van Gennep, t. I, Vol. II, pp. 614–620).

As for the din that is made at the time of an eclipse, its ostensible purpose is to frighten away the animal or monster that is about to devour the heavenly body. The custom has been recorded the world over: in China, Burma, India, and Malaysia; in Africa, especially in Dahomey and the neighboring territories; in America, from Canada to Peru by way of Mexico. It was also known among the Greeks and Romans, since Livy and Tacitus refer to it; and it seems to have lasted until fairly recent times, either in its traditional form or in the reduced form of the explanatory belief, current in Italy, Scandinavia, and even France, that eclipses are caused by a wolf attacking the moon or the sun.

If we ask ourselves what these two manifestations of noise had in common and what people hoped to achieve by it, the answer at first sight seems easy. Charivari punishes reprehensible unions, while an eclipse would seem to be the result of a dangerous conjunction—that of a devouring monster taking a heavenly body as its prey. The current interpretation of the din that occurs at the time of an eclipse would seem to complete the proof that the noise is supposed to drive away, in one case, the cosmological monster who is devouring the sun or moon and, in the other, the sociological "monster" who is "devouring" his or her no less innocent prey. Nevertheless, we have only to glance through the examples given by Van Gennep to see that this explanation does not apply in all instances. Sometimes the charivari is directed at the supposed victim, rather than at the person, male or female, who is behaving improperly.

Let us therefore try to define the situation in greater detail. The difficulty arises from the fact that, to judge by the instances we are considering, the noise seems to penalize either a reprehensible conjunction or a highly dangerous disjunction. But is it not true that the conjunction does not constitute the primary phenomenon? In the case of both marriages and eclipses, it can, in the first place, be defined negatively: it represents the disruption of an order ensuring, in regular sequence, the alternation of the sun and the moon, day and night, light and darkness, heat and cold; or, on the sociological level, of men and women who are in a relation of mutual suitability in regard to civil status, age, wealth, etc.:

$$a, b, c, d, e, \ldots f, g, h, \ldots l, m, n, \ldots$$

What is punished by the din is not just a simple conjunction between two terms in the syntagmatic sequence—that is, a situation of the following kind:

$$a, b, c, \overgroup{d\ e} \ldots f, g, h \ldots l, m, n, \ldots$$

but something much more complex, which consists, on the one hand, of the *breaking* of the syntagmatic sequence, and on the other, of the *intrusion* of a foreign element into this same sequence—an element that *appropriates,* or tries to appropriate, one term of the sequence, thus bringing about a distortion.

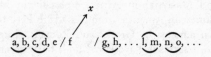

The concept of appropriation makes it possible to overcome the antinomy between disjunction and conjunction, especially if we realize that it can affect either one term of a potential pair or a term acting as an intermediary between the terms of this potential pair.

An unpublished survey of the practice of charivari, which was carried out by P. Fortier-Beaulieu and has been kindly placed at my disposal by M. Georges-Henri Rivière, chief curator of the Musée des Arts et Traditions populaires, supplies empirical proof of this analysis. Although it mentions, among the grounds for charivari, disparity in age between spouses, improper behavior by one or the other of them, the marriage of a pregnant girl, and the refusal to hold a ball to celebrate the wedding, it is remarkable that 92.5 per cent of the cases examined deal with *re*marriage accompanied by disparity in age or wealth, or between individuals who are both too old, or after improper conduct during widowhood. Remarriages of this kind no doubt appear abnormal. But they also illustrate the fundamental nature of remarriage, which consists always in the appropriation—by an individual who, having been married once, should, as it were, be out of circulation— of a spouse who ceases to be generally available, and whose misalliance breaks the ideal continuity of the sequence of matrimonial conjunctions. This is what an informant (B. du R. d'Eyguières) quoted in the survey means when he says that the purpose of the charivari is to carry out "reprisals against a widower or a widow who is depriving young girls and young men of a bachelor or a spinster."

The preceding demonstration is tantamount to a lemma. It enables us to establish, as a preliminary step, the true function attributed to noise both in the charivari and on the occasion of an eclipse. The function of noise is to draw attention to an anomaly in the unfolding of a syntagmatic sequence. Two terms of the sequence are in a state of disjunction; and, correlatively, one of the terms enters into conjunction with another term, although the latter is outside the sequence.

The question now is what bearing does this conclusion have on my general argument?

In the course of the present work I have often referred to the equivalence, which is found practically everywhere, between the male/female polarity and the sky/earth polarity. The Ge myths about Star, the wife of a mortal (M_{87}–M_{93}), attribute a feminine connotation to the sky and a masculine connotation to the earth. The relation is reversed in the corresponding myths of North America and sometimes even in South America (cf. for instance M_{110}). Only the form of the equation remains unchanged:

$$\text{sky} : \text{earth} :: \text{sex } x : \text{sex } y$$

Now, according to all the myths we are studying, the discovery of cooking had a profound effect on the relations previously existing between the sky and the earth. Before they learned about fire and the cooking of food, men simply placed meat on a *stone* and exposed it to the *sun's* rays (the connotations here are admirably terrestrial and celestial).[2] Meat was therefore a sign of the proximity of the sky to the earth, and of the sun to mankind. One myth says so explicitly: "A long time ago the Tenetehara did not have fire. Meat was cooked in the sun, *which at that time was closer to the earth*" (my italics; Wagley and Galvão, p. 133).

It is no accident that the Ge, who implicitly formulated the same hypothesis, should include a tribe that at one time was obsessed with the proximity of the sun to the earth. The Sherente believed that periods of drought were caused by the sun being angry with men. In order to divert its wrath, they used to perform a ceremony which, because it was so long and arduous, was given pride of place among their rites. For three weeks the adult men fasted and chanted almost without interruption and went without sleep. They were not allowed to wash either—or, to be more precise, they were not allowed to use water. At the end of this period of mortification the

[2] This mythological hypothesis is not self-evident. The tribes of the states of Oregon and Washington in North America, who express mythological problems in terms astonishingly like those used by the Ge, say that before fire was stolen by the civilizing hero, men used to put meat under their armpits or sit on it in order to heat it. But their neighbors along the Thompson River in British Columbia have the same theory as the Ge; whereas in South America, the Jivaro, the Tucuna, and the Mundurucu combine the two theories.

penitents, who by this time were emaciated, dirty, and burned by the sun's rays, were supposed to see and hear two black wasps bearing arrows. Immediately the entire population of the village lowered their eyes and hid their faces; but if one of the penitents failed to see the insects, the fast had to continue until the wasps made a fresh appearance.

From this point on, the wasps would appear more frequently, and they dropped miniature arrows which were picked up by the penitents. When each one had obtained an arrow, the first bath took place, followed by the haircutting and other bodily requirements that accompanied the return to the family huts.

The next stages included a collective hunt, a distribution of food, and a "log" race. After this a pole 10 meters high and 40 centimeters in diameter, called "road to the sky," was erected during the night. The first man to get to the top, who was always a member of the Kuze clan of the Shiptato moiety (cf. above, p. 75 and p. 217), would beg the sun to give him fire, and the handful of fibers he was holding would immediately burst into flames. The fibers were then used to relight all the fires in the village. The men then climbed the pole in turn, and each one inquired of the souls of his deceased relatives who appeared to him at the top how long he still had to live (J. F. de Oliveira, p. 23). Each one also dropped an object from the top of the pole—a feather, a leaf, a seed, etc.—illustrating the visible form in which he would be reincarnated. The last man to climb received the sun's reply, through the medium of a celestial herald: the sun would express satisfaction at the orderly way in which the ritual had been conducted, and would give an assurance that it would send rain as a mark of compassion.

The next morning the pole was dismantled before daylight and thrown into the water. Then for the last time the penitents "sit down in two rows, separated by moieties, and the director or precentor who had collected the souls steps up before each one with the covered bowl. Extracting the man's transformed soul, he rubs it between his palms, exhibits the object, and via the tonsure, rubs it back into the owner's body" (Nim. 6, pp. 93-8). The Kayapo, too, look upon the sun as a former persecuter of humanity (Banner 1, p. 49).

Two phases of the ritual are especially worthy of attention. The penitents were divided into two main groups: *awakbonikwa* and *aimbati*, with the addition of another small group comprising a few old men. The latter had to undergo a fast lasting only five days. Their main function was to offer a sip of water to the penitents every night and every morning. Now this group of old men bore the name *asare*, which is the name of the thirsty hero of M_{124}, a fact that would confirm, were this necessary, that there is a close connection between the rite and the myth. Moreover, at the close of the last Great Fast that the natives can remember, the part of the sun's herald was played by χ *Orionis*—that is, Asare.

Secondly, water was distributed to the men assembled round the pole, by three personages representing respectively Venus, Jupiter, and Mars. The first two offered clear water: one in a gourd of the *Lagenaria* species; the other in a gourd of the *Crescentia* species. But the drinkers refused to drink the stale water offered by Mars in a cup decorated with feathers (the *Lagenaria* gourd was decorated with cotton). Venus and Jupiter belonged to the Shiptato moiety; Mars to the Sdakran moiety. Here again the ritual refers to a social structure and to myths we have already discussed (M$_{93}$ and M$_{138}$).

Following Nimuendaju, M. I. de Queiroz saw in this ceremony proof of the fact that the Sherente formerly lived in a region where drought was more to be feared than it is in the territory they occupy today. However, this overlooks the point that the theme of the maleficent sun moving dangerously near the earth and causing a drought, and perhaps even a general conflagration, also exists in Amazonia (Amorim, pp. 459–60), notably among the Mundurucu (Strömer, pp. 136–7), and that it was of paramount importance in the mythical conceptions of the natives of eastern and western Canada, the Montagnais-Naskapi and Kwakiutl, and also of so-called village tribes of Missouri (Pawnee and Mandan), none of whom are likely to have experienced climatic conditions corresponding to the belief.

First and foremost, the Great Fast of the Sherente seems to respect a pattern that is made clear in the enactment of the ritual and is based on a distinction between "good" fire and "bad" fire. Only the second kind of fire results from a too direct action of the sun on the earth. So men must persuade the sun to move farther away, and after achieving this result through various mortifications, they must approach within reasonable distance of the sun (by climbing a pole) so that it may grant men the two complementary elements capable of acting as mediators between sky and earth: on the one hand, cooking fire, thanks to the burning fiber that was used to light all domestic fires; and on the other, rain, which is promised by the sun. These are the very elements whose origin the Bororo and Ge myths purport to explain—the former dealing with fire, the latter with water—and which they attribute in both instances to a child who climbed to the top of a pole. . . . And like the men who climb the pole in the Sherente rite, the bird-nester meets with a symbolic death before coming back to life again and returning to his own people.

Confirmation of this interpretation of the Great Fast is provided by a set of Ge myths that have not yet been studied, although they, too, deal with the origin of fire: but not this time with beneficent cooking fire; the fire we are now concerned with is maleficent, since it burns up the earth. These myths belong to the cycle of the two civilizing heroes Sun and Moon, who, as we have already seen from a Kraho version (M$_{11}$), also played a part in the origin of cooking fire, which they took from men when they decided to abandon them. Consequently there exists a very real link between the two groups of myths. The numerous Ge versions resemble each other so closely that they can be conveniently grouped together in the following composite summary:

M_{163}. Central and eastern Ge tribes. "Destructive fire"

Long before men existed, Sun and Moon lived on the earth. One day, unknown to his brother, Sun set off into the savannah (or steppe) and arrived at the "foot of the sky" (Kraho). There he heard the characteristic sound of the woodpeckers piercing the bark of the trees with their beaks. One of the birds had just made a red head ornament of feathers, which gleamed like fire. Sun asked the bird for the headdress, and the latter agreed to give it to him but warned Sun that he would throw it down from the top of the tree; Sun must catch it as it fell and not allow it to touch the ground.

The red feather crown came whirling down, flickering so brightly that it looked like real fire. Sun caught it and threw it from one of his hands to the other until it grew cold.

Shortly after, Moon discovered the ornament in the hiding place where Sun had put it, and begged his brother to obtain a similar one for him. Somewhat reluctantly Sun led Moon to the woodpeckers, who agreed to supply another ornament. But as Sun was preparing to catch it, Moon insisted on doing so himself, in spite of the warnings uttered by his brother, who feared some disastrous accident. Moon was, as it happened, very clumsy. As Sun had predicted, the ornament burned his hands, and he let it fall to the ground; the entire savannah caught fire, and all the animals were burned. (Timbira: Nim. 8, pp. 243–4; Apinaye: Nim. 5, pp. 160–61, C. E. de Oliveira, 82–6; Kraho: Schultz, p. 57 ff.; Pompeu Sobrinho, pp. 204–5.)

The theme of the burning headdress is extremely widespread: it is found in the cosmogony of both the ancient Tupinamba and the ancient Mexicans. The fire-creating part played by woodpeckers also occurs in North America, particularly the Zuni, and among the Caddo, the Wichita, the Jicarilla and Mescalero Apache, and always in the "bungling host" cycle, of which the preceding myth is a good South American example. The woodpecker is master of fire in several myths of British Columbia (cf. for instance Boas 2, pp. 894–6). It is well known that most species have red head feathers. I have already referred to the function (p. 206) by virtue of which—and no doubt as "wood-eaters"—the woodpeckers were the polar opposites of the "water-drinking" aquatic birds. This, at all events, is what is suggested in a Bororo myth already quoted (M_{120}), which deals with the moving away of the Sun and the Moon (and not with celestial fire coming nearer), also caused by a clumsy action—in this case the spilling of water, not the spreading of fire (p. 193).

Behind the farcical, and sometimes even scatological, misadventures that befall the bungling host, one can clearly discern metaphysical conceptions, such as those to which the Sherente have given tragic ritual expression.[3] Celestial fire must not enter into conjunction with the earth, because if they come into contact, they would cause a general conflagration of which drought constitutes a moderate, but empirically verifiable, initial symptom. Nevertheless, primitive humanity used to enact in mime the conjunction of sky and earth—and may even have believed that such a conjunction actually occurred—before cooking fire, which is doubly "domesticated," appeared to act as mediator between the sky above and the earth below, since it manifests the qualities of celestial fire here below but spares man its violence and excesses; and at the same time moves the sun away from the earth, since their proximity is no longer required for the purpose of heating food.

But whereas the Sherente were afraid of a catastrophic coming together of the sun and the earth, the Kraho seemed chiefly concerned about the opposite danger, which was also present, incidentally, in the minds of the Sherente (Nim. 6, pp. 87–8, 93): they were afraid (M_{164}) that each eclipse of the sun might be the sign of a return to the "long night" which occurred in ancient times, and during which men were reduced to feeding on bark and leaves and were exposed to mortal attacks from every kind of creature —even mosquitoes and grasshoppers—so that many preferred to end their days rather than brave the monsters (Schultz, p. 159).

The mediatory function of cooking fire therefore operates between the sun and humanity in two ways. By its presence, cooking fire averts total disjunction, since it *unites* the sun and the earth and saves man from the *world of rottenness* in which he would find himself if the sun really disappeared; but its presence is also *interposed;* that is to say, it obviates the risk of a total conjunction, which would result in a *burned world*. The adventures of Sun and Moon combine both eventualities: after the world conflagration had been put out, Moon proved incapable of cooking his food, and he was obliged to eat rotten, worm-infested meat; being alternately a skunk and an opossum (p. 177), he oscillated between the two extremes of *burned meat* and *decomposed meat* and never succeeded in finding a balance, through the cooking of food, between destructive fire and the absence of fire which also destroys.

It is beginning to become clear why, in all the myths we are studying, the acquisition of cooking fire demands a cautious attitude toward noise, which is the contrary of the attitude required in face of the cosmic disorder brought about by an eclipse or the social disorder brought about by reprehensible marriages. When it is a question of obtaining cooking fire, noise is dangerous—whether the subject originates it or perceives it. Evi-

---

[3] It is therefore understandable that certain North American tribes believe the stories belonging to the "bungling host" cycle to be especially sacred (Swanton, p. 2). They look like a kind of rustic *Roman de Renart,* mainly intended to amuse young and old—but there may be more to the *Roman de Renart* than that.

dence of this incompatibility between cooking and noise is found even in the Western world, in traditional precepts; for example, "Silence between meats is necessary," in a twelfth-century French treatise (Hughes de Saint-Victor, *De Institutione Novitiarum,* quoted by Franklin, p. 154). In order to interpret the equation: Latin *nausea* > Old French *noise,* it is therefore unnecessary to reflect as arduously as some linguists have done, or to appeal to a complex semantic evolution (as Spitzer does, for example). The isomorphism between the gustative and the auditive categories is also instantly, and hardly less vigorously, conveyed in the pejorative use of the word *gargote* (low-class eating house) to describe a place where the cooking is disgusting, since the word comes from *gargoter,* whose original meaning is "to boil noisily."

But let us now leave Europe and go back to tropical America by way of New Mexico, if only for the purpose of adding a final example. The Zuni Indians cook maize cakes, which form their staple diet, on stone slabs which have to be heated gradually while oil and resin are rubbed into them. During this essential operation, "no word must be spoken above a whisper. . . . Should the voice of anyone present be raised above a whisper, the stone would crack" (Stevenson, p. 362).

If the mediatory action of cooking fire between the sun (sky) and the earth demands silence, it is normal that noise should mark the reverse situation, whether it occurs in the literal sense (disjunction of the sun and the earth) or figuratively (disjunction, as the result of a reprehensible union, of two people who were a potential married couple by virtue of their position within the normal marriage system): in one instance, the eclipse is greeted with a din; in the other, charivari is organized. However, it must not be forgotten that, as I have shown, the "anticulinary" situation can occur in two ways. It is an absence of mediation between sky and earth, but this absence may be thought of as a lack (disjunction of the poles) or as a form of excess (conjunction):

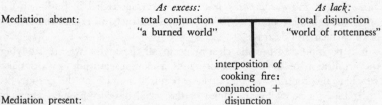

	As excess:	*As lack:*
Mediation absent:	total conjunction "a burned world"	total disjunction "world of rottenness"
	interposition of cooking fire:	
Mediation present:	conjunction + disjunction	

There are then, in all, three possibilities: one of them implies mediation; the others exclude it. Only the first demands silence.[4] On the other hand, as

---

[4] Cf. Dumézil's theory about the Latin goddess of silence: "Might it not be through silence, through a strict abstention from speech that the original Angerona achieved the work expected of her during the constraint of the winter solstice?" (pp. 52–3).

has just been proved, noise is called for every time two paired terms (sky and earth, or a potential married couple) are in a state of disjunction. It is already clear that, contrary to the rationalizations put forward by the natives themselves, and subsequently by ethnologists, the true function of the din is not so much to drive away the appropriator (either the monster devouring the celestial body, or the improper suitor) as to fill in symbolically the void left by the appropriation. But what happens in the third case—that is, when the absence of mediation is the result of an excessive proximity of the paired terms?

The Sherente ritual is particularly instructive in this respect, since its aim was to put an end to this kind of situation or to try to avert it. The participators did so in three ways: they fasted (eating nothing except a few maize cakes); they allowed themselves only two sips of water (one in the morning, one in the evening); and they chanted almost without a break. The first two actions raise no problem. They follow on quite simply from the circumstances in which the ritual is supposed to take place, and which in theory exclude cooking fire and rain, because of the imminent conjunction between the sun and the earth. Domestic fire and rain will be restored to man only after the sun has agreed to move farther away.

The acoustic nature of the third action is obvious. What else is there for the penitents to do except chant, since both silence and noise would be equally out of place here in this third set of circumstances, having been already prescribed, respectively, for each of the two others? They therefore have to resort to an acoustic behavior, which is, as it were, halfway between silence and noise. Such behavior exists in two forms: speech, which constitutes its profane modality; and chanting, which is its sacred modality.[5] In their version (M_1) of the bird-nester myths the Bororo do not openly express the culinary aspect. On the other hand, they lay emphasis on an incestuous act that the Ge, in their turn, hint at in an attenuated form. In the Ge myth the antagonism is between two brothers-in-law of different generations, instead of between father and son; but they are still two men brought together through the medium of a woman, who is a blood relative of one and a relative by marriage of the other. The Ge stress the discovery and the conquest of cooking fire. So in the one instance we have an initial situation—incest—similar to the eclipse and at the same time the reverse of the preculinary situation, in a myth that inverts the theme of the origin

[5] Unfortunately it is not possible to give an interpretation of the wasp episode purely in terms of the syntagmatic context. It is nevertheless curious that the wasps appear in the first place as humming insects, whose characteristic noise informants are careful to describe: "Ken! ken! ken-ken-ken!" (Nim. 6, p. 95), especially when we remember that in Guiana another unidentified insect, which might be one of the Hymenoptera or Hemiptera (sun bee, wamong bee), because of its "powerful voice" has a part in the initiation of the shaman, so as to make the latter a good singer or chanter (Butt). Cf. p. 314, n. 18.

of fire (since it purports to explain the origin of water);[6] and in the other, a preculinary initial situation, the reverse of the eclipse, in a myth that deals openly with the problem of the origin of fire. The initial conjunction which is social with the Bororo (the coming together of mother and son) is cosmic with the Ge, since for them it consists in the coming together of the sky and the earth by direct (= incestuous) exposure of the meat to the heat of the sun, before the existence of cooking fire.[7] Yet all these various aspects are so carefully worked into the myths that the Ge, prompted, it seems, by a logical scruple, are at pains to include incest but, as might be expected, in an inverted form: the murdering of the jaguar's wife by the hero, after he becomes the jaguar's adopted son. This only makes it even more remarkable that the episode, which is already an inversion, should reappear, with a further twist, in the Bororo myth about the bird-nester: the father is murdered by his son, by being devoured (it is an actual devouring and not just a threat) by fish (aquatic, instead of terrestrial, cannibalism). The myths are thus re-established in a negativized form on their respective axes, and the cannibal function is an inherent characteristic either of the mistress of fire (origin of fire) or of the master of water (origin of water).

What I have just said may appear conjectural and speculative. Yet there is a myth, which is known throughout the whole of America, from southern Brazil and Bolivia to the Bering Strait (and farther still, in the northern region of Asia, northern Russia, and the Malay archipelago) via Amazonia and Guiana[8] and which establishes a direct equivalence between eclipses and incest. This is a myth about the origin of the sun and the moon; and the following Eskimo version of it comes from the Bering Strait region:

M₁₆₅. *Eskimo (Bering Strait). "The origin of the sun and the moon"*

Long ago a man and his wife lived in a village on the coast. They had two children, a girl and a boy. When the children grew up, the boy fell in love with his sister. He pursued her unceasingly with his attentions, so she finally took refuge in the sky, where she became the moon. Ever since then the boy

---

[6] Huxley, using a different approach, arrives at the same theory of the congruence between incest and water (*Affable Savages,* p. 145).

[7] It is a fact of some relevance that in Africa, too, cooking is associated with coitus between husband and wife: "to put fuel into the fire and to blow it is to cohabit; the hearthstones are the posteriors; the cooking pot is the vagina; the pot ladle is the penis" (Cory, p. 87). For similar details, cf. Dieterlen and Calame-Griaule, *passim;* cf. also, in North America, the phallic symbolism of the poker among the Pueblo Indians.

[8] Southern Brazil: Nim. 1, p. 331; 14, p. 148; Borba, p. 69; Cadogan, pp. 77–80. Northeastern Brazil: Huxley, pp. 165–6. Guiana: Roth 1, p. 256; K.G. 1, pp. 54–5. Venezuela: Osborn, pp. 79–80; etc. Bolivia: Cardus, p. 78.

has never stopped pursuing her, in the form of the sun. Sometimes he catches up with her and manages to embrace her, thus causing an eclipse of the moon.

After the children left him, the father became gloomy and full of hatred toward humanity.[9] He traveled across the world, scattering disease and death, and feeding off the people who fell victim to the diseases; but he became so evil that his desire could not be satisfied in this way. He then started to kill and eat healthy people, too. . . . (Nelson, p. 481.)

In an Ingalik version (M_{166}) the sister herself predicts the coming of diseases (Chapman, p. 21); whereas among the Mono of California (M_{167}), the incestuous sister becomes a cannibal (Gayton and Newman, p. 59). An Eskimo version (M_{168}) states that the sister in her anger deprived her brother of food and offered him instead her severed breast:

"You wanted me last night so I have given you my breast. If you desire me, eat it!" But the boy refused. The woman rose into the sky, where she became the sun. He changed into the moon and pursued her but was never able to catch her. The moon, being without food, waned slowly away through starvation until it was quite lost from sight. So Sun reached out and fed it from the dish in which the girl had placed her breast. After the moon is fed and gradually brought to the full, it is then permitted to starve again, so producing the waxing and the waning every month (Nelson, p. 482; cf. Rink, pp. 236–7; cf. also a much weaker South American version, Taurepan, in K.G. 1, p. 55).

Not only does this myth, of which I could quote several other versions, establish a link between incest and eclipse but, like the Bororo and the Ge myths, it introduces a second equivalence with cannibalism, which is the ultimate result of the advent of diseases.

The Ge, along with many other peoples, believe there is a link between eclipses and epidemics. The Spanish influenza epidemic which killed so many natives of South America in 1918 was attributed by the Sherente to an eclipse of the sun whose lethal slime spread all over the earth (Nim. 6, p. 93). The same belief is found in the Gran Chaco: "An eclipse of the sun or the moon foretells disease. When either the sun or the moon becomes angry with men, it covers itself. To have it uncover, it is necessary to beat drums, shout, sing, and make all kinds of noise. When the sun is covered, one may expect smallpox" (Métraux 3, p. 97).

These remarks do not invalidate what I said previously about the link between the rainbow and diseases (p. 278). I showed (p. 246) that the rainbow has two aspects—one diurnal, the other nocturnal—and that the nocturnal rainbow occupies, as it were, a negatively outlined space in the sky: a black area in the center of the Milky Way—in other words, an "eclipse" of the stars. By day as well as by night, therefore, the rainbow is characterized by the most emphatic coincidence of phenomena. During the day,

[9] It will be remembered that the Kayapo (M_7) use exactly the same terms to describe the feelings of the jaguar after men have stolen fire from him.

when the color enriches the light; during the night, at a point where a local absence of light intensifies the darkness. Thus congruence between the eclipse and the rainbow is confirmed.

Secondly, the slime, to which I have just referred and other instances of which will be quoted later, seems to provide, in terms of the nocturnal code, a kind of tangible equivalent of the visual chromaticism that it is the rainbow's function to signify during daytime. There is a finely graduated scale of the tangible, from the doughy to the viscous, from the viscous to the sticky, from the fluid to the volatile. . . . Chromaticism, therefore, is not eliminated by darkness; it is transposed from one sense category to another. When we say that the night is thick (*la nuit est épaisse*) or that the fog could be cut with a knife (*un brouillard à couper au couteau*), we are recognizing the fact that the absence of light, no less than the presence of iridescent coloring, forces the human mind to think in terms of short intervals. The ancients were in no doubt on this point: ". . . brightness and daylight is single and simple: and as Pindar says, we see the sun through pure air, whereas the night air is a composition and mixture of several lights and several forces . . ." (Plutarch, § xlii).

Starting from the problem of the mythic origin of cooking, I have thus been led to verify my interpretation of domestic fire as a mediatory agent between sky and earth by reference to the myth describing incest between blood relatives as the origin of the eclipse. The demonstration is strengthened by the fact that the peoples who are acquainted with this myth suppose the existence of a direct relation among eclipses, culinary utensils, food, and domestic fire. Let me first give a few North American examples.

The populations of the lower Yukon believe that a pervasive essence, a maleficent influence, spreads across the earth when an eclipse of the moon occurs, and that if by chance a small particle happens to get inside some utensil or other, sickness will ensue.[10] So, as soon as an eclipse begins, the women hurriedly turn all their pots, pails, and dishes upside down (Nelson, p. 431). When an eclipse of the sun or moon occurred, the Alsea Indians of Oregon threw out their reserves of drinking water: "All the buckets are usually upset, because it is not desired that the water should become bloody whenever the sun is killed" (Frachtenberg, p. 229). After an eclipse the Wintu of California would throw out all their food, and even water, in case they had become polluted by the blood of the sun or moon (Du Bois, p. 77). Among the Serrano to the south: "It was believed that such phenomena (the eclipse of either the sun or the moon) were caused by the spirits of the dead eating the celestial body, hence all food was forbidden at such times on the theory that eating would assist the spirits" (Strong, p. 35).

In South America, in Guiana, "the Lolaca and Atabaca Indians . . . were

---

[10] As in the Hawaiian Islands, where all vessels containing water were kept covered during storms accompanied by lightning (Handy and Pukui, p. 118, n. 19).

convinced that, if the moon really died, all domestic fires would be extinguished. The women, weeping and shrieking—while the men too swelled the noisy outburst—would each seize a burning brand and hide it in the sand or in the ground. Moved by their tears and entreaties, the moon would become visible once more; and the hidden firebrands would immediately go out. But, had the moon really died, the buried sticks would have continued to burn" (Gumilla, Vol. II, p. 274). Conversely, a Chiriguano myth (M₁₆₉) states that a prolonged eclipse of the sun would cause the half-burned logs to become green again and burst into bud. When things came to such a pass that even gourds had to be burned because there was no more dead wood, then this would mean that the "long night" was about to start (Métraux 2, p. 158).[11]

[11] It seems to me possible to consider this natural incompatibility between eclipses and culinary utensils as the weak form of the theme of the revolt of objects against their masters. The Eskimo provide an illustration of the transition between the two themes: when an eclipse occurs, the Ingalik immediately collect all their utensils, in case they should fly away (Osgood, p. 65). In the Northwest of the United States, Sahaptin-speaking tribes and their neighbors believe the revolt of household objects took place during the period of chaos preceding the ordering of the world by the moon. The Tacana of Bolivia believe that it occurred after the moon's death (Hissink and Hahn, pp. 84–5). The belief in the ordering function of the moon is found in northern Brazil, among the Bare of the upper reaches of the Rio Negro (Stradelli; pp. 753–62). In South America, Métraux (2, p. 128) had already noted that the Chiriguano, like the ancient inhabitants of Huarochiri (Davila, p. 110), link the rebellion of household objects with a solar eclipse. The same association is found among the Tacana (Hissink and Hahn, p. 85). If my hypothesis is correct, it might be the case that the absence of the belief over a wide intermediary zone is explained by the fact that it is replaced in the South and the North by the weak form (incompatibility between eclipses and culinary utensils) and in the center, by what is tantamount to an inversion of the myth about the revolt of household objects—that is, the myth about "self-working agricultural implements." In America this myth is found chiefly in an area stretching from the southeastern United States (Natchez) to the Gran Chaco (Chane), via Mexico (Quiche), Guiana (Taurepan), and northern and central Brazil (Tembe, Timbira, Apinaye). The discussion of this important problem would require a separate volume.

2

Bird Chorus

With the last quotation, we come full circle. A myth about the origin of
storms and rain (M_1) led me to myths about the origin of fire and the cooking of foodstuffs (M_7–M_{12}). I was able to establish that all these myths belong
to one and the same set, thanks to various arguments, the most significant
of which proved to be the function that all versions attribute to noise or to
the absence of noise. When approached from this angle, the problem of noise
led to the problem of reprehensible unions—the occurrence of which in the
Bororo myths M_1, M_2, and M_5 had already aroused my curiosity—punished
by charivari, and also to that of eclipses which give rise to noisemaking. And
now eclipses, by way of incest, then culinary utensils and prepared food
bring us back to the domestic hearth.

Nevertheless, one question still remains. How does it come about that the
two great noisemaking rites should be so unevenly distributed? Charivari,
in the strict sense of the term, belongs to the European popular tradition. The
efforts of Saintyves to generalize the institution do not seem very convincing.
As the comparative basis is widened, the customs discussed lose their homo-
geneity. In the end, one is not at all certain that one is dealing with a set.
On the other hand, noisemaking on the occasion of eclipses is practically universal, and its area of distribution includes the much narrower range of
charivari.

The problem is a difficult one, since its solution would demand a negative
proof. I venture nonetheless to suggest that in illiterate societies the mythical
category of noise is invested with too lofty a significance and its symbolic
intensity is too strong for it to be used with impunity in the humble sphere
of village life and private intrigues. To act otherwise would, in a sense, be
to make "much ado about nothing," or to make too much noise—not, perhaps, for too slight a cause, since reprehensible unions often call for cosmological sanctions, but at least in relation to the use men may allow themselves
to make of so important a power as noise. Noise only becomes available in
all circumstances and is entirely at the disposal of mankind when mythical
thought has been to a large extent secularized. We might see an argument

in favor of this theory in the fact that, conversely, even where charivari is no longer practiced, noise up to a point retains its general function. In twentieth-century Europe, where scientific knowledge is so widespread, it is no longer conceivable that an eclipse should be greeted by noisemaking. Nevertheless the practice still survives in cases where there is a break, or a threatened break, in the cosmological sequence, but only when the interruption is considered as a social, and not a cosmic, event. In Lithuania, where even up to the present century, children were told to beat pans and other metal utensils with sticks in order to drive away evil spirits during eclipses, the spring festivities are still marked by a certain rowdyism. On Good Friday young men create a din by breaking furniture, such as tables, bedsteads, etc. And in the past it was customary to break the furniture of deceased persons with a great deal of noise. It is believed that noise, water, and fire are effective in driving off the powers of evil (Gimbutas, p. 117). Customs such as these are part of a universal system, unmistakable vestiges of which still survive in Western countries—for instance, the smashing of china and exploding of fireworks in Italy on New Year's Eve, and the chorus of automobile horns that ushers in the New Year in Times Square, Piccadilly Circus, and the Champs Elysées. . . .

There exists, incidentally, a group of American myths that provide unmistakable evidence of the link between the social order and the cosmic order. They originate for the most part along the northern shores of the Pacific Ocean:

M_{170}. Tsimshian. "The story of Nalq"

In early times young people used to meet in the evening behind the houses. They used to amuse themselves by playing noisy games far into the night. The sky was irritated by the din and sent down a beautiful magic plume, which a young man tried to catch as it fell. But as soon as he caught it, he was carried off into the air; then in a long chain all the others were, too, since each one attempted to hold back the one in front by hanging on to his or her feet. All the people were taken up by the plume; and at last they fell, and all died. Not one of them survived.

However, one young woman had remained indoors, because she had been in labor. She gave birth to a series of miraculous children. After telling them of the fate that had befallen their family, she warned them against playing outdoors. But they provoked the sky into sending down the plume again, and succeeded in catching it. Using it as a talisman, they embarked on a journey around the world, reached the city of the Air, and finally married the daughters of the winds of the four cardinal points; they settled how and when these winds should blow. (Boas 2, pp. 125–31.)

I have given a very brief summary of this myth in order to apologize for the fact that its geographical source is far removed from tropical America.

Nevertheless, without its help we should have difficulty in fitting in a Brazilian myth that, in spite of the distance between them, corresponds to it very closely:

M₁₇₁. Caduveo. "How birds got their colored plumage"

Three children used to play in front of the hut until past midnight. The father and mother paid no attention to them. One night when they were playing—it was very late—an earthenware pot descended from the sky; it was lavishly decorated and full of flowers.

The children saw the flowers and wanted to take them, but as soon as they put out their arms, the flowers retreated to the other side of the pot, with the result that the children had to climb into the pot in order to reach them.

The pot started to rise into the air. When she saw what was happening, the mother just managed to grab the leg of one of her children. The leg broke, and from the wound flowed a lake of blood in which most of the birds (whose plumage was at that time uniformly white) dipped either all or some of their feathers, thus acquiring the different-colored plumage they have today. (Ribeiro 1, pp. 140–41.)

The similarity between these two Canadian and Brazilian myths makes it possible to introduce at this point an important group of South American myths also dealing with the colored plumage of birds, and to suggest an interpretation. We have already come across one of them—the Arecuna myth about the origin of fish poison (M₁₄₅), to whose penultimate episode I said I would return later (cf. pp. 261–2). After the rainbow/snake had been killed by the birds, all the animals assembled and shared out the multicolored skin. In accordance with the particular color of the piece allotted to each one, the animals acquired their characteristic cries, skins, or plumage:

M₁₄₅. Arecuna. "The origin of fish poison" (continued)

The white egret took its piece and sang, "ã-ã," a call that it still has to this day. The maguari (Ciconia maguari, a stork) did likewise and uttered its ugly cry: "a(o)-a(o)." The soco (Ardea brasiliensis, a heron) placed its piece on its head and wings (where the colored feathers are) and sang, "koro–koro–koro." The kingfisher (Alcedo species) put its piece on its head and breast, where the feathers turned red, and sang, "se-txe-txe-txe." Then it was the toucan's turn. It covered its breast and belly (where the feathers are white and red). And it said: "kión-he, he kión-he-he." A small piece of skin remained stuck to its beak which became yellow. Then came the mutum (Crax species); it put its piece on its throat and sang, "hm-hm-hm-hm" and a tiny remaining strip of skin turned its nostrils yellow. Next came the cujubim (Pipile species, a piping guan), whose piece turned its head, breast, and wings white:

it sang, "krr" as it has done every morning. since. Each bird "thought its own flute made a pretty sound and kept it."

The richly colored plumage of the macaw is explained by the fact that it seized a large piece of skin and covered its whole body in it; it was imitated in this by the parrots and the yellow parakeets. The oazabaka bird (an unidentified savannah bird) acquired a charming song: "oazabaka-oazabaka-ku-lu-lu-lu-lu." And all the birds, including the jacu and the nightingale, received in this way their plumage and their "flute."

Then came the turn of ground game—the tapir, the capybara (*Hydrochoerus capibara*), and the deer. Each one chose a piece of skin. The part the deer received as its share sprouted antlers. As a matter of fact, the antlers of the forest species formerly belonged to the savannah species, and vice versa: since the first were bothered by the size of their antlers because they became entangled in creepers and branches, the two species decided to swap.

The agouti (*Dasyprocta aguti*) acquired reddish and white fur on its breast and belly, and its little "flute": "king-king"; the paca (*Coelogenys paca*) likewise. The tapir was given its warning cry, which was like a whistle. The caititu (*Dicotyles torquatus*) placed the skin on its shoulders, which accounts for its black hair; and it also received its call "hx-hx"; while the peccary (= quiexada : *Dicotyles labiatus*) said "rr-rr." Finally, the great anteater (*Myrmecophaga jubata*) stretched the skin over its arms and spine where the fur became yellow, and was allotted the cry "rr-rr" (clearer than the gutteral and muted "rr-rr" of the peccary). Each species of monkey was also given a cry, and in this way all the wild animals obtained their colored coats and their "flutes." (K.G. 1, pp. 73–5.)

This is an admirable lesson in ethnozoology, and Koch-Grünberg, with his acute feeling for ethnographic substance, has preserved its vividness and wealth of detail. It should be compared, as he himself suggests, with another Guianian version:

M$_{172}$. *Arawak. "How birds acquired their colored plumage"*

Men and birds joined forces to destroy the huge watersnake, which dragged all living creatures down to his lair. But the attackers took fright and cried off, one after the other, offering as their excuse that they could only fight on dry land. Finally, the duckler (K.G.: a diver) was brave enough to dive into the water; he inflicted a fatal wound on the monster which was at the bottom, coiled round the roots of an enormous tree. Uttering terrible cries, the men succeeded in bringing the snake out of the water, where they killed it and removed its skin. The duckler claimed the skin as the price of its victory. The Indian chiefs said ironically, "By all means! Just take it away!" "With pleasure," replied the duckler as it signaled to the other birds. Together they swooped down and, each one taking a piece of the skin in its beak, flew off with it. The Indians were annoyed and angry and, from then on, became the enemies of birds.

The birds retired to a quiet spot in order to share the skin. They agreed that each one should keep the part that was in its own beak. The skin was made up of marvelous colors—red, yellow, green, black, and white—and had markings such as no one had ever seen before. As soon as each bird was provided with the part to which it was entitled, the miracle happened: until that time all birds had had dingy plumage, but now suddenly they became white, yellow, and blue. . . . The parrots were covered in green and red, and the macaws with red, purple, and gilded feathers, such as had never before been seen. The duckler, to which all the credit was due, was left with the head, which was black. But it said it was good enough for an old bird. (K.G. 1, pp. 292–3; Brett, pp. 173–5; Im Thurn, pp. 382–3; Roth 1, pp. 225–6.)

The Vilela of the Bolivian area of the Gran Chaco (who are therefore comparatively close to the Caduveo) have a similar myth:

M₁₇₃. Vilela. "How birds acquired their colored plumage"

A widow had an only son who was fond of catching birds, especially hummingbirds. This was his only occupation, and he was so absorbed by it that it was always late at night before he came home. This obsession worried his mother, who had a presentiment that it might lead to disaster, but he paid no heed to her.

One day he found some small stones of different colors at the water's edge. He carefully collected them in order to pierce them and make himself a necklace. Hardly was the necklace around his neck when he changed into a snake, and in this form took refuge at the top of a tree. He grew bigger and fatter and turned into a cannibal monster which began exterminating the villages one after the other.

An Indian resolved to kill him, and a fight started between them. In spite of the help given him by the dove, the man was on the point of succumbing, when all the birds together came to his aid. "They arranged themselves in groups, according to their families, and sang, for at that time, so it is said, song was the language of birds, and all birds could speak."

The attack launched by the birds was unsuccessful until a powerful family, the dwarf owls (*Glaucidium nannum* King),[12] which had so far remained in the background, joined in the fray. They attacked the monster, uttering their cry of "not, not, not, pi," and blinded it. The other birds finished it off, disemboweled it, and set free its victims, many of whom were still alive. Whereupon the birds withdrew, each family going in a specific direction.

Shortly afterward it rained, and the monster's corpse appeared in the air

---

[12] The *Glaucidium* species includes tiny owls: the wing span of the *Glaucidium brasilianum* does not exceed 13 centimeters. Unlike other owls, they are *diurnal* birds, and "although they are the pigmies of the family, they are very pugnacious hunters" (Ihering, Vol. XXXIV, pp. 516–17).

in the shape of the rainbow, which ever since that time has always existed and always will exist. (Lehmann-Nitsche 2, pp. 221–6.)

These myths come from very different geographical sources, since M_{170} belongs to northwestern Canada, M_{145} and M_{172} to Guiana, and M_{171} and M_{173} to the southwestern area of tropical America. It is nevertheless clear that they are all variations on one theme—the establishment of a natural order, which is both meteoric and zoological. The heroes of the Tsimshian myth decided the direction of the winds—that is, the periodicity of the seasons; furthermore, they put the skeletons of their dead parents together clumsily, which explains the present (anatomical) diversity of human types. The two aspects appear also in the Caduveo myth, which gives an explanation of the diversity of birds (the zoological order), but in which the blood of the dismembered child accounts for the particular color of the sky at the end of the rainy season just before the start of the dry season, according to one version (Ribeiro 1, p. 141), and in another version (Baldus 4, p. 124) accounts for the colors of the rainbow. The Guianian myths, too, link the rainbow with the colored plumage of birds; whereas the Vilela myth, which is also concerned with the rainbow, defines the zoological order according to an acoustic, rather than a visual, criterion: birds are divided into different groups according to their songs. The Jivaro versions, which I have left out for the sake of brevity, also do this (Karsten 1, pp. 327–8; Farabee 2, p. 123). We have seen that the Arecuna myth simultaneously explains the different kinds of fur or plumage and the different bird songs and animal calls. A Toba version (M_{174}), which has its exact counterpart in Amazonia (Amorim, pp. 277–9) and in Guiana (Ahlbrinck, "nomo" entry), can be compared in other respects with the Tsimshian myth, since the rainbow's anger at the pollution of its water which was drunk by a menstruating girl caused a flood in which all the Indians perished: "The corpses turned yellow, green, or black, and birds of all colors, black, white, and green, flew up" (Métraux 5, p. 29). The zoological order, which is linked with the rainbow, is therefore doubly defined, in respect to men and to birds.

To explain the origin of the colored plumage of birds, the Toba and the Mataco have a different myth which seems to have no connection with the preceding one. This raises a problem that cannot be disregarded.

M_{175}. Mataco. *"How birds acquired their colored plumage"*

The demiurge and trickster, Tawkxwax, was walking along the banks of a river and spent the night there. When he awoke, he was very hungry; he resumed his journey, and about noon he arrived at a house that was surrounded by many pots full of water. An old woman lived there. Tawkxwax went up to her and asked for a drink. The old woman pointed to the jars and told him to drink as much as he wished.

But Tawkxwax made the water very warm and asked the old woman to go and get fresh water from the river. Since she was anxious about her grand-daughter, whom she was nursing, Tawkxwax advised her to put her into the hammock. He then murmured magic words, so that the old woman's jar would not fill up before he had had time to finish eating the child. When she reached the river, the old woman tried in vain to draw the water. Meanwhile, Tawkxwax took the child, grilled her, and ate her, then put a stone in her place (Toba version: Fox put his mouth to the baby's anus and sucked out all its substance; only the skin was left). He then lifted the spell, the jar filled with water, and the old woman returned.

When she saw the stone, she wept and became angry. The old woman was a wild bee of the moro-moro species (in another version a mason bee). She put the trickster into a deep sleep, and while he slept, she blocked all the orifices of his body—mouth, nostrils, eyes, armpits, penis, and anus—with wax; and she also smeared over the spaces between his fingers and toes.

When the demiurge awoke, he realized that he was swelling up in a dangerous manner. The birds (who at that time were men) came to his aid and tried to open the apertures with axes—that is, with their beaks—but the wax was too hard. Only a very small woodpecker succeeded in breaking through it. The demiurge's blood spurted through the hole and stained the birds with beautiful red colors—all except the crow, which was soiled by the dirt that blew out from the anus. (Métraux 3, pp. 29–30; 5, pp. 133–4; Palavecino, pp. 252–3.)

In interpreting this myth we are faced with two kinds of difficulty. If we consider only the syntagmatic sequence—that is, the unfolding of the story—it appears incoherent and very arbitrary in construction. And if we try to fit the myth into the paradigmatic whole formed by the other myths dealing with the colored plumage of birds—including M₁₇₄, although it, too, origi-nates with the Toba and the Mataco—we are still no nearer to understand-ing, since the story it relates seems to be quite different.[13]

Let us begin by studying the latter aspect. The myths explaining how birds acquired their colored plumage are concerned with the sharing of the skin of a cannibalistic monster. Now in the myth we have just dealt with, the trickster does in fact assume the role of a cannibalistic monster, since he eats a child alive. By considering, for the time being, only the last part of the myth, we arrive at the following transformation:

[13] For reasons I have already indicated (p. 177, n. 18) I do not propose to com-pare the contemporary myth with ancient Peruvian myths (Davila) and with a passage from the Popol-Vuh (Raynaud, pp. 50–1).

M_{145} etc. $\begin{cases}\text{cannibalistic monster} \\ \text{skinned;}\end{cases}$	hostile birds share out the skin:	(centrifugal action)	$\left.\begin{array}{c} \\ \\ \\ \end{array}\right\}$ birds' colored plumage
$M_{175} \begin{cases}\text{cannibalistic monster} \\ \text{blocked up;}\end{cases}$	bird helpers open up his orifices:	(centripetal action)	

Must we therefore conclude that the sole aim of the first part of M_{175}, with its careful construction and its wealth of apparently gratuitous detail, is to justify the function of the trickster as a cannibalistic monster? The conclusion would seem to be inevitable, if we take into account only the syntagmatic relations. But I am dwelling at considerable length on this particular myth because it illustrates an essential rule of the structural method.

Considered purely in itself, every syntagmatic sequence must be looked upon as being without meaning: either no meaning is apparent in the first instance; or we think we can perceive a meaning, but without knowing whether it is the right one. In order to overcome this difficulty, we can only resort to two procedures. One consists in dividing the syntagmatic sequence into superposable segments, and in proving that they constitute variations on one and the same theme (L.-S. 5, pp. 227–56; 6). The other procedure, which is complementary to the first, consists in superposing a syntagmatic sequence in its totality—in other words, a complete myth—on other myths or segments of myths. It follows, then, that on both occasions we are replacing a syntagmatic sequence by a paradigmatic sequence; the difference is that whereas in the first case the paradigmatic whole is removed from the sequence, in the second it is the sequence that is incorporated into it. But whether the whole is made up of parts of the sequence, or whether the sequence itself is included as a part, the principle remains the same. Two syntagmatic sequences, or fragments of the same sequence, which, considered in isolation, contain no definite meaning, acquire a meaning simply from the fact that they are polar opposites. And since the meaning becomes clear at the precise moment when the couple is constituted, it did not exist previously, hidden but present, like some inert residue in each myth or fragment of myth considered separately. The meaning is entirely in the dynamic relation which simultaneously creates several myths or parts of the same myth, and as a result of which these myths, or parts of myths, acquire a rational existence and achieve fulfillment together as opposable pairs of one and the same set of transformations. In the present case the proof will be rendered even more conclusive by the fact that it has to be given in two stages, each stage repeating, and helping to throw light on, the other.

As it happens, there is a myth whose syntagmatic sequence can be said to "explain" that of the Toba-Mataco myth, since it is its polar opposite in every

particular. I am referring to the Carib myth of Guiana about the origin of
fish poison and diseases (M_{162}), a summary of which was given above, on
page 279:

M_{175}	A deceiving male spirit is walking near a river not far from which is a hut;	the owner of the hut is a grandmother looking after a baby;	the owner of the hut does not conceal, and generously offers, her water supply.
M_{162}	An honest female spirit visits a hut, not far from which is a river;	the woman visiting the hut is a mother suckling her baby;	the owner of the hut hides, and selfishly refuses to share, her water supply.

M_{175}	The spirit asks for a drink (although he is hungry);	the visiting spirit makes the drink offered him too hot;	the owner of the hut goes off to the river to get cold water for her visitor, and leaves her baby.
M_{162}	The spirit accepts food (but will become thirsty);	the human owner of the hut makes the food offered too hot;	the woman visiting the hut herself goes to seek cool water in the river and leaves her baby.

(Cf. p. 307)

M_{175}	The spirit grills and eats the baby belonging to the owner of the hut, or devours it raw;	. . . . . [M^{175}]	origin of the birds' colored plumage.
M_{162}	The owner of the hut boils (but does not eat) the spirit's baby;	. . . . . [M^{145}]	origin of fish poison.

I shall give later (pp. 326-7) another example of transformation by inversion, culminating in the one instance in poison, in the other in bird plumage.
For the moment, the important point is that the first part of M_{175} is isomorphic to M_{162}, and the second part is isomorphic to M_{145}, which is an entirely different myth. We may therefore ask whether there is some connection
between M_{145} and M_{162}; and if there is, what kind of connection it is.

M_{145} and M_{162} are both myths about the origin of fish poison, but they carry out their common mission by following inverted paths. M_{145} attributes the origin of fish poison to the rainbow, which the other myths we have studied describe as a cannibalistic monster causing suffering and death to prevail among men. On the other hand, M_{162} starts off with a description of an age in which suffering and death were unknown. A supernatural being, a male and cannibalistic snake, is counterbalanced by a female spirit who assumes the role of wetnurse. The snake persecutes men (and birds in M_{172}); the spirit shows affection for them. In the person of a child, men are victims of the snake's malevolence (M_{145}); again in the person of a child, the spirit is the victim of men's malevolence (M_{162}). The snake/rainbow lives at the bottom of the water, of which it is master. The spirit is deprived of water and parched with thirst. In M_{145} the major antipathy is between the rainbow and the birds (aerial beings) which exterminate it; the spirit in M_{162}, like all its fellow spirits, has a strong aversion for the sweet potato (chthonic being?), and the mere mention of the word is enough to make it disappear.[14]

It is clear that M_{162} occupies a special position: it is a "critique"—in the Kantian sense—of M_{145}, since the problem that is presented and solved in the myth can be formulated in the following way: what is the totality of conditions required to induce a supernatural being, who is the polar opposite of the rainbow, to act exactly like the rainbow? Although my analysis is concerned with form, it allows me to put forward a theory regarding the respective ages of the two myths and their primary or derivative function: for the syntagmatic sequences to be intelligible, M_{145} must be earlier than M_{162}, and the second myth must appear to be the result of a kind of meditation, no doubt unconscious, on the first. The opposite theory would have no explanatory value whatever. Similarly, M_{175} would appear to be derivative in relation to M_{145} and M_{162}, since its presupposes both of them, and since its originality lies in the fact that it juxtaposes and at the same time inverts them. But the mode of inversion is different in each case: M_{175} conveys

[14] I am willing to admit that this last interpretation is very speculative, but it could perhaps be reinforced by another myth from Guiana (M_{176}) of Arawak origin. It deals with a fisherman who captures and marries the female spirit of the waters. Everything goes well until the mother-in-law becomes drunk and discloses her daughter-in-law's supernatural origin, thus breaking the vow of secrecy insisted on by the siren. The latter is offended and resolves to leave men and to return to her aquatic abode with her husband. But before doing so, she replaces the fish with which she has kept her human family generously supplied by a jug of cassiri—beer made from manioc and "red potatoes" (*Dioscorea?*)—and a supply of sweet potatoes, which she sends from underneath the water. After they have eaten their fill, the Indians throw the empty jug and potato peelings back into the water. The siren changes the jug into a gigantic catfish (*Silurus* species) and the peelings into imiri (*Sciadeichthys*), which are small, squat fish. For this reason, the Arawak call the catfish "fisherman's water jug" and the imiri "fisherman's potatoes" (Roth 1, pp. 246-7). If we accept the fact that fish are in the same relation to water as birds are to air, the equivalence, which the myth postulates between fish and potatoes, could be generalized as follows:

$$(\text{potatoes} : \text{earth}) :: (\text{fish} : \text{water}) :: (\text{birds} : \text{air})$$

the same message as M_{145} (the coloring of birds' plumage) by means of a straightforward lexical inversion; and it conveys the opposite message to M_{162} by means of a preserved code. By assuming half of the function of the rainbow (essentially evil) and half of the function of the spirit (essentially good), the trickster, who is both good and bad, reveals his duality on the formal level in several ways: by the achievement of a kind of "crossing over"[15] between two myths; the adoption, in the case of one of these myths, of its inverted version; an original reversal of this version; the adoption of a "straight" version of the other myth; and an original reversal (but on a different axis) of this straight version.

Although the above conclusion is complex enough, we have not by any means exhausted the problem. There exists a Caraja myth (M_{177}) which in the interests of brevity I have not attempted to analyze, although in certain respects it appears to be an inverted version of the Kachuyana myth about the origin of curare (M_{161}). It tells of a hero whose ulcers are cured by a snake which, in addition, gives him magic arrows with which he destroys a race of cannibalistic monkeys of the howler species. These arrows are not poisoned; on the contrary, they have to be tempered with a magic ointment, or they will turn against their user (Ehrenreich, pp. 84–6; Krause, pp. 347–50). A curious symmetry can be noted between one detail of this myth and M_{175}. And we have just seen that M_{175}, too, is an inversion (but in a different way) of the myths about the origin of poison. In M_{177} the hero is given instructions to simulate coitus with a frog, whose collusion he must obtain, by rubbing his penis in the spaces between the frog's fingers and toes—that is, by treating the latter as if they were orifices.[16] Conversely, in M_{175} the bee or wasp blocked up the orifices and filled in the folds formed by the joints, treating them, too, as if they were orifices.

On the other hand—and comparing now M_{175} and M_{162}—it will be remembered that the supernatural heroine of M_{162}, although she is the reverse of the rainbow, ends by behaving like the rainbow, since she reveals herself as responsible for introducing death, diseases, and fish poison. Correspondingly, the heroine of M_{175}, who is congruous with the rainbow when she appears in human form—as mistress of water—proves in the end to be a wasp or a moro-moro bee: a word of Quechua origin, in which language the word *muru-muru* means "multicolored," a fact that is itself not without significance. Like the frog in M_{177}, the bee makes no distinction between the folds formed by joints and orifices but obtains the opposite result: the frog imagines that someone will be able to "pierce" the folds formed by his joints; the bee is a victim of the opposite illusion when it tries to block up

---

[15] TRANSLATORS' NOTE: This expression is in English in the original.

[16] These details again point to the *cunauaru* (cf. pp. 264–5), whose body "is covered with an unpleasant-smelling slime, which it seems particularly difficult to remove from the enlarged toe pads" (Schomburgk, Vol. II, p. 335).

the orifices of another creature. Like the rainbow, the frog is connected with water; and the heroine of M₁₆₂ is described from the outset in terms of her thirst and in relation to drought, since she is deprived of water. If we continue to apply the same transformational rules, we can deduce from them that the bee or wasp of M₁₇₅, which behaves in the opposite way from the frog in M₁₆₂, possesses an "arid" connotation, which confirms in advance what I shall say (p. 314, n. 18) about the semantic function of wasps in the Sherente ritual.

Let us go back for a moment to the Tsimshian version (M₁₇₀), which was the starting point of the present discussion. In itself, it was interesting for two reasons. Before I introduced it, we saw that noisemaking occurred in two quite distinct contexts: on the social level (charivari) and on the cosmic level (eclipse). The originality of M₁₇₀ was that it combined the two: the myth began by describing improper behavior on the part of youths—that is, a social disorder, but one that marked the beginning of a long series of adventures culminating in the setting up of a meteorological and cosmic order.

Now when we look at them closely, we notice that the Caduveo and Vilela myths (M₁₇₁ and M₁₇₃) do exactly the same thing. The first associates children's noisy behavior with the color of the sunset and the rainbow. In the two versions of the Vilela myth that we know of, the hero's misdeed consists either in returning home too late or in shunning the society of girls and boys of his own age (Lehmann-Nitsche 2, p. 226). Such antisocial behavior leads ultimately to the appearance of the rainbow and the division of the birds into species, which are clearly defined both as regards habitat and call.

Secondly, M₁₇₀ is linked to a vast and complex set of myths, the study of which cannot be embarked on here, and which deals with the punishment meted out to young people guilty of unruly behavior. Certain myths relate to noise: nocturnal disturbances, insults hurled at the stars, or at the sky because it is snowing, or at human excrement; others, which are widespread in America, deal with the punishment of a scornful or casual attitude toward food products. If it is accepted as a working hypothesis that food is a terrestrial modality (terrestrial including in this case both terra firma and water —that is, the "low" as opposed to the "high"; cf. L.-S. 6), the fact—evidenced by the myths—that the sky reacts to noise *as if it were a personal insult,* encourages us to postulate an equivalence about which I shall have more to say later. If noise is a violation of the sky, and the lack of respect toward food (or drink; cf. M₁₇₄) a violation of the earth (or of water: we have only to think back to the previously quoted Toba myth and the miraculous draughts of fishes obtained by the incarnate hyper-poisons), it follows that:

[noise (=violation of x) : sky] :: [violation of food : earth (or water)].

The equivalence above, in its still problematic form, can be proved in two ways. There is at least one Brazilian tribe that, in the space of a single myth, covers the complicated course we have followed by putting several myths end to end in order to move from noisemaking to eclipses, from eclipses to incest, from incest to unruliness, and from unruliness to the colored plumage of birds:

M₁₇₈. Shipaya. *"How birds acquired their colored plumage"*

Two brothers lived with their sister in an abandoned hut. One of them fell in love with the young girl; he lay with her every night without telling her who he was. The other brother discovered that his sister was pregnant, and commanded her to rub the face of her nocturnal visitor with genipa juice. When the guilty brother realized that the stains betrayed him, he fled up into the sky with his sister. But after arriving there, they quarreled; the man gave the woman a push, and she fell like a meteor and landed on the earth *very noisily* (my italics; cf. M₁₇₂ in which men drag the snake onto the shore, "uttering terrible cries," p. 303); she turned into a tapir, while the incestuous brother, who had remained in the sky, became the moon.

The other brother summoned the warriors and ordered them to shoot arrows at the moon and kill it. Only the armadillo succeeded in wounding it. The moon's blood was of all colors, and men and women were bespattered with it as it streamed earthward. The women wiped themselves with an upward movement, so they came under the moon's influence. The men, however, wiped themselves clean with a downward movement. The birds bathed in the different colored pools, and each species thus acquired its characteristic plumage. (Nim. 3, p. 1010.)

On the other hand, looking back over the ground we have covered, we might say that we began with myths whose hero was a bird-nester (M₁, then M₇–M₁₂), and that, for the time being at least, we have arrived at myths (M₁₇₁–M₁₇₅, M₁₇₈) that are concerned with the origin of the colored plumage of birds. In order to justify this circuitous course, I have just shown that while the myths featuring bird-nesters are myths about cooking, those that deal with the colored plumage of birds present, in sociological, zoological, meteorological, or cosmological terms, a problem that, from the formal point of view, is the same kind of problem as that posed by the advent of what might be termed alimentary order. We thus come back to the remarks I made earlier (p. 294) about cooking fire being mediatory between high and low, between the sun and the earth. Consequently, the bird-nester, who is stranded halfway between the sky above and the earth below, and who—in his capacity as brother-in-law or son—is a mediator between a man and a woman, between alliance and kinship, can be the introducer, or the remover—but at all events the master—of cooking fire, which, on the cultural level, establishes an order congruous with other orders—whether sociological, or cosmic, or situated at different intermediary levels.

When we bear this in mind, it is even more startling to discover that certain myths directly juxtapose the theme of the bird-nester and that of the colored plumage of birds:

M₁₇₉. Parintintin. "How birds acquired their colored plumage"

Two old Indians, who were close friends, decided to go into the forest in order to collect eggs from the nests of harpy eagles (*gavião real, Thrasaetus harpyia*). They improvised a ladder, and one of them climbed a tree containing an eyrie they had previously located. On seeing that his companion had found an eaglet, the old man who had remained at the foot of the tree asked, "What's the little eagle like?" To which the other man replied, "As hairy as your wife's——"[17] The old man, whose name was Ipanitegue, was angry and outraged. He broke the ladder and went off. For five days his companion, who was called Canaurehu, remained at the top of the tree without water and food, plagued by wasps and mosquitoes (*cabas e carapanans*), which stung him day and night. Finally, about midday, he heard in the distance the call of the eagle, which was bringing back sloth meat to its young. The old man was terrified and climbed right to the top of the tree, where he crouched without uttering a word. The eagle flew to the nest, and while its offspring was eating, it noticed the man. Startled by his presence, it flew to a near-by tree and questioned the Indian, who told his story. When the old man recounted his jesting reply to his companion, the eagle went into fits of laughter. It expressed a wish to move nearer so as to hear better, and insisted on being told the story again. But the man was afraid that the eagle would kill him. Eventually he was reassured and told his story over again. The eagle found it so funny that it laughed and laughed and laughed. . . .

The eagle then suggested to Canaurehu that it should help him to get his revenge. It shook its feathers over him, until he was completely covered with them and changed into an eagle. Once the metamorphosis was complete, the bird taught the man to fly and to break off bigger and stronger branches.

Together, and in order to attract attention to themselves, *uttering loud cries* (my italics), they flew over the village square, in the center of which Ipanitegue was busy making an arrow. The two birds swooped down on him, attacking him with beak and claw, and carried him off, one holding him by the head, the other by the legs. The Indians fired arrows which wounded only the victim. An attempt to hold him back by pulling the thread that had unwound from his arrow met with no success, for the arrow broke at once. In the square was a pool of blood, full of pieces of intestine and brain.

The eagles took their prey to the eyrie and invited all the birds to the feast, on condition that each agreed to be "tattooed." They painted the macaw with the blood. The beak and wing tips of the mutum were smeared with brain, the beak of the *tangara-hu* (a manakin) with blood, the feathers of the parrot and the parakeet with bile, the egret's feathers with brain, too. The breast of the *surucua-hu* (a trogon) and the neck of the *jacu-pemun-hu* were smeared with the blood. . . . Thus all the birds, great and small, were tattooed; some

[17] For a rejoinder in the same vein, see Murphy and Quain, p. 76.

had a red beak or red feathers; others had green or white feathers; because all colors were present in the blood, bile, and brain of the old man who had been murdered. As for the flesh, the birds ate it. (Pereira, pp. 87–92.)

In comparing the material given by Nunes Pereira with the texts he himself had collected from other tribes, Nimuendaju accuses Pereira of making faulty and incomplete transcriptions (Nim. 11, Vol. III, pp. 293–4). The following discussion will, I believe, show that one should never be in a hurry to criticize a text that has been obtained at first hand. In mythological analysis, differences between versions cannot be rejected *a priori*. The remarkable thing about the highly colored Parintintin version of the bird-nester is that, point by point and with a systematic exactness that could not be the result of negligence on the part of the collector or of some whim on the part of the narrator, it reverses every detail, and even the structure, of the corresponding Ge myth:

M_{179} { two old men of the same age,	bound by friendship,	hunt eagles (carnivorous);
M_7– M_{12} { two men who are not the same age (adult and child),	related by marriage,	hunt parrots (fructivorous);

M_{179} { one insults the other by means of an absent social relation (wife of $x \neq$ sister of y);	hero abandoned, persecuted by venomous[18] insects.	
M_7– M_{12} { one insults the other by means of a present, natural relation (bird present, allegedly absent; egg changed into stone);	hero abandoned, covered with excrement, and crawling with vermin.	

[18] This remarkable contrast confirms the interpretation already suggested by the wasp episode in the Sherente ritual of the Great Fast (cf. pp. 295, n. 5 and p. 311). If vermin denotes "a world of rottennesss," then venomous insects must denote the "burned world" (in the sense I attributed to these terms pp. 293–5). Now the aim of the Great Fast was to relieve mankind of the threat of a burned world, and its end is heralded by the appearance of the wasps, which are therefore messengers of this world, but in a twofold capacity as "singers" (granted to men who sing or chant) and as givers of miniature arrows, which are their stings, changed from their natural form, which is hostile to mankind, into a cultural form which is at the service of mankind. This may well be symbolic of the taming or domestication of the burned world. Banner (2, pp. 20, 27–8) has recently described a Kayapo ritual game in which adolescents, sometimes imitated by children, wage war on wasps, the native term for which means "enemies."

M_{179}	{ mediation by the sloth, a symbol of a cosmic conjunction;[19]	the eagle feeds its young and does not adopt—but becomes "the ally" of—the hero;	the hero *makes the eagle laugh* at his expense (object of laughter, +).
M_7–M_{12}	{ mediation by the caititu (M_8), symbol of a social conjunction (cf. p. 91);	the jaguar has no child, adopts and feeds the hero;	the hero is *careful not to make the jaguar laugh* (subject of laughter, —).

M_{179}	{ The eagle confers a bird's nature on the hero (feathers);	the eagle bestows a natural faculty on the hero (power to fly, superhuman force),	he helps him to take revenge on a friend (who has remained human).
M_7–M_{12}	{ The jaguar relieves the hero of a birdlike nature (excrement and vermin);	the jaguar endows the hero with a cultural force (weapons, cooking fire),	he helps him to take revenge on a relative (mother) who has become an animal.

M_{179}	{ The setting-up of a natural and zoological order;	cannibalistic meal, outside the precincts of the village;	making a noise in order to be heard.
M_7–M_{12}	{ The setting-up of a cultural and alimentary order;	meal of cooked meat, within precincts of village;	not making, or not hearing, noise.

We may now ask what reason there can be for these various inversions. I have already defined a very large set of myths whose common denominator is that they attribute the same relevant function to various attitudes toward noise, or to attitudes that can be recognized as transformations of

[19] In connection with this particular function of the sloth, which is of only indirect interest here and which I have not had occasion to establish independently, reference can be made chiefly to the myths of Tacana and Bolivia, in which the sloth is a master of destructive fire which sets the world alight; and its excrement, if it cannot defecate on the ground and is forced to do so from the top of a tree, "acquires the force of a comet," shattering the world and wiping out all living beings (Hissink and Hahn, pp. 39–40). An echo of these beliefs is found in Guiana, where the star called "the sloth's star," which appears on the horizon at the beginning of the long dry season, is supposed to come down to earth to perform its natural functions (Ahlbrinck, "Kupirisi" entry).

such attitudes. The semantic function of these myths is to bear witness to the fact that there is an isomorphic relation between two types of order, which may be either the cosmic order and the cultural order; the cosmic or meteorological order and the social order; or one or other of the orders above and the zoological order, which is situated on an intermediary level in relation to them. In the Bororo myth about the bird-nester (M₁) the meteorological order is explicitly expressed (the origin of wind and rain), and the cultural order (the origin of cooking) is implied. The opposite occurs in the Ge myths belonging to the same set. But none deals with the zoological order, which is very much to the fore in the myths of the Gran Chaco and Guiana (as for them, we thus again confirm that they are closer to each other in respect to their armature than they are to the myths of central and eastern Brazil, although this area lies halfway between the Gran Chaco and Guiana). We can now see that the Parintintin version acts as a link between the versions of central and eastern Brazil on the one hand and those of the Gran Chaco and Guiana on the other. With the help of a code borrowed from the bird-nester cycle, the Parintintin version "transmits" a message belonging to the cycle about bird plumage:

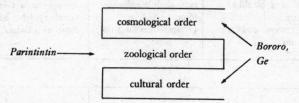

But, for the inversion to take place, M₁₇₉ must be carried out as a kind of caricature of the other versions. Since it aims at describing a natural order, family relations and social regulations (whose lexical material is inherited from the Bororo and Ge versions) are negativized or made ridiculous. The two brothers-in-law—one a young man, the other an adolescent—are replaced by two old men who are simply "friends," and not kinsmen or affines: in other words, they are bound by the weakest of social ties, instead of by the strongest. And yet in insulting his companion in the person of his wife (who is not a sister, since the old men are just friends), the ridiculous hero of M₁₇₉ testifies to the logical force of the absent relationship. The same allusive form of expression occurs later in the myth where the specific colorings of the birds, which belong to a natural order, are referred to as "tattooing," and compared therefore with distinctive markings associated with a cultural order. The Parintintin myth intercalates *the bird as fisher of man* as a third section in the center of the diptych formed by *man the bird-nester* (central and eastern Brazil) and *man the fisher of fish* (Guiana).

The Mundurucu, who speak a Tupi dialect, form a transition between the tribes belonging to the Ge linguistic group in the east and the Parintintin—

Tupi-speaking like the Mundurucu—in the west. Their geographical and linguistic position perhaps explains why their myth about the colors of birds carefully omits any reference to the one about the bird-nester. The Mundurucu myth is, one might say, completely "dehumanized"; it is situated on two levels only: the zoological (explicit) and the cosmological (implicit).

M_{180}. *Mundurucu. "How birds got their colors"*

A royal eagle mother lived with her child in a nest at the top of a tree. One day, she flew down to the water to seize a terrapin which was surfacing; but the terrapin was too heavy; it dragged the bird down to the bottom, and the eagle was drowned.

By its cries the motherless eagle attracted the attention of a black eagle which at first took care of it, but soon wearied of the task and flew away. A "rapina" eagle took its place, and when the eaglet grew up, its two protectors trained it to lift heavier and heavier tree trunks so that it would be able to get even with the terrapin and avenge its mother's death.

When it was ready, it lay in wait for the terrapin. The terrapin came up to the surface, its whole body decked out in the dead eagle's feathers, and provoked the young one. The bird dived and seized the terrapin which tried to pull it into the water, but the other terrapins pushed their fellow terrapin back to the surface. The bird flew off to the nest with its prey.

The eagle invited all the birds to eat the terrapin, whose shell had first to be broken. The toucan had a try, and its beak became flattened, whence its present shape; the woodpecker succeeded. Then the birds painted themselves with the red blood, the blue fluid from the gallbladder, and the yellow fat. The toucan smeared blue all around its eyes, and yellow on the end of its tail, and a band of yellow across its breast. It also put a daub of blood on its tail. The woodpecker painted its head red; the pipira (a tanager) daubed itself all over with blue. The mutum stained its legs and its beak with blood, and in order to deprive the galsa (*garça?*—"a wading bird," Murphy I, p. 143) of the animal dyes, it suggested that it should use white clay. The galsa did as the mutum suggested, but when the mutum's turn came, it flew away. The galsa could only catch the tip of its tail, which has remained white to this day.

As a token of thanks for its services, the royal eagle offered the "rapina" eagle the terrapin's head, with which it made a trumpet, which produced the noise: "Toc, toc, poat, poat." The tawato eagle (*Astur* species (?), cf. Ihering, "Tauatu pintado" entry) was jealous, because in a spite of its size, it had a shrill cry. It therefore insisted on an exchange. Ever since, the tawato eagle has had a deep voice, and the "rapina" eagle cheeps, "Eee, eee, eee." (Murphy 1, pp. 128–9.)

It is difficult to analyze this myth because of the uncertainty about the three species of "eagle" and their place in native taxonomy. According to Murphy (1, p. 143), the "rapina" eagle is *Cerchneis sparverios eidos,* and the tawato *Hypomorphnus urubitinga urubitinga.* Another version calls them *ii* and *uayuptauhu* or *puatpuat*, respectively (Kruse 2, p. 633). The helpful eagles are not present in an Amazonian version of uncertain source (Barbosa Rodrigues, pp. 167–71). I shall therefore do no more than stress the fact that M_{180} and M_{179} are largely isomorphic. The man in M_{179} and the bird in M_{180} train themselves to lift pieces of wood as heavy as their adversary; the bird, when it is abandoned, calls loudly for help; the man does not utter a word; the man covered with feathers in M_{179} has his counterpart in the feather-decked terrapin of M_{180}; in the first instance the attackers, who are "up above," shout and insult their adversary who is "down below"; in the second the reverse occurs: the eagle remains silent and waits for the terrapin to provoke and insult it; lastly, the human companions of the victim try to hold him back (M_{179}), whereas the animal companions push the victim up to the surface (M_{180}). A link with the Guianian versions can be detected in the episode of the head which is handed over to the most deserving animal.

Above all, it is clear that, unlike the Parintintin myth, the Mundurucu myth takes place entirely in an animal world, although like the Parintintin myth, it deals with predatory eagles and not with parrots dislodged from their nests: they are pugnacious rather than peace-loving birds; meat-eating rather than fruit-eating; and in the Mundurucu myth, birds associated with water, whereas parrots are associated with dry land, on which grow the trees where they find their food. This last contrast is strongly in evidence among the Bororo, whose priests are sometimes supposed to change into birds, in order to help in the search for food: as macaws, they gather fruit, and as harpy eagles, they catch fish or kill other birds (Colb. 3, p. 131).

3

The Wedding

(If, if she were to have a child,
she could be worth twice as much.)

IGOR STRAVINSKI, *Les Noces,* SCENE IV.

All the rainbow myths we have examined associate the phenomenon either with the origin of fish poison and diseases or with the colored plumage of birds. But the way in which the rainbow is introduced varies according to the type of link chosen: it may be an agent, or it may be the passive object of an action that is done to it.

It is, directly or indirectly, because of its malevolence that the living rainbow causes poison and disease to appear: it acts as their moral cause. Of the colored plumage of birds it is merely the physical cause, since the birds were not to acquire their distinctive plumage until they had previously killed the rainbow and divided its skin among themselves. To use a different kind of vocabulary, we might say that the rainbow signifies poison and diseases, but that its logical function, when it applies to the colored plumage of birds, changes from signifying to being signified.

When we met this problem for the first time, we solved it by appealing to a dialectic of short and long intervals. We had seen that disease and poison present a dual character. Both imply that life and death, nature and culture, are in a transitive relation, and that the changeover from one to the other takes place progressively without there being any means of detecting the intermediary stages. Furthermore, disease and poison are essentially "chromatic" entities, producing what might be called "diatonic" effects; since fish poison, like epidemics, creates large gaps in the populations affected by it. The Guarayu of Bolivia draw a rational conclusion from the similarity between fish poison and epidemics; they believe that all diseases are the result of poisoning, and that if men were not poisoned, they would never die (Cardus, p. 172).

Because poison and disease can be seen as "chromatic" entities, they have a feature in common with the rainbow, which makes the latter appropriate to signify them. On the other hand, empirical observation of the havoc they cause leads to the inference—or confirms the hypothesis—that the continuous contains the discontinuous and even gives rise to it. But as soon as the rainbow is no longer considered as an agent and is turned into an object of action, the preceding relation is reversed. A signifying chromaticism, the negative form of the diatonic order (since this order is merely the residue of a wrecked continuum), gives way to a *signified* chromaticism: positive raw material out of which an order, which is also diatonic, can be constructed, and which, like the other, will be credited to nature. The decimation of any given population (whether it is a human population killed off by epidemics, or fish destroyed by poison) is symmetrical with the general discontinuity of the species: it is isomorphic with it, within any one genus. I had already arrived at this conclusion earlier by means of a different argument (Part One, I, *d*).

Let us recall the circumstances in which the Vilela hero of M_{173} changed into a chromatic entity "whose colors could be seen gleaming from afar, in spite of the darkness of the night" (Lehmann-Nitsche 2, p. 222). The transformation occurred after he had picked up different-colored stones at the water side and made himself a necklace with them—in other words, a multicolored entity composed of previously scattered elements, between which the intervals became very small once the elements were threaded together. The process, as described in the myth, is all the more significant, since I think it would be difficult to find a necklace answering to this description in any ethnographic collection emanating from tropical America, where the necklaces worn by the natives are notably sober in color and regular and repetitive in pattern.[20] They are almost invariably made from black and white beads—small disks carved out of the shells of either aquatic mollusks, or palm nuts. The many varieties of trade beads are more or less disregarded: white and black, used alternately, remain the most highly prized colors. Beads of a different color are sometimes accepted and used to make monochrome necklaces—blue, for instance, when this color (which the native languages rarely distinguish from black) has a religious connotation (Huxley, p. 47; Nino, p. 197). I never saw the natives of the seven or eight tribes with whom I lived make use of the (quite superfluous) variety

[20] They are so even among the Chiriguano, who live not far from the Vilela, and who, according to certain travelers, had necklaces made of coral and malachite; this assertion was, however, disproved by B. de Nino (p. 197). It is not impossible that the curious invention of the Vilela myth was suggested to the natives by old necklaces of Andean origin. But as the colored stones theme also occurs in Guiana, where it is associated with the spirit of the rainbow (Goeje, p. 33)—and we know from other sources that the Carib name for rainbow also denotes the opossum (cf. above, p. 249) —it seems that the origin of the theme belongs to the realm of speculation rather than to that of experience.

of beads we distributed among them (L.-S. 3, p. 260) to make multicolored necklaces, as the imprudent hero of the Vilela myth does. . . .

It was noted that formerly Bororo women were reluctant to accept striped or flowered material that was offered to them:

> At first, we blamed fashion or whim. We learned that their attitude was determined by religious ideas. The priests . . . explained that striped or flowered materials belonged to the kingdom of souls, and that for this reason the women were forbidden to accept them, even as presents, unless it was to adorn the person who represented the deceased man's soul during the funeral rites, or to reward the priest entrusted with the conjuring up of souls; and even he could not wear them until he had informed the souls of his intention to do so.

The same author adds that the Bororo prescribed the use of light- or plain-colored materials (Colb. 3, p. 131; EB, Vol. I, p. 174). In 1935 the natives put forward arguments of the same kind to explain to us why their pottery was dark colored and totally devoid of decoration.[21] Such hatred of polychromaticism is no doubt a rather exceptional phenomenon in South America. Yet the Bororo are merely carrying to extremes an attitude they share with other communities, who display it in a more subtle way. In one of their myths (M_{181}) the Tucuna relate that ritual musical instruments used always to be painted a uniform red. A god ordered the civilizing hero to use instead "clay of different colors" which was to be found not far from a stream, but he must not touch it with his hands. He was to collect it in his blowgun by thrusting the latter into the ground several times, until he had obtained samples of every variety. After that he had to extract the colors by cleaning out the gun with a rod, and then use them to paint with. It is further stated that this kind of painting is the chief cause of the taboo affecting musical instruments, at which women are not allowed to look. Another myth (M_{182}) explains that a woman hid in a tree in order to satisfy her curiosity. But as

---

[21] The ancient Egyptians also seem to have made use of the contrast between chromaticism and monochromaticism, but to evolve a liturgy of costume that was the opposite of the Bororo's: "As to the sacred vestments, that of Isis is parti-colored and of different hues; for her power is about matter, which becomes everything and receives everything, as light and darkness, day and night, fire and water, life and death, beginning and ending. But that of Osiris has no shade, no variety of colors, but only one simple one, resembling light. For the first principle is untempered and that which is first and of an intelligible nature is unmixed; which is the reason why, after they have once made use of this garment, they lay it up and keep it close, invisible and not to be touched. But those of Isis are used often. For sensible things, when they are of daily use and familiar to us, afford us many opportunities to display them and to see them in their various mutations; but the apprehension of what is intelligible, sincere and holy, darting through the soul like a flash of lightning, attends but to some one single glance or glimpse of its object" (Plutarch, "Of Isis and Osiris" lxxviii, trans. by William Baxter).

soon as the instruments appeared, she was fascinated by the way in which they were decorated. She mistook a trumpet for an alligator: "She urinated much, and pa! fell." The musicians rushed at her and cut her into little pieces, which they cured. And they forced even her mother and sister to take part in the feast (Nim. 13, pp. 77–8, 134).

These stories call for several comments. First of all, it will be remembered that the Tucuna regard one of the two rainbows as the master of potter's clay (cf. pp. 246 ff.). Secondly, the very special method imposed on the hero with regard to the preparation of the colors, would seem to lead inevitably to a partial mixture, so that the colors on the instruments would blend into each other, like the colors of the rainbow. Finally, the description of the guilty woman's death—she sits fascinated on the branch of the tree, then urinates, and falls—corresponds exactly to what happens when a monkey is hit by an arrow poisoned with curare, as I myself have observed among the Nambikwara; the fact is, moreover, confirmed independently by the source I am using: "The effect (of the poison) on the wounded animal is to produce immediately incontinence of feces and urine, the creature falling in about three minutes." (Nim. 13, p. 30). Here again, then, we have the triple association of the rainbow, chromaticism, and poison; the difference between the Bororo and the Tucuna is that the latter seem to restrict to the female sex the poisonous effects of chromatic decoration.

Tucuna pottery is crudely decorated with brown designs on a white ground. These designs may be geometrical, or zoomorphic; and Nimuendaju does not think that even in former times they were any more delicately drawn (13, plate 6 and pp. 47–8). This is not true of other Amazonian tribes, who used to make very beautiful and intricate polychrome pottery. Now technical and artistic skill of this kind is accompanied by a significant bent of the mythology of the rainbow:

M₁₈₃. Amazonia (Teffe Lake). "The origin of painted earthenware"

There was once a young woman who had no manual skill whatever, and the pottery she made was shapeless. To mock her, her sisters-in-law molded clay around her head and told her to bake this clay to make a pot.

One day an old woman appeared and the young woman told her of her misfortunes. The old woman was a tender-hearted sprite who taught the young woman how to make magnificent pots. On taking leave of the young woman, the sprite told her that she would henceforth appear in the form of a snake, and that the young woman should not be afraid to embrace it. The heroine did as she was told, and the snake at once turned into a sprite, who showed her protégée how to paint earthenware pots: "She took some white clay and smoothed it evenly around the pots. Then, with yellow clay, brown clay, and rucu (urucu: *Bixa orellana*) she drew beautiful variegated patterns and said to the young woman: 'There are two kinds of painting: Indian painting and flower painting. The kind of painting that draws the lizard's head, the

Great Snake's tracks, the branch of the pepper tree, the breast of Boyusu the rainbow serpent, etc., is what we call Indian painting, and the other is the kind that consists in painting flowers.'

"Then the sprite took black varnish and used it to decorate and give luster to numerous gourds, on the insides of which she drew a variety of patterns: the shell of the land tortoise, shafts of rain, a meandering river, a fishhook, and a great many pretty designs. . . ." (Tastevin 3, pp. 192–8.)

Consequently, in a culture that produces polychrome pottery, the rainbow takes on an ambiguous and equivocal meaning. Its awesome power can become protective and indulgent. In this second aspect the poison (which was distilled by the rainbow in its other aspect) regresses, as it were, to the state of excrement that must not be thought repulsive: the umbrian brown used for brown painting is called the "Great Snake's excrement" (*Ibid.*, p. 198). While the female potters thought of the rainbow in the guise of an old sprite, men did likewise but with erotic intent: to them the rainbow appeared as a bewitching mistress (*ibid.*, p. 197).[22] We notice here, then, a movement which is the reverse of the one that led us (pp. 274, ff.) from the love philter to the death philter and from the seducing animal to poison. This retrograde movement is the characteristic feature of an aesthetic which, unlike that of the Bororo, compromises with chromaticism.[23]

But there is in tropical America one field in which polychromaticism seems to be universally and unreservedly accepted. I am referring to the feather ornaments, of which the Bororo offer sumptuous examples.[24] There is a good reason why the myths of this part of the world should present the problem

[22] It is curious, to say the least, that according to a Maya tale, which is no doubt a relic of some old myth, an abandoned fiancée whose name could mean "Aunt Rainbow" was changed after her death into a deceitful divinity who charms travelers, then turns into a snake with a forked tail, whose prongs she thrusts into her victim's nostrils while she crushes the body under her weight (Cornyn). This inverted copulation corresponds symmetrically to the act of copulation described in M_{95}, in connection with an opossum god. It follows, then, that in Mexico there is a connection between the snake, the rainbow, and the opossum as seducer (transformed, in this case, into an anti-seduced virgin, then into a female snake which seduces men in the same way as a male opossum seduces females). Incidentally, it is well known that the skunk— along with the weasel and the dung beetle—had its place in the religious imagery of the ancient Mexicans (cf. Seler, Vol. IV, p. 506) as one of the forms in which ordinary dead people were reincarnated.

[23] It is relevant at this point to recall the charming Brazilian love song quoted by Montaigne (*Essays*, Book I, chap. 30, translated by Florio): "Adder, stay good adder, that my sister may, by the patterne of thy partie-coloured coat, drawe the fashion and worke of a rich lace, for me to give unto my love; so may thy beautie, thy nimbleness or disposition be ever preferred before all other serpents." Cf. also de Goeje (p. 28, n. 24) in connection with the Jurimagua, whose women used to call forth snakes in order to copy the patterns on their skins in the decoration of earthenware jars.

[24] They are a male speciality, unlike polychrome pottery which, where it exists, is always considered a female speciality. In connection with this contrasts among the Bororo, see above, p. 47.

of the diversity of species by referring initially (M_{145}) or exclusively (M_{171}, M_{172}, M_{173}, etc.) to birds. The use of feathers for practical purposes no doubt raised a theoretical difficulty that the myths help to overcome.

It may be objected that, according to certain myths of Guiana, the burned and dismembered body of a snake gave rise, not to birds endowed with their distinctive plumage, but to vegetable talismans (Roth 1, pp. 283–6; Gillin, pp. 192–4; Orico 2, pp. 227–32). These talismans consisted mainly of varieties of *Caladium,* each of which was given a specific magic function. Here again, then, it is a question of specific diversity being used to express significant contrasts. The terminology of scientific botany, which groups the numerous varieties of aroids with their brilliant and variegated leaves under the one heading of *Caladium bicolor,* underlines in its own way the most remarkable characteristic of these leaves, which can be looked upon as the vegetable equivalents of feathers. So in spite of this apparent exception, the problem still centers around the question of feathers.

The way feathers are chosen for making adornments would seem to be inspired by a veritable chromatic frenzy. Green shades into yellow, then into orange or red, which finally ends in blue through a sudden return to green, or through the medium of purple; or blue merges into yellow, which in turn fades into an ashen gray. The least likely transitions occur: from blue to orange, from red to green, from yellow to violet. . . . When the feathers are uniform in color, artistry makes good the deficiency by means of clever pasting, or by the juxtaposition of differently tinted feathers (D. and B. Ribeiro). However, the myths exist and proclaim the priority of the universal discontinuity of the species over the internal continuity of the chromaticism peculiar to each one. Unlike the art-lover, the Indian does not look upon a feather as an aesthetic object which must be described, and whose every nuance must be analyzed. Each type of feather is, on the contrary, apprehended in its totality; and in that totality the distinctive identity of a particular species is conveyed in tangible terms, so that it cannot be confused with any other species, for ever since the fragmentation of the rainbow's body, each species has been inevitably determined in accordance with the part it played in the dismemberment.

Consequently, every time colors occur in myths, we must consider what type of polychromaticism is involved: do the colors shade into one another, so that it is impossible to say where one ends and the other begins; or on the contrary, do bold colors or groups of blended colors form a series of contrasting sets? An Amazonian myth (M_{184}) provides a striking illustration of the first type, in a description of the signs preceding the flood that destroyed humanity: "The sun and the moon became red, blue, and yellow; and the wild beasts, even the jaguar and other fierce animals, moved fearlessly among men . . ." (Barbosa Rodrigues, p. 214). The Mundurucu refer to the same predominance of short intervals in graphic and acoustical terms when they relate that the serpent Muyusu—that is, the rainbow—being anxious to teach men how to write, attracted their attention by imitating the voices of all kinds of animals (Kruse 2, p. 623). It is, incidentally, worthy of note that when the natives imitate writing, they do so by drawing wavy lines, as if writing consisted, not of differently shaped characters, but of a series of fluxions (Figure 19). On the other hand, a Mundurucu myth (M185) ostentatiously chooses a visual code to illustrate the other type of polychromaticism, which is expressed by means of long intervals; it tells how the demiurge, by painting men various colors—green, red, black, and yellow—divided them out among the tribes and turned some into animals (Barbosa Rodrigues, pp. 245-51). According to one of their traditions, the Bororo descended from the

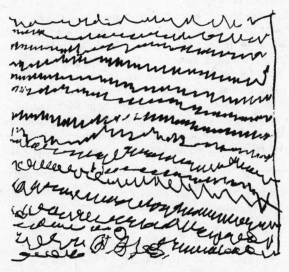

Figure 19. A page of "writing" by a Nambikwara Indian
(cf. L.-S. 3, pp. 314-15).

larva of a lepidopteron which they called *aororo* or *aroro*. And as the larva were marked with three bold, vivid colors—red, yellow, and black—the Bororo adopted these colors as their distinctive emblem (Colb. 1, p. 51; EB, Vol. I, p. 175). Each type of polychromaticism corresponds to either confusion or differentiation.

As additional proof of the reality of this dialectic of long and short intervals, we could quote a Guianian myth about the origin of the colored plumage of birds (M186; Brett, pp. 29-30; Roth 1, p. 212). Unfortunately it would be impossible, as Koch-Grünberg clearly realizes (1, p. 278 ff.), to analyze this myth without putting it into its context within the vast pan-American set known as "the visit to the sky"; and this would require a separate volume. No doubt we should arrive at the conclusion that the marriage of a mortal and a vulture-woman who is "covered in bugs" (Van Coll, p. 482), or who fouls the floor of the hut with her excrement (Wirth in Baldus 2, p. 23), can be interpreted as a transformation of the marriage of a mortal with an opossum-star, since both wives have the same celestial nature and the same ambiguity. The comparison seems to be made spontaneously in an Amazonian myth of uncertain origin (M_{187}), which tells the story of a woman who spurned an odious suitor and called him an "opossum." But when the latter persisted and finally seduced her, he proved to be a vulture, and the woman was impregnated with his foul smell. According to the same myth, the vultures fish with poison and feed on carrion swarming with worms (Amorim, pp. 435–40).

While I do not propose to embark on such a vast subject as the "visit to the sky" myths, I can at least compare M_{186} and M_{161} in order to show that the first, which deals with the colors of birds, is completely symmetrical with the second, which explains the origin of the use of poison for hunting —and probably for warlike purposes, too (cf. pp. 273–4). The comparison therefore confirms that, in accordance with what the "dialectic of intervals" would lead us to deduce *a priori,* a myth about the origin of the colored plumage of birds, in its inverted form, becomes a myth about the origin of poison; and therefore that it is possible to commute, so to speak, from the short interval register to the long interval register, and reciprocally.

M_{161}	The hero marries a monkey-woman;	he visits his parents (human);	he is abandoned at the top of a tree when he visits his parents-in-law (animal).
M_{186}	The hero marries a vulture-woman;	he visits his parents-in-law (animal);	he is abandoned at the top of a tree on the occasion of a proposed visit to his parents (human).

M_{161}	He is able to climb down with the help of sticky lianas,	helped by birds of prey (≡vultures);	he is adopted by the birds.
M_{186}	He is able to climb down in spite of a thorny trunk,	helped by spiders and birds (≢vultures);	he becomes the leader of the birds.

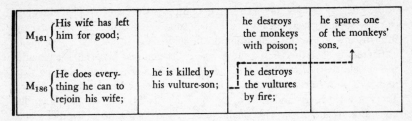

M_{161} { His wife has left him for good;		he destroys the monkeys with poison;	he spares one of the monkeys' sons. ↑
M_{186} { He does everything he can to rejoin his wife;	he is killed by his vulture-son;	he destroys the vultures by fire;	

M_{161} { By agreeing to hunt in conjunction with the eagle, man obtains curare;	origin of poison for hunting. ↗
M_{186} { By quarreling over their share of the booty, the birds acquire their plumage;	↘ origin of the colors of birds.

At the beginning of this fifth section I discussed the contrast between silence and noise. Once the problem of noise had been broached from this angle, I was led to reflect on the circumstances in which noise is prescribed by custom. They turned out to be linked to either the social or the cosmic order. Between these two types of order there soon appeared a third which acts as a mediatory term: this is the zoological order. I showed that this order is also mediatory on another level, too, and does not differ from those instruments of disorder—the rainbow, epidemics, and fish or hunting poisons —except through the widening of the gaps among their constituent elements. Biological discontinuity therefore manifests itself in the myths in two ways —one positive, the other negative: as zoological discontinuity it provides a transition between the cosmic order and the social order: and as demographic discontinuity it fulfills the same function between order and disorder. At the same time as along these two new axes we perceived fresh links between myths which I had already been prompted to compare for very different reasons, we discovered unexpected shortcuts which brought us back to our starting point—that is, to myths whose hero is a bird-nester. I thus established the objective existence, in mythological thought, of patterns that had had to be laboriously reconstituted when I was viewing mythological thought from the outside.

In connection with silence and noise we came up against a difficulty that related to the unequal distribution of noisemaking rituals in illiterate societies and in the Western popular tradition; the latter applies them indiscriminately to cosmological or sociological situations; the former seems to restrict them to cosmological situations. I therefore put forward the suggestion (pp. 300 ff.) that the explanation why reprehensible unions were not punished by charivari in illiterate societies was the inappropriateness of the category of noise for such humble purposes. It is as if people belonging to these societies were afraid that such a moralizing utilization of noise by humans might constitute an immoderate abuse.

There are nevertheless instances where the contrast between silence and noise is clearly indicated. Among the Warramunga of Australia, when a sick man was on his deathbed, noise was prescribed before his death, and silence afterward (Spencer and Gillen, pp. 516–17, 525–6). Correspondingly, the great Bororo rite of the visit of the souls (which is a kind of symbolic and temporary resurrection of the ancestors) begins at night in darkness and in total silence and after all fires have been extinguished. The souls are frightened of noise; but their arrival is greeted by a tremendous outburst of noise. The same thing happens when an animal that has been killed during a hunt is brought into the village, and when the shaman invokes the spirits so that they may take possession of him (Colb. 3, pp. 93, 100–102).

On the other hand, noise has its opposite: silence, which has been used not only in the popular tradition of the West, but also in a considerable number of illiterate societies to mark certain kinds of social relations. I am thinking, in particular, of a set of customs to which Frazer (1, *passim;* 2, Vol. IV, pp. 233–7) refers on two occasions, and which consisted in the imposition of a period of silence on widows or widowers, and even more frequently on newly wedded couples.

In various regions of Australia, Oceania, and Africa, young married couples had to remain silent for a period of time varying from two months to a year, according to the locality. A similar custom has been observed in America, the Caucasus, and Sardinia. The ban on speech was usually lifted on the birth of the first child. Discussing the significance of this custom, Frazer concludes: "More probably the silence of the wife till her first child is born rests on some superstitious belief touching her first pregnancy which as yet we do not understand" (2, Vol. IV, pp. 236–7).

The question at issue is not pregnancy but birth. If, as I have tried to show elsewhere (L.-S. 2 and 4, *passim*), every marriage disturbs the equilibrium of the social group, as long as the family is restricted to the husband and wife and remains childless (for although marriage is part of the great game of matrimonial alliances, it temporarily withdraws pawns from the board before restoring them in the form of descendants), it follows that the conjunction of a man and a woman is, in miniature and on a different level, an event that, symbolically speaking, bears some analogy to the much-feared union of the sky and the earth. The birth of a child, who is a potential, available spouse for a future spouse procreated in a different family, does more than merely testify to the re-entry, into the cycle of matrimonial exchanges, of a family that had been outside it as long as it remained sterile; it marks the emergence of a third term, which acts as mediator between the two poles and establishes a certain *distance* between them, with the result that the group is given a double security at once social and psychological. The child (especially the first-born) plays, between husband and wife, a part similar to that played by cooking fire between sky and earth. The nonmediatized couple is discordant, and noisemaking is appropriate to it, as is testified by the rowdy celebrations on wedding nights. So the couple itself must become silent before the contrast between silence and noise can be transcended through the birth of the first child, which re-establishes the dialogue. This explains partly at least why charivari was carried out by the age class of the young, and why the "Abbot of Youth" was entrusted with the task of collecting the dues that had to be paid in order to obtain exemption.

Several facts confirm that a marriage that is still sterile and also a first (or recent) birth are isomorphic with astronomical phenomena. The silence that precedes the first birth could correspond to the old Lapp belief that the new moon and the aurora borealis must not be annoyed by any kind of noise (Hastings, Vol. VII, p. 799a). Conversely, in various American communities, eclipses that were marked by noisemaking were also the particular concern of pregnant women and young mothers. During an eclipse the Micmac of eastern Canada made their women go outside the huts and take care of their children (W. D. and R. S. Wallis, p. 98). At Jemez, a pueblo in New Mexico, it was believed that eclipses caused abortions, so pregnant women had to remain indoors, or if they were absolutely obliged to go out, they had to put a key or an arrowhead in their girdles to prevent the moon from devouring the fetus or to keep the child from being afflicted with a harelip; according to Parsons, this belief was of Spanish origin, but during the pre-Columbian period also, the Indians were afraid that any pregnant woman rash enough to go out during an eclipse would give birth to a monster (Parsons 2, Vol. I, p. 181, n. 1). Even today, the Maya-speaking Pocomchi have the following rules which must be obeyed during an eclipse: "First your head is covered. And if you are a (pregnant) girl or even a boy who has just married and has a wife, you should go into the house. . . . It is not good to observe the moon in its struggle." The informant also comments that the time of "the new moon is not good for any kind of planting. . . . It is best at the time of the full moon. . . . When the moon begins to wane, it is not good, for it becomes wormy" (Mayers, pp. 38–9).

There are, then, occasions when illiterate societies mark certain sociological situations by stipulating silence or, conversely, establish a link between certain sociological situations and cosmological phenomena that call for noisemaking. Nor are the traditional societies of Europe indifferent to the metaphysical and cosmological projection of their social customs. It is a striking fact that the songs sung during charivari sometimes make use of metaphors similar to those employed by so-called primitives to explain eclipses. In Brittany people used to shout, "Charivari, an old cat and a young mouse!" (V.G., *l.c.*, p. 626). To quote a fact of quite a different order, it is well known that in the old days the ringing of bells was supposed to avert atmospheric disasters.

Although it did not actually give rise to charivari, the marriage of a younger son or daughter was viewed with disfavor if it preceded that of the older children. On the other hand, special celebrations marked the marriage of the youngest child. One such ceremony could be interpreted in the light of the foregoing remarks, although I am aware that its documentary basis is rather uncertain.

> In the wooded district of La Vendée and further to the north, when the youngest child is married, on the morning of the wedding, friends and relatives plant an alder tree along the route which the wedding procession is to follow on its way to church. They decorate it with a crown of foliage and natural flowers and surround it with bundles of sticks and faggots. A huge bladder filled with water is placed at the top of the tree. On her return from the religious ceremony, the young bride is asked to light the fire and the husband has to shoot at, and burst, the bladder. If he succeeds with the first or second shot, he opens the ball with his young wife: if not, the honor of the first dance goes to the best man. (V.G., *l.c.*, pp. 639–40.)

The same author also mentions that the custom occurs elsewhere in La Vendée and in Anjou and Le Poitou, but perhaps in connection with all marriages (cf. pp. 484–5).

Unlike the reprehensible unions punished by charivari, the marriage of the youngest child is eminently desirable, since it marks the close of a cycle. It is the opposite of remarriage, which removes a partner from the normal cycle of marital exchanges, instead of completing that cycle. The last marriage ensures the union of a man or woman who ought to be married, all the more so since he or she was the last member of the family after his or her brothers and sisters to remain in a state of disjunction. Now the rite described by Van Gennep links this desirable social conjunction with a conjunction between the elements, water and fire, to which one is tempted to attribute cosmological significance. Admittedly in the Vendean custom, water is "above" and fire "below." But French society is definitely patrilineal, and this is not true of the Ge, with the exception of the Sherente, whose patrilineal system is not nearly as clearly defined as the French one. This difference would explain why in the French custom the man deals with the bladder full of water which occupies a celestial position at the top of the tree where it represents the atmospheric sky, whereas the woman deals with fire—terrestrial among the Ge also—but here one degree lower and indeed chthonic, since the wood to be kindled is placed below a crown of greenery decked with natural flowers, representing the earth and its vegetable adornment:

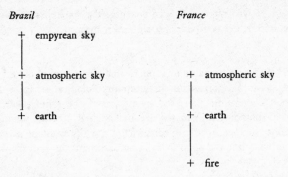

It will quite justifiably be objected that what I have just formulated is an oversimplification of relations that are much more complex. We have only to refer back to the myth of the star who married a mortal (M87–M93) to confirm that among all the Ge tribes, whether they are matrilineal or patrilineal, the woman is in the sky position, and the man in the earth position. The reversal imposed by the infrastructure occurs elsewhere: from being a benefactress of humanity and the introducer of cultivated plants, the Sherente heroine changes into a cannibalistic princess. Whereas in the other versions she was disgusted by the rotten food eaten by prehorticultural men, now it is the man, on reaching heaven, who feels revulsion at the sight of the smoked and roasted bodies. Therefore I have emphasized that among the Sherente another myth deals with the origin of cultivated plants (M108), and that in it mother's milk appears as a correlative term within an implicit pair of polar opposites; the blood from defloration is the other term, according to a Kraho myth (M89; see pp. 166–7).

Conversely, if we compare two matrilineal tribes like the Iroquois and the Mandan of North America, whose mode of life includes both agriculture and hunting, we are at first surprised to discover that, in spite of the features they have in common, their respective mythological systems link the high and the low with opposite sexual poles:

	sky	earth
Iroquois	O	Δ
Mandan	Δ	O

But the direction of the original movement that brought about the birth of humanity is correspondingly reversed in each system: for the Iroquois, it is a descent or a fall; for the Mandan, it is an ascent or an emergence. By integrating the two patterns, we can confirm that the apparent contradiction is resolved within the compass of a single formula:

$$O > \triangle$$

It would therefore be naïve to suppose that there is always and in all circumstances a simple correlation between mythological imagery and social structures—a correlation expressed by means of the same polar opposites; for instance, that dioscuric myths are the normal accompaniment of dual organizations; or that in patrilineal societies the sky must be masculine, the earth feminine, while the opposite relation automatically prevails in matrilineal societies.

To argue in this way would be to disregard a significant fact: the number of contrasts used by mythological thought varies from set to set. Certain sets merely contrast sky and earth, the high and the low. Others subdivide these unitary categories into subsets, which they use to convey contrasts no less fundamental than the previous ones. Thus the male/female polarity can belong entirely to the "high" category where the two principles coexist (or perhaps clash), in the form of the moon and the sun if these celestial bodies are endowed with different sexes, the evening star and the morning star, the atmospheric sky and the empyrean sky, etc. Or it may be that the male/female polarity is shifted completely into the "low" category: earth and water, the vegetable covering of the world and the chthonic kingdom beneath, etc. In systems such as these the contrast between high and low, which is essential in other contexts, may either cease to be relevant or function only as one transformation among others, relevance occurring in such a case at the level of the set or "bundle" of polar opposites, rather than at the level of each of them considered separately.

Often also it is not sufficiently taken into account that the mythological system is relatively autonomous when compared with the other manifestations of the life and thought of the group. Up to a point all are interdependent, but their interdependence does not result in rigid relations which impose automatic adjustments among the various levels. It is a question rather of long-term pressures, within the limits of which the mythological system can, in a sense, argue with itself and acquire dialectical depth: that is, be always commenting on its more direct modalities of insertion into reality, although the comment may take the form of a plea in favor or a denial. It is thus very rare for a mythological system, if it is at all resourceful, not eventually to exhaust all the possible codings of a single message, even if this is achieved through the apparent inversion of certain signs.

The same community—or communities that are geographically, linguistically, or culturally close to each other—sometimes invents myths that systematically tackle a given problem by envisaging, in one variant after another, the several different ways in which it may be solved. There is, for instance, the problem of mediation, from the Messiah to the Manichean opposite, by way of the androgyne, the trickster, and the Dioscuri; or the problem of dioscurism itself, which may be treated by trying out all possible formulas, one after the other: a divisible hero, identical twins, mutually hostile brothers, a grandmother and a grandson, or an old sorcerer and a young hero; or again, the problem of the duality of the sexes, by switching around the male and female principles in a succession of different relations: sky and earth, ascension and descent, activity and passivity, beneficence and maleficence, the vegetable and the animal, etc.

Have we to conclude that, this being so, no structural study is possible? For if the myths of a particular society admit of every kind of combination, the set as a whole becomes a nonredundant language; since all combinations are equally meaningful, at a pinch each one could be made to convey anything we liked. In this case mythography would be reduced to a form of lallorhea.

The difficulty is a real one, as we can see from reading certain works that purport to be studies of myths. But the fact is that most authors have failed to recognize the three methodological rules that make it possible to rediscover the indispensable redundancy of mythic language without which there can be neither grammar nor syntax. However, this redundancy must be sought in those places where it actually exists.

To begin with, the numerous versions—which may at times be so different as to seem to contradict each other—are not all situated on the same level of mythological thought. They must be put into an order that itself varies according to the particular context but is a "natural" property of the given society. Among the Pueblo three levels are easily discernible: first, myths of origin and emergence, which, in theory, are common to an entire community, although each religious brotherhood gives them a slightly different meaning in accordance with its functions and prerogatives, and although there may also exist esoteric or exoteric variants; next, migration myths which have a more legendary character and use identical themes and motifs but are skillfully adjusted so as to account for the privileges and obligations of each individual clan; finally, village tales which are part of the common heritage like the first set of myths, but in which the great logical or cosmological contrasts have been toned down and reduced to the scale of social relations. It can frequently be noticed that when we move from the first set to the second and from the second to the third, the high/low axis becomes interchangeable with other axes: first, north/south, then east/west. Similarly, among the Bororo and the Ge, the moon and sun cycle remains distinct from the cycle of the other great cultural heroes, and the system of permutations is not exactly the same for each of them.

Secondly, the formal analysis of each version allows us to fix the number of variables it uses, and its relative degree of complexity. All the versions can therefore be arranged in a logical order.

Finally, each version provides a particular image of reality: social and economic relations, technical activities, relation to the world, etc.; and ethnographic observation must decide whether this image corresponds to the facts. External criticism thus allows us, at least as a working hypothesis, to replace the relational orders we have already obtained by an absolute order, constructed according to the rule that the myths, whose subject matter expresses directly observed reality, are myths of the first rank, the others being myths of the second, third, and fourth ranks, etc., and further removed from the type that is logically the most simple (since there is no question here of historical priority) in that they have to be subjected to a greater number of transformations—unwound, as it were—to be brought back to the simple type. Thus, redundance, far from being expressed in the subject matter of the myth, as is too often believed, is revealed at the end of a reductive or critical process; the formal structure of each version provides the raw material, which is treated by means of a methodical comparison of content and context.

Having made the methodological remarks above, I can continue more confidently with the comparison of those customs that are called, respectively, primitive and traditional. From various areas of France we have evidence of identical customs intended to hasten the marriages of young men and young women who have remained celibate too long (these young people are "Baitogogos" according to the meaning I have given to the term on page 57, customs that Van Gennep finds puzzling. At the beginning of the nineteenth century, in the St. Omer district:

> If a younger daughter was married first, this was a sad day for her poor elder sister, for at some point during the celebrations, she would, willy-nilly, be seized upon, lifted up and laid on the top of the oven, so that she might be warmed up, as the saying was, since her situation seemed to indicate that she had remained insensitive to love. A similar custom existed during Napoleon III's reign, at Wavrin, in the Lille area. . . .

In the Somme district, the Pas de Calais, the north, Hainault, Walloon Brabant, and the Belgian part of the Ardennes and Luxemburg, "all that remains is a set phrase which varies from one locality to another: it is said that the elder sister must *danser sur le cul du four* or must be *portée sur la voûte* or *sur la culotte du four*. These expressions are used almost everywhere in the Pas de Calais and the north, although no one can now explain their origin." Not unreasonably, Van Gennep rejects the erotic interpretation that Saintyves put forward, and expresses his preference for a different one, based on the use of the top of the oven as a storage place for discarded objects (*l.c.* t. I, Vol. II, pp. 631–3). In several areas of England the penalty was different: the unmarried elder sister was obliged to dance barefoot (Frazer 3, Vol. II, p. 288; Westermarck, Vol. I, pp. 373–4); whereas in France, in the

Upper Forez, Isère, Ardèche, and Gard areas, the unmarried elder brother and sister were forced to eat a salad consisting of onions, nettles, and roots, or of clover and oats; this was termed "making them eat salad" or "making them eat turnip" (Van Gennep, Vol. II, pp. 630–2; Fortier-Beaulieu 1, pp. 296–7).

Instead of interpreting these customs separately, we must compare and contrast them before we can isolate their common features and hope to understand them. They all seem to depend, more or less explicitly, on the contrast between the cooked (the oven) and the raw (salad), or between nature and culture, the two contrasts being readily confused in linguistic usage. In eighteenth-century French "to dance barefoot" might have been expressed by the phrase *danser à cru* ("to dance raw"); compare *chausser des bottes à cru* "to wear boots without stockings" and *monter à cru* "to ride bareback." In English, "to sleep naked" can still be expressed colloquially as "to sleep in the raw."

On the other hand, it may be that the symbolic "roasting" of the elder,

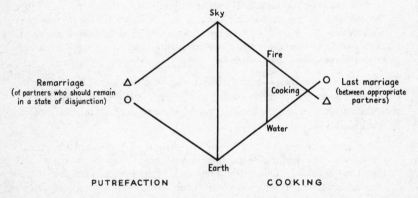

Figure 20. The cosmological and sociological connotations of the processes of putrefaction and cooking.

unmarried sister should be linked up with other beliefs and customs long prevalent in remote societies. In Cambodia—as well as in Malaysia, Siam, and various regions of Indonesia—a woman who had just given birth was laid on a bed or a raised grill under which there burned a slow fire. But, on the contrary, when a young girl had her first period she had to "go into the shade" and remain away from sunlight (Porée-Maspero, pp. 31, 39). In America, Pueblo women gave birth over a heap of hot sand, which was perhaps intended to transform the child into a "cooked person"—in contrast with natural creatures and natural or manufactured objects, which are "raw persons" (cf. Bunzel, p. 483). It was the habit of various Californian tribes to put women who had just given birth and pubescent girls into ovens, hollowed out in the ground. After being covered with mats and hot stones, they were conscientiously "cooked"; the Yurok, incidentally, used the same expression "cooking the pains" to refer to all curative rites (Elmendorf, p. 154). This practice was accompanied by others, even more widespread: for instance, pubescent girls were required to use combs and head-scratchers, so as to avoid touching their hair or their faces with their hands, as well as drinking tubes and tongs with which to pick up their food.

This rapid summary of customs, which ought to be systematically noted down and classified, does at least allow us to suggest a tentative definition: the individuals who are "cooked" are those deeply involved in a physiological process: the newborn child, the woman who has just given birth, or the pubescent girl. The conjunction of a member of the social group with nature must be mediatized through the intervention of cooking fire, whose normal function is to mediatize the conjunction of the raw product and the human consumer, and whose operation thus has the effect of making sure that a natural creature is at one and the same time *cooked and socialized*:

> Unlike the deer, the Tarahumara does not eat the grass, but he interposes between the grass and his animal hunger a complicated cultural cycle involving the care and the use of domestic animals. . . . Nor like the coyote does the Tarahumara avail himself of meat torn from a scarcely dead animal and eaten raw. The Tarahumara interposes between his meat and his hunger a cultural system of cooking. (Zingg, p. 82.)

This perceptive analysis, which is based on the observation of a Mexican tribe, could be applied to many other communities, as is suggested by the fact that almost identical conceptions expressed in very similar language are to be found in a Philippino tribe:

> The Hanunoo regard as a "real" food only that which is prepared for human consumption by cooking. Hence, ripe bananas which must be eaten raw are considered as "snack" foods. Real foods such as pre-ripe bananas, root crops, cereals, cucumbers, tomatoes and onions are never eaten raw. A *meal* must include cooked food. In fact, meals are usually enumerated by the term: pag'apuy, "fire making." (Conklin, p. 185.)

We must add the mediatory function of utensils to that of symbolic cooking: the head-scratcher, the drinking tube, and the fork are intermediaries between the subject and his body, which is now "naturalized," or between the subject and the physical world. Although normally unnecessary, their use becomes indispensable when the potential charge of the two poles, or of one of them, has increased to such an extent that insulators must be inserted to prevent the possibility of a short circuit. This function is also performed by cooking, in its peculiar way: when food is cooked, meat does not need to be directly exposed to the sun. Exposure to the sun is generally avoided by women who have just given birth and by pubescent girls.

Among the Pueblo Indians an individual who had been struck by lightning —that is, who had entered into conjunction with celestial fire—was treated by means of raw food. It often happens, too, that conjunction is manifested in the form of a saturation of the individual by himself: he is too full of humors that threaten him with decay, hence such necessary practices as fasting, scarification, and the swallowing of emetics—at puberty or on the birth of the first child. In the Carib speech of the West Indies the phrase that was used to refer to a first-born child meant literally "my fasting-matter." Even today the Carib Negroes of British Honduras forbid pregnant women to bathe in the sea in case they should provoke a storm. The old Carib communities of the West Indies referred to the periods of retreats and fasting prescribed at puberty or at the birth of a first child, and also on the loss of a close relative or the murder of an enemy, as *iuenemali* "withdrawal from exposure": the exposure results from an excess of body heat, which makes the subject too directly and intensely "vulnerable" to others and to the external world (Taylor, pp. 343-9). In this sense the problem is how to prevent over-communication.

It will be objected that traditional customs are less logical than primitive customs. The latter always operate along the same lines: the "cooking" of women and adolescent girls corresponds to the need for their relations with themselves and the world to be mediatized by the use of "hypercultural" utensils; whereas in Europe the placing of the unmarried elder sister on the stove, on the one hand, and the removal of the shoes and the feeding with raw food, on the other, should, according to my interpretation, be given opposite meanings.

It should be noted, in the first place, that the unmarried elder sister is in a symmetrical but reverse situation to the one in which the young mother or pubescent girl finds herself. The unmarried sister calls for mediatization because of the deficiency from which she is suffering, and not because of a superfluity of which she might be the temporary source. To repeat a formula I have already used for the solution of a difficulty of the same kind (cf. p. 293), the unmarried elder sister belongs to "the world of rottenness," whereas the young mother and pubescent girl belong to the "burned world." In the case of the first, cooking and even raw food supply something that was lacking: they move her one or two places up the scale, as it were. Cooking and raw food have the opposite effect on the others: by regulating or dulling their ardor, they correct its excesses.

The explanation above seems to me to be acceptable, if incomplete: it has some bearing on the subject matter but fails to deal with the form. Now, in this last respect, the rites appear as a "paralanguage" which can be employed in two ways. Either simultaneously or alternatively, rites provide man with the means either of modifying a practical situation or of characterizing and describing it. What usually happens is that the two functions overlap or translate two complementary aspects of the same process. But where the power of magical thought is tending to weaken, and when the rites take on a vestigial character, only the second function survives, and the first is lost. To come back to the charivari, it would be rash to suppose that even deep in the folk subconscious, noisemaking fulfilled the same function as that ascribed to it by the native at the time of an eclipse—that is, to scare away a devouring monster, whether that monster is carrying out its ravages on a social or a cosmological level. In French villages the din of the charivari perhaps did not *serve a practical purpose* (except that it had the secondary effect of humiliating the guilty person), but it is clear that it still had a *meaning*. It signified the breaking of a chain, the emergence of a social discontinuity which could not be really corrected by the compensatory continuity of noise, since the latter operates on a different level and belongs to a different code; but which it indicates objectively and which it seems at least to be able, metaphorically, to counterbalance.

The same goes for the customs I have just been discussing. The putting onto the oven, like the roasting of women in childbirth or pubescent girls, may be a symbolic gesture intended to mediatize a person who, still unmarried, has remained imprisoned in nature and rawness, and perhaps even destined to decay. But the barefoot dance and the giving of the salad do less to change this situation than to signify it, in relation to the "low" and to the earth. In the same way, the symbolical demediatization of the bride, which is an anticipation of the wedding night, consists of stealing her garter which is connected with the "middle" world.

We can derive a certain comfort—or, on the other hand, become convinced of the futility of so much effort—from the fact that these interpretations, which have been so laboriously deduced from remote and initially incomprehensible myths, link up with universal analogies which are immediately perceptible in our use of words, whatever our native language happens to be. I pointed out a little earlier that in French and no doubt in other languages, too, the implicit equivalence of the two contrasts—nature/culture, raw/cooked—was openly expressed in the figurative use of the word *cru* to denote, between the human body and material objects, the absence of the normal cultural intermediary, such as a saddle, stockings, clothes, etc. We also say, when speaking of those people whose behavior would formerly have provoked charivari because it deflects marriage toward ends other than those desired within the given culture, that they are *corrompus* "corrupt, tainted." When we use the term in this way, we rarely think of the literal meaning. The physical sense may, however, be more conscious in the mind of someone who silently insults an old maid by calling her *sexe moisi* "moldy vagina." Be that as it may, we are careful not to reverse the epithets and so re-establish, within the category of decay, the fundamental contrast between rapid destruction and slow destruction by means of which the myths distinguish between the categories of the rotten and the burned:

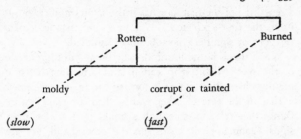

When the myths that were the starting point of this study describe a hero covered with bird droppings and vermin or changed into stinking carrion, they are not embroidering "crudely" on metaphors that are still used today even in our societies, as is indicated by this adverb which suggested itself spontaneously. In fact, the opposite is true: thanks to the myths, we discover that metaphors are based on an intuitive sense of the logical relations between one realm and other realms; metaphor reintegrates the first realm with the totality of the others, in spite of the fact that reflective thought struggles to separate them. Metaphor, far from being a decoration that is added to language, purifies it and restores it to its original nature, through momentarily obliterating one of the innumerable synecdoches that make up speech.

It follows, therefore, that when myths and rites display a predilection for hyperbole, they are not making an artificial use of rhetoric. Emphatic statement is natural to them; it is a direct expression of their properties; it is the visible shadow of a hidden logical structure. Mythic thought, when it inserts the pattern of human relations into a cosmological context which seems to extend beyond them on all sides but which as we have proved, is, when taken in its entirety, isomorphic with them and in its way able both to include them and to imitate them, is echoing a linguistic process the importance of which does not need to be stressed.

I am thinking, for instance, of reduplication, which is common to all languages, although present to a greater or lesser degree. It is more often noticeable in childish language (Jakobson, pp. 541–2); this is certainly not because of any illusory primitive character, but because, since it is a fundamental process, it is one that the child cannot avoid once he begins speaking. Moreover, no other process makes a greater contribution to the establishment of linguistic behavior.

Even at the babbling stage the phoneme group /pa/ can be heard. But the difference between /pa/ and /papa/ does not reside simply in reduplication: /pa/ is a noise, /papa/ is a word. The reduplication indicates intent on the part of the speaker; it endows the second syllable with a function different from that which would have been performed by the first separately, or in the form of a potentially limitless series of identical sounds /papapapapa/ produced by mere babbling. Therefore the second /pa/ is not a repetition of the first, nor has it the same signification. It is a sign that, like itself, the first /pa/ too was a sign, and that as a pair they fall into the category of signifiers, not of things signified.

When this is borne in mind, it becomes still more obvious that duplication of the root syllable, triplication, and sometimes even quadruplication are mainly observable in words formed on an onomatopoeic basis. The reason is that in the case of other words, their arbitrary nature in relation to the things they refer to is enough to make it clear that they are to be taken as signs. Onomatopoeic terms, on the other hand, are always ambiguous in nature because, being founded on a resemblance, they do not clearly indicate whether the speaker, in pronouncing them, is trying to reproduce a noise or to express a meaning. As a result of reduplication the second element ostentatiously emphasizes the meaningful intention, which might have been doubtful in the case of the single element had it remained unaccompanied. /Pan!/ "bang!" is an exclamation that causes a break in the sense; but in the expression *je vais te faire panpan* "I'll give you a spanking," when addressed to a child, *panpan* is a word indicating a series of actions of which none perhaps will be accompanied by the threatened noise. Here again, therefore, the second term acts as a sign to show that the first one, too, was a sign and not a gratuitous or merely imitative noise. Other forms of emphatic statement can be interpreted in the same way. To give only one example, caricature consists in the emphatic exploitation of a visual feature, a process that is prompted not by the desire to reduplicate the model, but by the intention of making some function or aspect meaningful.

It can thus be understood how mistaken those mythologists were who supposed that the natural phenomena which figure so largely in myths for this reason constituted the essential part of what myths are trying to explain. This mistake forms a simple counterpart to another, committed by those mythologists who, in reacting against their predecessors (the latter were themselves reacting against the other type of interpretation), tried to reduce the meaning of myths to a moralizing comment on the situation of mankind and made them into an explanation of love and death or pleasure and suffering, instead of an account of the phases of the moon and seasonal changes. In both cases there was a failure to grasp the distinctive character of myths, which is precisely emphatic statement, resulting from the multiplication of one level by another or several others, and which, as in language, serves to indicate areas of meaning.[25]

The layered structure of myth to which I drew attention in a previous work (L.-S. 5, chap. 11) allows us to look upon myth as a matrix of meanings which are arranged in lines or columns, but in which each level always refers to some other level, whichever way the myth is read. Similarly, each matrix

[25] TRANSLATORS' NOTE: The words of the original text are: [*le caractère distinctif*] . . . *a pour fonction de signifier la signification* (signify signification).

of meanings refers to another matrix, each myth to other myths. And if it is now asked to what final meaning these mutually significative meanings are referring—since in the last resort and in their totality they must refer to something—the only reply to emerge from this study is that myths signify the mind that evolves them by making use of the world of which it is itself a part. Thus there is simultaneous production of myths themselves, by the mind that generates them and, by the myths, of an image of the world which is already inherent in the structure of the mind.

By taking its raw material from nature, mythic thought proceeds in the same way as language, which chooses phonemes from among the natural sounds of which a practically unlimited range is to be found in childish babbling. For, as in the case of language, the empirical material is too abundant to be all accepted indiscriminately or to be all used on the same level. Here again, it must be accepted as a fact that the material is the instrument of meaning, not its object. For it to play this part, it must be whittled down. Only a few of its elements are retained—those suitable for the expression of contrasts or forming pairs of opposites.

But, as with language, the discarded elements are not thereby eliminated. They are always present in latent fashion, behind those that have been singled out, and are always ready to answer in the name of the whole row behind them and, on occasion, to bring forward one or another of the concealed elements. In other words, the virtually unlimited totality of the elements always remains available. The internal order of each row may be modified, and their numbers may vary through fusion or fission on the part of some of them. All this is possible, on two conditions: any internal change affecting the organization of one row is accompanied by a change of the same kind in the others; and the principle of arrangement in rows continues to be respected. It is vitally necessary that the terms separated by the shortest intervals should be grouped together and reduced to the state of reciprocal variants, so that each series of rows can have room in which to operate and to maintain an adequate distance between itself and the other rows.

The multiplicity of levels appears then as the price that mythic thought has to pay in order to move from the continuous to the discrete. It has to simplify and organize the diversity of empirical experience in accordance with the principle that no factor of diversity can be allowed to operate for its own purposes in the collective undertaking of signification, but only as a habitual or occasional substitute for the other elements included in the same set. Mythic thought only accepts nature on condition that it is able to reproduce it. By so doing, it limits itself to the choice of those formal properties by which nature can signify itself and which consequently are appropriate for metaphor. That is why it is pointless to try to discover in myths certain semantic levels that are thought to be more important than others. Either the myths treated in this way will be reduced to platitudes, or the level we imagine we have singled out will elude our grasp and auto-matically resume its place in a system involving a multiplicity of levels. Then, and then only, can the part be fitted into a figurative interpretation, through the operation of a whole capable of fulfilling this function, because a tacit synecdoche has in the first place isolated the part that the more eloquent metaphors of the myth now refer back to the whole for significance.

June 1962–July 1963

BESTIARY

1. Harpy Eagle

2. Egret

3. Tortoise

4. Howler Monkey

5. Capuchin Monkey

6. Deer

7. Spider Monkey

8. Coati

9. White-Lipped Peccary

10. Collared Peccary

11. Woodpecker

12. Agouti

13. Capybara

14. Toucan

15. Anteater

16. Macaw

17. Jacu

18. Inhambu

19. Jaguar

20. Irara

21. Mutum

22. Skunk

23. Jaó

24. Parrot

25. Sloth

26. Paca

27. Piranha

28. Prea

29. Puma

30. Rat

31. Water Rat

32. Seriema

33. Opossum

34. Tapir

35. Nine-Banded
Armadillo

36. Hairy
Armadillo

37. White-Bristled
Armadillo

38. Giant
Armadillo

39. King Vulture

40. Rhea

Bibliography

ABBREVIATIONS:

ARBAE   *Annual Report of the Bureau of American Ethnology*
BBAE   *Bulletin of the Bureau of American Ethnology*
Colb.   COLBACCHINI, A.
EB   ALBISETTI, C., and VENTURELLI, A. J. *Enciclopédia Boróro,* Vol. I. Campo Grande, 1962.
HSAI   *Handbook of South American Indians*
JAFL   *Journal of American Folklore*
K. G.   KOCH-GRÜNBERG, TH.
L.-S.   LÉVI-STRAUSS, C.
Nim.   NIMUENDAJU, C.
RIHGB   *Rivista do Instituto Historico Geographico Brasileiro*
RMDLP   *Revista del Museo de la Plata*
RMP   *Revista do Museu Paulista*
UCPAAE   *University of California Publications in American Archaeology and Ethnology*

ABBEVILLE, CLAUDE D'. *Histoire de la mission des pères Capucins en l'isle de Maragnan et terres circonvoisines.* Paris, 1614.
ABREU, J. CAPISTRANO DE. *Rã-txa hu-ni-ku-i. A Lingua dos Caxinauas.* Rio de Janeiro, 1914.
AHLBRINCK, W. "Encyclopaedie der Karaïben," *Verhandelingen der Koninklijke Akademie van Wetenschappen te Amsterdam, afdeeline Letterkunde Nieuwe Reeks Deel 27, 1,* 1931. French translation by DOUDE VAN HERWIJNEN, mimeographed, Paris, 1956.
ALBISETTI, C. "Contribuições missionarias," *Publicações da Sociedade brasileira de antropologia e etnologia,* Nos. 2–3. Rio de Janeiro, 1948. (See also COLBACCHINI and ALBISETTI, and EB.)
AMORIM, A. B. DE. "Lendas em Nheêngatu e em Portuguez," *RIHGB* Tomo 100, Vol. 154 (2° de 1926). Rio de Janeiro, 1928.
ANDERSEN, J. C. *Myths and Legends of the Polynesians.* London, 1928.
AUGUSTINOS. "Relacion de idolatria en Huamachuco por los primeros—," *Informaciones acerca de la Religion y Gobierno de los Incas* (Colección de libros y documentos referentes a la Historia del Peru, Tomo 11). Lima, 1918.
BALDUS, H. (1) *Ensaios de Etnologia Brasileira.* São Paulo, 1937.
———. (2) *Lendas dos Indios do Brasil.* São Paulo, 1946.

————. (3) "Lendas dos indios Tereno," *RMP*, n.s., Vol. 4, 1950.

————. (4) (ed.) *Die Jaguarzwillinge. Mythen und Heilbringersgeschichten Ursprungs-sagen und Märchen brasilianisches Indianer*. Kassel, 1958.

BANNER, H. (1) "Mitos dos indios Kayapo," *Revista de Antropologia*, Vol. 5, No. 1. São Paulo, 1957.

————. (2) "O Indio Kayapo em seu acampamento." *Boletim do Museu Paraense Emilio Goeldi*, n.s., No. 13. Belém, 1961.

BARBEAU, M. "Huron-Wyandot Traditional Narratives," *National Museum of Canada*, *Bull. No. 165, Anthropol. Series No. 47*. Ottawa, 1960.

BASTIDE, R. "La Nature humaine: le point de vue du sociologue et de l'ethnologue," *La Nature humaine, actes due XIe Congrès des Sociétés de Philosophie de langue française* (Montpellier, September 4-6, 1961), Paris, 1961.

BATES, H. W. *The Naturalist on the River Amazon*. London, 1892.

BAUDELAIRE, CHARLES. "Richard Wagner et *Tannhäuser* à Paris," *Ouvres Complètes*. Pléiade edition, Paris, 1961.

BEAGLEHOLE, E. and P. "Ethnology of Puka-Puka," *B. P. Bishop Museum, Bull. 150*. Honolulu, 1938.

BECHER, H. "Algumas notas sôbre a religião et a mitologia dos Surára," *RMP*, n.s., Vol. 11. São Paulo, 1959.

BECKWITH, M. W. "Mandan-Hidatsa Myths and Ceremonies," *Memoirs of the American Folk-Lore Society*, Vol. 32. New York, 1938.

BENVENISTE, E. "Communication animale et langage humain," *Diogène*, I. Paris, 1952.

BOAS, F. (1) "The Central Eskimo," *6th ARBAE* (1884-1885). Washington, D.C., 1888.

————. (2) "Tsimshian Mythology," *31st ARBAE* (1909-1910). Washington, D.C., 1916.

BORBA, T. M. *Actualidade Indigena*. Coritiba, 1908.

BOTELHO DE MAGALHÃES, A. *Impressões da Commissão Rondon*. Rio de Janeiro, s.d. (1921).

BOULEZ, P. "Serie," *Encyclopédie de la musique*, 3 vols. Paris, 1958-1961.

BRETT, W. H. *Legends and Myths of the Aboriginal Indians of British Guiana*. London s.d. (1880).

BUNZEL, R. L. "Introduction to Zuñi Ceremonialism," *47th ARBAE* (1929-1930). Washington, D.C., 1932.

BUTT, A. "Réalité et idéal dans la pratique chamanique," *L'Homme. Revue française d'anthropologie*, Vol. 2, No. 3, 1962.

CADOGAN, L. "Ayvu Rapita. Textos míticos de los Mbyá-Guarani del Guairá," *Antropologia*, No. 5, Boletim no. 227. *Universidade de São Paulo*, 1959.

CAMPANA, D. DEL. "Contributo all' Etnografia dei Matacco," *Archivio per l'Antropologia e la Etnologia*, Vol. 43, fasc. 1-2. Firenze, 1913.

CARDUS, J. *Las misiones Franciscanas entre los infieles de Bolivia*. Barcelona, 1886.

CARTER, T. D. "The Opossum—Our only Pouched Mammal," *Natural History*, Vol. 56, No. 4. New York, 1957.

CASPAR, F. (1) "Some Sex Beliefs and Practices of the Tupari Indians (Western Brazil)," *RMP*, n.s., Vol. 7. São Paulo, 1953.

————. (2) "Puberty Rites among the Tupari Indians," *RMP*, n.s., Vol. 10. São Paulo, 1956-1958.

CAVALCANTI, A. *The Brasilian Language and its Agglutination*. Rio de Janeiro, 1883.

CHAPMAN, J. W. "Ten'a Texts and Tales from Anvik, Alaska," *Publication of the American Ethnological Society*, Vol. 6. Leyden, 1941.

CHERMONT DE MIRANDA, V. DE. "Estudos sobre o Nheêngatú," *Anais da Biblioteca Nacional*, Vol. 54 (1492). Rio de Janeiro, 1944.

CHRISTIAN, F. W. *The Caroline Islands*. London, 1899.

COLBACCHINI, A. (1) *A Tribu dos Bororos*. Rio de Janeiro, 1919.

————. (2) *I Bororos Orientali "Orarimugudoge" del Matto Grosso, Brasile* (Contributi Scientifici delle Missioni Salesiane del Venerabile Don Bosco, 1). Torino, s.d. [1925].

COLBACCHINI, A., and ALBISETTI, C. *Os Bororos Orientais.* São Paulo-Rio de Janeiro, 1942.

COLL, P. C. VAN. "Contes et légendes des Indiens de Surinam," *Anthropos,* Vols. 2 and 3, 1907–1908.

CONKLIN, H. C. "The Relation of Hanunóo Culture to the Plant World." Doctoral Dissertation, Yale University 1954 (microfilm).

CORNYN, J. H. "Ixcit Cheel," *The Maya Society Quarterly,* Vol. I, No. 2. Baltimore, 1932.

CORY, H. "Jando, II," *Journal of the Royal Anthropological Institute,* Vol. 78, Nos. 1–2 (1948). London, 1951.

COUDREAU, H. *Voyage au Tapajoz, 1895–1896.* Paris, 1897.

COUTINHO DE OLIVEIRA, J. *Lendas Amazonicas.* Pará, 1916.

COUTO DE MAGALHÃES, J. V. *O Selvagem.* Rio de Janeiro, 1876.

CREVAUX, J. *Voyages dans l'Amérique du Sud.* Paris, 1883.

CROCKER, W. H. "The Canela since Nimuendaju: A Preliminary Report on Cultural Change," *Anthropological Quarterly,* Vol. 34, No. 2. Washington, D.C., 1961.

CRUZ, M. (1) "Dos nomes entre os Bororos," *RIHGB,* Vol. 175 (1940). Rio de Janeiro, 1941.

————. (2) "Mitologia borora," *Revista do Arquivo Municipal,* Vol. 91. São Paulo, 1943.

DAVILA, F. "Relación de idolatrias en Huarochiri," *Informaciones acerca de la Religión y Gobierno de los Incas* (Colección de Libros y documentos referentes a la Historia del Peru, Tomo 11). Lima, 1918.

DIETERLEN, G. and CALAME-GRIAULE, G. "L'Alimentation dogon," *Cahiers d'Etudes africaines,* No. 3. Paris, 1960.

DIETSCHY, H. "Das Häuptingswesen bei den Karaja," *Mitteilungen aus dem Museum Für Völkerkunde in Hamburg,* XXV. Hamburg, 1959.

DU BOIS, C. "Wintu Ethnography," *UCPAAE,* Vol. 36, No. 1. Berkeley, 1935.

DUMÉZIL, G. "Déesses latines et mythes védiques," *Collection Latomus,* Vol. XXV. Brussels, 1956.

DURKHEIM, E. *Les Formes élémentaires de la vie religieuse.* 2ᵉ edition. Paris, 1925.

EHRENREICH, P. "Beiträge zur Völkerkunde Brasiliens," *Veröffentlichungen aus dem Kgl. Museum für Vülkerkunde,* t. II. Berlin, 1891. (Portuguese translation by E. SCHADEN in *RMP,* n.s. Vol. 2, 1948.)

ELMENDORF, W. W. "The Structure of Twana Culture," *Research Studies, Monographic Supplement No. 2.* Washington State University, Pullman, 1960.

FARABEE, W. C. (1) "The Central Arawak," *Anthropological Publications of the University Museum* 9. Philadelphia, 1918.

————. (2) "Indian Tribes of Eastern Peru," *Papers of the Peabody Museum, Harvard University,* Vol. 10. Cambridge, Mass., 1922.

————. (3) "The Central Caribs," *The University of Pennsylvania, The University Museum, Anthropological Publications,* Vol. 10. Philadelphia, 1924.

FENTON, W. N. "The Iroquois Eagle Dance," *BBAE 156.* Washington, D.C., 1953.

FIRTH, R. *We, The Tikopia.* New York-Chicago, 1936.

FORTIER-BEAULIEU, P. (1) *Mariages et noces campagnardes.* Paris, 1937.

————. (2) "Enquête sur le charivari." Manuscript in the Musée National des Arts et Traditions Populaires, Paris.

FRACHTENBERG, L. J. "Alsea Texts and Myths," *BBAE 67.* Washington, D.C., 1920.

FRANKLIN, A. *La Vie privée d'autrefois. Les Repas.* Paris, 1889.

FRAZER, J. G. (1) "The Silent Widow," *Transactions of the Third International Congress for the History of Religions.* Oxford, 1908.

————. (2) *Totemism and Exogamy.* 4 vols. London, 1910.

———. (3) *Folk-Lore in the Old Testament.* 4 vols. London, 1919.

FREISE, F. W. "Plantas Medicinaes Brasileiras," *Boletim de Agricultura*, Vol. 34. São Paulo, 1933.

FRIGOUT, A. Personal communication (December, 1962).

FRIKEL, P. (1) "Kamani. Costumes e Preceitos dos Indios Kachúyana a respeito do curare," *RMP*, n.s., Vol. 7. São Paulo, 1953.

———. (2) "Agricultura dos Indios Munduruku," *Boletim do Museu Paraense Emilio Goeldi*, n.s., *Antropologia*, No. 4. Belem, 1959.

GAMELON, S. "Contribution à l'étude des Indiens Gê: les Kayapo du Nord." Manuscript.

GAYTON, A. H., and NEWMAN, S. S. "Yokuts and Western Mono Myths," *Anthropological Records*, 5, 1. Berkeley, 1940.

GENNEP, A. VAN. *Manuel de Folklore français contemporain.* 9 vols. Paris, 1946–1958.

GILLIN, J. "The Barama River Caribs of British Guiana," *Papers of the Peabody Museum, Harvard University*, Vol. 14, No. 2. Cambridge, Mass., 1936.

GILMORE, R. M. "Fauna and Ethnozoology of South America," HSAI, Vol. 6, *BBAE 143.* Washington, D.C. 1950.

GIMBUTAS, M. "Ancient Symbolism in Lithuanian Folk Art," *Memoirs of the American Folklore Society*, Vol. 49. New York, 1958.

GOEJE, C. H. DE. "Philosophy, Initiation, and Myths of the Indian of Guiana and Adjacent Countries," *Internationales Archiv für Ethnographie*, Vol. 44. Leiden, 1943.

GUALLART, J. M. "Mitos y leyendas de los Aguarunas del alto Marañon," *Peru Indigena*, Vol. 7, Nos. 16–17. Lima, 1958.

GUBERNATIS, A. DE. *Zoological Mythology or the Legends of Animals.* 2 vols. London, 1872.

GUMILLA, J. *Historia natural . . . del Rio Orinoco.* 2 vols. Barcelona, 1791.

GUSINDE, M. (1) *Die Feuerland-Indianer.* 3 vols. Mödling bei Wien, 1931–1939.

———. (2) Compte-rendu de; Murphy, R. F., "Mundurucu Religion," *Anthropos*, Vol. 55, fasc. 1–2, 1960.

HAILE, Father B., and WHEELWRIGHT, M. C. *Emergence Myth according to the Hanelthnayhe Upward-Reaching Rite*, Navajo Religion Series, Vol. 3. Sante Fe, New Mexico, 1949.

HAMILTON, W. J., JR. "Success Story of the Opossum," *Natural History*, Vol. 72, No. 2. New York, 1962.

HANDY, E. S. CRAIGHILL. "The Native Culture in the Marquesas," *B. P. Bishop Museum, Bull.* 9. Honolulu, 1923.

HANDY, E. S. CRAIGHILL, and PUKUI, M. KAWENA. "The Polynesian Family System in Ka-'u, Hawai'i," *The Polynesian Society.* Wellington, New Zealand, 1958.

HARRINGTON, J. P. "The Ethnogeography of the Tewa Indians," *29th ARBAE* (1907–1908). Washington, D.C., 1916.

HARTMANN, C. "Traditional Belief concerning the Generation of the Opossum," *JAFL*, Vol. 34, No. 133, 1921.

HARTT, C. F. *Os Mitos Amazônicos da Tartaruga.* Translation and notes by L. DA CAMARA CASCUDO. Recife, 1952.

HASTINGS, J. (ed.). *Encyclopaedia of Religion and Ethics.* 13 vols. New York, 1928.

HENRY, J. *Jungle People. A Kaingáng tribe of the Highlands of Brazil.* New York, 1941.

HISSINK, K., and HAHN, A. *Die Tacana*, I *Erzählungsgut.* Stuttgart, 1961.

HOEHNE, F. C. *Botanica e agricultura no Brasil (seculo 16).* São Paulo, 1937.

HOFFMANN-KRAYER, E. *Handwörterbuch des deutschen Aberglaubens*, Vol. 9. Berlin, 1941.

HOHENTHAL, W. "Notes on the Shucurú Indians of . . . Pernambuco, Brazil," *RMP*, n.s., Vol. 8. São Paulo, 1954.

HOLMER, N. M., and WASSEN, H. *Muu-Igala or the Ways of Muu. A Medicine Song from the Cunas of Panama.* Göteborg, 1947.

HURAULT, J. "Les Indiens de la Guyane française," *Nieuwe West-Indische Gids 42.* The Hague, 1963.

IHERING, R. VON. *Dicionário dos animais do Brasil.* São Paulo, 1940. (Some of my quotations are taken from the first version of this work, which appeared under the same title in the *Boletim de Agricultura,* São Paulo, 1931–1938.)

IM THURN, E. F. *Among the Indians of Guiana.* London, 1883.

JAKOBSON, R. (1) *Selected Writings. I—Phonological Studies.* 'S-Gravenhage, 1962.

——. (2) *Essais de Linguistique générale.* Paris, 1963.

KARSTEN, R. (1) "Mitos de los indios Jibaros (Shuara) del Oriente del Ecuador," *Boletin de la Sociedad ecuatoriana de estudios historicos americanos,* No. 6. Quito, 1919.

——. (2) "The Head-Hunters of Western Amazonas," *Societas Scientiarum Fennica. Commentationes Humanarum Litterarum,* t. 7, No. 1. Helsingfors, 1935.

KEMPF, F. V. "Estudo sôbre a Mitologia dos Indios Mundurucus," *Arquivos do Museu Paranaense,* Vol. 4. Curitiba, 1944–1945.

KOCH-GRÜNBERG, T. (o) *Anfänge der Kunst in Urwald.* Berlin, 1905.

——. (1) *Von Roroima zum Orinoco. Zweites Band. Mythen und Legenden der Taulipang und Arekuna Indianer.* Berlin, 1916.

——. (2) *Zwei Jahre bei den Indianern Nordwest-Brasiliens,* n. ed. Stuttgart, 1921.

——. (3) *Indianermärchen aus Südamerika.* Jena, 1921.

KOZAK, V. "Ritual of a Bororo Funeral," *Natural History,* Vol. 72, No. 1. New York, 1963.

KRAUSE, F. *In den Wildnissen Brasiliens.* Leipzig, 1911.

KRUSE, A. (1) "Munducurú Moieties," *Primitive Man,* Vol. 8, 1934.

——. (2) "Erzählungen der Tapajoz-Mundurukú," *Anthropos,* tomes 41–44, 1946–1949.

——. (3) "Karusakaybë, der Vater der Mundurukú," *Anthropos,* tomes 46 and 47, 1951 and 1952.

——. (4) "Pura, das Höchste Wesen der Arikéna," *Anthropos,* Vol. 50, fasc. 1–3, 1955.

LEHMANN-NITSCHE, R. (1) "La Astronomia de Los Matacos," *RMDLP,* t. 27 (3ª serie t. 3). Buenos Aires, 1923.

——. (2) "La Astronomia de los Vilelas," *RMDLP,* t. 28 (3ª serie, t. 4). Buenos Aires, 1924–1925.

——. (3) "La Constelación de la Osa Mayor," *RMDLP,* tomo 28 (3ª serie, t. 4). Buenos Aires, 1924–1925.

——. (4) "La Astronomia de los Tobas," *RMDLP,* t. 27 (3ª serie, t. 3). Buenos Aires, 1923.

——. (5) "La Astronomia de los Tobas (segunda parte)," *RMDLP,* t. 28 (3ª serie, t. 4). Buenos Aires, 1924–1925.

LÉRI, JEAN DE. *Histoire d'un voyage faict en la terre du Brésil.* Gaffare, 2 vols. Paris, 1880.

LÉVI-STRAUSS, CLAUDE. (o) "Contribution à l'étude de l'organisation sociale des Indiens Bororo," *Journal de la Société des Américanistes,* n.s., tome XVIII, fasc. 2. Paris, 1936.

——. (1) "Tribes of the right bank of the Guaporé River," HSAI, *BBAE 143.* 7 vols. Washington, D.C., 1946–1959.

——. (2) *Les Structures élémentaires de la parenté.* Paris, 1949.

——. (3) *Tristes Tropiques.* Paris, 1955.

——. (4) "The Family," *Man, Culture and Society* (ed. H. L. SHAPIRO). New York, 1956.

——. (5) *Anthropologie structurale.* Paris, 1958.

――――. (6) "La Geste d'Asdiwal," *École Pratique des Hautes Études, Section des Sciences religieuses*, annual (1958–1959). Paris, 1958.

――――. (7) *Leçon Inaugurale*. Inaugural lecture delivered on Tuesday, January 5, 1960 (Collège de France, Chair of Social Anthropology). Paris, 1960.

――――. (8) *Le Totémisme aujourd'hui*. Paris, 1962.

――――. (9) *La Pensée sauvage*. Paris, 1962.

LIMBER, D. NELSON. "The Pleiades," *Scientific American*, Vol. 207, No. 5, 1962.

LIPKIND, W. (1) "Caraja Cosmography," *JAFL*, Vol. 53, 1940.

――――. (2) "The Caraja," HSAI, *BBAE 143*, 7 vols. Washington, D.C., 1946–1959.

LUKESCH, A. (1) "Uber das Sterben bei den nördlichen Kayapó-Indianern," *Anthropos*, Vol. 51, fasc. 5–6, 1956.

――――. (2) "Bepkororôti, eine mythologishegestalt der Gorotire-Indianer," *Wiener Völkerkundliche Mitteilungen*, Vol. 7, jahrgang Band 2, No. 1–4. Wien, 1959.

MACIEL, M. *Elementos de Zoologia geral e descriptiva de accordo com a fauna brasileira*. Rio de Janeiro, Paris, 1923.

MAGALHÁES, A. A. BOTELHO DE. *Impressõs da Commissão Rondon*. 5th ed., São Paulo, 1942.

MAGALHÁES, B. DE. "Vocabulario da lingua dos Bororos-Coroados do Estado de Mato-Grosso," *RIHGB*, t. 83 (1918). Rio de Janeiro, 1919.

MAHR, A. C. "Delaware Terms for Plants and Animals in the Eastern Ohio Country: A Study in Semantics," *Anthropological Linguistics*, Vol. 4, No. 5. Bloomington, 1962.

MAYERS, M. *Pocomchi Texts*. University of Oklahoma, Norman, 1958.

MÉTRAUX, A. (1) *La Religion des Tupinamba*. Paris, 1928.

――――. (2) "Mitos y cuentos de los Indios Çhiriguano," *RMDLP*, t. 23. Buenos Aires, 1932.

――――. (3) "Myths and Tales of the Matako Indians," *Ethnological Studies* 9. Göteborg, 1939.

――――. (4) "A Myth of the Chamacoco Indians and its Social Significance," *JAFL*, Vol. 56, 1943.

――――. (5) "Myths of the Toba and Pilagá Indians of the Gran Chaco," *Memoirs of the American Folklore Society*, Vol. 40. Philadelphia, 1946.

――――. (6) "The Botocudo," HSAI, *BBAE 143*, 7 vols. Washington, D.C., 1946–1959.

――――. (7) "Ensayos de Mitologia comparada Sudamericana," *America Indigena*, Vol. 8, No. 1. Mexico, 1948.

――――. (8) "Mythes et Contes des Indiens Cayapo (Groupe Kuben-Kran-Kegn)," *RMP*, n.s., Vol. 12. São Paulo, 1960.

MONTOYA, A. RUIZ DE. *Arte vocabulario, tesoro y catacismo de la lengua Guarani (1640)*. Leipzig, 1876.

MOONEY, J. "Myths of the Cherokee," 19th *ARBAE*. Washington, D.C., 1898.

MURPHY, R. F. (1) "Mundurucú Religion," *UCPAAE*, Vol. 49, No. 1. Berkeley–Los Angeles, 1958.

――――. (2) *Headhunter's Heritage*. Berkeley–Los Angeles, 1960.

MURPHY, R. F., and QUAIN, B. "The Trumaí Indians of Central Brazil," *Monographs of the American Ethnological Society*, 24. New York, 1955.

NANTES, MARTIN DE. *Relation Succinte et Sincère . . .* Quimper, undated. (1706).

NELSON, E. W. "The Eskimo about Bering Strait," 18th *ARBAE*. Washington, D.C., 1899.

NIMUENDAJU, C. (1) "Die Sagen von der Erschaffung und Vernichtung der Welt als Grundlagen der Religion der Apapocúva-Guarani," *Zeitschrift für Ethnologie*, Vol. 46, 1914.

――――. (2) "Sagen der Tembé-Indianer," *Zeitschrift für Ethnologie*, Vol. 47, 1915.

———. (3) "Bruchstücke aus Religion und Uberlieferung der Šipaia-Indianer," *Anthropos*, Vols. 14-15, 1919-1920, and 16-17, 1921-1922.

———. (4) "Os Indios Parintintin do rio Madeira," *Journal de la Société des Américanistes*, Vol. 16. Paris, 1924.

———. (4a) "Die Palikur-Indianer und ihre Nachbarn," *Göteborgs Kungl. Veten skapsoch Vitterhets-Samhalles Handligar*, Fjarde Foljden, Band 31, No. 2, 1926.

———. (5) "The Apinayé," *The Catholic University of America, Anthropological Series*, No. 8. Washington, D.C., 1939.

———. (6) "The Šerente," *Publication of the Frederick Webb Hodge Anniversary Publication Fund*, Vol. 4. Los Angeles, 1942.

———. (7) "Šerenté Tales," *JAFL*, Vol. 57, 1944.

———. (8) "The Eastern Timbira," *UCPAAE*, Vol. 41. Berkeley–Los Angeles, 1946.

———. (9) "Social Organization and Beliefs of the Botocudo of Eastern Brazil," *Southwestern Journal of Anthropology*, Vol. 2, No. 1, 1946.

———. (10) "The Mura and Piranhá," HSAI, *BBAE 143*, 7 vols. Washington, D.C., 1946-1959.

———. (11) "The Cawahib, Parintintin, and their Neighbors," HSAI, *BBAE 143*, 7 vols. Washington, D.C. 1946-1959.

———. (12) "The Tucuna," HSAI, *BBAE 143*, 7 vols. Washington, D.C., 1946-1959.

———. (13) "The Tukuna," *UCPAAE*, Vol. 45. Berkeley–Los Angeles, 1952.

———. (14) "Apontamentos sôbre os Guarani," *RMP*, n.s., Vol. 8 (translation and notes by EGON SCHADEN). São Paulo, 1954.

NINO, B. DE. *Etnografia chiriguana*. La Paz, 1912.

NORDENSKIÖLD, E. (1) *Indianerleben, El Gran Chaco*. Leipzig, 1912.

———. (2) *Indianer und Weisse in Nordostbolivien*. Stuttgart, 1922.

OGILVIE, J. Creation Myths of the Wapisiana and Taruma, British Guiana," *Folk-Lore*, Vol. 51. London, 1940.

OLIVEIRA, C. E. DE. "Os Apinagé do Alto Tocantins," *Boletim do Museu Nacional*, Vol. 6, No. 2. Rio de Janeiro, 1930.

OLIVEIRA, J. F. DE. "The Cherente of Central Brazil," *Proceedings of the 18th Congress of Americanists*. London, 1912. Part II; London, 1913.

[OLIVEIRA, DE] FELICIANO, J. "Os Cherentes," *Revista do Instituto Historico e Geographico de São Paulo*. São Paulo, 1918.

ORICO, C. (1) *Mitos Amerindios*. 2nd ed., São Paulo, 1930.

———. (2) *Vocabulario de Crendices Amazonicas*. São Paulo-Rio de Janeiro, 1937.

OSBORN, T. "Textos Folkloricos Guarao II," *Antropologica* 10. Caracas, 1960.

OSGOOD, C. "Ingalik Social Culture," *Yale University Publications in Anthropology*, Vol. 53. New Haven, 1958.

OVID. *Metamorphoses*.

PALAVECINO, E. "Takjuaj. Un personaje mitológico de los Mataco," *RMDLP*, n.s., No. 7, *Antropologia*, t. 1. Buenos Aires, 1936-1941.

PARSONS, E. C. (1) "Zuni Tales," *JAFL*, Vol. 43, 1930.

———. (2) *Pueblo Indian Religion*. 2 vols. Chicago, 1939.

PEREIRA, NUNES. *Bahira e suas experiências*. Edição popular. Manaus, 1945.

PIERINI, F. Mitología de los Guarayos de Bolivia," *Anthropos*, Vol. 5, 1910.

PISO, G., and MARCGRAVI DE LIEBSTAD, G. *Historia naturalis Brasiliae* . . . Leyden in Holland and Amsterdam, 1648.

PITOU, L. A. *Voyage à Cayenne, dans les deux Amériques et chez les anthropophages*. 2 vols. 2e ed., Paris, 1807.

PLUTARCH. "De Isis et d'Osiris," *Les Oeuvres morales de* . . . (translated by AMYOT). 2 vols. Paris, 1584. English version, *Morals*, edited by W. W. Goodwin. London, 1870.

POMPEU SOBRINHO, T. "Lendas Mehim," *Revista do Instituto do Ceará*, Vol. 49. Fortaleza, 1935.

PORÉE-MASPERO, E. *Cérémonies privées des Cambodgiens.* Pnom-Penh, 1958.

PREUSS, K. T. (1) *Religion und Mythologie der Uitoto.* 2 vols. Göttingen, 1921–1923.

———. (2) *Die Nayarit-Expedition. Textaufnahmen mit Beobachtungen unter mexikanischen Indianern.* 3 vols. Leipzig, 1912.

QUICHERAT, L. *Thesaurus Poeticus Linguae Latinae.* Paris, 1881.

RAYNAUD, G. *Les Dieux, les héros et les hommes de l'ancien Guatemala.* Paris, 1925.

REICHEL-DOLMATOFF, G. *Los Kogi.* 2 vols. Bogota, 1949–1950 and 1951.

RHODE, R. "Einige Notizen über dem Indianerstamm des Terenos," *Zeit. d. Gesell. f. Erdkunde zu Berlin,* Vol. 20, 1885, pp. 404–10.

RIBEIRO, D. (1) "Religião e Mitologia Kadiveu," *Serviço de Protecão aos Indios,* Publication no. 106. Rio de Janeiro, 1950.

———. (2) "Noticia dos Ofaié-Chavante," *RMP,* n.s., Vol. 5. São Paulo, 1951.

RIBEIRO, D., and B. G. *Arte plumaria dos índios Kaapor.* Rio de Janeiro, 1957.

RINK, H. *Tales and Traditions of the Eskimo.* Edinburgh–London, 1875.

RIVET, P., and ROCHEREAU, H. J. "Nociones sobre creencias usos y costumbres de los Catios del Occidente de Antioquia," *Journal de la Société des Américanistes,* Vol. 21. Paris, 1929.

ROCHEREAU, H. J. "Los Tunebos. Grupo Unkasia," *Revista Colombiana de Antropologia,* Vol. 10. Bogota, 1961.

RODRIGUES, J. BARBOSA. "Poranduba Amazonense," *Anais de Biblioteca Nacional de Rio de Janeiro,* Vol. 14, 1886–1887, fasc. 2. Rio de Janeiro, 1890.

ROTH, W. E. (1) "An Inquiry into the Animism and Folklore of the Guiana Indians," 30th *ARBAE* (1908–1909). Washington, D.C., 1915.

———. (2) "An Introductory Study of the Arts, Crafts, and Customs of the Guiana Indians," 38th *ARBAE* (1916–1917). Washington, D.C., 1924.

ROUGET, G. "Un Chromatisme africain," *L'Homme. Revue française d'Anthropologie,* tome 1, No. 3. Paris, 1961.

RUSSELL, F. "The Pima Indians," 26th *ARBAE* (1904–1905). Washington, D.C., 1908.

RYDEN, S. "Brazilian Anchor Axes," *Etnologiska studier* 4. Göteborg, 1937.

SAHAGUN, B. DE. *Florentine Codex. General History of the Things of New Spain.* In 13 parts. (Translated by A. J. O. ANDERSON and C. E. DIBBLE.) Santa Fe, New Mexico, 1950–1963.

SAINTYVES, P. "Le Charivari de l'adultère et les courses à corps nus," *L'Ethnographie.* Paris, 1935.

SAMPAIO, T. "Os Kraôs do Rio Preto no Estado da Bahia," *RIHGB,* Vol. 75 (1912). Rio de Janeiro, 1913.

SANTA-ANNA NERY, F.-J. DE. *Folk-lore brésilien.* Paris, 1889.

SCHADEN, E. (1) "Fragmentos de mitologia Kayuá," *RMP,* n.s., Vol. 1. São Paulo, 1947.

———. (2) "A Origem e a posse do fogo na mitologia Guarani," *Anais do 31 Congr. Intern. de Americanistas.* São Paulo, 1955.

———. (3) *A Mitologia Heróica de Tribos Indígenas do Brasil.* Rio de Janeiro, 1959.

SCHOMBURGK, R. *Travels in British Guiana 1840–1844.* (Translated and edited by W. E. ROTH.) 2 vols. Georgetown, 1922.

SCHULTZ, H. "Lendas dos indios Krahó," *RMP,* n.s., Vol. 4. São Paulo, 1950.

SELER, E. *Gesammelte Abhandlungen zur Amerikanischen Sprach- und Altertumskunde.* 5 vols. n.ed. Graz, 1961.

SIMPSON, G. G. "A Carib (Kamarakoto) Myth from Venezuela," *JAFL,* Vol. 57, 1944.

SPECK, F. G. "Catawba Texts," *Columbia University Contribution to Anthropology,* Vol. 24. New York, 1934.

SPENCER, B., and GILLEN, F. J. *The Northern Tribes of Central Australia.* London, 1904.

SPENCER, R. F. "The North Alaskan Eskimo," *BBAE 171.* Washington, D.C., 1959.

SPITZER, L. "Patterns of Thought and of Etymology. I. Nausea > of (> Eng.) Noise," *Word, Journal of the Linguistic Circle of New York,* Vol. I, No. 3. New York, 1945.

STEINEN, K. VON DEN. (1) "Plejaden' und 'Jahr' bei Indianern des nordöslischen Sud-amerikas," *Globus*, Vol. 65, 1894.

———. (2) *Entre os aborigines do Brasil central*. São Paulo, 1940.

STEVENSON, M. C. "The Zuni Indians," *23rd ARBAE*. Washington, D.C., 1905.

STONE, D. "The Talamancan Tribes of Costa Rica," *Papers of the Peabody Museum of Archaeology and Ethnology, Harvard University*, Vol. 43, No. 2. Cambridge, Mass., 1962.

STRADELLI, E. "Vocabulario da lingua geral portuguez-nheêngatu e nheêngatu- portuguez, etc.," *RIHGB*, t. 104, Vol. 158. Rio de Janeiro, 1929.

STRÖMER, C. VON. "Die Sprache der Mundurukú," *Anthropos: Collection Internationale de Monographies Linguistiques* 2. Vienna, 1932.

STRONG, W. D. "Aboriginal Society in Southern California," *UCPAAE*, Vol. 26, 1926.

SWANTON, J. R. "Myths and Tales of the Southeastern Indians," *BBAE 88*. Washington, D.C., 1929.

TASTEVIN, C. (1) *La Langue Tapïhïya dite Tupï ou N'eêngatu* . . . (Schriften der Sprachenkommission, Kaiserliche Akademie der Wissenschaften, Band II). Vienna, 1910.

———. (2) "Nomes de plantas e animaes em lingua tupy," *RMP*, tomo 13. São Paulo, 1922.

———. (3) "La Légende de Bóyusú en Amazonie," *Revue d'Ethnographie et des Traditions Populaires*, 6e année, No. 22. Paris, 1925.

TAYLOR, D. "The Meaning of Dietary and Occupational Restrictions among the Island Carib," *American Anthropologist*, n.s., Vol. 52, No. 3, 1950.

TESCHAUER, P. C. "Mythen und alte Volkssagen aus Brasilien," *Anthropos*, Vol. 1, 1906.

THEVET, A. *La Cosmographie Universelle*. 2 vols. Paris, 1575.

TOCANTINS, A. M. G. "Estudos sobre a tribu Munduruku," *Revista Trimensal do Instituto Historico, Geographico e Ethnographico do Brasil*, tomo 40, 1st part. Rio de Janeiro, 1877.

VALDEZ, J. FERNANDEZ. *Novo Diccionario Portuguez-Francez e Francez-Portuguez*. 8th ed., Rio de Janeiro–Paris, 1928.

VANZOLINI, P. E. "Notas sôbre a zoologia dos indios Canela," *RMP*, n.s., Vol. 10. São Paulo, 1956–1958.

WAGLEY, C. "World View of the Tapirapé Indians," *JAFL*, Vol. 53, 1940.

WAGLEY, C., and GALVÃO, E. "The Tenetehara Indians of Brazil," *Columbia University Contributions to Anthropology*, No. 35. New York, 1949.

WALLIS, W. D., and R. S. *The Micmac Indians of Canada*. Minneapolis, 1955.

WASSEN, H. (1) "Cuentos de los Indios Chocós," *Journal de la Société des Américanistes*, Vol. 25. Paris, 1933.

———. (2) "Mitos y Cuentos de los Indios Cunas," *Journal de la Société des Américanistes*, Vol. 26. Paris, 1934.

———. (3) "Some Cuna Indian Animal Stories, with Original Texts," *Etnologiska Studier* 4. Göteborg, 1937.

———. (4) "De la Identificación de los Indios Paparos del Darien," *Hombre y Cultura*, tomo. 1, No. 1. Panamá, 1962.

WATSON, J. B. "Cayuá Culture Change: A Study in Acculturation and Methodology," *Memoir No. 73 of the American Anthropological Association*, 1952.

WESTERMARCK, E. *The History of Human Marriage*. 3 vols. New York, 1922.

WILBERT, J. "A Preliminary Glotto-chronology of Ge," *Anthropological Linguistics*, Vol. 4, No. 2. Bloomington, 1962.

WIRTH, D. M. (1) "A mitologia dos Vapidiana do Brasil," *Sociologia*, Vol. 5, No. 3. São Paulo, 1943.

———. (2) "Lendas dos indios Vapidiana," *RMP*, n.s., Vol. 4. São Paulo, 1950.

WISSLER, C., and DUVALL, D. C. "Mythology of the Blackfoot Indians," *Anthropological Papers of the American Museum of Natural History*, Vol. II. New York, 1908.

ZERRIES, O. (1) "Sternbilder als Ausdruck Jägerischer Geisteshaltung in Südamerika," *Paideuma* Band 5, Heft 5. Bamberg, 1952.

———. (2) "The Bull-roarer among South American Indians," *RMP*, n.s., Vol. 7. São Paulo, 1953.

———. (3) "Kürbisrassel und Kopfgeister in Südamerika," *Paideuma* Band 5, Heft 6. Bamberg, 1953.

ZINGG, M. "The Genuine and Spurious Values in Tarahumara Culture," *American Anthropologist*, n.s., Vol. 44, No. 1, 1942.

Index of Myths

Numbers in **boldface** indicate complete myth.

a. NUMBER ORDER AND SUBJECTS

b. TRIBES

General Index

Maize, 115
  origin of, 104, 165–169, 179, 185, 217 *n.* 7
Malinowski, B., 29
Mallarmé, Stéphane, 17 *n.* 6
Mandan, 224, 291, 331
Manioc:
  fermented paste, 75
  origin of, 126, 166, 181, 188, 193 *n.* 29, 217 *n.* 7
Manioc beer, 158–159, 309 *n.* 14
Mankind:
  after flood, 51, 140
  origin of, 115, 171, 269
Manufactures, origin of, 92–94
Marquesas Islands, 230
Marriage:
  charivari, 286–289, 294, 300, 327–330, 338
  cooked and raw food associated with, 334–335
  European customs, 328–330, 334–335, 338
  silence after, 328
  of younger daughter before elder, 334–335, 337
  of youngest child, 330
Mars (planet), 291
Marsupialia, 170–171; *see also* Opossum
Masks, 28
Mataco, 142 *n.* 16, 225
Maya, 323 *n.* 22
Mea (cotia, *Dasyprocta aguti*), 37, 47; *see also* Agouti
Menomini, 139
Message, definition of, 199
Methodology, three rules, 333–334
Micmac, 329
Milky Way, 246–247, 249 *n.* 22, 297
Modoc, 55
Mojos, 222
Monkey, 200, 203, 205, 206, 303
  capuchin (*Cebus* species), 260, 266–267, il. 346
  howler (*Alouetta* species), 121, 273–274, 310, il. 346
  marimondo (*Ateles paniseus*), 122

Monkey (*continued*)
  and origin of fire, 126–128, 131–133, 143, 204
  spider, 122, 274, il. 348
  as wife, 273–275
Montagnais-Naskapi, 291
Montaigne, M. E. de, 323 *n.* 23
Moon, 161, 329
  halo, 158–159
  origin of, 296–297, 312
  see also Eclipses
Moon (personified), 189, 193, 256, 264, 291–293
Mundurucu, 57, 61, 85, 131, 151, 180 *n.* 20, 258 *n.* 26, 277 *n.* 40, 289 *n.* 2, 291
  fish poisoning, 256, 260 *n.* 27
Mura, 247
Music:
  color and sound compared, 18–19, 22
  musique concrète, 22–23
  myth as parallel to, 14–18, 26–30
  painting compared with, 19–23, 25
  poetry compared with, 18
  serial, 23–27
  singing and speech related, 28–29
Musical instruments, forbidden, 321–322
Mutum (bird, curassow), 73–75, 204 *n.* 3, 302, 313, 317, il. 354

Nambikwara, 152 *n.* 6
Names, personal, 42–43
Nantes, Martin de, 102
Natchez, 174, 205, 299 *n.* 11
Navajo, 243
Necklaces, 320–321
Nimuendaju, C., 70, 74, 75, 216, 248, 314
Noise, 147–150, 285, 300–301, 311
  charivari, 286–289, 294, 300, 327–330, 338
  cooking fire and, 293–295
  eclipses and, 286–288, 294, 297, 300–301
  European and American customs, 301, 329–330
  silence and, 327–329

ABOUT THE AUTHOR

CLAUDE LÉVI-STRAUSS has served on the faculties of the New School for Social Research in New York and the University of São Paulo (Brazil) and is currently professor of social anthropology at the Collège de France. Among his books which have been translated into English are *Tristes Tropiques, The Elementary Structures of Kinship, The Savage Mind, Totemism,* and *Structural Anthropology.*